Sex in Transition

Sex in Transition

Remaking Gender and Race in South Africa

Amanda Lock Swarr

Published by State University of New York Press, Albany

For information, contact State University of New York Press, Albany, NY
www.sunypress.edu

Production by Kelli Williams-LeRoux
Marketing by Kate McDonnell

Library of Congress Cataloging-in-Publication Data

Swarr, Amanda Lock.
    Sex in transition : remaking gender and race in South Africa / Amanda Lock
Swarr.
        p. cm.
    Includes bibliographical references and index.
    ISBN 978-1-4384-4406-2 (pbk. : alk. paper)
    ISBN 978-1-4384-4407-9 (hardcover : alk. paper)
    1. Transsexualism—South Africa—History. 2. Transsexuals—Legal status, laws,
etc.—South Africa. 3. Intersexuality—South Africa. 4. Gender identity—South
Africa. I. Title.

    HQ77.95.S6S93 2012
    305.30968—dc23   2011047984

10 9 8 7 6 5 4 3 2 1

Contents

Acknowledgments   vii

Introduction: Transition Matters   1

1   Prescribing Gender and Enforcing Sex   43

2   Medical Experimentation and the Raced Incongruence of Gender   77

3   Redefining Transition through Necropolitics   109

4   *Stabane*, Raced Intersexuality and Same-Sex Relationships in Soweto   183

5   Performing Hierarchies and Kinky Politics: Drag in South Africa's Transition   207

Conclusion: "Extra-Transsexual" Meanings and Transgender Politics   231

Notes   261

Bibliography   285

Index   319

Acknowledgments

This book has developed over fifteen years and was a collective labor in every way. Without many people in South Africa, this work simply would not have been possible. Midi Achmat, Theresa Raizenberg, Bass John Khumalo, Conny Mchunu, Phumla Masuku, Donna van der Walt, Michelle Asburner, Barbara Rass, Dawie Nel, Juan Nel, Flo Belvedere, and Prudence Mabele opened their homes to me and allowed me to become part of their lives. Others in South Africa who went out of their way time and time again to offer assistance include Zackie Achmat, Pieter Dirk-Uys, Walter Dominique-Dunn, Sally Gross, Simone Heradien, Evert Knoesen, Premesh Lalu, Jack Lewis, Zanele Muholi, Tebogo Nkoana, Sophie Old-field, Yvonne Shapiro, Carrie Shelver, Funeka Soldaat, and Liesl Theron.

Spending time with and in organizations, groups, and workplaces taught me more than I can measure and allowed me to be part of meaningful actions. Thank you to members of the Treatment Action Campaign, AIDS Law Project, Association of Bisexuals, Gays, and Lesbians (ABIGALE), Umanyano, Gender DynamiX, Behind the Mask, Forum for the Empowerment of Women, FreeGender, Hope and Unity Metropolitan Community Church (HUMCC), Sistahs Kopinang, Gays and Lesbians of the Witwatersrand (GLOW), Triangle Project, Sex Workers Education and Advocacy Taskforce (SWEAT), National Coalition for Gay and Lesbian Equality/Equality Project, Gay and Lesbian Legal Advice Center (GLLAC), International Gay and Lesbian Association (ILGA)–Africa, Womyn, Pride Committee, Gay and Lesbian Organization of Pretoria (GLOP)/OUT, Uthingo, Gay and Lesbian Film Festival, Idol Pictures, The Glitter Sisters, The Brunswick Follies, Mince, Centre for the Book, Rape Crisis–Cape Town, and United Sanctuary for our conversations and collaborations over the past fifteen years.

Financial support for early stages of this research came from the University of Minnesota Graduate School in the form of a Graduate School Fellowship, President's International Predissertation Fellowship, Grant for Research Abroad, Doctoral Dissertation Special Grant, Doctoral Dissertation Fellowship, and Graduate Research Partnership Program Fellowship (with Richa Nagar), as well as from funding provided by the Anthropology Department, the Center for Advanced Feminist Studies, and the Schochet Center. The MacArthur Interdisciplinary Program on Social Change, Sustainability, and Justice/Interdisciplinary Center for the Study of Global Change supported this work financially, as well as serving as my intellectual home; within this program, thanks go especially to Allen Isaacman, as well as Karen Brown, Bud Duvall, Mary Gervais, Dave Henrikson, Jim Johnson, Linda Littrell, and Claudia Shores Skue and to the faculty who dedicated their time to mentoring MacArthur scholars.

I am grateful to participants in the MacArthur Gender Consortium for providing invaluable feedback and helping me think through these chapters at many stages, particularly Lisa Disch, Jennifer Pierce, Richa Nagar, Karen Brown Thompson, Amy Kaminsky, Libby Lunstrum, Hoku-lani Aikau, Leila Harris, Keiko Inoue, Tina Chen, Sally Kenney, and the late Susan Geiger. Feminist intellectual community at the University of Minnesota based in the department of Gender, Women and Sexuality Studies was also invaluable, and I'm especially grateful for the support of my co-advisors, Amy Kaminsky and Richa Nagar, as well as Naomi Scheman, Helen Longino, Jigna Desai, Jacquelyn Zita, Janie Jurgens, and Myrna Klitzke. Other mentors who have supported me over many years include Kathleen Barlow and the late Janet Spector.

A Mellon Postdoctoral Fellowship from Barnard College also supported my research and writing, based in the Women's Studies Department. During years spent in New York, I was immensely appreciative of the engagement of Chi-ming Yang, Chris Cynn, Janet Jackobsen, Rebecca Jordan-Young, Alison Wylie, Elizabeth Bernstein, Maxine Weingrau, Elizabeth Castelli, Natalie Kampen, and Lila Abu-Lughod.

Support from the University of Washington in the form of a Royalty Research Fellowship, as part of the Simpson Center's Society of Scholars, and from my home department of Gender, Women and Sexuality Studies helped me to complete this work. I owe a particular debt of gratitude to colleagues at the University of Washington, including Rebecca Aanarud, David Allen, Jerry Baldasty, Miriam Bartha, Clare Bright, Jeanette Bushnell,

Rachel Chapman, David Domke, Angela Ginorio, Michelle Habell-Pallán, Gillian Harkins, Danny Hoffman, Judy Howard, Ralina Joseph, Nancy Kenney, Kari Lerum, Shaun Lopez, Priti Ramamurthy, Luana Ross, Lynn Thomas, Shirley Yee, Sasha Su-Ling Welland, and Kathleen Woodward.

Assistance in the archival and technical research for this book came in varied locales. Graeme Reid, Ruth Morgan, Anthony Manion, and Busi Khwesa of the Gay and Lesbian Archives/Gay and Lesbian Memory in Action at the University of the Witwatersrand pointed me to critical sources. Librarians Kathy Robbins, Judy Wells, and Becky Hoffman at the University of Minnesota, Yuusuf Caruso at Columbia University, and especially Cass Hartnett at the University of Washington were consistently helpful in obtaining obscure resources. Myrna Klitzke at the University of Minnesota, Sierra Ortiz at Barnard College, and Carol Langdon and Elaine Haig-Widner at the University of Washington provided invaluable staff support. Engaged research assistance on final revisions was provided by graduate students Kai Kohlsdorf, Kate Mottolla, and Sean Jarvis, who were vital interlocutors in this project. SUNY Reviewers, including William Leap, and staff, including Beth Bouloukos, Andrew Kenyon, Kate McDonnell, Larin McLaughlin, Ryan Morris, and Kelli Williams-LeRoux, pushed this book toward publication, even when I resisted. Thanks to Dave Prout for conscientious work on the index.

Friends like Desiree Fintel, Tambra Donohue, Shari Geistfeld, Beth Mitchell, and Adam Sitze all helped in important ways in the process of research and writing. I am always already grateful for Joel Wainwright; his friendship, encouragement, and resilient faith in me have inspired me for over twenty years. Richa Nagar has been so much more than a mentor and collaborator; she's been my touchstone in reminding me of the political commitments that must always come first.

My family has endured long absences and supported me unconditionally. My parents—Barbara "CL" Harvey, Daniel Harvey, Fred Swarr, and Valerie Swarr—made me who I am. My sister, Jessica Stout, provided perspective on the things that really matter, like Nate Stout, Drew Stout, and Gabe Williams. My brothers and their families inspire me; Gabe, Karla, Zach, Maribeth, and Declan all make me proud to be a Swarr. Kathleen and Frank Smoker, Elsie and John Swarr, Alice Harvey, and Arna and Mark Kaufman have given me lifelong stability. Without my partner T Steele, and our kids Theo Johnson, Matthew Steele, and Jennifer Johnson (and granddaughter Aubrey), I would be sitting alone in a turret in Seattle. T translates my academic language to point out what these words really mean to me and to others, and her excitement about my work, politics, and ideas consistently reinspire me.

Finally, I am appreciative of Sam Bullington; we worked together in conceiving our dissertation topics, carried out most of the work in South Africa as research partners, and figured out connections together. During over a decade of research Sam organized photographs and tapes, maintained relationships, and kept meticulous notes. His constant support and companionship, focus and thoroughness, welcome distractions, careful readings, historical memory, patience, insights, and strength made this work possible, and my appreciation for this and all it has meant in shaping this work goes beyond words.

While all of this collaboration and help was essential, I take responsibility for any errors of omission or commission in this book. Any proceeds from its publication will be donated to South African organizations working on issues addressed here.

An earlier version of Chapter 4 was published as:
Swarr, Amanda Lock. "*Stabane*, Intersexuality, and Same-sex Relationships in Soweto," *Feminist Studies*, 35 (3), fall 2009: 524–548.

An earlier version of Chapter 5 was published as:
Swarr, Amanda Lock. "*Moffies*, Artists, and Queens: Race and the Production of South African Gay Male Drag," *Journal of Homosexuality*, 46(3/4), spring 2004: 73–89. Reprinted by permission of Taylor and Francis Ltd.

Introduction

Transition Matters

In 1994, transsexual Simone Heradien underwent sex reassignment procedures funded by the South African state. The timing of her personal
transition was significant:

> 1994 . . . was also the year we were going through the de-
> mocracy, the transition, so it was a lot of things. . . . When
> we were going through our transition stage, there was what
> we call the RDP, getting water and electricity to those who
> didn't have [them]. The RDP stands for the Reconstruction and
> Development Programme, and that was 1994, the same year
> that I had my op. So I said to everybody, well you've heard
> of the RDP, that's me! . . . I was definitely reconstructed and
> developed. (Heradien 1997)[1]

As Simone indicates, South African gender liminality is intimately connected to the histories and political economy of South Africa itself. Under
apartheid, many South African transsexuals had access to free sex reassignment surgeries and, following surgeries, were able to legally alter
the sex listed on their birth certificates. Transsexuals' transitions were,
in some ways, sanctioned by the state. But since the end of apartheid,
publicly funded sex reassignment programs like the one accessed by
Simone have largely ceased. And while the South African Constitution,
one of the most progressive in the world, promises freedom from discrimination based on sex, gender, and sexual orientation, during the
transitional years of South Africa's new democracy (1993–2003) it was
legally impossible to change one's sex.[2]

What circumstances led to these apparent paradoxes, and what do
they tell us about the materialization of sex and gender with race? This

question is the foundation for *Sex in Transition* and its exploration of the raced and classed contradictions constituting gendered boundaries. To date, gender liminality and transgender in South Africa, particularly their concurrence with South Africa's political transition from apartheid to democracy, have been largely unexamined. *Sex in Transition* exposes and analyzes cracks in the man/woman binary by investigating raced and classed challenges to dichotomous gendered norms. It does so through explication of the medical constitution of gender and sex, legislation under the apartheid and transitional states, specific instances of social discrimination, and narratives of gender liminality.

This book focuses centrally on concepts of transition. Dr. William Bridges begins his well-known series of books on life's transitions with an observation that transitions usually constitute three phases—an ending, a period of confusion and distress, and a new beginning (1980: 9). This formation is also replicated in understandings of transition in the social sciences. The political transition in South Africa has been well-documented over the past two decades, with the ending of apartheid, the simultaneous euphoria and panic that followed, and the promise of the new South Africa that has yet to be actualized. William Spurlin argues that the disruption of normalized social and political categories offered by the ending of apartheid, ". . . marks the transition as a *queer* space of analysis" (2006: 19). Gender transitions, while usually explained in medical terms, have much broader manifestations. During a group meeting of contributors to the important recent anthology, *Trans: Transgender Life Stories in South Africa*, participants described their understandings of this concept:

> We had a lengthy discussion at one of our meetings defining what transition means and when this process begins. Robert felt that transitioning starts, "the moment you have confessed to *yourself* that your body doesn't match your gender identity," and ties with the permission to think and feel about yourself in a different way. Tebogo felt that transitioning starts, "when a person starts to change living as their biological gender, when they start *living as the opposite gender* . . . maybe by binding and cross-dressing." Robert reflected that in the stories we have collected, "all these people are *living* it, not *thinking* it. *Living* is a nice word, because living can be in a closed space

or an open space, it can be in your home." (In Morgan et al. 2009: 11, emphasis in original)

It is the broadest sense of transition on which I focus in *Sex in Transition*. I am not interested in replicating medical models of linear and temporally-bound movement from one gender to another; instead I focus on the space of transition and its parallels and connections to South Africa's political transition. One psychologist I interviewed who works with transsexuals explained the impetus for understanding gender during this political period:

> I think because South Africa is kind of transitioning itself, it gives opportunities for debate. And because we're transitioning society, I would think it makes it easier in some ways. But even within [gender] transition within this transitioning society, we still have very set ideas about our people. (Ryland 2007)

As Karen Ryland explains, the period of transition produced contradictory spaces for individual and social change. These contradictions are the subject of this book.

Also critical and related to the concept of transition is my focus on gender liminality in this text as an alternative to terms with medical histories or more widely-used notions of transgender, gender variance, or gender nonconformity. The concept of "liminality" originated with anthropologist Arnold van Gennep (1909) and was further popularized by Victor Turner (1967 and 1969) to describe passage from one cultural state to another. Its use has grown to common parlance as a way to explain spaces between existential planes and sociocultural uncertainty that surpasses the individual. Central to this concept, and especially to my use of it here, are the ways that liminality works within hierarchies and institutions as both unsettling and formative. I prefer this concept to other alternatives because it is not geographically or disciplinarily bounded, nor does it assume a particular static gendered norm or a political position (e.g., conservative or radical). Further, it is important that liminality does not necessarily rely on movement—even Turner's original formulation describes the potential for "permanent liminality" (1909)—though it has spatial and temporal components that allow for various and differing expressions of it. For these reasons, gender liminality in this text works hand in hand with transition to describe spaces that both fall between and unsettle established orders while reworking them simultaneously.[3]

Throughout *Sex in Transition*, in different ways, I argue that South Africa's apartheid system of racial segregation relied on an unexamined but interrelated paradigm of sexed oppression that was at once rigid and flexible. Seemingly oppositional regulations of gender binaries and encouragement of gender liminality form South Africa's history of apartheid and political transition. Self-defined transsexuals, transvestites, intersexuals, butch lesbians, drag performers, and those who defy these categories speak to the violent ways that the borders of race, sex, and gender were policed under apartheid, as well as the creative ways that they have been subverted, articulating tensions between constraint and freedom. Further, varied narratives of South Africans living between sexed binaries provide opportunities for understanding the complex ways sex and gender are articulated with race.

Sex in Transition provides a threefold exploration of how multiple genders are formed through intersections with political economy, race, and colonialism. First, this text specifically *reconceptualizes apartheid as reliant on gendered disjunctures*. Apartheid's well-known racial policing was interwoven with gendered restrictions and manipulation, and apartheid's practices reveal similarly contradictory and complex ideas about race and gender. Gender was contradictory in the transitional state, as well; paradoxical social, medical, and legal treatment of gender liminal South Africans undermines generalizations about the "new" South Africa as a panacea or a catastrophe. This work expands important scholarship concerned with same-sex sexualities in South Africa by analyzing inconsistencies in trans/gendered categories. Critical to this growing field is the late Glen Elder's (2003) critique of South Africa's migrant labor system, in which he cogently evaluates ways that "heteropatriarchy"—the conjunction of heterosexuality with patriarchy—was critical to the apartheid state. *Sex in Transition* extends Elder's discussions by addressing how both sexuality and contradictory means of both encouraging and punishing gender liminality among different racial groups and in different periods were critical to the maintenance and composition of apartheid and the transitional states.

The second contribution of *Sex in Transition* consists of a *theorization of the paradoxes of raced gender* in varied contexts. The inseparability of gender from sexuality, race, class, history, and location has been well-established, and within this context, gender is comprised of innate contradictions. Far from being surprising or unsettling, varied inconsistencies explored in *Sex in Transition* foreground the ways that paradoxes are at the heart of gender production. Gender and race function as norms, and normality relies on abnormality. Focusing on narratives of gender liminal South Africans within the context of the nation's colonial history of racial policing highlights narrators' own understandings of the contradictions of gender.

Third, *Sex in Transition* extends the emerging field of Transgender Studies from perspectives of those in the global South and highlights what South African legal scholar Angelo Pantazis calls *"extra-transsexual meanings*—meanings for people who are not transsexuals" (1997: 468, emphasis added). South African theorizations of trans/gender both utilize and challenge Northern-based terminology, such as "transgender" and "transsexual," and the compartmentalization it affords, refiguring and undermining Northern hegemonic categories simultaneously.[4] And, at the same time, the nascent South African transgender political movement, initiated in 2005 primarily through the emergence of a Cape Town-based organization called Gender DynamiX, further develops and puts into conversation Transgender Studies and the burgeoning field of transnational sexualities by attending to the role of racism and globalized medicine in participants' lives.[5] The simultaneous locally-grounded and transnational meanings of gender liminality are critical to this project.

I. Transdisciplinary Situations

Although dualistic binaries (such as subject/object, mind/body, white/black) have been widely critiqued, the dichotomy of man/woman remains the bedrock of much work on gender. Further, while academic studies have addressed both drag and transsexuality, historically there has been scant discussion of the importance of race and class in shaping opportunities for gender expressions. Medical, legal, and academic discourses have tended to objectify gender liminality, paying little attention to the perspectives that individuals hold regarding their own lives. And rarely have any of these domains devoted significant attention to scholarship and activism based in Africa. *Sex in Transition* brings these divergent fields together to intervene into debates in Women's and Gender Studies, Transgender Studies, and African Studies.

Contemporary Women's and Gender Studies rests on two unstable concepts: woman or man (categories conceptually and practically tenuous) and location (often considered within the problematic boundaries of nation states). Developing these two directions for the field, *Sex in Transition* reads feminist theories of embodiment with transnational feminist theory. I put scholarship undermining biological expectations of gender into conversation with that focused outside of the global North.

Within the newly emerging field of Transgender Studies, two bodies of literature serve as inspirations for this research. In the past twenty years, books with strong autobiographical currents by activists from the United States and Europe have combined experimental writing styles with important contributions to transgender theory. The South African narratives highlighted here complement this scholarship and build on the recent contributions of *Trans: Transgender Life Stories from South Africa* (2009). Simultaneously, academic texts centered on trans narratives and activism have persuasively argued for the necessity of the inclusion of gender liminal voices in theorizing and historicizing gender liminality. Perhaps the most exciting directions in this field have been found in studies that address postcolonial/transnational concerns, gender, and sexuality simultaneously. Taken together and put into conversation, works such as these that are concerned with gender liminality and transnational sexualities promise to take LGBTQ/Queer/Sexuality Studies in exciting directions that inform this text.

Within African Studies, most conventional scholarship still depends on clear distinctions between women and men. While many texts concerned with gender in African contexts provide complex documentation of the lives and experiences of African women, they rarely explicitly theorize the constitution of sex—the body.[6] *Sex in Transition* attempts to advance understandings of colonialism and apartheid offered by South African scholars and to offer new discourses about gender liminality and race. As Andrew Tucker has pointed out, "while the regulation of difference based on 'race' has been well-documented in South Africa, the direct effect it had on different queer communities has yet to be systematically explored" (Tucker 2009: 2). *Sex in Transition* is part of emerging texts being published on and in South Africa that look at sexuality and gender in the so-called "new" South Africa, illuminated by growing numbers of works by and about queer South Africans that are attentive to race (e.g., Hoad, Martin, and Reid [2005]; Hoad [2005]; Van Zyl and Steyn [2005]; Morgan and Wieringa [2005]; Arnfred [2004]).

Conversations among theorists based in the global North and those based in South Africa have been increasingly articulated in significant scholarship emerging from and about South Africa. Some of the theorists most critical to this text are well-known worldwide; for instance, Michel Foucault's ideas of power, biopower, and the state; Judith Butler's conceptions of gender and performativity; and Achille Mbembe's notions of necropolitics and the postcolony are central to the organization and framing of *Sex in Transition*. How do these ideas travel and map onto South African ideas about gender liminality and race?

Of these theorists, Judith Butler has had perhaps the most notable influence on South African scholars of sex and sexuality. In 2004, the prominent South African feminist journal *Agenda* published a special issue on sexualities that included an interview with Butler by South African feminist scholar Vasu Reddy:

> The interview considers, in part, how ideas and problems in relation to the empirical context of "Africa" could enter into a meaningful dialogue with Butler's work. Likewise, the issues and ideas in this issue provide Butler with an understanding of how her work is understood and interpreted within this continent. (Reddy with Butler 2004: 115)

Reddy strives to make Butler's work accessible and relevant to *Agenda* journal readers—a mixed academic, political organizing, and popular audience based in South Africa—asking readers to engage with her ideas from an activist perspective. For example, Reddy queries Butler about the ways she intentionally unsettles categories including "man" and "woman" and the significance of her perspective. Butler replies, "You ask that the categories such as 'man,' 'woman,' 'male' and 'female' are displaced, and we have to consider what that displacement means. They may have lost their traditional place in a kind of political argument, but that does not mean that they cease to be an urgent political theme" (116). In this instance, the meaning of Butler's sometimes ephemeral work pointing out the instability of categories of sex is grounded in the political contexts of discrimination.

The influences of and conversations about Butler's work in South African contexts have been significant in other ways, as well. Equally notable, Mikki van Zyl and Melissa Steyn's (2005) publication, *Performing Queer: Shaping Sexualities, 1994–2004—Volume One* informs readers,

"The book derives its title *performing queer* from Butler's (1999) notion of gender and sexuality as performance, and the inescapable fluidity of identities" (Van Zyl 2005: 20). Such dialogues within South Africa are increasingly common and quite important and indicate the extent of critical dialogical theory-building. Van Zyl further draws on Reddy's interview with Butler in *Agenda* in her framing and descriptions of the chapters that comprise the anthology, *Performing Queer: Shaping Sexualities, 1994–2004—Volume One*.[7]

These representations of the utilization and reconfiguring of Butler's work in South African contexts demonstrate the interplay and motion of academic theories. Neville Hoad's analysis of South African interpretations of Gayle Rubin's famous essay, "Thinking Sex: Notes for a Radical Theory of the Politics of Sexuality," suggests that, "the reception of [Rubin's] essay in South African sex scholarship reveals something more like what Edward Said has termed 'traveling theory'" (Hoad 2010: 120). "Traveling theory" is similarly useful to my articulation of the framework for this text. Said's conception of traveling theory consists of the following trajectory:

> First, there is a point of origin, or what seems like one, a set of initial circumstances in which the idea came to birth or entered discourse. Second, there is a distance transferred, a passage through the pressure of various contexts as the idea moves from an earlier point to another time and place where it will come into a new prominence. Third, there is a set of conditions of acceptance or, as an inevitable part of acceptance, resistances—which then confronts the transplanted theory or idea, making possible its introduction or toleration, however alien it might appear to be. Fourth, the now full (or partly) accommodated (or incorporated) idea is to some extent transformed by its new uses, its new position in a new time and place. (Said 2000 [1982]: 196)

Taken together, these four points of consideration guide my use of the work of Foucault, Butler, and Mbembe in *Sex in Transition*. Applying and transforming theorists' ideas across time and space and grounding them in the specificities of gender liminality in South Africa comprise one of the objectives of this book. This kind of mobile and transformative work been increasingly accomplished in transnational contexts.[8]

One of the most notable characteristics of the theoretical framework that underpins *Sex in Transition* is a commitment to foregrounding African (and Africanist) scholarship. Mbembe's notions of necropolitics and the postcolony, and my interpretations of the ways his theories travel, are one effort in this direction. The work of scholars specifically working on gender, sex, and sexuality in South Africa also provide ideas and concepts that are critical to this text. For instance, I have already mentioned the importance of Glen Elder's (2003) notions of "heteropatriarchy" as a way of articulating the heterosexist and gendered inconsistencies of apartheid and the transition.

Kopano Ratele's conception of "kinky politics" similarly links race, gender, and sexuality within the framework of South African histories and colonialisms. He explains the concept this way:

> By kinky politics I want to indicate racial perversion. Kinky politics follows the fetish of, and refetishises, race. There can be no racism without this constant refetishisation. Indeed, one could say racism is kinky politics as it always involves a sexual warping of identity politics. Racism, together with (hetero) sexism, then, is what keeps us in awe, or fear, or ignorance of black and white, male and female bodies and sexualities in this society. (Ratele 2004: 142)

For Ratele, racism, sexism, and heterosexism are inseparable. And all three of these slippery categories are perverted. Perversion designates abnormality, usually along sexual lines, in this case indicating the sexualization of race. Further, to fetishize something is to attribute unwarranted power to it; or, in the Marxian sense (as with commodity fetishism), to transform social relationships between people to objectified relationships between things. And "kinky" is alternately used to refer to tightly curled hair or to deviance, especially sexual deviance. In all of these overlapping aspects of kinky politics, there is a reduction of personal relationships to ones dictated by and merged with the broader articulations of racism, sexism, and heterosexism in distorted ways. Ratele elaborates:

> Kinky politics is personal and institutional practices, politics, programmes, cultures that naturalise, objectify, and stabilise difference, refusing to allow for its characteristic of movement

> and change. In respect to racial difference, kinky politics
> shows itself when that difference is held permanently constant
> and becomes an explanation of what the idea of race or the
> policy of racial domination generates in the first place. (Ratele
> 2004: 143)

Ratele's kinky politics highlight the specific ways that the politics of apart-heid have "inscribed race indelibly on the landscape of sexual identities for South Africans, at least for the moment" (Van Zyl 2005: 21). Queer theory, based in the global North, refuses heterosexism and is similarly focused on nonnormativity; however, it is not consistently attentive to the ways that race and nation shape sexual subjectivities. Kinky politics provide a different but parallel way to explain the instability of social categories within a specific South African context whereby the temporal consistency and immutability of race and sexuality are exposed in the places where they meet.

Another foundational concept to *Sex in Transition* is found in Marc Epprecht and Neville Hoad's significant scholarship concerned with sexu-alities in Africa. Epprecht's *Heterosexual Africa?: The History of an Idea from the Age of Exploration to the Age of AIDS* (2008) is primarily concerned with the development of the conception of heterosexuality, as the title indicates. Epprecht is not simply interested in documenting the exis-tence of same-sex sexuality in Africa—as he points out, this has been done elsewhere over decades and largely overlooked. Instead, he traces patterns of heteronormativity and silences in the historical record that have been endemic and harmful. Neville Hoad, in his exploration of *African Intimacies: Race, Homosexuality, and Globalization*, similarly focuses on "the place of an entity that comes to be called 'homosexuality' in the production (discursive, material, imaginary) of a place called 'Africa'" (2007: xvi). Foucault's capacity to travel is again relevant here, since Hoad's discussion of this idea draws specifically on his and others' his-torical conceptualization of "heterosexuality" (59). Like these theorists' charting of an idea—in these cases, heterosexuality and homosexuality (and even Africa)—in some ways *Sex in Transition* also traces the idea of "sex," more than its tenuous reality. Unlike almost all analyses of sex in African Studies, however, I focus on sex not as sexuality, comprised of interactions and desire, but as the sexed body, encompassing physicality, appearances, and assumptions.

Sex in Transition is thus part of scholarship that integrates analyses of heteronormativity and gender normativity with apartheid and transitional literature, offering a comparative perspective on these periods in South African history. As Hoad put it in another context, "Arguably, apartheid places the question of sex as central to national and social as well as racial definition" (Hoad 2005: 23). And the aftermath of apartheid has led to similar revelations about the immediacy of race to sexuality during the transition. Mikki van Zyl reminds us, "to understand the workings of gender and sexualities in Africa we must always be sensitive to the issue of race in discourses concerning Africa—whether from the West or from within Africa" (Van Zyl 2005: 22–3). To accomplish these multifaceted objectives, my intention is not to focus on one theorist or disciplinary approach but to highlight various perspectives on and nuances of gender liminality in South Africa. Multiple and connected approaches to theory in this text are the core of this book, and use of this dialogic strategy foregrounds theorists' juxtapositions and similarities through attention to the constitution of sexed and gendered bodies within the specifities of Africa.

II. Historicizing Gendered and Political Transition

The simultaneous importance and troubles of creating an historical account of gender liminality mirror the contradictions facing historians of sexuality in the same context. Neville Hoad explains some of the difficulties he and his collaborators Karen Martin and Graeme Reid encountered in anthologizing *Sex and Politics in South Africa* (2005), a compilation of academic and activist articles, narratives, interviews, and archival material from Gay and Lesbian Memory in Action in Johannesburg. The text focuses on historical accounts of lesbian and gay organizing, about which Hoad expresses the following reservations:

> Obviously this is an overdetermined history, where one narrative line . . . will not suffice; and the documents, analyses and testimonials from the recent archiving of the history of lesbian and gay organising stand in various relations to the emergent historiographies of what is variously termed the post-apartheid state and civil society, or South African in an era of internally led structural adjustment. (Hoad 2005: 18)

Similarly, the narrative line of gender liminality is not clear and consecutive, best expressed in multiple forms and contradictions. The complexities of temporality, and critiques of dominant assumptions of the workings of time based in the contemporary global North, are also critical to understanding both individuals' narratives and the assumption of an historical queer progress narrative. Here, temporality figures as an historical metanarrative, circumscribed by colonial relations of power.

Gender liminal South Africans have had both notable raced and classed degrees of public visibility and acceptance and faced significant discrimination in various time periods. Concurrent with critiques of varied narratives lines and queer temporalities, attention to historical and geographic particularities helps to provide a context for these disparities. Further, as Gayle Salamon writes, following Foucault and others, "Bodies can only be understood, become legible, though their historically contingent specificity" (2010: 79). In South Africa, mainstream media accounts in the 1950s often featured flamboyant drag performers and accounts of coloured "drags" (private drag parties) (Jeppie 1990), as well as sensationalized narratives by black and coloured transsexuals (Williams 1994). Sex reassignment surgeries for many transsexuals were funded by the state beginning in the 1960s (South African Law Commission 1995), whereas laws like the Prohibition of Disguises Act 16 of 1969 made dressing in drag with "criminal intent" illegal (Cameron 1994). But what preceded and complemented these documented instances of gender liminality and how are they similar and different?

Colonial histories of the development and production of gender and the development of strict racial categories in South Africa are critical to this analysis. While European explorers sailed around modern-day Cape Town beginning in the 1400s, it was not until 1652 that Table Bay, in the southwest corner of South Africa, was settled by Dutch colonizers (Thompson 1995). From the origins of colonialism, two parallel themes emerged that shaped South African colonial and apartheid history—the struggle for control of land and labor. Colonization spread north through a series of wars between those indigenous to the region and white settlers. Despite their victories, colonizers were largely unable to force local populations into servitude, and they began to import slaves from West Africa and Asia to the Cape by the thousands beginning in 1658, establishing classes of landless poor people and promoting European superiority.[9]

In 1795, global struggles for economic and political power led the British into bloody combat with the Dutch for control of South Africa, but despite the regime change, both powers had similar goals: to prevent "native wars" (particularly with the Xhosa), advance settler societies, and exploit the natural resources of the region (Fredrickson 1981). Tension between Dutch and British settlers complicated these objectives and increased "ethnic" and class distinctions between the British and the *Boers* (white Dutch Afrikaner farmers), while consolidating whiteness as a cornerstone of colonial power. The Great Trek (1836–1854), a mass migration of at least 10,000 *Boers*, exemplified colonizers' continued struggles over control of land and labor, as it was initiated by Dutch settlers who were angry about their loss of land, slave labor, and status in the Cape (Thompson 1995: 87). The Great Trek greatly extended the geography of white colonization. White migration resulted in the violent displacement of indigenous black South Africans, and colonists merged race and class by forcing blacks to work or pay them for rights to live on marginalized rural lands.

National and class-based tensions among whites and blacks' resistance to increasing state-led subjugation were only heightened by the discovery of diamonds in Kimberly and gold in Johannesburg in 1886 at the height of British imperialism. Together, capitalist and state leaders controlled migration, kept wages low, and managed black male labor within this emerging white-dominated capitalist economy (Kanfer 1993). Passes, initially instituted to control slave labor in the Cape in 1760, formed an integral and elaborate instrument of raced and gendered labor control beginning in 1895 and continuing through the period of apartheid (Harsch 1980), an issue to which I will return.

One of the lesser-known means of maintaining low wages and managing black male labor was state acceptance of gender liminality and same-sex sexuality in the form of what scholars label "mine marriages." Mine marriages were gendered relationships between black male miners that provided companionship, sex, domestic service (for masculine "husbands"), and protection (for feminine "wives"). Such relationships were quite common in the region; for instance, according to Marc Epprecht, one study suggests that 70–80 percent of Zimbabwean men working on mines took male wives (Epprecht 2004: 80–81). One of the arguments central to *Sex in Transition*, building on the work of Glen Elder, is that the degree of acceptance of gender liminality by state institutions often rested on the extent to which gender liminal bodies were under state control and supported institutional gendered ideologies. Further, this state acceptance can be a means of analyzing the extent to which class and race are interpolated into citizenship. Beginning in the late 1890s, mine marriages served state and capitalist interests by organizing male workers in mining compounds away from their heterosexual families (Moodie 1989; Wa Sibuye 1993; Elder 1995; Epprecht 2004). As Epprecht cogently explains,

> These temporary male-male unions often served (and were often self-consciously intended by the men themselves) to strengthen traditional marriage with women back in the rural areas. That is, "boy wives" allowed the men to avoid costly and potentially unhealthy relationships with female prostitutes, hence to be able, eventually, to retire as "real men" ruling over successful rural homesteads. (2009: 1266)

In this case, gender liminality was temporarily acceptable in broader contexts of labor, poverty, geography, and state interests.[10]

In this same period, the intersections of global imperial tensions, competing racial agendas, and capitalist greed (especially British fears of losing control of South Africa's immense wealth) resulted in the violent Anglo-Boer War (1899–1902). Britain's victory consolidated colonizers' political power in South Africa (with the four white settler states in the Cape, Natal, Transvaal, and the Orange Free State incorporated as provinces), and in 1910 what was a British colony became the Union of South Africa.[11] Colonists continued to violently subjugate black South Africans, systematically retracting black people's political rights and options for land-ownership through measures such as the 1913 Native Land Act, which severely restricted black people's rights to purchase or lease land (Thompson 1995).

Black and coloured South Africans mounted multiple forms of resistance to colonial rule, but segregation policies and growing colonial political and military power largely overwhelmed the efficacy of their protests. Throughout the 1920s and 1930s, the National Party, formed to serve Afrikaner farming interests, gained support. In 1948 the National Party was elected, fueled by conjunctions of white Afrikaner disillusionment with British rule, class-based repression of striking white miners, and racist fear of growing black dissent. National Party leaders developed apartheid, literally "separateness" and based in British segregation policies and Afrikaner *baasskap* (supremacy), into a regime of strict but contradictory political, economic, and social segregation of blacks and whites and violent suppression of enemies of the state. Apartheid's supporters aimed to regulate all aspects of South Africans' daily lives, separating people according to race (Population Registration Act, 1950), outlawing marriage between people from different racial groups (Prohibition of Mixed Marriages Act, 1949), restricting land usage (Group Areas Act, 1950), and racializing education (Bantu Education Act, 1953). Whiteness was again consolidated through these policies, despite the "ethnic" political separations of Afrikaner and British citizens.

Deborah Posel argues that tensions between culture and biology were part of what made these apartheid measures of race so strong.

> "Race" had both cultural and biological markers, each providing tautological evidence for the other (as mutually both the cause and effect of the other). It was this hybrid conceptualisation of race that lay at the core of apartheid's racial project, and which enabled a practice of racial differentiation far more insidious and tenacious in its grip on everyday life than might otherwise have been the case. (2001a: 59)

Like race, gender is commonly theorized as comprising social components (behaviors, attitudes, appearances) as well as somatic ones (conceived of as biological sex). The hierarchical relationality of race and gender and their connection to apartheid conceptions of order contributed to their virulence. Posel points out that versions of racial restriction and definition were authorized by the law that relied more on science and violent policing at some times and were more deliberately flexible and elastic at other times (2001a, 2001b).[12]

These restrictive measures instituted by apartheid leaders were met with intense resistance in multiple forms, led particularly by the African National Congress (ANC) and the Pan Africanist Congress (PAC). Though demonstrations were initially nonviolent, the apartheid government responded by brutally repressing grassroots protests such as the Sharpeville pass resistance of 1960 and the 1976 Soweto demonstrations against racist education. By the late 1960s, liberation movements turned to armed insurgency. Again, leaders of the apartheid government responded by declaring a state of emergency and by passing multiple pieces of repressive legislation that gave the white police flexible powers to arrest South Africans at will.

Not surprisingly, gender liminality converged with the powers of state control during this time. In the 1970s, according to historian

Denis-Constant Martin (1999), the apartheid state's acceptance of Cape Town's Coon Carnival, and the *moffies*[13] that were an integral part of this annual festival, contributed to growing state-led hierarchies among racial groups, positioning coloured people as humorous and "deviant" when compared to "normal" whites and "threatening" blacks. In this same period medical postulations that black South Africans were far more likely than whites to be intersexed (Grace 1970) also formed part of the scientific racism and pathologization of black bodies integral to apartheid.[14]

While gender liminality was used by the state to give further evidence of the deviance of black and coloured people, gender liminality among whites was especially alarming to the apartheid government. Gender liminality within the context of black same-sex relationships was tolerated, and even encouraged, by the apartheid state, such as in the form of the previously mentioned mine marriages, but gender liminality within the context of white homosexuality was usually stringently policed. For example, in 1966 police raided a large gay party in Forest Town, "a quiet and respectable old suburb to the north of Johannesburg" (Gevisser 1994: 30) and several men were arrested for "masquerading as women." The party, which was called a "mass sex orgy" in the media, was the catalyst for a parliamentary investigation of homosexuality.[15] The interests of the white Afrikaner state were greatly undermined by white homosexuality for two reasons. First, Afrikaners were very concerned with racial purity and reproduction as a small white minority in the midst of a black majority. Second, same-sex sexuality among whites was perceived as morally tainting the Afrikaner nation.[16]

Although Afrikaner nationalism and the apartheid state were violently repressive, they were hardly monolithic. Even the epitome of state apparatus, the military, treated gender liminality in a contradictory manner. For instance, during the 1980s when apartheid came to crisis and the government issued states of emergency, utilizing unprecedented levels of military repression to maintain control of South Africa and the region, those in command manipulated military drag shows to reinforce gender stereotypes (Krouse 1994).[17] This deployment coexisted with homophobic discrimination and medical abuse of white gay conscripts, including electroshock therapy to "cure" homosexuality and forced sex reassignment procedures that sought to eliminate gendered nonconforming expressions by reinforcing gender binaries and the necessity of their congruence (Van Zyl *et al.* 1999). Though these strategies appear contradictory, institutionally they both served similarly repressive goals.

How did race and gender materialize together during apartheid? Many people have theorized the critical differences between race and gender, but Deborah Posel's cogent analyses of components of apartheid racial reasoning (2001b: 70–73) can help us theorize their similarities to the boundaries of gender during this period, as well. This is particularly important to highlighting gendered bodies (sex) as constituted by apartheid. First, Posel represents "race and racial difference as self-evident 'facts' of experience." The presumed reality of gender and sex binaries and divisions similarly remained the bedrock of all debates about their parameters. Second, she identifies race as "a mix of biology, class, and culture." Posel contends that apartheid conceptualizations of race relied on phenotypical differences, social components of everyday life, and class privilege. In the latter, "products of a more 'civilised' 'way of life'—were considered to be markers/evidence of biological superiority." As we will see in Chapters 1 and 2, apartheid conceptions of gender were similarly reliant on socioscientific designations along raced and classed lines. In Posel's view, under apartheid race was also "ubiquitous" and came to be attributed to things including choice of hairdresser, food and alcohol, sport, clothing, styles of dress, and interactions with neighbors. "By elasticising the official definition of race beyond merely biological factors, the apartheid state created a mechanism for investing all facets of existence with racial significance." Similarly, policing the boundaries of gender was located in and on everything; this book will speak to various forms of this policing in detail.

Posel further claims that under apartheid, race was "essential rather than accidental or contingent." Ways of thinking about both race and gender under apartheid relied on the idea that all races are different from each other and, I suggest, that men and women are different from each other. This was the basis for ideas of racial separation upon which apartheid was based. Posel also asserts that race was "the primary determinant of all experience"; this is a difference between gender and race. I'm not convinced that race always superseded sexuality, gender, or class, or that we can hierarchize social categories, but it certainly worked in concert with them. Finally, Posel identifies "race as the site of white fear." Anxieties about racial mixing were paramount under apartheid. As we will see, gender-based fears, including those rooted in heterosexism, occurred within racialized frameworks.

Apartheid's simultaneously restrictive and flexible designations of gender and race met with continued defiance from South Africans as well as international supporters of the anti-apartheid movement, with waves of economic sanctions imposed globally. The 1980s were repeatedly marked by uprisings and recession, and eventually apartheid became fiscally and politically untenable. In 1990, ANC leader Nelson Mandela was released, and despite widespread violence and negotiations in this period, he became South Africa's first democratically elected President in 1994.

Since 1994, the economic and racial divisions and inequities of colonialism and apartheid have been difficult to dispel. Initial optimism about the transition to democracy has given way to disillusionment with the failure of the ANC to make material changes in South African's daily lives. Mikki van Zyl notes, for instance, that "apart from the creation of new black elites, the dynamics of economic power have remained mostly unaltered for the majority of South Africans—whites (12% of the population) still earn more than half the country's income" (2005: 26–7). Reconciliation (particularly through the Truth and Reconciliation Commission) and nation-building have posed new sets of challenges. As Van Zyl reflects, "[t]he ten years of democratisation have brought about major shifts in the way we South Africans see ourselves and others [and] . . . we have all had to reorient ourselves to a new political order" (19).

Since the end of apartheid, visibility, medical treatment, and legal protection have increased for some groups and decreased for others. While same-sex sexuality became legally protected by the 1996 Constitution with varied ramifications, medical sex reassignment programs were increasingly difficult to access. And whereas the repeal of laws outlawing sodomy initially brought greater expectations of safety for gay South Africans when the transition began, the simultaneous repeal of laws that allowed transsexuals to change the sex listed on their birth certificates in 1993 left those who underwent medical sex reassignments without legal rights after their physical transition. South African progress narratives of freedom and the hopes based in rights discourses have been undermined by these contradictions.

III. Simone Heradien: July 24, 1997

The movement to and in this transitional period is the focus of *Sex in Transition*. Two life historical interviews conducted ten years apart provide a particularly poignant theoretical and analytic framework through which to conceptualize the dual meanings of "transition." In 1997, I met Simone as she was in the midst of her surgical sex realignment transitions in Cape Town. She was in her late twenties and identified as a "so-called coloured." At this time, she made important connections between her life and the political economic histories of South Africa, linking the transitions she experienced as a South African and a transsexual. She also personally utilized the power of the new South African Constitution to force changes in her legal identification during the political transition. Simone articulated a theory of self-acceptance and confidence that guided her decisions and ran counter to prevailing medical and legal accounts of transsexuals' supposed illness and instability. Here I share her thoughts from 1997, and I return to her narrative from 2007 in the Conclusion. Simone reviewed both of these narratives in 2011.

Groote Schuur hospital where Prof. Barnard performed the first heart surgery . . . [did] realignment surgery since 1970 . . . up till about 1994.[18] There were two others after me but very close, we were all like one month apart. Because with our health, going through all this process and transformation and budget cuts here and budget cuts all over the show, those ops have been suspended until further notice. . . . So for psychiatric treatment, assessment, and the actual surgery, Groote Schuur was your most viable option.[19] . . .

In South Africa, or actually at Groote Schuur, [the sex realignment procedure] was covered by health expenses, which most South Africans do not want to believe. . . . In South Africa, even in our apartheid years, if you passed the test it was seen as a necessary procedure and not cosmetic.[20] Therefore, the state would pay if you couldn't afford to pay for it. They still did up till '94, but I was on medical aid, a private patient. The state was going to pay for me, but then my medical aid decided they would pay for the operation when they were confident that it's not purely cosmetic. . . . But most of the cases are state [-financed]. You would pay a nominal amount, like maybe your visitations, after-care, and when you go every six months for . . . your hormonal prescription, which you have . . . to take for the rest of your life. So suppose for that, you pay your 34 Rand or it's now 35, but for the actual surgery the state covered it.[21] But it wasn't a widely publicized procedure [and] that is why even up to today if you tell people that you've had your operation done at Groote Schuur, a lot of South Africans won't believe you. Because it's always thought that you had to go overseas for these operations, and they don't even know that. . . .

The process took me about a year. And it was also because of it being postponed and not knowing when [the attending physician] was coming back . . . and strikes and things like that. That was also the year we were going through the democracy, the transition, so it was a lot of things. Anyway, when we were going through our transition stage, there was what we call the RDP, getting water and electricity to those who didn't have water and electricity. The RDP stands for the Reconstruction and Development Programme, and that was 1994 the same year that I had my op. So I said to everybody, well you've heard of the RDP, that's me! . . . I was definitely reconstructed and developed. . . .

At the moment [doctors at Groote Schuur are] doing pure cosmetic procedures with respect to sexual realignment. Like I've still got too much skin on my labia, so they're going to remove it. It was going to be done six months ago, and I was on the operating table when I started putting on my Joan Collins prima donna act and said, "I don't want to go in [for] this operation!" <with affected accent, laughing> So they're going to do it now in the next month. But you know everything [else] is done, everything is over. It's just excess tissue that I want them to remove. It's not a necessity. I don't have [to have] it done, it's not gonna kill me. And they all said to me, "You've been through the major part of surgery, you've been in hospital for the first part for something like twenty days. This is like nothing. . . . Two stitches, in two days you're out and about." I just couldn't take one more day of lying in hospital with anesthesia in my system and stitches and pain, and I just couldn't.

I just have to bite through the last part because I'm also having my nose done as well. I know you're going, "There's nothing wrong with your nose!" I suppose like in my case or a lot of TSs would feel this way . . . for instance, the doctors agree with me that to refine my nose is going to feminize my face more. So that is why I feel unhappy with my nose, and after that just have my chin chiseled a bit, just about a few millimeters shorter. Once you have your breasts and your vagina and you can dress the way you want to, I don't think you ever get out of that euphoric state totally. I don't think so. . . . I've always been this way, I've always looked this way, I mean since the age of 18, I'm 34 now. . . .

Since the age of 18 I've dressed up like a female and lived as a female, I've worked as a female. . . . I was employed as a secretary, full knowing that I was still a so-called male. That was in the apartheid era when we still had blacks and whites and coloureds, and different houses of Parliament and everything. I was employed as a female secretary with them full knowing. And, also, I went through my surgery while still in the government employ. My op itself wasn't that painful like a lot of girls or guys whichever way say it's *painful. It was more uncomfortable. So I think that was the only disconcerting thing about going through the op.*

But as far as my employment at this stage with the [government] was concerned, they were very supportive. In fact, my boss, he was the senior superintendent. I went to my boss and I said to him, "You know . . . it's been about a year now, and I'm always off sick for about six weeks, two weeks, two months here, there. And you're probably wondering by now what the devil is going on with me." So I said to him, "Well I think I'm going to tell you now, I've been going through sexual alignment surgery." He says, "Oh?" And his face drops like that. I said, "Yes." And he says to me, "Now, just tell me one thing, are you going to come back to work dressed as a man?" . . . I had been working for him for two years, and he didn't even know that . . . <laughing> He thought I wanted to become a man. . . . I was fortunate that in the [government department] I worked with professionals. I worked with . . . managers and superintendents . . . So they were very supportive. I wasn't working in the admin section or with clerks and stuff like that. So I didn't have problems as far as my work was concerned. . . .

When I had my ID changed, they even changed my ID number to now indicate that I am female. So all my male records are then, except for one lousy thing on microform somewhere up in Pretoria, that's the only evidence there is, but anything else has been erased which couldn't have been done. There was sort-of an impasse for about ten years where, actually, like in the '70s, you could have your ID changed, it said female, but you couldn't have your ID number changed. So if it was still in the computer, it would still come up as male. And then you couldn't have your ID changed at all for about five years.

Since the new Constitution, actually you still can't have your ID changed. The law has not been promulgated yet. But I threatened Constitutional Court action and I went [through the Gender Research Unit at the University of the Witwatersrand.] And they were going to represent me in the Constitutional Court. And because I threatened Constitutional Court, the Department of Justice then and Department of Home Affairs, they sort-of knew that it would be a win situation [for me] in the case. So instead of going through that process, they just decided to change my ID book. . . . But I suppose, you know, the others after me could just as easy [threaten legal action] until they change the law. . . .

Things actually started changing way before the Constitution. The Constitution made [living as a transsexual] a lot easier. Cape Town has always been a progressive city. Life here, apart from sexuality, otherwise was much easier than anywhere else in South Africa. . . . In Cape Town people accept you more if you cross-dress because they feel more comfortable, as they say, if they know what you are. Because you know, people think in this limited way. . . . They tell you, "Make up your mind, do you want to be a man or woman?" I would walk into [a] company and . . . I still had major anxiety, but because they feel comfortable with the way I project myself, the way I look, I come in there with [a] dress and make-up and long hair and jewelry hanging to my ankles. They can relate to me as a woman so they would accept me. That is generally still the case. . . .

I've got a steady boyfriend now, for, it's going in for two years. I met him about six months after my op, and before that I've had relationships with guys. I'm quite sure they were straight [and the relationships] . . . were quite successful, you know, like relationships lasting for about anything from about six months to two years. . . . I think that sort of encapsulates it. I must say that I am extremely happy, I've got no regrets. . . . I would go through all that trauma, all that pain, all that discomfort. If I were ten, say five years back, . . . in the same male's body wanting to be a woman, I would do it all over again. Definitely. And I would recommend anyone, whichever way you want to go, to go for it. If that's what you really want and you've been assessed by a good psychiatrist and plastic surgeons and urologists, and [gynecologists] . . . I would say, "Go for it."

My boyfriend is 14 years younger than me, and I think for a young man he coped quite well. He knew right from the start that I'd had a [gender realignment]. Generally I find that guys in Cape Town . . . a few of them are shocked, but . . . I've [only] had one negative reaction that you read about in magazines where I thought I was going to lose my life. And it was an Australian, from Australia. I haven't had that type of reaction from South African men. It's either, "I'm sorry, I'm not interested," or "Wow!" or "You're kidding," you know, that type of reaction and then you don't hear from them for about two weeks to three months and then they warm up to you. But I wouldn't say I've had a negative reaction in that sense, except this Australian guy. . . .

I would say that in Cape Town, there is quite a large transsexual community, a pre-op transsexual community. And the transsexual community, or the, let's term them the cross-dressing community in Cape Town, since the early '70s were very out. There was no hiding. If you wanted to walk like that you would walk like that. And you would just face people's taunts. It's very strange that was sort-of always out in Cape Town, cross-dressing or transgenderism, but the gay scene was very closeted. . . .

The communities are very closely knit. . . . If you're TS you get a lot of support from the gay community, and if you're gay you get a lot of support from the TSs, and if you're transvestite you get a lot of support from the gays and the TSs.[22] *There's a lot of support with the out community of all of the transgenders. Cape Town is small, as well. So it's very closely knit, and in the end if you are an out gay person and socialize a lot, you end off knowing almost each and every TS and TV and TG in the Cape Peninsula. Honestly. Because, like you all go to the Bronx, you all go to Moulin Rouge and to Angels and at that time to Caesar's.*[23]

Look, to be quite honest, even I don't want to associate myself with the screaming queens. Okay, let's put it this way. On the whole, I am the type of person, I'll be friends with whoever wants to be my friend. If they respect me, I will respect them for whatever they are. If my friend is a screaming queen, I'll walk with her in the street, and she can scream as much as she wants to. <laughter> But there are two types of screaming queen elements in Cape Town. I'm sure you probably find them over the world, as well. You've got your . . . lower class of screaming queen and your more upper class. So the lower class of screaming queen, they sort of put you more to shame and, not because they're screaming queens, but it's their behavior, their rudeness, their lewdness. I'll walk with a screaming queen with pink feathers in her hair look-ing like Priscilla, Queen of the Desert. *But as long as she's got manners and if people taunt her, just shrug it off like that. But I'm not gonna walk with a screaming queen that's gonna start screaming and shouting back.*[24]

But I think now, after the [gender realignment], I'm more ready. I'm more prepared to walk with a screaming queen because I know within myself now that I'm a woman. You see? I don't have to prove anything to anyone anymore. Whereas before, I wanted to show the world that I'm a transsexual, I am woman, although I'm in a man's body, and I'm not a screaming queen. So . . . before I would sort-of try and avoid screaming queens, not to be stig-matized or categorized with that. But now because my [gender realignment] has given me confidence, now I couldn't be bothered. If people want to say, "Ah, that's another screaming queen," well fine. You know? I'll give them a peep show at one of the hanky panky shops and they can see whether I'm a screaming queen or not. <laughing> Then they can judge for themselves.[25]

I can honestly say that I don't think I would have ever committed suicide if I didn't have the [operation]. I probably would have resigned myself to the fact that I couldn't have the op.[26] *Because I was living a relatively successful life before—I mean, good heavens, what more could you want to be employed as a woman and accepted as one? That's really like 80% of the battle won. And*

I think if I couldn't have it, or if I had to pay for it or something, I probably would have resigned myself to live that for the rest of my life. I've got a friend at the moment who . . . she's fifty years old already and she's only on hormone treatment. I don't think she's going to get the treatment because actually she's very masculine. But even if I had to go that route with just having breasts, I don't think I would kill myself because to me . . . there's such a lot to live for, you know, than to kill yourself because of the damn [gender realignment]. There were stages, I think, in my early teens when, the teens, I think that we all go through that in your early teens, that sometimes you want to commit suicide. Thank goodness that was just a phase. . . .

I can just imagine a few TSs out there who are now 16, between 16 and 25, going through the same trauma I went through, not knowing where to turn to, who to go to. And I think we need, in Cape Town and in South Africa, we need a [lifeline for transgendered and transsexual people facing emergencies] like if you are on the verge of committing suicide . . . if you've got family problems, you know you can contact [it]. . . . Well-publicized. . . . [Transsexuals also need a place to get advice about] where to go from the stage where they have decided that they want to have a [gender realignment]. You know, which channels to go through. That, I think, is desperately needed.

Twelve years ago I was going to have my surgery, but at that time I wasn't working. So the only criteria was that I had to work for a year to show them that I'm now totally stable and then come back. And when I had worked for a year, I came back and [the realignment program] was suspended, due to lack of funds, and then I had to wait ten years. It was from phoning this one, that one, and all over the country that I heard through the grapevine that Groote Schuur's doing the ops again. And if I wasn't that determined or that tenacious type of person then maybe . . . it still would have passed me by. So I think it just needs to be made easier; [people could call and find out], "Here's at least two numbers of contact if you need assistance" and that's it. And I would say it's time now I've got my life settled. Basically I'm happy. I'm happy with my career, happy with my life . . . I would like to play a major role in setting up that support group in Cape Town.

People in South Africa often associate transsexualism with prostitution. They criticize [people who] . . . have a [gender realignment] and they end up being a prostitute. Personally, I don't have anything against that, because to me, if you want to be a sex worker, then be it. But I just feel from my side that perhaps the growing TS needs a more normal role model to look up to, to know that you don't have to. Because a lot of transsexuals, especially pre-op, in Cape Town are sex workers. You know, generally because it's difficult *to find a job, that type of thing. So I think a lot of them need to know that, depending on your personality, and I'd even say depending on some luck, you can find a normal job out there and live a normal life. Get married have 2.5 kids and a dog. I think it's important and then they can make the decision whether they want to live a normal life with the 2.5 kids and a dog or they want to live a street life, 500 men and no dogs. Five hundred men and lots of dogs? <laughing> . . .*

I was unemployed for nine years, and some people would probably say this is stupid but I'm glad that I stuck it out. I wasn't prepared to take a job as a hairdresser, or beautician, or designer, or a typical gay or transsexual job. I wasn't prepared to do it, because I wanted to move away from that. I sort of see myself, stupid me, I see myself as a martyr. You know, for the TS community. Show the world that you can live as much a normal life as the next, the next person. And, sorry to say, I think my life has turned out more normal than straight people. I'm more happy and at peace with myself and what I am and what I'm doing and how I dress and how I live and how I walk and talk and speak. I'm not walking around with a mask. And to a certain extent, yes, like I mean at work I can't use my foul language the way I want to, that's sort-of like the world over, but I would say generally I don't think I walk around with a mask. I'm an open book.

Simone's narrative encompasses many of the critical themes of this book—emphasizing the importance of transition, medical and legal discrimination in related inconsistencies facing transsexuals, and the range of gender liminal communities in South Africa. Uniquely South African concerns and debates also emerge from her narrative, including the role of apartheid, public medicine, and hospitals in transitioning; balancing political economic concerns with the medical necessity of sex reassignment; the role of government-issued identification numbers in transitions and employment; regional and temporal considerations; the South African Constitution and its potentials and pitfalls; sex work and suicide; and degrees of acceptance in racialized communities. These themes are interspersed throughout the five chapters that follow.

IV. Toward Sex in Transition

Many scholars have spoken for gender liminal people. However, in academic accounts they rarely describe their own lives and discuss what gender means to them. The first challenge of this research thus lay in developing methodologies in which the narratives of such South Africans would be central. *Sex in Transition* also falls at the center of a number of academic and popular discourses that are not frequently in dialogue with each other. The second challenge, therefore, was to develop a research strategy in which competing discourses could be heard simultaneously.

To achieve these goals, *Sex in Transition* employs narratives, interviews, participant observation, and archival and media analyses. Over the course of twelve years, from 1997 until 2009 (including fourteen consecutive months from 1999–2000), I collected over 250 interviews and life histories. Participatory research and interviews were undertaken primarily in urban areas in South Africa and their surrounding townships in the Western Cape, Gauteng, and KwaZulu-Natal, especially Cape Town and nearby townships, Johannesburg, Pretoria, and Soweto. I describe my approach to participant observation and interviews below and detail the process of collecting life histories in Chapter 3. I also drew on archival and library resources in Cape Town and Johannesburg and on extensive media records. The National Library of South Africa provided vital sources about the history of transsexuals' medical treatment in South Africa, as well as critical newspaper accounts. The Mayibuye Centre, an archive documenting the apartheid era in South Africa and previously housed at the University of the Western Cape (now on Robben Island), has large collections of activist materials that provided background for this book. The library of the University of the Witwatersrand in Johannesburg was essential to my review of African feminist materials. South African media analyses in *Sex in Transition* focus on mainstream newspapers, popular magazines, and gay and lesbian media. Perhaps the most significant resource is Gay and Lesbian Memory in Action (GALA, formerly the Gay and Lesbian Archives), housed at the University of the Witwatersrand in the Historical Papers Archive of the William Cullen Library. GALA holds relevant archival materials on military medical abuses, accounts of gender liminality, and activist organizations' histories. I was not interested in the trans* past as something to be discovered in archives to support the "uneasy and sometimes impossible portability" (Arondekar 2009: 9) of gendered categories based in the global North, but in an approach that highlighted politics of creating gender liminality in the past and the present as a means of attention to gendered colonialism. Taken together, these methods and sources allowed the development of an interdisciplinary analysis based in multiple and comparative locations.

An important challenge facing Marc Epprecht in writing *Hetero-sexual Africa?: The Making of an Idea from the Age of Exploration to the Age of AIDS* (2008) that I also faced with this work was how to find substantive information on a subject that has been so widely overlooked by researchers. In his text, Epprecht tries to create and reshape histories of sexuality, despite the obvious material gaps that exist in the historical record, forcing him to take risks in his text that might unsettle traditional historians. As Anjali Arondekar cautions in her analysis of contemporary work on similar subjects, "For scholars of colonialism and sexuality (of which I count myself), the references to homosexuality troublingly reiterate the very colonial dynamic one attempts to exceed: homosexuality remains obvious and elusive—undeniably anecdotal . . . yet rarely sustainable in any official archival form" (2009: 14). Critiques of fields such as history and anthropology necessitate a refiguring of research purposes and of evidentiary claims regarding sexuality and, I argue, gender liminality. Consequently, the choices I made about the kinds of material to include here were not based on traditional disciplinary prescriptions or academic expectations regarding sources or methodology, but were broad and wide-ranging in response to the subject of this book and its politicized subject.

One of the most difficult methodological decisions to make in framing this work was how to clearly define terminology and simultaneously undermine it both conceptually and linguistically. For instance, I rely on words such as "gender" and "sex" throughout this book. In common usage, *gender* is how we present ourselves in the world as masculine or feminine, while *sex* is simplified as "the body." However, as feminist theorists have increasingly asserted, while sex and gender are socially constituted, neither rely on simple biological fact. Whenever possible, I rely on *gender* to refer to varied forms of gendering, including the gendered body, as a way to minimize the false distinction between gender and sex. However, in some places unsettling the corporeal composition of *sex* and distinctions made among sex, gender, and sexuality are semantically useful.

I similarly depend on racial terms used by South African narrators to self-identify. But I also recognize the ways colonial and apartheid laws and practices created and codified these categories, as well as recognizing the inabilities of racial categories to neatly contain South Africans. Under apartheid the population was generally classified into four groups—White, Indian, Coloured, and Black—and contemporary racial categories and self-identifications stem from these imposed differences. Historically "white" has referred to those who are of English or Afrikaans descent, "coloured" included those who are of Cape Malaysian, Indian, or mixed descent (with apartheid law officially designating people as Cape Coloured, Cape Malay, Griqua, Indian, Chinese, Other Asiatic, and Other Coloured), and "black" or "African" encompassed those nations indigenous to South Africa, such as Zulu and Xhosa. In some time periods, "Indian" and "Chinese" were additional apartheid racial classifications and "black" was politically employed to include all people of color by those oppressed by the apartheid regime. I apply the terms people use to describe themselves in particular historical contexts here; these categories didn't emerge spontaneously but are imbricated in colonial projects and must be understood through the lens of the nation-state.

Gender neutral language underpins this text. I use gender neutral designators such as "s/he" and "hir" in place of she, he, his, or her to indicate ambiguity (or just the letter "e" when referring to an author who has chosen this). In an attempt to provide clarity, when possible I define gendered terminology used by authors or narrators in the text or in footnotes. "Cisgender" refers to people whose gender and sex assigned at birth match (masculine/male or feminine/female) and is often contrasted to "transgender" identifications as "[t]he Latin prefix cis means 'on the same side,' while the prefix trans means 'on the opposite side' . . . [and] has a more positive connotation than 'normal' or 'non-transgender'" (Morgan et al. 2009: 5).[27] In addition, I use medical terms such as "transsexual," "intersexual," and "transvestite" that often have divergent and objectifying/pathologizing meanings in different contexts and time periods, but only with careful attention to these meanings.[28] I choose not to use the term "transgender" descriptively, because over time it has come to hold much more meaning than the umbrella term of a gender spectrum it once designated (Valentine 2007) with geographic connotations; instead, I deploy it only in specific ways as chosen by individuals and organizations. The designator trans*—with an asterisk—has come to serve as a useful way to indicate the prefix trans and an open suffix (e.g., trans-sexual, trans-vestite, trans-gender), all possible suffixes, or another category altogether.[29] I use the word "queer" only very specifically, as it was rarely deployed by South Africans I interviewed.[30] The authors and editors of Trans: Transgender Life Stories from South Africa write of their collaboratively authored glossary,

> As we are dealing with issues concerning identity that are also politicised, the words, and how they are used, are always changing. These definitions are by no means final. The glossary was therefore the most problematic part of the book for the team to write. (Morgan et al. 2009: 5)

I hope that readers will recognize my similar need to constantly reference new terms and redefine words from chapter to chapter and also embrace the intangibility of many of the categories and terms used throughout this book.

As Richa Nagar and I detail in *Critical Transnational Feminist Praxis*, feminist scholars' attempts to engage with methodological concerns have led to the development of three specific practices:

1. *Engagement with positionality and reflexivity*, where the concept of positionality refers to the ways in which a researcher's position in terms of gender, race, class, sexuality, age, and ability shapes the content of research and critical self-reflexivity becomes a tool to produce a description of that positionality;

2. *Representational experiments* that seek to interrupt the researcher's own authority by incorporating or juxtaposing multiple "voices";

3. *Enacting accountability*, which for many interdisciplinary "social scientists" has included sharing of interview transcripts, life histories and finished academic products with "informants"/ "subjects"; and which has involved wide-ranging engagements with questions of how to write for multiple audiences. (Nagar and Swarr 2010: 7)

All three of these practices were important to me in my work and methodologies in different ways. However, Nagar and I also critique the limitations of these efforts to address feminist concerns. In the first instance, positionality can set researchers' identifications in space and time, "foreclosing an analysis of the manner in which identities and locations of those who produce knowledges are constituted and negotiated in and through the process of knowledge production itself." Representational experiments often do not advance dialogues and "run the risk of being dismissed by some academics as atheoretical narratives." Enacting accountability, in the increasingly professionalized context of academia, "rarely finds the legitimacy, encouragement, or resources that it deserves to prosper as a practice" (ibid.). Nagar and I argue that all three of these practices are further undermined by hierarchies of knowledge producers and knowledges.

Beyond the logistical details of what I did and the language and concepts that shape this work, there are a few considerations mindful of these critiques that are critical to my investments in this text. My research for *Sex in Transition* employed three components—collaboration, intimacy, and conflict—in particular ways, all of which are woven through complicated situations that I explore below. The most important aspect of this research and engagement with the critiques Nagar and I offer has been sustained involvement with individuals and communities. I have made a long-term commitment to working in South Africa; since 1997 I have returned approximately every other year for periods of time ranging from two months to almost two years in order to build and maintain relationships. I interviewed many people multiple times over the course of these years, gaining perspective on their own transitions and the effects of the changes happening in South Africa more broadly in their lives.

Much of this research was conducted collaboratively with Sam Bullington, a process that we write about extensively in *Critical Transnational Feminist Praxis* (Bullington and Swarr 2010) and that Sam eloquently analyzes in his dissertation (Bullington 2005). While my work focused on gender liminality, Sam examined contemporary nation-building, the political effects of post-apartheid constitutional protection for lesbians and gays, and connections among anti-apartheid, gay/lesbian, and HIV/AIDS activism that have emerged over the past fifteen years. Collaborative research, with other researchers or with members of communities in which we work, is a feminist ideal that is rarely practiced. While we may extol the benefits of working together in theory, individual achievement is expected and rewarded within academia.[31] However, Sam and I found that by working together we were able to overcome many of the impediments we would have faced as researchers alone and to enhance our individual projects. The first benefit was theoretical; talking about our research in the moment and being accountable to another academic's perspective helped us to better understand complexities. Our accounts and interpretations of the same experiences were often completely different, even unrecognizable, from each other. Constantly processing our interactions informed our decisions about how to proceed in our ongoing work in inestimable ways.

Methodologically, our collaborative work enhanced interviews and our rapport within communities where we worked and varied our knowledge of South African contexts and histories, though we simultaneously and constantly struggled with inherent power imbalances in these contexts and relationships (Bullington and Swarr 2010). We took advantage of mutually exclusive research opportunities by splitting up, had close bonds with different people, and created a meticulous division of labor between us that was far more extensive than either of us could have completed alone, allowing us to document and analyze research through dual sets of daily notes, binders of newspaper clippings and archival research, photographs, videotapes, tape recordings, and transcripts. We provided emotional support to each other, especially in the face of the difficult subjects we were researching, and felt safe traveling together in ways that we never would have attempted alone.

Confidentiality presents another serious concern underpinning this research and integral to these reflections on collaboration. Feminist researchers often struggle with how to represent important but potentially compromising details of narrators' lives, a consideration particularly poignant in small marginalized communities. A tension exists between positioning narrators as theorists and knowledge producers yet not using their names. But confidentiality is a prominent issue for researchers of same-sex sexuality and gender liminality, as breaches of secrecy may mean community ostracism or violence for narrators (Lewin and Leap 1996). Secrecy was often paramount in interviews with transsexual and intersexual narrators, for instance, as the medical details of surgical treatments, hormone therapies, and other procedures, as well as their social implications, are often not discussed, even with family members. Further, compromising anonymity in these contexts can prevent transsexuals from attaining medical treatment. Some doctors I interviewed explicitly caution patients that if they appear on television or in the media speaking about their transsexualism, they will no longer receive treatment (e.g., Williams 1997). Consequently, to protect narrators' privacy I use pseudonyms throughout *Sex in Transition*. I have also chosen not to reveal details of medical programs, especially locations and practitioners, in this text. While I have discussed these details privately with South African activists, many feel that sharing them publically might have the unintended effect of jeopardizing or undermining medical services that exist today.

Long-term relationship-building included close work with and collaboration in many groups in South Africa. Working with groups focused on gay and lesbians and gender rights, Sam and I were consistently involved in daily activities as varied as taking minutes, making protest signs, assisting in social spaces, providing manual labor, and writing research reports. On request, we spoke repeatedly on radio shows in Cape Town, Atlantis, and Durban ranging from the local "In the Pink" to the U.S.-based National Public Radio about topics including gay marriage, international women's day, HIV/AIDS activism, and drag. Our activities ranged from co-facilitating a safer sex training for the Department of Welfare—contributing an explicit discussion of lesbian sexual practices "much to the astonishment of the majority black African heterosexual group of government workers present" (Bullington 2005: 64)—to serving as ushers at a gay and lesbian film festival. We offered our skills and presence to organizations, content to help in specific ways or to be ordinary members of these groups.

We did not simply focus on one subject. While neither Sam nor I were researching domestic and child abuse, we established a consistent relationship with a shelter for women and children and its founder in a largely forgotten township outside of Cape Town. Much of this work involved bearing witness to violence, talking to women staying there, and helping with everyday tasks at the shelter. We became deeply involved in HIV/AIDS activism through the Treatment Action Campaign from the organization's inception. Sam, always excellent at documenting the details of our daily lives, explains that our "involvement with the Treatment Action Campaign took many forms, including participation in pickets, research for their court case against the South African government, making signs, taking photos to document their history, fundraising, gathering signatures, attending branch, regional, and national meetings, organizing for the march and rally that corresponded with the International AIDS Conference taking place in Durban in 2000, and serving as a small group leader for their mother to child literacy conference" (Bullington 2005: 41). Zackie Achmat, the founder of TAC and 2004 Nobel Prize nominee, likes to refer to us as "TAC's first American volunteers."

Our research took varied forms with individuals, as well. We took photographs that were used by TAC to document public protests. But other contexts for our photography ranged from providing pictures for drag artists who used them for self-critique and for publicity in a local newspaper (e.g., published in the *Cape Argus*) to providing gay and lesbian couples with photos they framed as validation of their relationships. I worked with people one-on-one, too, helping them write speeches, school assignments, and resumes, taking them to doctor's appointments, cooking constantly, and even teaching one person to swim. Only a fraction of this involvement is included in this book, but it all informs my thinking on these subjects in multiple, sometimes inexpressible, ways.

Working in collaboration over more than a decade and on intense subjects meant that narrators and interviewees were intimate in the details of their lives shared, both through daily intimacies of our years of living together and candid discussions. During everyday interactions and conversations, bodies were displayed, discussed, and compared. Sexual abuse and physical violence were regular topics of conversation, such as accounts of histories of incest and experiences of being robbed or raped. Explicit details shared about how and why people have sex, including hilarious conversations about desires and attractions, were common. Questions posed to Sam and me about our relationship and requests for advice about relationship angst were daily occurrences.

It's difficult to express the intimacy of the connections that were the basis for this research outside of specific examples. One of the most touching and difficult interactions I had while in South Africa was in 2005, when I was working in the shared offices of the Treatment Action Campaign, the Community Media Health Project, and Idol Pictures, then located in Muizenberg, outside of Cape Town. This was a space where I had spent a lot of time since 1997, and it formed a hub for local activists involved in projects ranging from campaigning for HIV treatment access to making films about gay and lesbian histories. On this day, though, Zandie, a friend from a community of strong black lesbians in Soweto who I hadn't seen in a few years, was in the offices. We looked at each other with surprise at finding ourselves both in Muizenberg—the white wealth of this oceanfront suburb of Cape Town and geographic distance makes it feel worlds away from Soweto—and then embraced. I asked her what she was doing in Cape Town, and we decided to take a walk on a nearby beach to talk.

Living in Soweto for her whole life, Zandie had never seen the ocean. As we walked, she told me how in Soweto she had been raped repeatedly by the same men because of her lesbianism and how her family had been targeted for violence and harassment, especially her grandmother with whom she lived. The police had ignored her case, even though she knew the rapists who lived in her community. A few days before our serendipitous meeting a network of activists had mobilized to move Zandie to Cape Town, where she didn't know one person, to try to help her escape the campaign of terror waged against her. She had to go into hiding from the men who raped her, almost as if she were in a witness protection program or traveling on the underground railroad in U.S. historical terms. As we walked, Zandie saw the expanse of the ocean for the first time, a miraculous moment for me to share with her but made bittersweet by the circumstances. I found a giant shark's tooth, something I've never seen before or after this time, which I gave to her so she could remember her first time at the ocean as she reclaimed her life. The joy and the sorrow that I felt on that day touched and stayed with me. These kinds of intimacies marked my relationships in South Africa.

Trauma was an unfortunate theme to the intimacy of this research, as well. As Adam Ashforth puts it, concerning his own research in Soweto: "I can think of no way to adequately convey the sense of insecurity that the prevalence of violence in Soweto arouses other than to report that the only friends I have mourned as murdered have died in that place and no one I have known over the past decade has seen a year go by without seeing a year go by without being called to a funeral of someone connected to them who died another's hand" (2005: 36). Most, if not all, of the people interviewed discussed experiences including witnessing murder, sexual violence, intentional HIV infection, medical experimentation, community persecution, and suicide attempts. Sam and I were part of this trauma and felt it viscerally. I was physically and emotionally sick when I took anti-retrovirals prophylactically after being exposed to HIV. I cried when someone with whom I worked closely tried to commit suicide. I ran home with collaborators in a collective panic, as was their practice to avoid potential violence after dark, when we lost track of the time and stayed too late talking at a neighbor's house. I relived the experience of having a brick thrown at my head by a group of youths when Sam and I rode in an otherwise vacant train car in Cape Town. I lost sleep after a friend lagged behind our group traveling in Soweto to buy cigarettes and overheard men discussing plans to come and rape Sam and me later that night.

But the rewards of the intimacy and intention of the research out-weighed these traumas. One narrator who discussed medical experimentation on transsexuals and drag queens in her community with me explained at length that part of the reason she and her friends wanted to speak with me, as a researcher and activist, was that they hope more research or a film can be made to alert those in her community to the dangers of surgeries. The reason, as Brandy Roeland observed, was that "this is actually a very serious situation. It's terrible. And it's something very important and it's an issue that must be brought out and people must know about it" (2000). The concern expressed by Roeland and other narrators during my interviews forms an important part of why I continue to research and write about these issues. In 1996, Sam was on the short list for a prestigious dissertation research fellowship and was asked to interview with a committee of faculty. His work was dismissed by a committee member who told him, "There are no black gays and lesbians in South Africa." When we got to South Africa (without the support of any major funders), we told those we worked with about this comment. One person repeatedly asserted, "You have to do this work and show her that I exist!"

However, such intimacies were consistently unsettled. For example, one drag bar was a site of both intimacy and conflict. We spent many months at this location, conducting interviews and observing drag shows. The dressing room access we were consistently granted allowed us to observe and interview performers as they prepared to go on stage. We talked to them about their characters, miming (lip synching), and gender, and one said the photographs we took, "made us feel like supermodels." But our class, race, and national privileges structured these interactions and created conflicts for us. The owner of the bar was originally interested in speaking to us because he overheard our "American accents," and his enthusiasm about the United States translated into awkward benefits for us. We were given complimentary tickets to drag shows and reserved front-row seating for the sold-out performances, and small handwritten signs were placed on our chairs, which read "Reserved for USA." We came to represent the entire nation. We were young student researchers, excited to be welcomed, yet ambivalent and critical of the context of this acceptance.

The unsettling national privilege of being Americans was something we could not avoid, but it sometimes contrasted with our underestimation as students. My role as an American student and then professor also allowed me to interview doctors in Gauteng, the Western Cape, and KwaZulu-Natal who told me about successes and failures as extreme as patients dying in their gender reassignment programs. One doctor sat with Sam and me for hours and sifted through his years of medical records working with transsexuals, reading from these documents about the interviews he conducted with his patients and sharing one case after another, recounting patients' reasons for seeking surgery and his shockingly subjective criteria for "true transsexualism." Another doctor insisted on taking Sam and me to a white female-to-male transsexual's bedside just hours after his phalloplasty to speak about his life, decisions, and medical experiences. We were shown explicit photographs of patients' bodies and asked for our evaluation of their attractiveness; we heard details of doctors' transnational connections and allegiances, especially to medicine in the United States and Europe. This kind of frankness was a consequence of our privilege and implicit commentary on doctors' views of students that made us very uncomfortable yet provided insights into hidden biases.

The valorization we experienced as Americans sometimes went in the opposite direction, as the reputation of exploitative researchers from the global North caused many South Africans to be rightfully skeptical and guarded. The trust and long-term relationships built with people like Midi Achmat and Theresa Raizenberg, two long-time activists and close collaborators, facilitated this research by allowing us to live in their home for months at a time and connect with their amazing network of friends. And, as Sam put it, "Theresa and Midi went to great lengths to demonstrate to people that Amanda and I were not like other researchers. As a result, we were allowed to witness and participate in activities and conversations from which others were explicitly excluded" (Bullington 2005: 53). Similarly, our close collaboration with Bass John Khumalo, a young Sowetan lesbian who took great pride in sharing her twin bed with us while her sisters slept on the floor of the same room over many years, introducing us to those in her community, and shepherding us on minibus taxis all over Soweto both built intimacies and connected us to communities with histories of mistrust of outsiders. These experiences of collaboration, intimacy, and conflict shaped and guided always awkward, dangerous, and transformative interactions. While Sam and I were not able to overcome the hierarchies and conundrums that Nagar and I raise concerned with positionality and reflexivity, representation, and accountability, we undertook our research with all three of these critiques and cautions at the forefront of our work and engagements.

It is integral that I connect Sam's own gendered transition to the title and concepts of this book. When we began this research in 1997, Sam went by a different name and identified as a lesbian, and our romantic relationship was an important part of this work. Sam and I also identified with the newly emerging transgender movement that we were finding in Minnesota and growing across the United States at the time. But over the following years, Sam changed his name, changed his gender pronouns from feminine to gender neutral to masculine, and eventually began taking testosterone and living as a man. He was fired from his academic job primarily due to his gendered transition, which created a public battle at his former university. Sam's transition reflected the upheaval of the changes taking place around us in South Africa and unsettled our assumptions about who and what we were.

Sam was in varying places in his own transition during our years of research. During our time in South Africa from 1997 to 2000, most of our research and relationships were based on perceptions of us as a lesbian couple, especially in Soweto and Cape Town, so our planned returns together in 2003 and 2005 raised a lot of questions. How would Sam's identity as a trans man and his name change, new beard, and deeper voice impact our research? Who would feel closer to us and who would feel alienated? When Sam had shared personal writings with one collaborator previously about his transgender identity, she swatted him on the head with a newspaper and asked, "What were you thinking?" We were nervous.

What we didn't realize was that circumstances in South Africa were changing around gender liminality. On these later trips I was interviewing people who identified increasingly overtly as transsexual and working with newly formed transgender organizations, so Sam's transition and his openness about it proved to be an asset and to enhance trust and understanding with narrators and activists. Plus, we had underestimated the rapport we had already built through our many years in South Africa, which seemed to outweigh discomfort people may have felt. Sam's process of transition helped us both to identify with gender liminal people in important ways; gender liminality was not an objectified subject of study to us but something we thought about daily. Being able to relate to the practical and emotional aspects of transitions was critical to this work.

The research that comprises the chapters of this book intersperses conceptual interventions, medical accounts, and legislative and media analyses through each chapter's engagement with a particular question, contradiction, or tension. Why were transsexuals' transitions encouraged under apartheid and illegal during the political transition to democracy? Why do white South African doctors claim that intersexuality is more common among black South Africans than whites, with scant research to substantiate their claims? How do white, black, and coloured butch lesbians and drag queens reshape race and gender simultaneously? These and related questions form the fabric of this book.

Each chapter of *Sex in Transition*, while addressing different sets of gendered and raced practices, works in concert to create a picture of the ways these categories have been produced under apartheid and during South Africa's political transition. I claim that gendered ambiguity (such as intersexed bodies, transsexuals' transitions, drag queens' performances, and butches' contested masculinities) was often encouraged among black and coloured South Africans by the state, as it buttressed dominant perceptions of their "abnormality." Experimental and botched sex reassignment procedures on coloured South Africans are perhaps the most striking example of this. Simultaneously, white South Africans were forced into embodiments that cohered gender, sex, and sexuality. Accounts of forced sex reassignment surgeries performed on white gay conscripts provide a vivid demonstration of imposed adherence to dichotomous gendered normality. The means through which the enforcement of these patterns can be traced are varied—ranging from medical experimentation to legal prohibitions—but concurrently they give us new ways to think about the scope and contradictions of apartheid and democratic South Africa, as well as the contradictions of race and gender more broadly. The social implications of apartheid and the transition to democracy for those between genders whose bodies are debated form a consistent theme joining these chapters together.

My first chapter addresses the history and temporal development of the idea of "transsexuality" through medical and legal frameworks. It does so by analyzing the conundrum of the legal promise of the "new" South Africa and the increased gendered restrictions it brought, exploring understandings of sex and gender binaries under apartheid and the co-production of medical and legal practices of transsexuality with race and state politics. The apparent paradox of legal shifts made it impossible to change one's sex on legal documents during South Africa's transition from 1993 to 2003. I demonstrate that gender ambiguity and homosexuality were policed to enforce the congruence of sex, gender, and sexuality. The racialization of physical gender liminality and same-sex sexuality— encouraged or discouraged in particular times and places—served the complex and fluid objectives of apartheid.

Why were free sex reassignment surgeries offered to some South Africans while the same surgeries were forcibly performed on others?

Utilizing Foucault's work on biopower and Africanists' critiques of it, the second chapter explores how the apartheid government conceptualized and manipulated the differences between "specials"—coloured transsexual sex workers often left without functioning genitals after free, experimental sex reassignment surgeries—and white conscripts in the South African Defense Force forced to undertake sex reassignment procedures to "cure" them of their homosexuality. For apartheid's architects, race and gender were inextricable: white homosexual conscripts were forced to align sex with compulsory heterosexuality, while specials' liminally sexed bodies reinforced the perceived abnormality of black and coloured South Africans.

Chapter 3 reconceptualizes and links gendered "transitions" beyond medico-legal and political definitions. Narratives collected from 1997–2009 detail transitions mediated through inconsistencies in legal rights and employment opportunities, incongruous access to medical treatment, and unpredictable relationships. Dominant trends in scholarship about transsexuality speak in medical terms and enforce gender boundaries. By contrast, these narratives are conceptualized through a framework of what Achille Mbembe terms "necropolitics," his way to explain the states of exception and siege that have normalized violence and trauma and to detail the relationships among resistance, sacrifice, and terror. Taken together, these narratives highlight tensions between violence and agency and between risks of death and visions of freedom. In sum, this third chapter examines the intimacy of decisions about what constitute personal transitions in South Africa's political transition.

The fourth chapter of *Sex in Transition* interrogates the concept of *stabane*—literally, intersexual—and its effects on those who express same-sex desire. In contemporary Soweto there is a widespread notion that those who self-identify as lesbian or gay may have both male and female genitals. This tension is most commonly expressed through *stabane*. *Stabane* functions as an accusation often violently leveled at those engaged in same-sex sexual practices, an assumption that bodies cannot transition or change but must retain congruence among gender, sex, and sexuality. Further, these accusations are connected to colonial ideals and current medical research that pathologize and racialize the bodies of those who express same-sex desire. This chapter explores Judith Butler's heterosexual matrix in conversation with Africanists theorizations of *stabane*, ultimately arguing that not only is the meaning of *stabane* contingent, but it cannot be understood apart from the broader implications of race in South Africa.

Chapter 5 theorizes drag as both shaped by and productive of race and gender. This chapter considers drag in the urban centers and surrounding townships of Cape Town, Johannesburg, and Pretoria from the perspectives of its participants focusing on South Africa's period of transition to democracy. Two distinct raced understandings of the relationships among sex, gender, and sexuality emerged in drag communities during this time with differing interpretations of how gender transition is imperative or impossible. In this chapter, I contend that an examination of whiteness in white drag and the intricacies of township femininity illustrates not only the ways that drag produces gender, but affects how we understand and define "drag," "audience," and "performance" through the framework of Kopano Ratele's "kinky politics."

Sex in Transition concludes by discussing the ways that the paradoxes of gender, sex, and race illuminate what South African legal scholar Angelo Pantazis calls extra-transsexual meanings. I explicate these emerging meanings through an analysis of the burgeoning transgender movement in South Africa. "Transgender" is a term with growing significance in the global South that functions paradoxically as a community-building tool and Northern imposition simultaneously. The Conclusion to this book explores the implications of bringing increasing attention to gendered and raced discrimination in both theoretical and grounded contexts. An historical analysis of the position of gender liminality via South Africa's political economy ties together themes of gendered and political transition that have structured this text.

In order to understand how these chapters fit together, I am asking readers to suspend their categorical assessments of gender liminality and attempts to put this research into familiar conceptual boxes. In Northern and medical terms, Chapter 1 is concerned with transsexuality, transvestitism, and homosexuality and boundary shifting among them in different times and with changing political and disciplinary stakes. Would we apply labels to those who are forced or coerced into sex reassignment in Chapter 2 as gays and lesbians or transsexuals? Narrators in the Chapter 3 discuss their gendered transitions, but most don't fit "true transsexual" definitions and some eschew these labels. Chapter 4 is concerned with intersex, gendered same-sex desire, and the instability of sexed bodies. But are butch lesbians who experience a penis during sex with women or gay men who have a vagina when they have sex with men "transgendered"? Are their partners who co-constitute these realities "straight"? Chapter 5 compares forms of drag but broadens its definitions to include drag queens who perform without a paying audience and might be pathologized as transvestites or transsexuals. In short, commonly held categories don't work in Sex in Transition.

The following chapters cover varied terrain, raising questions about South Africa's transition to democracy and gendered transitions of individuals that took place within them. My intention is to engage with conundrums and questions often marked by violence, resilience, and categorical recreations. This book endeavors to articulate new questions to fill lacunae and confront objectification surrounding gender liminality through careful attention to the effects this violence has had for South Africans most affected by it.

One
───────

Prescribing Gender and Enforcing Sex

Under apartheid, many South African transsexuals had access to publicly funded sex reassignment surgeries and were allowed to legally alter the sex listed on their birth certificates. But since the end of apartheid, most public sex reassignment programs have ceased, and while the new South African Constitution promises freedom from discrimination based on sex and gender, from 1993–2003 it was impossible to change one's sex legally. What circumstances led to this apparent paradox and what does it tell us about the constitution of gender in South Africa's political transition?

Apartheid allowed for a category—transsexual—that the post-apartheid state did not. This chapter explores reasons for this through an examination of the medical and legal treatment of transsexuals in South Africa from 1948 to 2003 and concludes that this apparent paradox is integral to ideas about the constitution of sex and gender as inseparable from South African politics and alliances. In short, the emergence of "transsexuality" as a medical and legal entity can be related to efforts to maintain apartheid order. To facilitate this consideration, I elucidate histories of medical sex reassignment procedures and their racialized and historicized sanction for particular groups of South Africans.[1] I compare these histories to legal developments concerning transsexuality in South Africa under apartheid and during the transition to democracy. Through this analysis, transnational discourse about the emergence of the category "transsexual" in South Africa is revealed, as is the temporality of this category itself. Temporality provides a useful framing of the movement and mobility of this category in conjunction with the politico-historical forces, considering how what it means to be a transsexual has changed over time.

This chapter also explores ideological differences about the fixity of gender versus the fixity of sex. These differences are reflected in dissimilar yet overlapping medical and legal histories and change over time through apartheid and the transition to democracy. Through this examination, Edward Said's notion of "traveling theories" is analytically useful to articulate the ways South African gendered and sexed categories work with theories emanating from the global North and South. The slippery importance of the idea of sex and its raced connection to heteropatriarchy are paramount here.

The medical and legal treatments of transsexuality and their contradictions must be mediated through an analysis of the co-production of sex, gender, race, and class. Like Foucault, who finds a "spontaneous and deeply rooted convergence between the requirements of *political ideology* and those of *medical technology*" (Foucault 1973: 38–9), I believe that certain forms of subjectivity can be explicated by understanding their genealogies. Consequently, tracing medico-legal discourses of gender liminality in apartheid and transitional South Africa exposes complementary and contradictory ways that challenges to sex and gender binaries were understood and policed. Following apartheid's adherence to order and simultaneous contradictions, discourses around transsexuality demonstrate conflicts over the raced constituition of gender.[2]

I. Foundations of "Transsexual"

As discussed in the introduction to this text, a number of recent and related works have traced the history of ideas and concepts. Within African Studies, Marc Epprecht's attention to the manifestation and movements of "heterosexuality" (2008) and Neville Hoad's focus on the production of "homosexuality" (2007) over time and space are particularly instructive. Epprecht explains the conceptual and methodological difficulties he faced this way:

> Charting the history of an idea that is often unspoken and unrecorded is inherently more difficult than uncovering evidence of human activity. I acknowledge that my principle sources leave significant gaps that often require extrapolation from scant and geographically uneven evidence. (2008: 26)

The challenges of Epprecht's work were replicated in constituting this chapter. However, this kind of project is also quite valuable in that it eschews potentially troublesome topical analyses of communities based on concepts or identities that may not be uniformly adopted or applicable. In this vein, anthropologist David Valentine explains how he began to rethink his project initially focused on "transgender communities" in New York City marginalized by race and class "in terms of examining the idea of transgender itself and how it is setting the terms by which people come to identify themselves and others" (2007: 21). Unpacking conceptions of "sex" and, more explicitly, "transsexual," can be politically salient in illuminating the borders, stability, and movement of this concept under apartheid and during the political transition in South Africa.

Within rubrics of gender liminality, people who have altered their physical bodies have been documented worldwide in various forms and time periods.[3] However, it was not until the 1940s that "transsexualism" emerged as a modern medical category. European scientists first recorded their attempts to perform "sex transformation" procedures on animals in the 1910s, basing their experiments in theories that all beings are "bisexual"—part female and part male—and sex reassignment surgeries on humans began to occur with increasing frequency in the 1920s (Meyerowitz 2002). Jay Prosser suggests that Michael Dillon was the first transsexual to undertake surgical and hormonal transition in the 1940s, and he did so before the inception of transsexual as an official medical category. Early cases such as this demonstrate "how transsexuality constitutes an active subjectivity that cannot be reduced to either technological or discursive effect" (Prosser 1998: 10). Transsexuals are thus not an effect of discourse or of technological innovation but have complex histories and materializations beyond these external factors.

Despite exceptional cases, surgical procedures did not become publicly recognized in the United States and Europe until Christine Jorgensen's widely publicized male-to-female sex reassignment transition in Denmark in 1952.[4] In the wake of the publicity surrounding Jorgensen's transition, endocrinologist Harry Benjamin brought international attention to transsexuality as a medical category. His text, *The Transsexual Phenomenon*, was published in 1966, the same year that the first sex reassignment surgery was performed in the United States.[5] Benjamin's work provides an essential backdrop to an analysis of South African transsexuality because of the enormous impact of his theories. Beginning in the mid-1950s, Benjamin began a campaign for recognition of transsexualism that differentiated him from other physicians of his time in two regards. First, by seeing gender "disorders" on a continuum, Benjamin distinguished transsexualism from transvestitism and homosexuality, writing: "The transvestite has a social problem. The transsexual has a gender problem. The homosexual has a sex problem" (Benjamin 1966: 28). Second, he perceived himself as a humanitarian who could save transsexuals from self-harm or suicide (Califia 1997). In this sense, Benjamin represented himself as trying to assist transsexuals in achieving their desired bodies.

As protocol surrounding the treatment of transsexuality developed, sexologist John Money emerged as the most prominent physician writing on and treating patients through sex reassignment surgery and arguing that gender is learned, not innate. Based in the United States but with global influence, feminist theorist Suzanne Kessler points out that almost all of the published literature on intersexed infant care management has been written or co-authored by Money. The overwhelming majority of U.S. physicians interviewed for her 1990 analysis of the medical construction of gender in terms of intersexuals and transsexuals "essentially concur with his views and give the impression of a consensus that is rarely found in science" (Kessler 1990: fn 9).[6] Those complicit in this consensus maintained that gender identity is changeable until an infant reaches eighteen months. Later research and Money's own patients eventually suggested otherwise.[7]

Nevertheless, in this time period emerging treatment protocols for transsexuality developed from treatments for intersexuality such as Money's. Among medical professionals, intersexuality is essentially linked to discussions of transsexuality, as these are the two most common gender "disorders" treated through hormone therapy and surgeries. They are also related historically and technically, as techniques used in sex reassignment surgeries and hormone therapy programs were developed out of (and are often the same as) those used to treat intersexuality. Clinical experience with intersexuals established surgical techniques of genital reconstruction and hormonal therapy as well as theories of gender-role learning and self-identification as independent from anatomy.

The ideas of those who promoted sex reassignment surgery such as Benjamin, Money, and Anke Erhardt were extremely unpopular among physicians when they were first introduced in the 1950s and 1960s.[8] Treating transsexuals with surgery was considered elective and dangerous, and such procedures undermined commonly-held beliefs that sex was immutable. At the same time, three factors increasingly motivated physicians to fight for the medical efficacy and desirability of sex reassignment treatments. First, physicians such as Benjamin saw themselves in the role of healing patients and attending to their considerable mental distress. Second, psychiatrists and surgeons recognized opportunities to conduct groundbreaking research on the treatment of gender disorders. Several surgeons interviewed by sociologists Billings and Urban from 1978–1982 asserted that they regarded sex-change surgery as a "technical *tour de force* which they undertook initially to prove to themselves that there was nothing they were surgically incapable of performing" (103).[9] Many physicians wanted to master the body; their ability to change sex proved the victory of science over nature. Furthermore, procedures on transsexual patients were often seen as experiments that could advance physicians' careers (Califia 1997: 72). Third, an excess of cosmetic surgeons in the United States resulted in competition for patients and an increased number of unnecessary operations; some authors suggest that transsexuality fit into this trend as an expensive elective treatment (Hausman 1995: 63).[10]

Moral and legal opposition to the removal of healthy organs initially prevented the recognition of transsexuality as a medical disorder, but eventually conflicting views were overwhelmed by legitimizing publicity. It is important to note transnational influences on the development of global medical opinion, including opinion in South Africa, which can largely be traced to medical networks of professional associations and internationally-circulated journals. For instance, the globally-focused Erickson Educational Foundation became a significant mediating force shaping medical opinion surrounding transsexuals. Founded in the United States in 1964 by Reed Erickson, a wealthy American female-to-male transsexual, one of the missions of this foundation was to convince physicians of the significance of transsexuality as a disorder (Meyerowitz 2002: 209).[11] This Foundation achieved enormous success by convening international medical symposia and conferences (attracting medical professionals from the U.S., Canada, Mexico, Morocco, and Australia [Devor and Matte 2007: 63]), sponsoring workshops at medical schools and professional meetings, and disseminating films and pamphlets about transsexuality to doctors, police, clergy, and social workers. The Erickson Foundation even funded publication of a major anthology on how to treat transsexual patients, which served as a handbook for doctors internationally.[12] Foundations, journals, and professional associations all contributed to commonalities in protocol and philosophies emanating from the United States and Europe.[13]

This powerful and influential advocacy, coupled with increasing numbers of publications outlining the medical necessity of sex reassignment treatment, eventually led to a shift in medical opinion. In the mid-1960s, the majority of physicians in the United States opposed sex reassignment surgery and said that they would refuse a request for it from a patient (Green 1969: 235–42); 94 percent of psychiatrists surveyed in 1967 said that they would refuse to grant sex reassignment surgeries on "moral and/or religious grounds" (Green 1969: 238). However, by the early 1970s, gender dysphoria was widely recognized and was eventually conceptualized in U.S. medicine as a "serious and not uncommon gender disorder" (Billings and Urban 1996: 101).[14]

In conjunction with this shift, physicians increasingly referred to patients' desire for sex-reassignment surgeries as an indicator of their mental illness. The origins of Gender Identity Disorder were perceived as psychological, not physical. Within this context, solidifying the distinctions among transsexuality, transvestitism, and homosexuality remained of great concern for physicians. This is clear in Norman Fisk's summary of what eventually came to be behavioral guidelines for recognizing "true transsexuals," characterized by:

1. A life-long sense of being a member of the opposite sex.

2. The early and persistent behavior of cross-dressing without erotic feelings attached to it.

3. Disdain for homosexual behavior. (Fisk in Billings and Urban 1996: 105)[15]

This emphasis on psychological causality allowed patients to exercise agency in obtaining their desired treatment. But the shift from physical designators (like measurements of hormone levels and chromosomal testing) to behavioral evaluation also granted increasing legitimacy to physicians' particular perceptions of gender and sex. This gatekeeping took place through a trope of "true transsexualism" that I explore below.

II. Prescribing Gender:
South African Medical Conceptions of Transsexuality

Sex reassignment surgeries in South Africa began to grow in numbers at the same time as did these surgeries in the United States—in the mid 1960s. Statistics for sex reassignment procedures from this time period are difficult to ascertain; anecdotally, between 1969 and 1984, 150 transsexuals were treated at Groote Schuur hospital in Cape Town (South Africa Law Commission 1994: 6), and between 1969 and 1993, 58 sex reassignment surgeries were performed by Dr. Derk Crichton of the University of Natal Hospital in Durban (Crichton 1993: 347). Like statistical estimates of many medical procedures in South Africa, inconsistent records of sex reassignment surgery were kept during apartheid. A few additional sources offer estimations. For instance, within this complicated context, transsexuality is estimated by some South African physicians to occur at 1/37,000 people (Taitz 1993), which would mean there were approximately 1,081 transsexuals in South Africa based on 1996 census reports. Other official estimates suggest that there are 2,500 transsexuals in South Africa (Minister of Home Affairs 2003). Precise numbers are impossible to ascertain and are probably quite understated because of the concealment of doctors and their patients, as well as those who are unable to attain medical treatment.

The discussions that surrounded the decision to begin to perform such treatment are largely undocumented; unlike in the United States, widespread public debates are not part of the history of transsexuality in South Africa. However, one anomalous article indicates the terms of early concerns with diagnoses of Gender Identity Disorder. The first published reference to medical debates about the constitution of sex attempts to differentiate between "transvestitism" and "transsexualism" and was published in the *South African Medical Journal* in 1963. In it, Alexander Don describes four South African cases and their extensive physical and psychological diagnostic and treatment protocols that utilize medical models based in the United States and Britain. All four of these case histories center on patients who are each only eighteen years old and who the researchers find to have significant mental deficiencies, including severe mental retardation and schizophrenia. Testing included blood and urine tests, "radiological examination of the skull and chest," searching for evidence of intersexuality and concluding that patients had psychological illnesses not physical disorders (Don 1963: 481).[16]

In all four of these cases, surgical sex reassignment was refused by attending physicians. Indeed, Don's conclusions categorically reject surgical sex reassignment and express "serious doubts about its value" (485), citing lack of proof of the efficacy of surgical treatments, except in cases of what he terms biological intersexuality, as well moral opposition to such procedures. Explaining his moral imperative, Don makes a comparison to physician-assisted suicide, suggesting "there would appear to be as little moral justification for operations on these patients, as there would be for assisting the depressed person who wanted to die" (484).

Instead, Don advocates for aversion therapy through the administration of electroshock therapy and hormonal interventions as the most promising treatment. He cautions that the success of aversion therapy rests in patients' openness to the treatment:

> It is important, though, to remember that this treatment is only likely to benefit the transsexualist who is willing to accept that no surgery is possible and who genuinely desires to stop his cross-dressing. Unfortunately, such patients probably comprise a small minority only, and the remainder, if adamant enough, will seek treatment in countries where surgical reconstruction is available or, failing that, suicide is not an unlikely outcome. (1963: 485)

In this view, patients' successful treatment rests on their willingness to dismiss surgery as an option, tautologically blaming patients for clinical failures. Don's statement also anecdotally indicates the veracity of patients seeking surgery outside of South Africa and the high rates of suicide found in other times periods, as well.

Despite opposition to surgery from Don and his colleagues, around the same time this piece was published surgeries were initiated and began to be practiced by a small number of surgeons and psychologists in South Africa. Secrecy was paramount for doctors who feared that sex reassignment surgeries could be seen as elective and unnecessary by their peers and for those involved in unethical medical experimentation (Vorster 2000). Those seeking treatment were also bound to a treatment protocol of silence that required them to change their names and social associations and often encouraged them to move to locations where they didn't know anyone to facilitate "passing" or "stealth." Otherwise, they risked doctors' refusal to treat them (Williams 1997).[17]

South African medical and legal literature on transsexuality draws heavily on literature from the United States, Europe, and Australia—little medical discussion of theories surrounding transsexuality has come directly out of South Africa. Don's 1963 article, for instance, does not cite one overtly South African source. However, the literature that does exist provides insight into the particularities of transsexuality in South Africa, especially when linked to the histories of apartheid. When South African sex reassignment surgeries began, the legal restrictions of apartheid established in the 1950s were also meeting increasing resistance from black and coloured South Africans. This was the same time period in which the extreme repression of apartheid and the institution of passes were growing and controlling all aspects of South African's lives. South African historian Keith Breckenridge (2005) reminds us of the importance of then-Prime Minister Hendrik Verwoerd's temperament to this development of the *Bantustan* policy: "Here was a politician for whom 'obstacles in human nature, must give way to regulation and systemization,' the leading newspaper editor of his time observed, 'The ideal must be imposed on the society'" (104). This view can be extended to apartheid treatment of transsexuals. The oppressive legislation in this period (including banning of the ANC and PAC) coincided with the inception of state-sponsored sex reassignments.

South African medical practitioners relied extensively on the work of Harry Benjamin and John Money in developing medical protocols. There was significant theoretical consistency in medicine based in both common reliance on medical literature from the United States and the tendency to conceptualize transsexuality rigidly and in a narrow scientific sense. For example, a prominent physician who performed sex reassignment surgeries in South Africa, Dr. R. E. Hemphill, preferred the term "transsexualism" to "gender dysphoria" because:

> "gender dysphoria" . . . means "gender discontent," [the term] is ambiguous, refers to feelings not facts, and should not be used. [Hemphill] defines transsexualism as: "A rare congenital defect or anomaly whereby a person of male, or of female, gender is born with the reproductive system and genitalia of the opposite sex, female or male respectively. Sex and gender normally concordant, are discordant." (SALC 1994: 4)

Within this definition, transsexualism is conceptualized as a physical disorder, like intersexuality, whereby the body of the patient does not match her/his gender. In this view, the body has not developed properly in a way that would allow gender consistency.

In stark contrast to many feminist theorists who have maintained that gender is socially constructed while sex is an anatomical given, or those who see both gender and sex as socially constituted, Hemphill and others maintain that a person's gender is fixed from birth and the body must be "corrected" to match this gender. While most South African physicians refer to "psychological" gender—gender based in the mind, not the body—some go even further: "For Dr Hemphill gender is not psychological, it is the quality of the 'self'" (SALC 1994: 5). The bulk of these conversations in the 1990s are presented in a report of the South African Law Commission (hereafter abbreviated as SALC), established by the SALC Act 19 of 1973. With members appointed by the President of South Africa, this body's objectives are to:

> [conduct] research with reference to all branches of the law of the Republic and to study and to investigate all such branches of the law in order to make recommendations for the development, improvement, modernization or reform thereof, including—the repeal of obsolete or unnecessary provisions; the removal of anomalies; the bringing about of uniformity in the law in the various parts of the Republic; and the consolidation or codification of any branch of the law. (SALC 1997)

This report, in working and final forms, is one of the only documents that directly addresses transsexuals in South Africa.

In this report and elsewhere during the transition, gender was conceptualized as innate and unchanging, coming from an unspecified place within the individual. One social worker who had treated South African transsexuals for twenty years explains that in her experience, "It's almost like your spirit and your soul and your whole being [are] in the wrong body" (Baker 1997).[18] Here we see the conjunctive complications of biology, psychology, and theology. This poetic means of explaining gender identification mirrors that of physicians and transsexuals transnationally and offers a theory of gender that has a psychological and internal basis, removed from the aesthetics of the body itself (usually thought of as "sex").[19]

In South Africa, as in the United States, discourses of transsexuality depend heavily on boundaries among the categories of transsexual, transvestite, and homosexual, which are defined oppositionally. Since the 1970s, most South African scholars have represented transvestitism as the psychological tendency to dress in the clothing of the opposite sex for sexual gratification, as opposed to a transsexual desire to be the opposite sex (Strauss 1970: 348; Taitz 1989: 468; Bruns and Kannelly 1995: 488). The SALC (1995) makes this distinction even more clear, with highly problematic assertions. Their explication of who fits into the category of "transvestite" includes:

(i)   Costume fetishists who wear the garments of the opposite sex, usually of an intimate nature, for sexual arousal or as sex objects (symptomatic transvestism);

(ii) female impersonation entertainers (drag artists);

(iii) prostitutes, sado-masochists and others who wear clothing of the opposite sex for deviant purposes (this group would include homosexuals who cross-dress for the purposes of prostitution);

(iv) criminals who would wear clothing of the opposite sex in order to carry out criminal acts. (SALC 1994: 7–8)[20]

The definition of transvestitism offered by the SALC does more than demonstrate the differences among medicalized categories. It broadly combines the intentions of costume fetishists, drag artists, prostitutes, sadomasochists, and criminals who broke apartheid laws. I return to its implications below.[21]

During the political transition to democracy, the SALC linked drag artists with criminals who cross-dress. The criminalization of cross-dressing has historical roots (Don 1963: 484) and was codified in the Prohibition of Disguises Act (1969), which targeted cross-dressing as deceptive and was based on assumptions that drag could be used to trick police. Justice Edwin Cameron uncovers the origins of this connection between drag and criminality, citing a Johannesburg case in 1965 in which a man in drag was arrested. The arresting officer was confused as to whether the plaintiff was a man or a woman. The judges in this case claimed that because this plaintiff's drag (referred to as a "disguise") had been so effective, ze must have "intended illegally to 'conceal his sex and pass himself off as a woman'" (Cameron 1994: 90). Following precedent set by this particular case, Parliament criminalized dressing in drag in 1969. Drag artists and criminals in disguise were fused in the same category—transvestite—and both were pathologized during this politically volatile and uncertain period. The co-production of class with deviance is also evident in the inclusion of sex workers who cross-dress professionally in the SALC's "deviant" category. In sum, individual's intentions in "wearing garments of the opposite sex"—described as sexual arousal, entertainment, prostitution, and criminal subterfuge—are merged under the same label.

In order to legitimize transsexuals, doctors medically distinguish them from transvestites. The SALC explains, "Dr. Hemphill is of the opinion that transsexuals do not show a preference to cross-dress as their dress is correct for their gender" (SALC 1994: 8). Again, Hemphill attempts to solidify gender as static and unchallenged by transsexuals and, as one of the only published medical authorities on the subject in South Africa and as someone who was interviewed by the SALC, Hemphill's opinion is weighted heavily. In this view, transsexuals' bodies are modified to fit their gender; they do not undermine the rigidity of the gender binary itself.

As in the United States, physicians also attempt to find material rationales for individuals' transsexuality. The case of the first South African female-to-male transsexual to apply for re-registration as a male in 1972 illustrates this point. In this particular case, the court required justification that Frederic X was a medical and social male, though he was born female.[22] The rationalization for a change in sex status given by the general practitioner attending to him included the following:

> My reasons include her masculine tastes in clothing, hobbies and recreation. Her mental outlook and mannerisms are masculine and she has a deep voice. Her facial features, physique, and gait are masculine and she has apparently never shown any social interest in men. On physical examination her general stature and hair distribution are more in keeping with those of a male than a female. (In Strauss 1974: 24–5)

Similarly his employer, who was also a "medical officer" (Frederic X worked as a nurse), gave the following statement concerning the need for Frederic's legal re-registration as a male:

> There are apparently physiological reasons for her being more of a male than a female type. From the glandular and chromosomal standpoint there is no complete sexual development of either male or female characteristics. For this reason Miss X wishes to change from female to male. (In Strauss 1974: 25)

In these two descriptions, social, psychological, and physical evidence of Frederic X's maleness are emphasized. Social components include Frederic X's attire, hobbies, and recreation, as well as his masculine mannerisms (e.g., his gait). Frederic X has a masculine "mental outlook" and lack of sexual interest in men, so as to be considered postoperatively heterosexual. Heterosexuality might be thought of as physical evidence of Frederic X's maleness, along with his facial features, physique, deep voice, and underdeveloped glands/chromosomes. In this analysis, both experts do not simply speak of Frederic X as having transitioned to maleness; instead, they stress his supposed preoperative physical intersexuality as justification for his re-registration. In this case we see a specific historical example of the ways that the material reasoning shaping medical practitioners' diagnoses of transsexuality and their legal recommendations are based in sociocultural understandings of what it means to be a man or a woman.

Within the context of medical analyses and expert legal opinions, homosexuality was distinct from transsexuality and transvestitism during South Africa's transition. "Homosexuals" were simply conceptualized as "individuals who are sexually attracted to persons that they know are of the same biological sex as themselves" (SALC 1994: 8). However, according to the SALC, there could be no overlap between transsexuality and homosexuality because, "Strictly speaking, a [preoperative] transsexual cannot be a homosexual, even if he is attracted to members of his own biological sex. By the very nature of gender dysphoria syndrome he genuinely regards such persons as being of the opposite sex to himself" (SALC 1994: 8–9). There was no discussion in South African medical literature regarding transsexuals who are postoperatively homosexual (e.g., trans women who are attracted to cisgender women following their transition).

In this time period and continuing to the present, ideas about what it means to be a "true transsexual" or to be, conversely, an unsuccessful transsexual, are revealing. In interviews conducted during this transition period in 1997–2000, individuals who were postoperatively homosexual were largely seen to be "failed" transsexuals by South African medical practitioners. For instance, when asked whether some of his patients were postoperatively homosexual, one surgeon responded, "No . . . they have no doubt in their minds who they are. They want to take up with the opposite sex, and the opposite sex is the same sex as they were. No, there's no homosexuality" (Williams 1997). Another doctor who psychologically assessed transsexuals used the likelihood of postoperative heterosexuality and lack of identification with gay communities as critical factors in determining whether someone was a good candidate for sex reassignment surgery. He stated,

> I wanted them to function in society as an ordinary straight man or woman. Transsexuals still hanging out in the gay clubs didn't seem to have been very good candidates. Most were postoperatively heterosexual. (Jooste 2000)

Following this reasoning, a postoperative transsexual who was homosexual was never a "true transsexual" in the first place. The concept of "true transsexualism" rests on postoperative heterosexuality as a measure of its success. This same doctor gave an example of a female-to-male patient whom he did not recommend for surgery because, "[s]he said that she had no interest in women and would like to live a gay life after her operation" (ibid.). Clearly for these physicians, postoperative sexual attraction must be heterosexual, demonstrating how treatment for transsexuals is not only embedded in ideas about gender and sex but also in the ways they intersect with sexuality.

There was an exception to this viewpoint among the medical practitioners I interviewed during the transition. One psychiatrist described how, based on recently published medical literature, he had begun to make clearer distinctions between gender identification (i.e., transsexuality) and sexual orientation (Vorster 2000). He explained that he started to accept transsexuals for treatment who were heterosexual, homosexual, and asexual, and distinguishing desire for sex reassignment from sexual attraction had been helpful to both his patients and himself. However, this physician also seemed to have few criteria for deeming patient ineligible for surgeries. Of the forty or fifty patients whom he had seen since making this distinction, he had only rejected two because of their supposed mental instability.[23]

Discussions of transsexuality in South African medical arenas in the transition concentrated on gender, sex, and sexuality, with implications about the impact of race and class in determining, for instance, who counted as "true transsexuals." However, the inseparability of race and class from gender were more overt in terms of treatment practices. As sex reassignment practices developed under apartheid, poor South Africans (most often those who were coloured or black, as a result of apartheid's linked racial and economic policies) were increasingly given access to free sex reassignment procedures. These procedures seemed to be a panacea for many of those living between gender categories, a way to fit into society by matching gender and sex, desirable in an apartheid political context that often severely punished difference. Unfortunately, these free procedures were experimental and, according to their recipients addressed in Chapter 2, often left lingering mental distress and physical complications. Such procedures had contradictory causes and effects; on the one hand, according to physicians, they legitimized gender binaries by shaping South Africans' bodies to fit them, and on the other hand, they allowed the advancement of medical science with little regard to the suffering caused to transsexuals who had to live with the consequences of failed procedures.[24]

III. Enforcing Sex: Transsexuals and South African Law

Many theorists, especially those attending to the complexities of gendered realities of the state, have pointed out the ways that gender is property. Gayle Salamon suggests that access to medical treatments and legal gendered changes often fall outside of individual control and agency, as "sex is treated as material property in trans peoples' dealings with medical and state bureaucracies and functions specifically as state property rather than private property for trans people in a way that it does not for the normatively gendered [cisgendered]" (2010: 8). In South Africa, not only did failed medical procedures present transsexuals with challenges during apartheid and the transition, legal changes were inconsistently available, as well. Legal reference to gender and sex ambiguity has fallen into two areas: prohibitions of cross-dressing and restrictions on changing sexed legal documents.

Since at least the eighteenth century, laws required some black South Africans to carry identity documents, restricting their movement and freedom (Thompson 1995: 37, 166–7). With the introduction of apartheid in 1948, racial control was increasingly codified. Under apartheid, pass laws were linked to the Population Registration Act (1950), which classified South Africans according to race, and the Group Areas Act (1950), which forced people to reside in racially zoned areas. South Africans were required to carry identity documents, or "passbooks,"

at all times. Colonial and apartheid land-based legislation disproportionately favored white South Africans. For instance, the 1913 Native
Land Act designated only 13 percent of available land for purchase and
residence by black South Africans, while blacks constituted more than
three-quarters of the population (Gilson and McIntyre 2001: 193). This
great disparity led black and coloured South Africans to rely on passes
to travel or live in most areas of the country.

As a means of enforcing racist land policies and controlling black
and coloured South Africans, the apartheid government attempted to
limit rural-urban migration and travel by authorizing the arrest of those
who could not produce identity documents. Consequently, beginning in
the late 1960s,

> [e]very year, more than 100,000 [black] Africans were arrested
> under pass laws; the number peaked at 381,858 in the year
> 1975–76. The government also removed [black] African
> squatters from unauthorized camps near the cities, placing those
> who were employed in segregated townships, and sending the
> rest either to the Homelands or to farms where white owners
> required their labor. (Thompson 1995: 193)

This complex and extreme form of control made the possession of identity documents for black and coloured South Africans hold potentially
life-changing consequences, and transsexuals were no exception. As mentioned above, the Prohibition of Disguises Act 16 of 1969 made cross-
dressing with "criminal intent" illegal for both men and women under
apartheid (Cameron 1994: 90),[25] and enforcement of this Act was largely
left to police officers' discretion.[26]

The interplay between the law and medicine was complex. Some
physicians actually cited repression by the police for cross-dressing under
apartheid as a rationale for recommending sex reassignment surgery. One
medical practitioner explains,

> I felt sorry for them because clearly within their community
> they tended to be ostracized and made fun of and the police
> tended to take delight in arresting them, putting them into
> custody, but being rather cruel and harsh. So for them it
> was important that they could undergo gender reassignment.
> (Vorster 2000)

Here, it is suggested that bodies should be changed to protect those between gender binaries from harassment and prosecution. Individuals' ability to "pass," their race, and their class were co-produced to shape the difficulties they faced. For instance, those who moved or lived in areas heavily policed by South African authorities, such as the townships, who did not "pass," and/or who were sex workers were more likely to be arrested than those who fit into conventional ideas of sex and gender and were not perceived as potential criminals, especially during the violence of the 1980s and early 1990s.[27] In short, these arrests disproportionately penalized black and coloured South Africans. Medical practitioners often provided transsexuals in transition, who were vulnerable to prosecution under the Prohibition of Disguises Act, with letters stating that they were undergoing treatment (Don 1963; SALC 1994; SALC 1995). These letters served as a bridge between the South African state and medical establishment, as physicians attempted to exempt their patients from the law.

The other Act of Parliament that directly affected transsexuals (and sometimes intersexuals) was the Births, Marriages, and Deaths Registrations Act 81 of 1963. Apartheid was losing its political efficacy and tightening everyday restrictions simultaneously in the 1960s. Within this context, legislation was codifying social categories. At the same time, this Act allowed South Africans to apply to the Registrar for correction of "any omission, defect, or inaccuracy" in the birth certificate (in Strauss 1974: 28). Frederic X, described above, relied on the Births, Deaths, and Marriages Act, as did a number of other transsexuals who re-registered under this legislation between 1963 and 1974 (Strauss 1974: 19).[28] This legislation allowed for the gender on birth certificates to be changed when represented as a defect or inaccuracy in its original recording. In this way, the documentation of control that South African administrators exercised worked to the advantage of those who wanted to change gendered identity documents.

However, soon after Frederic X's case was resolved, an amendment to the Births, Marriages, and Deaths Registrations Act 81 of 1963 was introduced. This 1974 amendment (section 7B) provided that:

> The Secretary (for the Interior) may on the recommendation of the Secretary of Health, alter in the birth register of any person who has undergone a change of sex, the description of the sex of such person and may for the purpose call for

> medical reports and institute such investigation as he may
> deem necessary. (Nzimande 1994: 52; Taitz 1993: 134; SALC
> 1994: 13)

This amendment still allowed for changes in birth certificates but was
now also the first specific recognition of transsexuality under South African law. The way this Bill was introduced in 1974 by the Deputy Minister
of the Interior gives an indication of the "dignified and professional"
(Taitz 1993: 134, fn 57) state approach to sex reassignment at this time:

> For the past few years the Department of the Interior has, on
> request, altered a person's sex description in his or her birth
> register after such person has undergone a change of sex as a
> result of medical treatment. . . . The Government law advisers
> have confirmed that no provision exists in the Act in terms
> of which the sex description of a person who has undergone
> a change of sex may be altered in his birth register. . . . It
> is consequently being proposed . . . that the Secretary for
> the Interior be vested with power to alter in a person's birth
> register the sex description of a person who has undergone
> a change of sex on the recommendation of the Secretary of
> Health. (In SALC 1994: 13)

The approval of this amendment allowed transsexuals to successfully
change the sex registered on their birth certificates and to change their
names following medical treatment.[29] It illustrates a close and mutually
substantiating relationship between the state and medical institutions as
legal recommendations followed medical opinion of the 1970s. The context of extreme and rigid state control and the collusion in codifying the
apartheid state are paramount and may indicate reasoning behind this
amendment.[30]

Court judgments following the passage of this amendment to the
Births, Deaths, and Marriages Registration Act 81 of 1963 tested the
relationship between the government and medical institutions and relied
heavily on British legal precedent, marking Britain's colonial influence on
South Africa. As legal scholar Jerold Taitz points out, "While there have
been a number of interesting decisions regarding the sex of transsexuals
in the United States, these are not as pertinent to South African law as

are the English decisions" (Taitz 1989: 469). This can be attributed, in part, to the history of British colonialism in South Africa.

One English case particularly stands out, as it was to have immeasurable influence on subsequent South African court judgments. In *Corbett vs. Corbett (orse Ashley)* (1970), Judge J. Ormrod (a former medical practitioner himself) "held that a marriage between a post-operative female, April Ashley, and a biological male was a nullity in law" (Taitz 1989: 469). The judge administered a test for "true" gender/sex, based on the congruency of a person's chromosomes, gonads, and genitalia at the time of his/her birth (Taitz 1989: 469; SALC 1994: 42; Nzimande 1994: 54), thereafter known as the "Ormrod Test." According to these criteria, Ashley was found to be male and her marriage was declared null, as under both English and South African law same-sex marriage was prohibited. The ideological and temporal differences between medical experts who treat transsexuals and Ormrod are articulated in the judge's conclusions that:

> [t]he biological sexual constitution of an individual is fixed at birth (at the latest), and cannot be changed, either by natural development of organs of the opposite sex, or by medical or surgical means. The respondent's [sex reassignment] operation, therefore, cannot affect her true sex. (Ormrod in SALC 1994: 17)

This decision obviously indicated an extreme departure from South African and United States medical literature, which held that while sex (the body) may change, psychological or "true" gender remains the same. This serves as an example of the fixity of social categories being juridically determined. The legal shift inspired by Ormrod's decision led to an increasingly apparent disjuncture between the state and medical institutions in South Africa. It also indicated a shift from U.S./medical dominance to British/legal influence affecting the lives of South African transsexuals.

The other English case to have significant effects on later South African court judgments was *R vs. Tan and Others* (1983). In this case, Gloria Greaves, a male-to-female transsexual, was charged with living off the earnings of another person's prostitution (referred to as pimping). Under English law, only a male could be charged with such an offense; however, the judge here also adopted the "Ormrod Test" (as formulated in *Corbett* above). Greaves was found to be male and charged with a fine of £10,000. From that time, the "Ormrod Test" became the sole judicial determinant of sexual identity in England (Taitz 1989: 470–1, SALC 1994: 43–44).

The English precedents described here had notable effects on the lives of transsexuals in South Africa, as the most important court decision affecting gender liminality in this period was modeled on the *Corbett* case. In the South African case of *W vs. W* (1976) the plaintiff, a postoperative male-to-female transsexual, sued her husband for divorce on the grounds of adultery. Following her surgery, the plaintiff re-registered her sex and changed her birth certificate in accordance with the Births, Marriages, and Deaths Act of 1963. However, Judge J. Nestadt found that the amended birth certificate was not sufficient proof of the plaintiff's sex, and he administered the British Ormrod Test. The judge then held that the plaintiff remained male in the eyes of the law and accordingly declared her marriage to be null and void (Taitz 1989: 469), given prohibitions of same-sex marriage. Because the plaintiff was born male, despite her transition and surgery, it was legally impossible for her to marry a man.

This case had significant effects on understandings of transsexuality by the South African state. Between 1976 and 1992, decisions about legal transitions were made on a case-by-case basis. But in 1992—at the inception of the transition from apartheid to democracy—the Births, Marriages, and Deaths Act of 1963, including section 7B, was repealed. The reason for this repeal was unrelated to sex reassignment; it was a means to streamline registration processes. Similar legislation was introduced in its place, referred to as the Births and Deaths Registration Act 51 of 1992. The advent of this new legislation raised the possibility of reconsidering the place of intersexuals and transsexuals under the law. Unfortunately, this Bill followed the precedent set in the *W vs. W* case (and its British counterparts) by rejecting "transsexuality" as a recognized legal category, and, effectively, reversing South African transsexuals' rights.

The new Births and Deaths Registration Act 51 came into operation on August 1, 1992, and "according to the new Act, it is not possible for any person who is currently undergoing a series of sex-change operations to alter his or her sex description in his or her birth register" (SALC 1994: 19). A social worker with twenty years of experience with transsexuals and a psychologist, interviewed ten years apart, similarly explained that, as a consequence of this Act,

A lot of these people were in limbo. They would have the one ID that would have this change, but they couldn't work because they didn't have the right papers. They couldn't go traveling, they couldn't get a passport, they couldn't marry. It was torture for them. They couldn't open a bank account. [It was] really, really hard. (Baker 1997)

That has so many implications. You can't get a driver's license. You can't get a job. There are so many. . . . Like the basic, basic human needs are quite limited in accessing. So there are all those other things that you need to deal with besides your sexual identity or gender identity. All of those things. (Ryland 2007)

The repercussions of the Act demonstrated the inseparability of class and gender. The transsexuals Baker and Ryland described could not work, gain credit, or have legally recognized relationships. They could not vote or obtain driver's licenses. Transsexuals were unable to change the legal documents they need to function in society and were effectively denied legal rights and citizenship in the transitional state.[31]

The Minister of Home Affairs, Gene Louw, introduced the new Bill with the following commentary that spoke to its underpinnings regarding the constitution of gender:

As a result of a court judgment [W vs. W] that a person's sex cannot be altered medically, the present power to record the fact in a person's birth certificate that he has undergone a sex-change, has been omitted in the [1992] Bill. The court did indeed rule that a sex-change operation brings only psychological relief and that a person's sex is not fundamentally changed by way of surgery. (Louw in Taitz 1993: 136)

This statement indicates fundamental differences between medical and legal understandings of gender as alterable or inalterable. Beginning in 1992, it was legally impossible to change one's sex in South Africa.[32]

The tone of the discussion introducing this Bill is illustrative. Jerold Taitz, an advocate of transsexual rights, points out that while the introduction of the 1974 Bill was characterized by a professional spirit, ignorance and ridicule dominated in the Parliamentary treatment of transsexuality in 1992 (SALC 1994: 18–19). The transcript of the discussion in Parliament reads:

> *The Minister* [Gene Louw]: Before I resume my seat, I just want to issue a final word of warning to those hon. members who have nevertheless considered undergoing a sex-change operation that the good old days when a man could become a woman after a sex change operation, and a woman a man, no longer exist as a result of court judgments in that regard.
>
> *Mr J H van der Merwe*: And if a Nat changes to become a DP?[33]
>
> *The Minister*: I am sorry the hon. member is so disappointed, but one cannot simply cut off or attach more organs and then expect one to be able to assume a different sex.
>
> [Interjections.]
>
> *Mr J H van der Merwe*: You are not cutting anything off me. (Taitz 1993: 136–7)

In this debate, we see a striking example of the connections between South African politics and perceptions of sex. Achille Mbembe reminds us that vulgarity in the postcolony, including references to the phallus, "must be located in the real world, in real time, as play, as fun, as mockery" (2001: 107). Mockery and humor are at the heart of these superficially lighthearted disputes with serious underpinnings and implications.

In this exchange, the rigidity of political identities and party affiliation is compared to rigid ideas about the immutability of sex. Van der Merwe ribs Louw about his comment suggesting that members may want to undergo surgery themselves, teasing him about the conversion of members of the National Party (NP) to the Democratic Party (DP). It shows the significance of the split between the NP and the DP and notably doesn't refer to the African National Congress (ANC), then coming into power. This dialogue during the transition came during a time of particularly violent turmoil and political negotiations, just preceding the first free national elections in South Africa in 1994 when the NP's white supremacism was losing support and power. It also suggests that surgeries were aligned with the "good old days" of apartheid, acknowledging a past wrong, or at least an eccentricity.[34]

Van der Merwe's final comment, "You're not cutting anything off me," expresses a common male fear of losing his penis and his masculinity, a fear perhaps too serious for him to entertain, even through joking comments. Here, we see white leaders losing power in the transition in a world of what Mbembe terms "anxious virility" (2001: 110). Perhaps Van der Merwe is speculating on his political, as well as his personal, castration during the end of apartheid and the pending rule of the ANC. Patriarchal politics, the attempt to codify social categories found in earlier days of apartheid (Posel 2001a, 2001b), and the immutability of sex converge in this new legislation. And politically, this paradox reflects the shift from the coherence of the racist logic of policy in the earlier period of the apartheid era to the increasingly incoherent vision in the legislative agenda of the National Party as apartheid came to an end.

IV. Politics and Medical Technology in Transition

Following medical and legislative changes in the early 1990s, transsexuals became fictional under the law as it was almost impossible to change identity documents legally.[35] The current South African Constitution, which is widely recognized as one of the most progressive in the world, did not thwart the legislative change that prevented legal sex re-registration from taking place.[36] In fact, the political and social turmoil of the 1980s and early 1990s in South Africa may have triggered a backlash against those seen as threatening to the efficacy of apartheid that became characteristic of the transition.[37] In the 1990s, the details of the new Constitution and other legislation were strongly debated by activists and representatives of the major political parties. The rights of gays and lesbians, for instance, obtained a place in the Constitution "largely due to the ability of a male-dominated gay rights movement to form strategic alliances with the anti-apartheid struggle, to mobilise the master narrative of equality and nondiscrimination and to lobby effectively during the constitution-making process" (Cock 2005: 188–9). But during this time, transsexuals had no activist presence in South Africa as part of this process or elsewhere. Commentary and rigidity concerning the definition of "sex" as recounted above went unchallenged. Does this indicate adherence to more restrictive ideas of gender and sex during the transition to democracy than during apartheid?

Following the legislative shift around sex re-registration in the early 1990s, a number of legal and medical professionals concerned with its implications for transsexuals put forth their own recommendations. The South African Law Commission's "Report on the Investigation into the Legal Consequences of Sexual Realignment and Related Matters," researched by the late Jerold Taitz, was a comprehensive publication on South African transsexuality; two hundred and fifty copies of this report in draft form were distributed to interested institutions, organizations, and individuals in June of 1994 (Working Paper 24, Project 52).[38] Comments from these readers were then incorporated into the 1995 publication, making it an exhaustive and important document despite the paucity of cited sources and overt biases. Four of the areas of recommendation contained in this report are of particular significance in understanding gender liminality in the transition.

First, the SALC report pointed out that if the 1992 Act were left to stand, it would affect legislation concerning marriage, criminal law, rape, prostitution, "statutory offences intended to protect the chastity and dignity of women," income tax, conscription, employment, and succession (SALC 1994: 21). The legal complications of denying the validity of transsexuality indicate the degree to which all laws are gendered and how social inclusion is predicated on gendered citizenship. As discussed previously, transsexuals became non-persons under the law following their transitions. Scholars were concerned that transsexuals would continue to be unable to marry postoperatively (as they legally retained the sex they were assigned at birth). Those who support rights to change identity documents were also concerned that male-to-female (MTF) transsexuals living as women might not be able to access the specific protections offered to women under South African law, such as being able to charge rapists with a crime (only women could be raped under the law). No scholars in this field at the time advocated more radical changes such as legitimating legal sex changes with or without medical justification, legalizing relationships between two consenting adults regardless of sex/ abolishing marriage protections and privileges altogether, or defining rape beyond gender to include any forcible sexual contact.

Second, physicians warned that transsexuals must be legally recognized in order to prevent them from harming themselves and others

(SALC 1995). Doctors asserted that suicide and genital self-mutilation are common among transsexuals when sex reassignment surgeries are not available. Again, marriage was represented as a necessity for postoperative transsexuals because, when it is not possible for legal or other reasons, physicians claimed,

> Prostitution is sometimes a tempting substitute for marriage. There is no greater confirmation of femininity than that of having normal heterosexual men again and again accept [a MTF transsexual] as a woman and even pay her for her sex services. (Block and Tessler in SALC 1994: 6–7)

Economic reasons that may motivate sex work, as well as the physical dangers it can pose, are ignored in this statement; instead prostitution is seen through a condescending lens as a logical alternative to marriage as a means for gendered acceptance and as a marital deficiency. Experts posit MTF transsexuals as requiring and desiring male affirmation and male control (presumably like cisgendered females, in their views), either through marriage or through sex work, and the two are positioned as analogous. Further, female-to-male (FTM) transsexuals are largely omitted from this consideration and trans women stand in for all representations of trans people.

Third, many physicians advocated setting up gender clinics to monitor transsexuals and their treatment in South Africa. Dr. Derk Crichton claimed, "Gender identity clinics proved their worth in many civilised countries . . . the experience of the clinicians involved, accuracy of diagnosis, strict and unhurried selection, and prolonged pre-operative support have largely been responsible for the good results" (Crichton 1993: 349). Taitz further suggests that such clinics would authorize sex reassignment surgeries and recommends punishing physicians working outside of these clinics with imprisonment and fines (SALC 1994: 63). Given the ideological and logistical conflicts between medical practitioners and some segments of the South African state, it is unclear why physicians such as Crichton advocated giving panoptic power to the state in determining the treatment of transsexuals. The SALC and many of the respondents to its Working Paper 24 (1994) opposed such institutionalization, primarily on the grounds of administrative expense and unnecessary bureaucracy (SALC 1995: 2–3, 57–69). However, while the establishment of gender clinics may be impractical and expensive, as well as subjecting medical practitioners to restrictions, it was the only proposal addressing wide-spread medical experimentation on South African transsexuals.[39]

Finally, the recommendation was set out by the SALC that sex reassignment surgeries be restricted in a number of ways:

> No sex-change procedure shall be commenced or carried out upon—
>
> (a) any person under the age of 21 years;
>
> (b) any married person;
>
> (c) any person who suffers from or is a carrier of a communicable disease;
>
> (d) any person who has been convicted of an offence relating to the offering of his or her body for material gain;
>
> (e) any person who is addicted to drug or alcohol;
>
> (f) any person who is considered psychologically incapable of or unsuitable for undergoing the necessary series of surgical procedures;
>
> (g) any person who has children. (SALC 1994: 64)

These suggested restrictions are so broad that were they enacted, most transsexuals would be excluded from medical treatment. Despite the length of the SALC report (73 pages), no rationale for choosing these particular criteria are given. They are, in part, a means by which the SALC hoped to legitimize transsexuality. However, they also point to the subjectivity of treatment decisions and the ways doctors and lawyers conceptualize ideal or "true transsexuals" with vivid effects mentioned in the previous section and addressed in Chapter 3.

Misperceptions concerning transsexuals' motivations for sex reassignment surgery form perhaps the most striking part of this report. For instance, some contributors expressed concern that homosexuals might try to have sex reassignment surgeries for the purposes of undertaking prostitution or that criminals in prison might want to have sex reassignment surgery in order to obtain lighter workloads. The reference to marriage in these prescriptions (i.e., prohibiting those who are married from obtaining surgery) is consistent with physicians' ideologies about what constitutes transsexuality; in their views, an individual born female who is married to a male is obviously not a "true transsexual" or she would not be attracted to men. Similarly, the mention of children assumes gender to be static (i.e., fixed from birth) and presumes that "true transsexuals" would not have relationships or children until after their sex reassignment surgeries. In fact, having children often disqualified potential candidates, because having a child was considered corporeal proof of the success of one's natal body. For example, one transsexual who consulted with two surgeons involved with the SALC a number of times between 1986 and 1990 was rejected because of her age (age 44 in 1986) and her prior marriage and children, despite her persistent, poignant, and articulate arguments to the contrary (Darling 2009). These comments by doctors also reflect the importance accorded to family relationships (especially marriages) and the desire to "protect" children from the confusion of having a parent undertake sex reassignment surgeries.

Thus, while this report provides a means to understand the constitution of sex, it also has specific material effects. In a recent meeting of more than twenty gender liminal people in South Africa, members of the group recounted instances in which they were denied medical treatment. They write, collectively:

> During the apartheid years, doctors consulted a list of criteria that was drawn up by the Law Commission, which effectively disqualified people from getting surgery. Criteria included having been married, having children, being unemployed and having a history of drug abuse. Joy recounted how a doctor at Groote Schuur hospital prevented her from getting treatment on the basis that she was married. . . . She felt that the list of criteria was used to get rid of people who wanted sexual reassignment surgery. Simone remembered that in 1976 she was denied surgery because she was self-employed—which wasn't considered the same as having a full-time job. Liesl heard of a person who had, as recently as 2006, been told by her doctor that it was illegal to transition and was refused help. (Morgan et al. 2009: 218)

Taken together, these anecdotal stories constitute a picture of the implications of the kinds of policing that took place as a result of the assertions described here. Overall, this report focused on how transsexuals can fit into society, instead of exploring the ways that they challenge gender/ sex norms and how these norms might be disrupted socially in order to make a larger space for transsexuals.

V. Transsexuals' Categorical Existence

So why did apartheid allow for a category—transsexual—that the transitional state did not? Transsexuals have existed throughout South Africa's history but have faced differing degrees of acceptance and discrimination. Through the analysis of specific understandings of sex and gender in relation to state politics illuminated here, we see that the apparent paradox of treating transsexuals and allowing their legal registration under apartheid and the diminished medical treatment and refused legal sex changes in the transition are not paradoxical at all. Instead, this treatment fits a pattern of contradictory and competing ideas about gender and sex linked to moments in South Africa's political history.

The relationship between legal and medical treatments of transsexuality in South Africa remained tenuous and contradictory throughout the transitional period. At the heart of conflicts were ideological differences about the fixity of gender in medical discourse and the fixity of sex in legal discourse, as well as conflicts between the dominance of U.S. influence in medical arenas over British precedent in legal ones. These superficially different conceptions of what it is to be a woman or a man are not as disparate as they may first appear. Both rely on the assumption that gender/sex is dualistic and unchanging over the course of a person's life. Further, medical and legal scholars and policy makers have shown little comprehension of the impact of their decisions for transsexuals' and intersexuals' lives, nor for larger ideologies of gender, sex, and sexual orientation. Instead, their treatments codify their own ideas of gender and sex in powerful embodied ways and the means through which they converge with race and class.

Medical practitioners have relied on the idea of "psychological" gender as fixed and sex as mutable, and, further, they have not looked beyond a binary conception of man/woman. In terms of transsexuals: "Most medical specialists believe that the only relief . . . [is] to bring [transsexuals'] bodies into alignment with the psychological sex, i.e., their gender" (Taitz 1993: 133). Doctors have attempted to bring people's bodies into congruence with their dualistic ideologies, even when patients have opposed their interventions, as we will see in Chapter 2.[40] These medical experts advocate conformity to existing gender and sex norms instead of tolerance of ambiguity.

Legal ideologies in transitional South Africa rested on similar premises of sex as dualistic. "South African common law is based on the fact that there are two immutable sexes. It does not recognize the phenomenon of transsexuality nor does it lend any support to the notion of sex change" (Bruns and Kannelley 1995: 490). South African judges increasingly relied on consistency among chromosomes, genitalia, and other physiological factors in determining "true" sex. Despite medical opinion and evidence to the contrary, the potential for intersexuality and transsexuality to suggest the multiplicity and mutability of sex did not exist under South African law during the transition. And British precedent loomed large in these discussions. While doctors medically shaped sex according to gender, lawyers posited sex as incontrovertible.

South African legal scholar Angelo Pantazis (1997) criticizes the conservatism of his profession in this regard, asserting that the South African Law Commission avoided the challenge posed by transsexuality by claiming that it is "better to allow a change of sex than a conflict of sex and gender" (1997: 473). During South Africa's transition, little productive dialogue took place between those involved in legal and medical institutions. Taitz argues, "In their attempt to alleviate the mental anguish of transsexuals through sex change surgery, the medical profession paid little heed to the legal consequences of a sex change, such as, in particular, the determination of sexual identity of post-operative transsexuals" (Taitz 1989: 469). Here, Taitz is frustrated by doctors' decisions to continue to undertake sex reassignment procedures despite the postoperative legal difficulties their patients face. Similarly, politicians intentionally dismissed transsexuality as a medical concept, ridiculing the suggestion that sex can be changed with little regard for those who have gone through this process. While medical scholars see gender as static and legal scholars see sex as static, both of these assumptions rested on the same concept, that of a rigid and dualistic sex/gender system of man/woman.[41]

Under apartheid, as historian Keith Breckenridge explains, "[t]he Apartheid state developed the first universal biometric order in the effort to control the labor and movement of African people" (2005: 105). This movement toward order coincided with the worldwide emergence of sex reassignment surgeries and the codification of scientific prowess. The apartheid state's legal endorsement and financial support of sex reassignment procedures may superficially appear to have undermined policies of stringent social control. In some ways rights to medical treatment and legal fairness that transsexuals seek and deserve were institutionalized. However, the following chapter addresses how apartheid-era raced and classed disparities in health care access created a culture of condoned medical experimentation on marginal bodies.

As Foucault and others have pointed out, ID documents are essential to establishing the surveillance and documentation that link identity categories to bureaucracies. Passports and drivers' licenses, among others, have garnered increasing attention in relation to political conflicts, immigration, and the rise of terrorist fears since 9/11 (see, for example, Puar 2007). The work of Helga Tawil-Souri on ID documents in contemporary Palestine/Israel is a useful point of comparison here. Tawil-Souri suggests that, "the materiality of ID cards *determines*—that is, gives meaning to, provides a limit on, fixes conclusively—the identity of and borders around Palestinians and determines their ensuing rights and privileges and lack thereof" (2011: 81, emphasis in original). Tawil-Souri points out that ID cards are decisive and can have fatal consequences, providing a one-way communication in which state apparatuses determine individuals' meanings (2011: 81–4), even as they are interpreted and appropriated by their users. Discussions of South African passbooks have similarly explored the quotidian biopolitics mediated through documentation. Considering discrimination against transsexuals in relation to these concerns points out how citizenship is always already provisional and determined through state property, of which gender is one form.

While the transition is known for its bold legislative challenges to apartheid's oppressive conventions, particularly through the new Constitution, it was legislatively characterized by contradiction.[42] Through examination of how this legislative shift took place, we see that conflicts in transitional South African politics and reliance on British precedent over U.S.-based medical judgments and vulgar gendered humor expressed by parliamentarians played roles in the shift affecting gender liminal South Africans. This shift left them in contradictory positions with the inability to match sex and gender. As the transition opened up space for greater freedoms, apartheid's architects retained adherence to the rigidity and order that shaped the period; these contrasting influences had effects on transsexuals' lives and gendered citizenship potential. In ideas about what constitutes "transsexuality," we see that forced heteronormativity served political and economic goals at various points in history, but sometimes encouraging sexed, gendered, and sexual liminality proved more important than heterosexuality.

VI. Movements Forward

Since the end of the period defined here as South Africa's transition, transsexuals' and intersexuals' legal statuses have changed significantly. Due in part to the efforts of activists, specifically the Cape Town Transsexual/Transgender Support Group of the Triangle Project and the Intersex Society of South Africa, and especially Sally Gross, Simone Heradien, and Estian Smit, in October 2003 a new bill was adopted that permits sex to be changed in birth registers (Minister of Home Affairs 2003).[43] The Alteration of Sex Description and Sex Status Act, No. 49 allows for a legal change of sex status and, despite evidence to the contrary, does not require proof of genital surgery. This legislation represents an amazing feat for activists. South Africa stands as a model in this regard, as trans activists elsewhere in the world have unsuccessfully called for similar legislation that would demedicalize identity documents, detaching gender classifications from medical control. As lawyer and trans activist Dean Spade notes in U.S. contexts, "Reducing and eliminating medical evidence requirements for gender reclassification directly addresses trans people's survival issues, especially low-income people, youth, and people of color who are disproportionately deprived of health care access" (2011: 159).

But while offering important relief to postoperative transsexuals, contradictions and concerns remain regarding this new legislation. Most significantly, the Department of Home Affairs, bureaucratically in charge of such matters, does not follow the law in changing identity documents.[44] Further, although birth certificates may now be changed in some circumstances, identity numbers, which are themselves gendered male or female, will not be altered. These unchangeable numbers allow problematic contradictions to exist between a transsexual's pre- and postoperative legal sex. As transsexual advocates point out, in some ways this Act reestablishes the collusion between medical and legal institutions.[45]

The perspectives and needs of those most significantly involved in these debates—those expressing gender liminality—have been largely absent from these discussions until recently. Their bodies became the sites for conflicts between medical and legal practitioners. For example, one physician I interviewed who had been working with transsexuals for thirty years as a psychologist discussed the difficulties he and his patients faced when attempting to change identity documents. While claiming that legal changes were not usually difficult, he gave an example of a legal problem that was "resolved" through a medical intervention:

> There was one doctor who was examining an FTM where there was no penis construction. He said that this male could have [heterosexual] sex with another male, though the vagina would have shrunken from the use of testosterone. We had to do a partial closure of the vagina to get the ID documents changed. (Jooste 2000)

In this case, a risky medical procedure was undertaken simply to fit a transsexual into legal conceptions of a man (i.e., a person who cannot be vaginally penetrated). Bodies are still being changed to fit sex/gender ideologies and vice versa today.[46]

In January 2006, a few activists were again able to effect related change through a little-known but legislatively significant act.[47] The Juridical Matters Amendment Act, 2005, amends the Promotion of Equality and Prevention of Unfair Discrimination Act, 2000, "so as to extend the application of the Act to expressly include intersexed persons within the definition of sex" (2006: 2) This piece of legislation is significant in its potential and defines intersexuality as "a congenital sexual differentiation which is atypical, to whatever degree" (2006: 16).[48] This legislation allows for space between discrete categories of "man" and "woman" under the law. While not specifically mentioning transsexuals, the potential for and shortcomings of broad definitions of sex and for changes to sex status, including changes to birth certificates and other legal documentation, are increasingly being put into place and are addressed at length in the Conclusion to this text.

I would like to end this chapter with a brief discussion of how medical, legal, and state conflicts detailed here challenge us to think more clearly about how gender and sex work, particularly with race. First, the conflicts detailed here point to the incoherence and inconsistencies of race, sex, and gender. How the nuances of womanhood, manhood, and the spaces between are mediated by racial and classed politics is illustrated by the treatment and experiences of transsexuals in South Africa.

The constitution of the *idea* of transsexuality, and debates about it, are part of these broader conversations about the complexes of sex, gender, and sexuality in South Africa (Epprecht 2008; Hoad 2007), and the temporality of transsexuality is critical to understanding its composition.

In this chapter, gender liminal people's lives do not simply answer questions about "binary gender" and such an assumption would be reductive. In later chapters, I return to the ways that Viviane Namaste and others have critiqued the work of Janice Raymond, Bernice Hausman, Judith Butler, and Marjorie Garber for using transsexuals to illustrate gender theories with inattention to the lives of transsexuals (2000). I am invested in avoiding these mistakes. However, as David Valentine points out, *conflicts* over the treatment of transsexuals—as those demonstrated here—can be revealing (Valentine 2007: 16).

Second, despite the instability of social categories, their effects are serious. As Deborah Posel points out: "The architects of apartheid racial classification policies recognized explicitly that racial categories were constructs, rather than descriptions of real essences—a version of the idea of race that contributed directly to the enormous powers wielded by racial classifiers" (2001a: 109).[49] Gender binaries, in conjunction with racial categories, are policed in severe ways with corporeal consequences for transsexual and non-transsexual South Africans alike; the resulting violence and patterns of these consequences will be explored at length in the following chapters. In U.S. contexts, important work in critical race and queer theories suggests that moves toward freedom from violence may actually create circumstances that necessitate and normalize violence against those perceived as abnormal or irrational (e.g., Reddy 2011). Rather than seeing the contemporary violence facing South African gender and sexual liminality in the transition as anonmolous, we might conceptualize this violence as inherent to the transitional state and the contradictions of rights claims.

Third, and finally, disruptions to "heteropatriarchy" and the "heterosexual matrix" are revealed in the ways gender ambiguity reinforces racial hierarchies. Glen Elder posits "heteropatriarchy" in South Africa as a means of explaining the heterosexist and seemingly contradictory junctures of gender and race and, for Judith Butler, the "heterosexual matrix" (1990) describes the necessary coherence among sex, gender, and heterosexuality that govern what it means to be a man or a woman. However, South African histories of gender transitions reveal complicated raced relationships and significant ruptures among sex, gender, and sexuality. These disjunctures notably unsettle heteropatriarchy and the heterosexual matrix and reveal the ways that theories travel or falter transnationally.

Further, as we will see in the following chapter's discussion of the grounded application of these medical ideologies in particular communities, bodies were manipulated to ensure sex and gender congruence when their coherence reinforced racial expectations. But bodies were construed as anomalous when gender "abnormalities" buttressed racism and racial hierarchies. This manipulation of transsexuals as apartheid property is critical to rethinking the parameters and outreach of this regime. Gayle Salamon, in her examination of Jan Morris's autobiography *Conundrum*, suggests, "Whether it is the knowledge of sex or whether it is sex itself, the assigned letter on the document functions as a kind of property. . . . Sex is not private property, but rather property *that belongs to the state itself*" (2010: 183, emphasis in original). Ideas of "sex" and "transsexual" under contestation in South Africa traveled and changed in their temporal and spatial applications and meanings, but within the framework of apartheid's attempted manipulation of transsexuals' bodies as state property.

Two

Medical Experimentation and the Raced Incongruence of Gender

[T]he military has a history of doing sex change operations—many sex changes were done in military hospitals. One has to ask to what extent it was experimental. Although in any medical advancement there is always a cutting edge of experimentation, in total institutions there is a captive audience. The question then reverts to one of "informed consent" and whether the choices people are given are limited because they cannot say "no." (Van Zyl et al. in Kirk 2000d: 4)

["Specials"] are experimental sex changes. . . . I saw it. [The vagina] was now laying up her legs . . . and [it] actually looks like a raw tomato that's sliced open and it's just a hole . . . It heals, it heals. It just becomes, it's almost like a piece of meat. It's just a slit and then some sort of a hole there that they urinate from, and then at the bottom there's some hole probably where penetration is supposed to take place, which they can't even do. Now tell me, would you have that? (Baard 2000)

During the transition to democracy, the Truth and Reconciliation Commission (TRC) revealed that apartheid medicine encompassed atrocities such as forced sterilization, nonconsensual experimentation, and medical torture. Africanist Meg Samuelson describes this context as providing "a space in which the liminal rituals of incorporation and group cohesion—rituals, in other words, of re-remembering—were performed" (2007: 2). In addition to changes concerning sexuality and gender mentioned previously, the 1996 South African Constitution brought new promises of health equity, including the rights "to have access to health care services" and "not to be subjected to medical experiments without . . . informed consent." These promises were not realized during the transition.

This chapter explores medical experimentation on those who did not fit normative ideas of gender and sexuality under apartheid and the continuation of such abuses during the transition. Within this context, I problematize "consent" through a discussion of the tenuous agreement of those who are not fully informed about the risk of medical procedures and the context in which information is transferred, while also attending to the complications of autonomy, agency, and consent. As Antonio Gramsci (1971) pointed out, the interdependence of consent and force is integral to the production of hegemony. I define experimental medical procedures as ones carried out under controlled conditions to discover unknown effects; examples of this include the administration of medications with untested results and surgeries performed to test hypotheses about sex, gender, and/or sexuality. I argue that apartheid and poverty created health inequities that compelled those in greatest need to routinely and often unintentionally risk serious health complications in order to get medical care. I further suggest that with the configuration of apartheid and transition described in Chapter 1, some medical professionals capitalized on this demand to facilitate scientific advances and training at the expense of two marginalized groups of patients.

Within African Studies, some of the most useful work in this realm has attended to the "traveling theory" of Michel Foucault's biopower—the application of political power to control human populations, especially the body—in South African contexts. Megan Vaughan's historical analysis of African medicine, for instance, considers the effectiveness of biopower, in terms of "how the body, in modern western society, has become both the site of, and constitutive of, power relations" (1991: 8). Vaughan outlines a critique of Foucault's concepts based in the differences between the contexts in which he wrote and the power and knowledge regimes of colonial Africa, with particular attention to historical means of control and capitalism.

More recent comparative analyses of Foucault's notions in terms of HIV/AIDS are particularly relevant, as well. For Africanist Ulrike Kistner, while biopolitics constitutes a useful framework for conceptualizing African colonial medicine,

> [c]olonial power does not provide a sufficiently neat fit with
> the mode of power for whose analysis Foucault (prescriptively)

describes a methodology. . . . Foucault's methodology rests, among other things, on the presupposition of the continuity between individualising bio-power and regulating bio-politics, producing the ingredients of a society of normalization. (2003: 149–150)

Similarly, Jean Comaroff, while noting the usefulness of Foucault and Giorgio Agamben's analyses, also points to their limitations in analyses of HIV/AIDS in South Africa. Among other critiques, Comaroff notes that the ambiguity of biopolitics, "blurs precisely what demands specification in the quest to plumb the shifting political significance of AIDS in contemporary Africa, for example" (2007: 209). The similarities in illness and death between HIV/AIDS and medical treatments for transsexuals and homosexuals, historically, allow us to think about Foucault's ideas in a different but parallel medicalized context here and are further developed regarding Mbembe's notions of necropolitics in Chapter 3.

In his recent review of studies of African sexualities, Marc Epprecht spoke to the importance of new initiatives in research since the 1990s, including "research by African scholars theorizing their work with reference to other African intellectuals (rather than, for example, Foucault)" (2009: 1271). As Africanist activist-scholars Annie Leatt and Graeme Hendricks succinctly put it, "Foucault's history has been criticised for neglecting the other side of Europe's political and economic rise: colonialism" (2005: 310). Epprecht goes on to suggest that new trends in this scholarship have undermined familiar dichotomies, categories, periodizations, and polemical positions. The importance of the work of African scholars relative to the academic overemphasis on those from the global North cannot be understated. Following Epprecht's edict, in this chapter I build on "biopower" as popularized by Foucault (1978) and the archaeologies of *The Birth of the Clinic* (Foucault 1973) but attend to colonialism and focus on Africanists' framings of gendered apartheid and the transition period relative to medical experimentation. Attention to the slippages and inconsistencies Vaughan, Kistner, Comaroff, and others identify, as well as the histories and specificities of African biopolitics in relation to medicalized gender liminality along racial lines, forms an important scaffolding for this chapter.

In addition to Africanists' critical reframing of the works of theorists like Foucault, equally important is the work of South Africanists who have theorized gender as an integral part of apartheid. State formation and gender form one critical aspect of these conversations. Linzi Manicom, for example, points out the importance of "understanding the South African state formation as a gendered and gendering process, of exploring the different institutional sites and ruling discourses in which gender identities and categories are constructed" (1992: 465). This process was particularly salient in racialized medical contexts where forced sterilization, abortion, and foci on reproduction dominated (Vaughan 1991; Marks 1994). This chapter extends these ideas by considering how, within the highly gendered and raced junctures of apartheid medicine, South African physicians' creation of "sex" undermines the "familiar dichotomies [and] categories" Epprecht describes (2005: 310).

Why were state-sponsored sex reassignment surgeries offered to some South Africans while the same surgeries were forcibly performed on others? In the previous chapter, I detailed the institutional and political forces that shaped the emergence of transsexuality as a medical and legal category in South Africa. In this chapter, I extend that analysis through a consideration of two practices of sex reassignment procedures. This chapter compares conceptualizations and manipulations of "specials," coloured transsexual sex workers left without functioning genitals after experimental sex reassignment surgeries, and white conscripts in the South African Defense Force, forced to undergo aversion therapy and sex reassignment procedures to "cure" them of their homosexuality. For apartheid's architects, race and gender were inextricable: white homosexual conscripts were forced to align sex with compulsory heterosexuality, while specials' liminally sexed bodies reinforced the perceived abnormality of black and coloured South Africans. This comparison of the two groups under consideration here draws on interviews with physicians and other medical professionals and with South Africans who experienced these programs as patients or community members, as well as media analyses. It analyzes the relationships between sexed surgeries and the state and suggests that the contradictions of sex reassignment treatments are not merely arbitrary, but are integral to the inherent contradictions of gender and race and their co-constitution.[1]

The metaphor of transition is again important here. The coercion and consent that underlie the medical transitions described in this chapter define temporal lines of race, gender, and (hetero)sexuality that continued into South Africa's political transition. This chapter ends with a consideration of the ramifications of these medical abuses during the transition, through the TRC and the potential prosecution of those involved, which has helped to define the goals and priorities of transitional South Africa.

I. Medicine in Apartheid and Transitional South Africa

Close relationships between some medical practitioners and the apartheid state have been well-documented by African historians and ethicists (Dubow 1995; Seedat 1994; de Beer 1986). Under apartheid, scientific discourse developed that used ideas about race and, I argue, the relationship between sex/gender, to justify experimental research to support apartheid policy objectives. Furthermore, as South African doctors themselves, such as Laurel Baldwin-Ragaven et al., point out, "Racist health care provision jeopardised the health of the majority of the population, but was allowed to continue with little comment and less protest from professionals, until well into the 1980s" (1999: preface).

Historian Premesh Lalu traces this relationship to its colonial origins, suggesting that beginning at the turn of the twentieth century there were considerable similarities between the perspectives of medical authorities and the South African colonial state (Lalu 1998: 135). As the colonial state increasingly granted authority to western medicine, basic life functions and illnesses were racialized. For example, in 1912 South African eugenics supporter Dr. G. D. Maynard claimed that tuberculosis was not an infectious disease spread through overcrowding and poor sanitation, but that it genetically targeted blacks as a means of natural selection (Dubow 1995: 142). In many cases, the physical and the social roots and manifestations of maladies and disorders were indistinguishable. Lalu writes:

> [T]he medical profession was increasingly consulted on matters related to social contagions—lunatics, criminals, inebriates, prostitutes, and "quacks." These groups, it seems, were subjected to scientific scrutiny and government control or action, and especially after 1896 became the focus of a joint medico-political effort. (1998: 135)

Intersexuals, transvestites, and homosexuals could be added to Lalu's list of lunatics and the like, as their experiences were similarly codified and pathologized.[2] Alliances between the South African colonial state and some medical practitioners were formed through behavioral boundaries that medically and legally specified those considered normal and abnormal.

The effects of colonial and apartheid ideals had fatal consequences for black and coloured South Africans. Decisions about resource allocation and illness made under the auspices of promoting health were based in attempts to further the economic privileges and interests of the white minority, and the connections between some white physicians and legal scholars continued to develop as apartheid was enacted in 1948. While health care for white South Africans improved during apartheid, black, coloured, and Indian South Africans suffered and died in vast numbers from malnutrition, tuberculosis, and other easily curable diseases (De Beer 1986; Seedat 1984; Lodge 1983).

Health and medical treatment in South Africa has not been monolithic; postcolonial theorist Partha Chatterjee argues, for instance, that in some contexts it might be more appropriate to speak of the ways colonial states and medicine were seeking state legitimacy rather than exercising hegemony (1994). The effectiveness of colonial medicine was perhaps found more in its intellectual and ideological successes than its quantifiable ones. There were always gaps in the monolith of apartheid medicine, often through the dual positions of health care providers as colonizer and colonized (Marks 1994). Historians like Alan Jeeves have pointed to the important contributions offered by health education programs around sexually transmitted diseases, nutrition, and disease prevention during colonialism (2001, 2003). As Zwi, Marks, and Andersson (1988) note, medicine under apartheid sometimes made important advances such as reducing infant mortality. However, these advances were too often based in broader efforts of the government to promote Northern medicine over indigenous medicine (Jeeves 2001) or "to diffuse urban resistance and to coopt the African, Asian and coloured middle classes through the provision of social welfare services" (Zwi et al. 1988: 664). Within this context, the role of missionary medicine and the juridical codification of medical protocol facilitated complicated conditions for coercion.

The development of a racially-based two-tiered system of health care in South Africa during colonialism and codified under apartheid served only to exacerbate divisions.[3] Beginning in the 1900s, "whites" and "non-whites" were treated in separate health care facilities, or in separate areas of the same facilities. As Baldwin-Ragaven et al. point out, "Segregation affected the quality of care adversely; the mythical idea of 'separate but equal' was unattainable" (1999: 36). The introduction of private health care played a part in undermining some doctors' attempts to increase health care provisions (Zwi et al. 1988). Funds were devoted to specialized treatment for whites, while blacks were intentionally neglected; South African physician Aziza Seedat makes this comparison: "expensive heart transplants are performed for the few while Soweto has the highest incidence of rheumatic heart disease in the world, a disease which could easily be eradicated by improving living conditions" (1994: 12).

Health care expenditures were similarly racially skewed under apartheid in ways that reflected the ideology of the regime; in 1980–81, for example, the government spent nearly four times as much on health care for the average white South African compared to the average black South African (Gilson and McIntyre 2001: 195). This disparity had clear material and sometimes fatal effects. Health care inequities were also rooted in geographic foci on urban areas. By the mid-1980s the *Bantustans* were home to nearly half the black population of South Africans, yet only three percent of practicing doctors practiced there (Baldwin-Ragaven et al. 1999: 21).[4]

Medically suspect procedures were an important component of apartheid rooted in social inequities. Those in detention, in the military, and in vulnerable groups were subjected to extreme forms of medical torture; South Africans protesting the apartheid government from the 1960s continuing through the 1980s were considered enemies of the state, and consequently chemical and biological weapons were used against them in medical settings and prisons. Coerced and forced sterilization were two of the many forms of medical abuse against South Africans outside of these institutions that were well-known by the late 1980s and created justified atmospheres of patient distrust. For example, as Baldwin-Ragaven et al. expound,

> The apartheid state embarked on a major programme of female surgical sterilisation. . . . One doctor recalls how, as a medical officer, he observed surgical registrars (surgeons in training) sterilising patients during appendectomies without their knowledge, let alone consent. Furthermore, he recollects

how surgeons regularly manipulated fallopian tubes with the intention of causing adhesions and subsequent infertility. These practices were commonly known. (1999: 33)

Medical abuses such as these were an integral part of apartheid. And within these contexts, gendered health was particularly neglected and problematic. The intentional and unwanted surgical sterilization of black women during apartheid demonstrates the co-production of racial and gendered oppression with state politics. During this period, white South Africans' fears of being outnumbered by resistant blacks led to justifications for eugenics and medical mistreatment.[5]

Following Foucault—and Africansts' modifications of his theories— we can see the complex interplay of power and coercion woven throughout colonial medicine. In his careful analysis of historical constitutions of medicine and the body in South Africa, Alexander Butchart describes the insidiousness of power in such settings:

Indeed, it is difficult to identify a single example of a colonial or post-colonial society in which the public-health official, the primary-health-care nurse, the hospital doctor, the psychiatrist and many other representatives of the socio-medical sciences are not a ubiquitous presence. It is equally impossible to identify any setting where the population has no knowledge of how to act and react in the ritual of medical examination by the doctor, inspection by the aid worker, interrogation by the anthropologist or enumeration by the census officer. Wherever such figures and rituals appear, the diagram of power cannot be reduced to a simple equation of power as that which is held and wielded by one group over another, since wherever they appear is also where discipline is at play, fabricating the human body and the social as its visible objects and effects. (1998: x)

These reminders about the reach and pull of medicine and the protocol and ritual that inform its practices shape our understandings of the body, medical experimentation, and complications of consent.

This is the politico-economic context from which medical ideas of transsexuality emerged in South Africa. In the 1950s Groote Schuur Hospital in Cape Town was the site of both the first heart transplant in the world and, reportedly, the first sex reassignment surgery on the African continent. Expensive services were reserved almost exclusively for white patients, but race was only one factor in this complicated equation of medical experimentation.

The medical inequities endemic under apartheid continued to plague South Africans during the transition. According to the 2000 World Health Report, South Africa ranked 175 out of 191 countries in terms of health care delivery and vital statistics of its citizens (Taitz 2000). The poverty and racial segregation shaped by policies of the apartheid regime that persisted often facilitated medical abuse. These abuses were combined with a public trust of doctors, despite undermining evidence to the contrary. As Baldwin-Ragaven et al. note, "It was the veneer of professionalism that covered the close partnership between 'science' and a repressive state and that allowed for many of the activities to continue without public censure" (1999: 128). Not all physicians were abusive, of course, and many actually fought apartheid and its effects. But this combination of health care inequalities and widely-known medical abuses had particular effects in relation to gender "disorders" that highlight the co-production of gender, sex, race, and class.

II. "Lots of Things Can Go Wrong": Medical Experimentation on Transsexuals

The conversion of sex reassignment surgeries with the politico-economic conditions of South Africa has been deadly for some transsexuals. In particular, a group of male-to-female transsexuals referred to by their peers as "specials," part of communities of self-identified drag queens, sought sex reassignment surgeries through one hospital's gender identity clinic in the 1990s.[6] However, according to my interviews these surgeries were largely unsuccessful, leaving most patients with serious medical problems and often without functioning genitals. These individuals were not forced to undertake sex reassignment surgery, and many of them traveled long distances at considerable expense to have such operations, known in Cape Town's gay communities to be available for only R35 (about $6 at the time)—hence the name "specials" (implying a sale at a store on "special"). The reasons these procedures were so cheap are not clear. In interviews, doctors and narrators make contradictory claims about why surgeries were made available to transsexuals at these prices: because the procedures were experimental, because doctors were sympathetic and wanted to assist poor transsexuals, and because the state (that paid for them) and the medical establishment had similar goals in aligning sex and gender. As we saw in the previous chapter in the development of the category of "transsexual," medical discourse had a number of uses. Megan Vaughan, speaking more broadly about colonial medical discourse, identifies two of these:

> First, it could be used to pathologize the African as a social being, and to represent difference in such a way as would provide a clear rationale for domination to those who wished to find it. Secondly, it was able to satisfy the liberal conscience by feeding on a partly secularized Christian ideology which represented anything "medical" as an act of benevolence, and even of salvation. (1994: 173–174)

It is likely that all of these rationales have some grounding here. However, social, economic, and political factors have facilitated the conditions that engendered serious medical complications, and interviews suggest that these patients did not realize the potential risks of their surgeries.

Within the situation of medical inequities described above, the treatment of transsexuals in South Africa has often been less than successful, according to patients and their peers. The first study to explore such complications in the United States was published by physicians at Stanford University in 1977. Although the Stanford gender clinic was "thought by many professionals to perform the finest sex-change surgery in the country . . . half of their male-to-female conversions involved complications" (Billings and Urban 1996: 108). And more recent publications by transsexuals themselves have anecdotally revealed the complications they face, even in ideal circumstances. Amy Hunter, for instance, speaks candidly about her own failed surgeries in the United States in order to expose the details of what happens when surgeries go wrong:

> Emergency surgeries [in Colorado], four more at home in Kalamazoo and another in Denver have all failed. Chronic pain, heavy narcotics addiction, and bouts of deep depression are the hushed legacies I have battled. Left with a possibly permanent colostomy and a painful, fibrous lump between my legs where a vagina should be, it is nearly impossible not to

revisit the devastation daily. It is now two and a half years later. (Hunter 2010)

Hunter's discussion of her ongoing physical difficulties informs her articulation of problems endemic to health care for transsexuals. She identifies lack of access to health care, primary or specialized, as well as lack of knowledge among health care providers as critical problems, noting that "documentation of protocols for care of patients undergoing transition is severely limited. Additionally, techniques for remedial care of complications are not well developed" (ibid.). Hunter further points to lack of training, lack of experience, and lack of interdisciplinary collaboration among surgeons related to sex reassignment surgery as contributing to the kinds of problems she faced. Such problems are not simply due to medical mistakes and inexperience; Hunter's own physician was trained extensively in sex reassignment surgeries and performs up to two hundred such procedures per year. But, Hunter argues, "even a surgeon as experienced as mine cannot overcome obstacles that she has no training for and little experience resolving" (ibid.).

While no statistics on success or failure rates are available, South African physicians have pointed out the shortcomings of similar surgical treatments over the past fifty years. For example, one physician writes, "From the results of operations done by the author and by other surgeons in South Africa, it appears that postoperative complications are not uncommon and that results are often disappointing" (Crichton 1993: 347). Some doctors do not take responsibility for complications themselves, blaming patients or "inadequate psychiatric evaluation beforehand" (Dewaele and Van Iddekinge 1987: 789), while others express great concern about their patients.

There are significant physical risks associated with sex reassignment surgeries in any context, including constructed vaginal canals closing and penises becoming detached, painful and even deadly infections, hormonal imbalances, and postoperative difficulties with urination and bowel movements. One South African physician who has conducted surgeries for over thirty years explains some of the problems he has seen:

Lots of things can go wrong, obviously, all along the line, and they do sometimes. You're doing a male-to-female, you know, anything can go wrong. One of the problems is that you have to make a hole where there has never been a hole before, between the bladder and the rectum, and it's a very difficult area to get into because it's very tightly closed off in the female. Well you have to get in the male with a narrow pelvis, the male android pelvis, as opposed to the female, which is a very [wide] pelvis. And now you have to try to turn in the skin and use it to line a new vagina. And it's difficult. And you can go into the bowel. I've had a few connections between the bowel and the vagina or the bladder and the vagina, that's one of the things that can happen. Infection can happen. . . . Of course [breast] prostheses can go wrong, although we've had very little of that. It's very easy to put a [breast] prosthesis in as large as it can take, but in the male it's obviously not, sometimes there's no skin on there. (Williams 1997)

Here, the surgeon describes many of the physical troubles male-to-female transsexuals face in his practice. Most commonly, transsexuals' vaginas collapse and need to be repeatedly reconstructed and fistulas develop that threaten their health.[7] Further complications can include breast cancer facing hormonally-treated transsexual women and the need to surgically reduce the size of limbs bloated from hormone therapy (Billings and Urban 1996: 108). Transsexuals' agency cannot be underestimated here, as many express great desire for surgeries. But in the context of the program where "specials" were treated, it seems patients did not receive adequate information about the risks such procedures pose to their health.

Perhaps the most relevant distinction in the racialized delivery of medical services for transsexuals in South Africa is that between public and private health care discussed previously. Since the 1960s, sex reassignment procedures have been performed privately in the major urban areas of South Africa for those who can afford them. But for poor and/or black and coloured South Africans, politico-economic conditions have meant that elective sex reassignment procedures are difficult to attain in the private sphere. Public hospitals have been the primary treatment sites because of the infrastructure required for such procedures and their high costs.[8] Lack of funds and more pressing medical emergencies result in regular cancellations of sex reassignment surgery in public settings. These cancellations occur even when patients have traveled across the country for their operations or are only partially through their transitions; waiting periods for surgeries or follow-up procedures can span decades. Such difficulties take great psychological tolls on patients that can include severe depression and suicide attempts. The putative effects of the denial of health care have been increasingly documented in the United States, in which context: "Depression, anxiety, and suicidality are conditions commonly tied to the unmet need for gender-confirming medical care" (Spade 2011: 149). Elizabeth Baker, a South African social worker, who at the time of this interview had worked with transsexuals for twenty years, expounds,

> It's a long process and it's very traumatic. Because the operations often, I mean they're so complicated that they often go wrong and at the moment they keep canceling operations because they have to. I mean it's a luxury in a way, and there's a lot of trauma here. So often they get all geared up [for surgery] . . . and then it gets cancelled. (Baker 1997)

The temporalities of trauma are apparent here, and the tension caused by lack of funds is based on the necessity for evaluations of which surgeries are most urgent. But the psychological effects of these decisions are difficult to measure. Many transsexuals are so frustrated by waiting that they choose not to undergo surgeries at all.[9] As Odessa Jansen, a transsexual who sought treatment in a program in the transitional period at a different hospital explains:

> When I signed up there were sixteen boys [MTF] and one girl [FTM]. After about a year the girl got her "yes." And she went for a sex change to become a man. After two years of seeing psychologists and psychiatrists, three of us were chosen out of the sixteen. But then you go on a waiting list and now you have to wait, because they do one, and until that person is finished the rest wait. That is why I couldn't take it in the end. (Jansen 1997)

Jansen's story is not unique. Many patients in public hospitals get frustrated with waiting years for operations and choose not to have surgeries that can be completed in a matter of months in private clinics overseas. Waiting takes its toll on those in the midst of reassignment, as well, especially when such surgeries are not successful. As a psychologist explained about the process, "I have a client, for example, who still comes here who it's seven years later and it's not being . . . whatever difficulties there had been—and this is a female-to-male—they're still trying to correct it. And that has really severe psychological implications and consequences" (Ryland 2007). Estian Smit, a South African author and activist who identifies as not belonging to sex or gender categories, describes some of the problems of public health care e has ascertained from applicants to public programs, which include the following complaints:[10]

- Having no choice but to make use of a particular psychiatrist approved by the programme in question;

- Very high psychiatric consultation fees;

- Rigid expectations about confirming to the gender stereotypes of the gender towards which one wished to be "re-assigned";

- Being denied treatment because of having been married and/ or having had children;

- Being discouraged by a psychiatrist from forming support groups and having contact with other gender reassignment applicants; and

- Long waiting lists. (Smit 2006: 279–80)

These problems identified by Smit replicate many found during this research about the expectations and timing/temporality associated with medical interventions.

The distinction between necessary and unnecessary medical treatment has also caused surgeons undertaking sex reassignment to downplay its existence. Judgment about whether or not transsexuals should even be treated in public hospitals has made it difficult for potential patients to find care and has also made researching South African transsexuality extremely difficult. As one doctor put it,

> Because of the problems of lack of money and so on, which every country's going through now as far as health is concerned, we play it low-key. . . . And not because there's any secrecy or because it's a horrible thing, but because it spoils it for the rest and you have this backlash. The public saying, "Well, how can you do that? How can our hospitals do that . . . using up all the money that could be used more usefully?" You see

the number of gangsters that we treat who have been involved in drunken fights, with stabs and gunshot wounds. And you wonder whether that is better treatment. (Williams 1997)

In the context of crises of violence, HIV/AIDS, and lack of governmental resources, controversial decisions must constantly be made as to which patients are most in need of medical attention and resources; worthiness is constantly renegotiated here.

Despite surgical drawbacks, during the political transition many patients were grateful to attain surgeries because they could not afford to pay for them otherwise. One surgeon explains: "If [transsexuals] can't afford it they go in as H-1 patients, which means that the state pays for it. . . . In general . . . no one is going to not get an operation or not get treated because he or she can't afford it" (Williams 1997). Smit similarly notes that despite the shortcomings of public health care, "there are applicants who fit the criteria and who are happy with and grateful for the help and treatment they obtain—treatment they would otherwise not be able to afford" (Smit 2006: 280). Various gender identity clinics were set up in public hospitals in South Africa for a few years at a time since the 1960s intended to fill needs demonstrated by transsexuals and in an attempt to close the gap between health care available to South Africans of different socio-economic statuses.[11] A physician from a public hospital explains:

Eighty percent of our patients, of the country's population, is indigent that needs hospital attention. So what has grown up here is a large number of doctors like myself who for many years worked at a salary in these teaching hospitals and so on; we're not allowed to do any private practice. And we felt that very strongly, that these people [transsexuals] should not be taken advantage of and have to pay thousands to have their operations done. . . . [First,] *it was still experimental*, if we can call it that, and . . . [second,] they should be treated, not used and abused. The third reason was we found that those that were done in private practice often were not done with psychiatric input; they were just, they would go into the doctor's office and say "I want to be female." And they would say "Yes, sure," and do it, which we didn't like also. And they paid a lot of money for it. (Williams 1997, emphasis added)

Here, the surgeon expresses opposition to experimental surgeries, high costs, and mistreatment of transsexuals in private contexts, particularly in the lack of psychiatric evaluation in that setting. His concern stems, in part, from his experiences with those whom he believes do not fit diagnostic criteria for gender dysphoria, as well as patients who have come to him to have privately completed surgeries reversed. Unfortunately, the serious problems raised here have not been confined to private facilities alone; they have been mirrored in much of the public hospital treatment of transsexuals in South Africa.[12]

The specific program where the majority of "specials" were treated was initiated in the 1990s by physicians who explained in interviews that they had received a number of requests for such treatment (Vorster 2000). Patients were evaluated by a psychiatrist or psychologist in a session that would last about one hour, and of the forty to fifty potential patients seen, only two were turned away.[13] These MTF patients then took estrogen and sex reassignment surgeries were performed. Medical practitioners claim that patients in this program took hormones for about six months postoperatively, but patients and their peers claim that hormone therapy was only required for two months.[14] Because of costs and patients' home locations relative to the hospital, there were no social workers or psychologists available to help them through the transition process. Further, there was no postoperative medical attention available following their transitions; as a physician involved explains, "[t]he usual thing was that once surgery was done they would never return for any follow-up or counseling. They just seemed to want to rather do their own thing" (Vorster 2000). In cases without medical complications, this arrangement offered patients freedom from doctors' interference. However, when problems arose, most patients lived hundreds of miles away from the hospital, which meant that they could not easily access critical services.

After only a few years, the experimental program ended. When asked about why the program was discontinued, one of the physicians involved with it explains:

> Well, we had a death. He underwent surgery, but apparently where they removed part of the bowel to do the vaginal side of it, the anastomosis broke down and there was a peritonitis that happened and they missed it. So the poor guy died. So they decided to then discontinue the surgery. (Vorster 2000)[15]

No surgical procedures are undertaken without risk of complications. As Jasbir Puar put it in her examination of biopolitics, "Death becomes a form of collateral damage in the pursuit of life" (2007: 32). However, the overall context of this treatment program, combined with the limited psychological services provided, proved disastrous for many of its patients. Members of drag queen communities in Cape Town—home to many "specials"—suspect that more deaths occurred than were reported, as members of their communities have little power and their lives are often considered expendable, and they are anxious to have attention brought to this issue. Sex reassignment procedures are already bound by protocols of secrecy, which were exacerbated by the secrecy of potential experimentation.

Medical problems following sex reassignment surgery are common in South Africa, but the extent to which "specials" and other patients consent to undertaking risky procedures and the relative degree of risk of this particular program treating "specials" is unclear. As a social worker explains:

> Some people, well, a few people sail through these ops. Most people have lots of complications and infections. So I always say to them, I mean the doctor's always saying, "Well, it will take this amount of time. This is what we're going to do." And [the doctors] never really tell them all the complications. (Baker 1997)

These complications, often unexpected by patients, can be life-threatening. The expectations for post-surgery care are also often misunderstood or difficult for some patients to adhere to. One of the most common problems facing South African MTF transsexuals is the collapse of the constructed vagina. One doctor explains:

> We always insist after the vagina is made that they wear a mold in the vagina for about a year, because as the skin settles down and the whole thing tends to, the idea of any hole anywhere that you make surgically is it tends to close down. So you've got to keep the mold in . . . it takes about a year. And some, they won't wear a mold, say it's uncomfortable, or they don't like it. And then they rue it, they regret it, they come back and say that it hasn't worked and we redo it. (Williams 1997)

Wearing a mold postoperatively is considered very painful and difficult by most South African transsexuals I interviewed. Some revealed that they did not understand the importance of this mold as a necessary part of keeping the shape and size of the postoperative vagina, and as indicated, later regretted it when their vaginas closed.

Transsexuals and medical practitioners speak of untenable expectations about what surgery can offer, hopes that are often unfulfilled. For instance, a psychiatrist recalls a potential patient who approached him with such a misunderstanding, based in gendered expectations on what it would mean to be female:

> Like one person who wanted a gender reassignment, and I said to him, "But why?" And he said, "Well, I would like to just sit at home and just sew and cook." I said, "But that's not the purpose, it's meant to make a readjustment to life and live life to the full." (Vorster 2000)

This patient was not treated as a transsexual as the doctor felt this patient had confusion about post-transition life as a woman. Other patients similarly expressed expectations about treatment outcomes that could not be met. According to South African psychiatrists, psychologists, and transsexuals themselves, many specials sought surgery because of the discrimination that they face from their communities and the state, especially the police. They hoped that treatment would allow them to "pass" more fully and to avoid harassment. Some also complained of the ways that their liminal statuses did not allow them to get jobs. One practitioner suggested that many of his patients wanted sex reassignment so they could attain employment. He described a patient who "found that he couldn't obtain employment because he cross-dressed and he said [sex reassignment] was an advantage" and another who "had been living as a woman for a long, long time and did domestic light work, and when they discovered that she was not a woman, because she dressed as a woman, then she was dismissed . . . she had been unemployed for many years, because it is clearly difficult to find work" (Vorster 2000). Many of these patients hope that living as women postoperatively and having legal documentation of their new status will provide important relief from overt discrimination.

The conditions of apartheid and the transition set the stage for justification of medical abuses of black and coloured people, poor people, and sexual minorities, with "specials" fitting into all three of these categories. Apartheid was not fixed and consistent with regards to race, gender, and sex. Racial categories were often represented as rigid, but individuals, even within the same families, sometimes moved among these categories or were forced into particular racial groups. The tautological nature of race, as explored in the Introduction, make its seeming contradictions remarkable. As Achille Mbembe put it, extending Foucault, those in the post-colony, "rule by simultaneously employing force and avoiding doing so, depending on the times and the contexts" (1992: 128). Similarly, gender and sex were dualistically conceived as masculine/feminine and male/female, but, as I describe in Chapter 1, for medical practitioners sex was mutable as long as it "matched" gender. Understanding relationships between gender and sex is a cornerstone to understanding apartheid patriarchy. In this chapter, we see how coordinating gender and sex (making individuals fully men or women) guided medical experimentation.

This context, combined with socioeconomic realities of apartheid and the transition, made those who actively seek out treatment and those who are coerced into having procedures done difficult to differentiate. One narrator describes her experience with this type of coercion. As a young self-identified drag queen, Brandy Roeland won beauty competitions all over the Western Cape. However, in 1990 she was stalked by a man who shot her when he found out that she was a gay man, not a woman as he had presumed.[16] Roeland was taken to a hospital in Cape Town, but doctors did not know whether to put her in the male or female ward and this caused a furor in the hospital, resulting in her eventual placement in a private ward. In this ward she was approached by doctors from the hospital; she recounts,

> They wanted to perform a sex change also on me that time and I didn't want them to. I was in a ward alone, a private ward with a bathroom and everything in it. The professors that came in wanted to. Because of the scars [from surgeries following her shooting] they told me it was almost like the same kind of scar it's going to be for a sex change op. But I didn't want to. I was too young, I was nineteen, I wasn't sure what I wanted to go through and whatever. But I'm glad I didn't go for the sex change, because a lot of sex changes kill themselves today. (Roeland 2000)

Roeland considers herself lucky to have decided against sex reassignment surgery and is outraged by what she sees as experimentation on "specials." As I describe in the Introduction, she and her friends spoke to me in hopes that attention will be brought to this issue through the media, research, or films.

Roeland's concern about "specials" is grounded in the experiences of transsexual women she knows. The problems she and others in her community perceive are two-fold. First, the medical complications of surgeries are multiple and often dramatic. Capetonian drag queens claim that "specials" treated in the 1990s do not have breasts and that their genital surgeries are more accurately described as disfigurement. Sandra Baard explicitly describes the results she saw after her friend Michelle Lottering had surgery in the epigraph to this chapter and her horror about the forced liminality facing "specials." Describing the surgical outcomes she witnessed in Lottering and other friends, Baard became overwhelmed; because sex reassignment is something that most of the drag queens in her community have considered and sometimes desired, she finds the results of this treatment shocking.[17]

The second component of "specials'" treatment is psychological. Drag queens and "specials" in this community are aware of the dangerous effects that medical complications bring. Baard, Roeland, and other drag queens express alarm at the lack of psychological counseling for young drag queens treated as transsexuals:

> You are supposed to go in for a year first for psychiatric evaluation and all these steps before you actually do it, [have the] sex change. These young stupid fools actually just go for two months on hormones and the hormones start taking over their bodies, and they're all flushed and hot and ten times more girly. They go lay down [for the surgery] and wake up, "Ooh, I'm a woman!" [But] afterwards they suffer the consequences of what they're going through now [physically] and . . . after half a year saying, "Oh God, why did I do it?" (Baard 2000)

Baard is frustrated both by the lack of ethical medical treatment as well as "specials'" lack of foresight and expectations. As she points out here, these individuals are often young and may not understand the medical complications they will face, the mental distress sex reassignment may bring when patients are not fully informed of potential risks, and the limitations of surgical interventions. Doctors expressed similar concerns about this program. Because of the lack of psychological counseling as part of the program where "specials" were treated, and lengthy hormone treatment as part of their transitions, implications for undergoing surgeries may not be thoroughly considered.

Although this medical experimentation, ostensibly intended to improve surgical techniques and assist patients in need, has its roots in apartheid, living in a society that continues to value white and upper-class lives above those of black and coloured poor South Africans makes some in gender liminal positions in Cape Town continue to be wary about surgery. With so little societal and family support, their abuse and even deaths are not considered significant in South Africa. Further, many "specials" are sex workers and therefore further criminalized. Baard articulates her theory of why doctors medically abuse her friends:

> You get young [people] . . . and they come here at the age of 17, 18, and [they say] "Ooh, doctor, I want to be a woman." The doctor's gonna think, oh my God. . . . I can experiment on your body . . . maybe you'll die tomorrow, I wouldn't care. That is what the government is . . . there's no [monetary insurance] claim from the families, no nothing. . . . [A friend] told me before they operated on her, they put a tag on her toe. So it's like you die, you just die, and they just close you up and no matter what they did to your body. (Baard 2000)

The ways that "specials" are considered expendable are closely linked to the medico-legal dismissal of transsexuals' lives described in the previous chapter. Again, the co-production of gender, sex, race, and class materialize overtly in the lives of "specials." I am not suggesting that transsexuals do not express agency; the following chapter details transsexual agency in this process. The disparities and tensions between transsexuals and drag queens discussed in Chapters 3 and 5 also form an important backdrop to these accounts; hierarchies and conflicts have high stakes among those with differing expressions of gender liminality. However, given the interdependence of force and consent in processes of hegemony, the parameters of "consent" must be interrogated, especially regarding comments of doctors involved in experimental programs. Transsexuals in South Africa's public health care system may be seen as potential subjects of experiments, while those in private settings are prized for their finances. More broadly, while Foucault's biopower can account for efforts to discipline and normalize apartheid bodies, we must also pay close attention to the ways that their abnormalization was also critical to advancing apartheid.

III. "Military Mutilation: How the SADF Forced Gay Soldiers to Become Women"[18]

In July 2000, this front-page headline of the South African *Mail and Guardian* accompanied a full page artistic representation of a masculine white man in military uniform, with women's breasts bloodily sewed onto his chest. The accompanying articles detailed a pattern of medical experimentation, torture, and abuse of white gay conscripts during the 1970s and 1980s, allegedly including forced sex reassignment surgeries.[19] The medical abuse of gays and lesbians in the South African Defense Force during apartheid was increasingly documented during South Africa's political transition (Van Zyl et al. 1999; Baldwin-Ragaven et al. 1999; Van Zyl and Steyn 2005; Morgan et al. 2009). Researchers have shown that the military culture of the SADF and the goals of apartheid coincided to create circumstances that were dangerous for many homosexual conscripts.[20] The treatment of these soldiers consisted primarily of "aversion therapy" that purported to cure them of their homosexuality.[21]

The first documentation of medical abuse of South African gays and lesbians in the military was an article published in *Resister: Journal of the Committee on South African War Resistance* (1986/1987).[22] However, the interest of human rights activists and researchers was not sparked until June 1997 following the transition to democracy by submissions to the health sector hearings of the TRC. These hearings exposed a collusion between the apartheid state and medicine that is relevant not only to uncovering abuse within the military, but to larger analyses of medical treatments of sex, gender, and sexuality "disorders." Specifically, the TRC hearings illuminated the myth of medical ethics under apartheid and "revealed a nepotistic, self-serving, and self-enriching group of people, . . . [who] conducted work they deemed to be scientific, but which was underpinned by ideas, suggestions and hypotheses that were bizarre and incompetent" (TRC in Baldwin-Ragaven et al. 1999: 128).

Through the TRC hearings, a pattern of medical abuse of gay and lesbian conscripts was uncovered, and a research team was assembled in an effort to document such abuse and recommend future actions. "Rumours of these activities circulated for years, but details of the programme first came to light at hearings of the Truth and Reconciliation Commission with submission of *The Aversion Project*, a detailed investigation of treatment of homosexuals in the South African Defense Force by a coalition of groups, including the Medical Research Council" (Kaplan 2004: 1416). As part of the research for *The Aversion Project* report, fifteen interviews were conducted with former gay and lesbian military personnel, their family members, and some staff (Van Zyl et al. 1999).[23]

Through these interviews, codified medical abuse emerged, most notable under a Dr. Villesky.[24] Physician Robert M. Kaplan explains: "Threatened with punishment if they did not comply, they [homosexual men] were admitted to the secretive Ward 22 at 1 Military Hospital, Voortrekkerhoogte, Pretoria. In later years, homosexual women were also selected" (2004: 1416). The abuse of conscripts took the form of administering behavioral therapy and unknown drugs, some of which were addictive and others which had irreversible hormonal effects such as impotence and sterilization. Electroshock therapy was also practiced on conscripts in many cases, and it was often so severe, for example, that one psychologist described the shoes flying off a patient's feet (Van Zyl et al. 1999: 73). Some of the long-term problems facing patients of Dr. Villesky included extreme mental instability, photosensitivity, hormone disorders, headaches, depression, and newly diagnosed medical conditions such as epilepsy. Patients were prone to drug addictions, experienced difficulties in future relationships, and some committed suicide during treatment and after they were discharged (Kaplan 2004). The surgery itself also sometimes proved fatal:

> The casualty rates were high. Patients died during surgery, and some were discharged before reassignment was completed, with extra surgery required. Preoperative or postoperative assessment was not done, informed consent was not obtained, and expensive hormone regimens were needed to maintain appearance. (Kaplan 2004: 1416)

A number of politically and ethically-based organizations are currently determining how to hold individuals and institutions accountable for these practices in post-apartheid South Africa, a point to which I return at the end of this chapter.[25] Medical abuse of conscripts not only illustrates one way sexuality was understood and policed under apartheid, it also points to the connections among conceptualizations of gender, sex, and sexuality. The hormonal treatment and chemical castration performed on gay men in the SADF might be considered a form of forced sex reassignment.

Perhaps most striking and objectionable, some accounts also indicate that this experimentation likely included forced or coerced sex reassignment surgeries. Journalist Paul Kirk claims that at least fifty operations were performed on conscripts each year for eighteen years between 1971 and 1989 (Kirk 2000d; Kaplan 2004). He suggests that 900 forced sex reassignment surgeries may have been performed during this time, and journalist Ana Simo similarly claims that "between 1969 and 1987, approximately 900 men and women had gender reassignment surgery and most appear to have been young, 16- to 24-year-old white males drafted into the apartheid army" (2000: 1–2). These numbers have not been publically contested but are not fully substantiated, either. However, despite specific statistics the existence of such procedures has been demonstrated through interviews.[26]

To illustrate the details of these procedures, Kirk describes the experiences of a number of individuals who were offered sex reassignment surgeries while military conscripts. One of the individuals Kirk interviewed is Jonathan, who was told he was an "incurable" homosexual who should have surgery to treat hir ailment.[27] Jonathan explains:

> I was told in no uncertain terms that I was a freak, and should be locked up for the rest of my life. I was told that, once I was given the operation the army would see to it that all my paperwork was changed to reflect I was a female—birth certificate and the works. I was told I could keep in touch with my parents, but that I should find a new circle of friends. And of course I would never have to go back to the army. It seemed a good way out. (Kirk 2000b: 4)

In this account, Kirk discloses that Jonathan was not given any psychological support or counseling during or after this process. It is not clear whether Jonathan would identify hirself as gay or as a transsexual (or as neither or both). Most research on this subject to date assumes that conscripts were gay or lesbian and forced to undergo sex reassignment procedures; however, it is also possible that some of these conscripts might have considered themselves transsexual and sought out or welcomed the opportunity for state-sponsored surgeries.

One transsexual narrator who rejected these surgeries because of the military program's reputation and objectives, Lyndsay, describes the intensity of her decision not to pursue surgery. At age twenty, Lyndsay was in the military and became so frustrated with her lack of options that she attempted to remove her own penis:

> There wasn't anybody I could find who had an answer to the questions I had, and I desperately wanted to be rid of the appendage I saw as representing everything that was wrong with my life. So, one night, I took a .357 Magnum and shot myself through my penis. I ended up in 2 Military Hospital, and some nine months later returned to have reconstructive surgery. The surgeon had also been involved with the military-sanctioned sex-change project on gay people, and he asked me outright if I wanted a sex-change. So I knew that was a possibility in terms of their programme. But I also knew enough about their agenda to understand that I didn't wish to become another negative statistic. It was a heart-stopping moment to have that offer for something that I've wanted all my life. . . . I knew by then that this was not a project designed to help people; rather it was for them a form of Aryan experimentation. (In Morgan et al. 2009: 42)

Significantly, even though Lyndsay was desperate to transition physically, she chose to reject the option when it was offered to her as part of The Aversion Project, as she did not have confidence in the intention and outcome.[28] Unlike others who have been interviewed about their experiences, Lyndsay expressed her choice in this process. This conflict Lyndsay faced demonstrates the severity of the program and the depth of the fear it inspired.

Part of what makes this kind of medical experimentation difficult to evaluate is the issue of informed consent. Like most "specials," conscripts were usually quite young—in South Africa white men were required to serve in the military when they were seventeen or eighteen years old. Furthermore, gay and lesbian conscripts were sometimes institutionalized in military asylums and subjected to interrogations intended to undermine their self-confidence and sureness about their sexual and gender identities. As Van Zyl et al. assert in the epigraph to this chapter, challenges to informed consent and the histories of sex reassignments in the military are well-known. Within these contexts, hormonal and sex reassignment procedures performed on conscripts had unknown results and effects on sex and sexuality.

Another narrator in Kirk's article, Mary, also underwent sex reassignment surgery.[29] However, Kirk claims that ze is "one of many victims of the military's sex-change programme who is stranded halfway between sexes" (Kirk 2000b: 4). Kirk writes that though ze had not completed hir transition, Mary, a FTM transsexual, was told that the SADF no longer performed such surgeries and that ze would have to have them done privately, which ze has not been able to afford to date. After the publication of this story, the National Coalition for Gay and Lesbian Equality (now the Equality Project) was also approached by a trans man whose surgery was not completed by the SADF in 1973 and who wanted to bring this issue to light (Kirk 2000d). Unfortunately, such incomplete surgeries are not as rare as Kirk postulates.[30]

As we have seen above, many South African transsexuals in both public and private sectors have been unable to complete their procedures or have had complications that left them not clearly male or female. It would be fruitless to try to discern between the subjective choices of particular agents and violence subjected upon patients. Instead, it is clear that South African transsexuals cannot be simply positioned as empowered agents or passive victims. Antonio Gramsci's conception of hegemony, whereby the ruling class seeks to win the "active consent" of subaltern social groups (1971: 370), is useful here. In this view, the historical processes brought to bear upon those addressed in this chapter were, as is so often the case, at once violent and creative, transformational yet reproductive of inequalities of power. And incomplete medical procedures reflect the unceasing, imperfect reproduction of hegemonic power relations in South Africa.

As Vincent and Camminga point out, military medicine was connected to apartheid power in ways the affected both doctors and patients; they note that in this context, "Medical personnel were expected to obey commands even when orders from superiors contradicted personal or professional ethics" (2009: 687). However, culpability for such experimentation is also important. The doctor accused of masterminding most of the surgical and psychological aversion therapy described here is Aubrey Levin (speculated to be Villesky in *The Aversion Project* accounts), and in his defense he responded to the *Mail and Guardian*, stating:

> Nobody was given electroshock therapy by me. We did not practise Russian communist-style torture. What we practised was aversion therapy. We caused slight—very slight—discomfort in the arm by contracting the muscles using an electronic device. Some people used elastic bands to shock patients. Nobody was hurt and nobody was ever held against their will. At no time were patients forced to submit to treatment. (Levin in Kirk 2000d: 5)

Levin, then living in Canada, threatened to sue the *Mail and Guardian* for publishing articles on his alleged role in this experimentation in the SADF (Kirk 2000a). At the time of the exposure of this issue, the Equality Project, with the support of Amnesty International and the South African Council of Churches, among others, called for an investigation of Levin that did not materialize, even as he continued to practice medicine (Wa Ka Ngobeni 2000).

This situation raises a number of important questions about the creation of sex and compulsory heterosexuality under apartheid within medical and military institutions. The relationship between consent and force among those subjected to multiple forms of medical torture and within the context of military control is characterized by coercive and violent complexities. The military abuse of gay conscripts also complicates the boundary between homosexuality and transsexuality. In the preceding chapter, the rigid distinctions between these categories and among medical and legal professionals were explored. But here, the experiences of conscripts themselves show how individuals, while fitting loosely under the rubric of gender liminality, do not correspond neatly with rigid categories.

State control expressed through the collusion of medical and military institutions was essential to the maintenance of apartheid, as Foucault predicted. As Jacklyn Cock put it in specific South African contexts, a hidden form of terrorism infused the military, and "[t]his 'terrorism' is evident in how an unknown number of gays and lesbians in the SADF between 1969 and 1980 were subjected to electric shock treatment and sex-change operations" (Cock 2005: 198). Again, the importance of congruence between gender and sex is paramount and can be traced along racial lines. Here, heterosexuality is conceptualized as essential to "normal" white gender; that is, a successful man must be attracted to women. In these institutional spaces, challenges to the gender/sex binary disrupted the solidity of apartheid and were thus unacceptable.

IV. Lasting Implications of Raced Gender Incongruence

In March 2010, Dr. Aubrey Levin was arrested in Canada for allegedly sexually assaulting a male patient and is being investigated in dozens of similar cases. Despite widespread knowledge of his apartheid past, Levin has been practicing medicine in Canada for the past fifteen years. His threats of lawsuits against news media, including the South African *Mail and Guardian*, are said to have contributed to his suppression of his past. During this time, he was employed as a professor of psychiatry at the University of Calgary in Alberta and has been regularly asked to assess Canadian convicted offenders' sexualities as a forensic psychiatrist.[31] The outrages of unprosecuted medical injustices by professionals still practicing are manifold. And fatal effects persist beyond Levin:

> A psychiatrist working under [Aubrey Levin] at Voortrekkerhoogte military hospital, who in the 1970's allegedly helped chemically castrate a young gay conscript named Jean Erasmus, still practices in Cape Town. A depressed Erasmus killed himself last year after telling his story to an Amnesty International representative in Pretoria. (Simo 2000: 3–4)

The medical experimentation of apartheid and the transition have many unexplored facets. They clearly remain unresolved in uncovering the effects of experimental procedures and those involved.

One question raised through this chapter is how to conceptualize "informed consent" in contemporary South Africa, particularly as it relates to sex reassignment procedures. In both situations described here, the multiple physical and psychological complications that arise from such procedures are not adequately communicated to patients and their families. For "specials," results of surgeries are often shocking and can leave patients more socially marginal than before their surgeries. In the case of military experimentation, patients were likely forced to submit to damaging procedures. The production of consent in South Africa cannot be separated from institutions of medicine and law. However, it is important to concurrently consider how to account for patients' vulnerability without objectification or condescension. Discussions about the difficulties of informed consent are critical to reducing medical abuses and mental distress among particular groups of patients. But these discussions also must take into account patients' abilities to make decisions about their own bodies.

In her important work on Iranian transsexuality, Afsaneh Najmabadi finds related pressures in contemporary Iran where the relationships among Northern conceptions of gender, sex, and sexuality are similarly blurred. Here, religion plays a significant role in gender liminality. She summarizes the interstices of social categories in a specifically Iranian context this way:

> Simply put, the religio-legal prohibition of same-sex practices does contribute to pressures on gays and lesbians to consider transsexuality as a religiously sanctioned legal alternative (which is particularly important for religiously observant persons), but instead of eliminating same-sex desires and practices, it has actually provided more room for *relatively* safer semipublic gay and lesbian social space and for less conflicted self-perceptions among people with same-sex desires and practices. As one pre-op FtM (female-to-male transsexual) succinctly put it: "Once I was diagnosed as TS (transsexual), I started having sex with my girlfriend without feeling guilty." (2008: 25, emphasis in original)

The heart-wrenching decisions and effects of the choices Najmabadi describes are further documented in the film "Be Like Others" (2008) and blur pathologized categories in conjunction with state politics. Contentious choices for contemporary Iranians, as similarly faced by "specials" and enforced for South African conscripts, often mean that matching sex and gender proves more acceptable than same-sex sexuality.

Further, sometimes troublesome intentions and biases inform physicians' motivations. For instance, Billings and Urban note that in the United States features and behaviors that have not corresponded with patients' claimed gender, as well as homosexuality, are taken as alarming signs. One physician told these researchers, for example, "We're not taking Puerto Ricans anymore; they don't look like transsexuals, they look like fags" (1996: 111). Racism clearly informs the constitution of appropriate gender. In addressing the misogyny that can infuse treatment, feminist theorist Marjorie Garber recalls one doctor's account: "In one case with which I am familiar, the patient's massive scars were probably the result of the surgeon's unconscious sadism and wish to scar the patient for 'going against nature' " (Lothstein in Garber 1992: 103). While these examples are anecdotal, future research in South Africa might investigate biases in medical mistreatment.

The comparison addressed in this chapter simultaneously disrupts the categories that medical and legal professionals define as transsexual, homosexual, and intersexual, as many of these patients fit into none or more than one of these designators. They also show how these categories are co-produced with race, class, and nation. Poor coloured "specials" engaged with the public health care system in South Africa to gain medical care including hormone therapy and sex reassignment procedures, but these treatments rarely met their expectations and sometimes left them physically liminal. For white conscripts, sex, gender, and sexuality are conflated under the control of military medicine. While targeted for "treatment" because of their sexual orientation, their sex and gender are relatedly thrown into question. Doctors sometimes attempt to force congruity among sex, gender, and sexuality to advance racial divides. Homosexuality disrupts gender, as men with same-sex desire are not considered "real" men and vice versa. Aversion therapy was intended to shock or drug conscripts into heterosexuality, but if the therapy was unsuccessful some gay conscripts were surgically made "female"; that is, if their gender could not be made to fix their sex, then sex would be changed to match their gender/sexuality.

As in the previous chapter, we see here how ideas expressed about sex, gender, and sexuality here are not fixed or immutable, they are contingent. Gender, sex, and sexuality merge and emerge in South Africa, and they also show how marginality intersects with sexed and gendered medical treatments. This locates Foucault's biopolitics in specifically South African contexts. "One of the bio-political functions of the state is the creation and policing of new lines of demarcation, by which immigrants are turned into aliens, protection transmutes into discrimination, cultural difference becomes a means of racial stigmitization, and techniques of identification come to resemble racial profiling" (Kistner 2003: 154). In this chapter, it is clear that poor coloured "specials" and white gays and lesbians in the military experienced different difficulties in their interactions with medical professionals. But a constant thread that runs through these examples is the expendability of gender and sexual minorities in larger apartheid and transitional projects and the legitimated use of their bodies to advance political objectives.

Three
_____

Redefining Transition through Necropolitics

This chapter develops the theoretical frameworks of Chapters 1 and 2 in a new direction. Foucault's notions continue to be useful and relevant to these considerations of mobile or restricted experiences of the temporality of sex, describing states' regulations of bodies. But how can his traveling theories be extended and challenged in relation to self-described sexed transitions in apartheid and transitional contexts? Chapter 3 reconceptualizes and personalizes gender transition beyond medico-legal definitions through attention to seven narratives collected from 1997–2009 which detail encounters mediated through inconsistencies in legal rights, incongruous access to medical treatment, and unpredictable relationships and employment opportunities. In so doing, these narratives complicate and redefine gender boundaries, unsettling medical designations of gender liminality and expectations of somatic changes to emphasize the intimacy of decisions about personal transitions in South Africa's political transition.

Part of what makes this analysis different from those of U.S. and European transsexuals' narratives can be articulated through Achille Mbembe's critiques and articulations of colonialism. For Mbembe, racism is a technology that facilitates biopower—the domain of life controlled by power—and the cruel relationship between life and death in colonial contexts that he deems *necropolitics*. He suggests that ultimately, "the notion of biopower is insufficient to account for contemporary forms of subjugation of life to the power of death" (2003: 39–40) and alternately identifies necropolitics as a way to relate biopower to the states of exception and siege that have normalized killing, especially in colonial contexts, and to understand the relationships among resistance, sacrifice, and terror.

According to Mbembe, the restrictions of racism have been and continue to be violently policed and tested under colonialism in necropolitical contexts. He intimates,

> in most instances, the selection of races, the prohibition of
> mixed marriages, forced sterilization, even the extermination
> of vanquished peoples are to find their first testing ground in
> the colonial world. Here we see the first syntheses between
> massacre and bureaucracy, that incarnation of Western
> rationality.[1] (2003: 22–23)

This violent and rationalized racism—often intersecting with sexuality—is critical to the stories of South Africans' gendered transitions and
the racialized lines along which they must be historicized. The related
boundaries concerning sexuality and sexed bodies, as well as the differences between them, are not fully articulated in Mbembe's work. But he
alludes to the connections between sexuality and violence/death, arguing
that "[t]he truth of sex and its deadly attributes reside in the experience of loss of the boundaries separating reality, events, and fantasized
objects" (2003: 15). It is the dissolution of boundaries of the body and
the troubling of sexed reality that are of particular interest here. And the
capacity to define who matters and who does not, whose life is worth
living, as Mbembe, Judith Butler (1993: 16), and Jasbir Puar (2007: 36)
put it in different contexts, is characteristic of sovereignty.[2]

As we will see the in the narratives that follow, the making of
reality along both raced and sexed lines is often violent in colonial and
postcolonial contexts and rests on vacillating notions. The varying perceptions and roles of the state in its many guises remind us that "colonial terror constantly intertwines with colonially generated fantasies of
wilderness and death and fictions to create the effect of the real" (2003:
25). Apartheid was predicated on the attempt to create social categories
of race—and sex—as reality. In the narratives in this chapter we see the
ability to constantly define and redefine what it means to be "real" (real
men or real women) within raced, classed, and located parameters.

The forced liminality described in Chapters 1 and 2 further fits
Mbembe's ideas of necropolitical initiatives. In the case of sex reassignment and medical experimentation, transsexuals are sometimes kept
in physically and legally liminal spaces, as Mbembe describes colonial
slaves, "alive but in a *state of injury*, in a phantom-like world of horrors
and intense cruelty and profanity" (2003: 21, emphasis in original). This
"state of injury" also speaks to the physical sexual liminality faced by
some who have gone through partial and botched sex reassignments, like
"specials" and conscripts addressed in Chapter 2, and the social limin-

ality of being forced out of gendered spaces, like those who physically transition but cannot change their identity documents.

However, as these narratives demonstrate, it is also the prerogative of those who articulate gender liminality to create lives outside of categories of man/woman or to confront death through their decisions to transition between rigidly policed boundaries of sex. This can be a space of agency and the amplification of power, despite contradictions and concerns about liberal notions of consent described in Chapter 2. Mbembe suggests that colonial subjects, such as slaves engaging in mass suicide, may convey feelings about death in this way: "For death is precisely that from and over which I have power. But it also a space where freedom and negation operate" (2003: 39). The resolve of those choosing risky paths that may lead to death needs to be better understood. Mbembe defines this decision-making space through its anticipation of the future, critical for those making gendered transitions.

The phenomenology of pain articulated here implicitly critiques liberalism through a focus on queer futurity (Muñoz 2009), a concept to which I return below. This aspirational vision of freedom and utopia is best represented as a constant transition. In some ways, gender liminality can be seen as individually and politically important in a necropolitical context even if its results may be read by some as ill-advised or even suicidal, as "the human being truly *becomes a subject*—that is, separated from the animal—in the struggle and the work through which he or she confronts death (understood as the violence of negativity)" (Mbembe 2003: 14, emphasis in original). The complications in this context are manifold, but this is to be expected given the parameters of biopower and necropower, under which "the lines between resistance and suicide, sacrifice and redemption, martyrdom and freedom are blurred" (2003: 40). These oppositions—resistance/suicide, sacrifice/redemption, and martyrdom/freedom—are both artfully and painfully navigated by those in gender liminal positions in the narratives discussed here in their confrontations of death in search of their visions of freedom. Further, Mbembe explains each decision as unexceptional, an important corrective to the objectification and exoticization of trans* narratives elsewhere.

This chapter's focus on narratives both extends and draws inspiration from genres of transsexual autobiography in the United States and Europe articulating a different version of Said's traveling theory in its sociopolitically grounded approaches, putting them into conversation with the characteristics of necropolitics described above. Texts within this body of literature have moved transsexual voices from the margins of academic discourse to the center of much of contemporary theory and scholarship. Kate Bornstein's 1994 text has been one of the most influential works in this genre, bridging the divide between autobiography and theory; other oft-cited works include Rees (1996), Spry (1997), Wilchins (1997), McCloskey (1999), Green (2004), Khosla (2006), Valerio (2006), and Kotula (2007).[3] Such autobiographical texts have had significant influence; not only are they referenced by the South African narrators cited in this chapter, one South African doctor I interviewed even credited his life-long career interest in treating transsexuals to reading Jan Morris' *Conundrum* (1974) as a graduate student.[4]

There are similarities among South African narratives addressed below and more commonly-known autobiographies published in the global North. The narratives highlighted in this chapter point to (1) parallels in personal struggles with gender, (2) knowledge of dominant medical discourses (especially with regard to Gender Identity Disorder, parameters of "true transsexuals," and treatment protocols), as well as, (3) transnational relationships that connect narrators to transsexuals outside of southern Africa. However, as William Leap points out in his own work on gay male public sex in South African contexts, the appearance of familiarity can be misleading and necessitates careful attention to local understandings (2002). This same caution is critical to our understandings of gender liminality in South Africa, where familiar terms, concepts, and ways of being often have divergent understandings and manifestations. Morgan and Wieringa's anthology, *Tommy Boys, Lesbian Men and Ancestral Wives: Female Same-Sex Practices in Africa* (2005), for instance, provides important representations of butch masculinities that may seem familiar to readers in the global North but actually retheorize such concepts based on local understandings.[5]

While similarities are notable, the narratives in this chapter also differ substantially from North American and European narratives in that they are distinctively grounded in the global South, addressing concerns including the politics of violence and cultural and spiritual specificities that are markedly South African. For example, they question and attend to gendered identification numbers, the temporal intricacies of public health care, and local organizations and their role in facilitating transitions. South Africans' gender transitions are intimately connected to the sociopolitical history of South Africa itself. This chapter demonstrates ways that medical sex reassignment procedures, access to legal rights, economic freedom, and social discrimination were shaped by apartheid and transitional ideologies and policies.

I. Approaches to Transition

Methodologically, narrators included here were not chosen to be representative of all South Africans who express gender liminality, an obvious impossibility. There is no way to evaluate the relative representivity of individual South African transsexuals, as their communities are fragmented and largely invisible and there is no quantitative research on which to base comparisons. But these narrations are not simply exceptional; they also make significant theoretical claims that often challenge academic conventions.[6] While narrators may not have opportunities for or interests in publishing academic accounts, highlighting their interventions can advance understandings of transition and its necropolitical connections. The previous chapters suggest multiple ways that individuals are constituted through political interpretation. As Joan Scott famously pointed out:

> Experience is at once already an interpretation *and* something that needs to be interpreted. What counts as experience is neither self-evident nor straightforward; it is always contested, and always therefore political. (Scott 1991: 797, emphasis in original)

In short, this chapter is not a simple representation of narrators' experiences. Instead, it draws on narratives of South Africans who consider themselves to have transitioned from their birth gender designation and who focus on their perceptions and interpretations of their own lives, and indeed their articulations of gender, race, and history. Thus narratives that constitute the bulk of this chapter avoid codifying and representing an authentic "trans* experience."

This chapter focuses on narratives from different time periods and circumstances but with the commonality of broadly-defined gendered transitions. For some, these transitions were medically sanctioned, while others defined transition outside of these parameters. Some changed their legal documents while others did not. And the degree to which narrators publicly discuss their transitions (which, when private, most refer to as "stealth") varies, as well. The time periods of narrators' transitions range from 1969 to the present. I selected seven of the narratives I collected on which to focus in this chapter, intentionally choosing narrators who presented a range of generation, means of transition, geographic location, self-defined racial and ethnic categories, economic class position, and chosen gender. I introduce these narrators and describe their self-perceptions of transition briefly here in order of their introduction in this chapter:[7]

- *Vita Edmunds* conceptualized her transition as taking place from 1963–1969. She was born in Cape Town in 1942 and considered herself a male-to-female transsexual, white with English ancestry, and upper class. She went through sex reassignment surgeries, the first of which was in 1969, and she lived fully as a woman since that time and chose not to take hormones.

- Transitioning in the early 1980s in Durban, *Carmella Riekert* was born in 1962. Identifying as coloured and a male-to-female transsexual, she lived in a township in the Western Cape known for high rates of poverty, crime, and domestic abuse. Carmella also fits into the category of "special" discussed in Chapter 2 and faced life-threatening medical complications since her surgeries.

- Although he lived fully as a man, *Herman Maart* considered himself as being in transition since 1978—over thirty years—taking hormones for almost two decades, obtaining a hysterectomy and ovarectomy in 1992, and most recently obtaining a mastectomy in 2009. Despite his interest, sex reassignment surgeries were largely inaccessible and unaffordable to him. Herman grew up in District Six and the Cape Flats and was classified as coloured under apartheid.

- *Nicole Steenkamp* was born around 1950 and lived as a woman in Gauteng since the late 1970s; she described herself as white with mixed English-Afrikaans ancestry. Her transition included electrolysis to remove her facial hair and hormone therapy for the following two decades. She chose not to go through a surgical sex reassignment. When this narrative was collected, she spent most of her time in gay male communities and educating medical students about treating transgendered clients; since this time Nicole has gone into stealth.

- Transitioning currently, *Giles Davids* was born in 1987 and self-identified as a white South African who has lived primarily in the Western Cape. As a teen, he faced disciplinary troubles, overdosed on drugs, ran away from home, encountered abuse, and was eventually sent to drug rehabilitation. But by 2007 when this interview was conducted, his life had shifted drastically; he was in the midst of his physical and medical transition and has since completed most of his planned surgeries.

- *Donna Hendricks* was born in 1962 and grew up Afrikaans and Baptist, as part of the Pentecostal movement. Donna's transition began when she was in her thirties, and she went through sex reassignment surgery in Thailand.

- *William Molobi* was born around 1975 and stayed in Soweto; he strongly identified as Zulu and black. William had been living as both a gay man and a woman simultaneously for a number of years and used both male and female pronouns to describe hirself. William chose not to undertake a medical transition for both religious and financial reasons.

I collected the narratives excerpted here over a period of twelve years, from 1997–2009, as part of the methodological approach described in the introduction to *Sex in Transition*. During my first few weeks in Cape Town, I found that the guest house where I was staying was coincidentally being managed by narrator Vita Edmunds, who graciously agreed to participate in a life historical interview. As I explained it to her at the time and explained to future narrators, as well, my approach was to ask her to share a narrative of her life, focusing on the events and perspectives that she found to be the most important. And narrators would always ask me questions, too; sometimes these were personal, but more often they were about gender liminality in the United States and what I was learning through my research in South Africa.

The narrations themselves ranged from thirty minutes to three hours and often focused on discussions of narrator's own bodies. For instance, Carmella Riekert's comparisons between surgeries done in South

Africa and Singapore speak to her self-criticism and quest for the body she has been seeking, as well as demonstrating a self-taught knowledge of medical treatment:

> I would really like one day to go to Singapore. Just so that they can have a look at me, my vagina, and even my breasts. Feel that! [She is referring to her breast and motions for me to feel it, which I did]. It's very hard. Alright it's silicon, it's understandable. And you've got to massage it every day. Not massage softly, but press it in! And I think after fifteen years it should be at least hanging on my stomach. You know like a big woman, you know, it's got to show that you are matured. But wherever I go I've got these virgin tits, you know what I mean? That's what I can't understand! . . . I would like mine to just drop a little. It must drop. . . . Naturally, the people must just see [I am] now a matured woman, not [with my tits] sitting there looking straight up. (Riekert 2000)

Carmella's request for me to feel her breast was unexpected, but it was not inappropriate or unusual in the context of her own objective evaluation of her own body. Explicit conversations like those in Carmella's narrative embody the intimacy of this research process. This was a comfortable part of our interactions for me, and my own background on the subjects of medical transitions and changing bodies facilitated easy and open conversations.

Each narration included unforeseen information, as well, including subjects as varied as narrators' intersexuality, suicidal pasts, and sex work. Narrators also often shared remarkable examples of collusions among medicine, law, media, political organizations, and family. One of the most memorable of these instances was Herman Maart's discussion of the options available to him in his transition when he was offered the chance to not only sell his story but to sell it in exchange for his new body. He recounts this opportunity and the decision he had to make in the 1980s when he was part of a political organization:

> So a lady from *Huisgenoot* came [to a meeting]. Then she must have gone back to *Huisgenoot* and *You* magazine and said something there because, next thing, I was told that, you know, they came up with an offer they would pay for the operation

if I allowed them to do before and after photographs and they wanted to do it in a sort of like a serial form. I couldn't do it. There was no way I was going to do that and get away with it. My family would be compromised. I mean, if it was just me, I probably would have gone for it, but, you know, the *Huisgenoot* and the *You*—I don't think there's a household in this country not reading one of those two magazines. The chances are that somebody who knows me or my family would see that. I often wonder if they were to come to me with the same offer now, what I would do. . . . I don't think I would even do it now because then I'd have to come out of stealth. (Maart 2009)[8]

For Herman, this is a decision that he has never forgotten. He doesn't regret turning down this chance because of the high personal costs it would have entailed, but trading his story to *Huisgenoot* was his opportunity to go through a full medical transition at the time. Herman has since been able to obtain some of the surgical interventions that he wanted, but this is clearly a decision that could have changed his life, both physically and in terms of his relationship with his family. I return to the unsettled realities and expectations of the ever-distant future Herman raises below and in Chapter 4. Following a traditional interview model, this topic would likely never have been raised, but Herman's own life story account allowed its emergence.

Herman also challenges medical and legal categories through his decisions. As Maynes et al. (2008) point out, in much of the social sciences, frameworks that rely on social categories reduce human agency to social position:

Social actors are treated as if they had little or no individual history, no feelings or ambivalences, no self-knowledge—in short, no individuality. Personal narratives analyses, in contrast, offer insights from the point of view of narrators whose stories emerge from their lived experiences over time and in particular social, cultural, and historical settings. (16)

While some narrators in this chapter share commonalities with transsexuals in other parts of the world, their life stories are also specifically related to the histories of colonialism and apartheid in South Africa, as well as the discourses and struggles described in Chapters 1 and 2. But while the circumstances facing the narrators presented here differ significantly from each other and from most published accounts in the global North, the importance of transitioning, relationships, and social discrimination figure significantly in all of them.

Life historical methods, while less favored in contemporary work in Queer Studies in the United States than in African Studies and with varying usage and reception across social scientific and humanities disciplines, have a strong base and value in contemporary work on sexuality and gender liminality in South Africa. Morgan and Wieringa's anthology *Tommy Boys, Lesbian Men and Ancestral Wives* (2005), for instance, grew from their African Women's Life Story Project, which trained women activists from different countries within the region to collect materials on same-sex sexuality in their own communities. Their intention was that "this project would stimulate new ethnographies and theoretical insights on sexuality and secrecy from African countries" (Morgan and Wieringa 2005: 11). Hoad, Martin, and Reid (2005), similarly approach the importance of narratives to this regional context intentionally:

> We provide this mix of analysis, testimonial, and archival material in the interest of encouraging future scholarship, as a way of acknowledging the multiplicity of possible stories that can and should be told about this time, and as a gesture to the deeply felt and ethically charged atmosphere in which these events occurred. We want these various voices, positions, genres, and passions to compete for the reader's attention. (Hoad 2005: 22)

For Morgan and Wieringa, as well as Hoad and his collaborators, genre is not incidental but a deliberate choice made by authors, editors, researchers, scholars, and/or activists. The variety and content of writing on sexuality in this region relies on and stresses the importance of multiple materials. Estian Smit (2006), writing an important historical analysis of the medicalization of gender liminality partly focused on South Africa, also intersperses life histories with more academic writing (e.g., Smit 2006: 267, 284).[9] Smit suggests:

> My historical knowledge of transgender and transsexual groups in South African communities is limited. However, there are currently individuals engaged in writing up their own life

stories and collecting those of others, and hopefully a South African trans history, including details about the first local cases of medical transition, will eventually emerge from collective efforts. (Smit 2006: 283)

Since this writing, Smit's hope has been realized in the collection of life histories that comprise *Trans: Transgender Life Histories from South Africa* (Morgan, Marais, and Wellbeloved 2009). And a few South African autobiographical texts have begun to emerge authored by those who fall outside of gender expectations (e.g., Nkabinde 2008 and Kuipers n.d.). Taken together, this work constitutes regionally-based arguments for narratives as part of contemporary activist and academic work on gender and sexually liminal southern Africa. This impetus is grounded in political commitments to people's stories and voices in the face of marginalization and lack of written records to bring attention to broader ways of constituting knowledge that do not rely on academia or the existence of traditional theory to define the parameters of gender and sex in South Africa.

Relying on narratives not as scientific and factual histories but as personalized and culturally significant texts is methodologically critical and connects to discussions of performativity. In his analysis of Nazi concentration camp survivors' oral histories, the influential Italian oral historian Alessandro Portelli put it this way:

> One of the differences between oral and written sources is that the latter are documents while the former are always acts. Oral sources are not to be thought of in terms of nouns and objects, but in terms of verbs and processes; not the memory and the tale but the remembering and the telling. Oral sources are never anonymous and impersonal, as written documents may often be. The tale and the memory may include materials shared with others, but the rememberer and the teller are always individual persons who take on the task of remembering and the responsibility of telling. (Portelli 2003: 14)

All oral sources, like these life stories, need to be evaluated for their contributions. And this is particularly important in research focused on marginalized and lesser known topics and communities (e.g., Sangtin Writers and Nagar 2006). In the analyses that are the focus of this chapter, there is limited scientific knowledge (demographics, statistics, and documentation) against which gender liminal narratives can be evaluated. Instead, this work, like many cross-disciplinary interventions, approaches life stories as challenging personal resources (Geiger 1986), providing a specific kind of information.

The challenges posed by narrators' interpretations of events that differed from my own were impossible to anticipate, but they pushed me to be open to categorically new ways of thinking and viewing the world. Temporality and chronology were methodologically and substantively undermined in these narratives as notions of simple forward progress, and the medical assumption that narrators progress over time from one gender to another prove inaccurate. Narratives took nonlinear forms and narrators came in and out of medical expectations of gender, often over decades. Many scholars have pointed to the specificity of notions of time; the work of Johannes Fabian (1983) was an early influence on my own conceptions of how temporality needs to be interrogated. Not only are chronologies culturally-specific, time creates boundaries between self/other that replicate colonial distinctions of otherness and Northern superiority (and Southern intentions and desires to progress toward this superiority).

More recent work like that of Elizabeth Freeman (2010) and Judith Halberstam (2005) queer notions of temporality in relevant ways. Halberstam suggests that queer temporality, especially transgender visibility,

> [d]isrupts the normative narratives of time that form the base of nearly every definition of the human in almost all of our modes of understanding, from the professions of psychoanalysis and medicine, to socioeconomic and demographic studies on which every sort of policy is based, to our understandings of the affective and the aesthetic. (2005: 152)

In this sense, queer temporality unsettles both disciplinary and methodological conventions. Freeman further challenges notions of temporality, focusing on possibilities for queer reconceptualizations of time that highlight gaps in chronologies and elaborating the importance of unbinding time and unbinding history from conceptual restraints.[10]

Allowing space for the disruption of multiple intersecting categories ranging from gender to time is methodologically challenging but conceptually essential. The narratives contained here test linear temporality through narrators' shifts among genders and corporeal expressions. Their extended transitions may not be contained within a medical model but instead push in fits and starts over decades, eschewing normative temporal narrative conventions and conceptions of transition. Transition can be seen as a form of spatial traveling. Further, savvy patients anticipate their doctors' expectations around gender and tell their stories in ways that fit medical truths, progressive notions of time, and parameters of gender. Narrators' own versions of these concepts and ideas, usually assumed to be easily defined and static, extend Halberstam and Freeman's calls for attention to queer time and space through their own reworking of chronology and linearity. Chronology, the science of measuring time in particular and regularized intervals, proves extraneous for South African narrators, focused on points of transition and on the future.

This chapter examines how transitions have been structured by access to the medical care and legal rights described in the preceding chapters, how South Africans have defined and redefined terms (including transsexual, transvestite, and transgender), and the intimacy of decisions about what constitute personal transitions within South Africa's political transition. Specifically, I extend themes articulated in the Introduction's examination of Simone's story here in connection to other narrators' descriptions of their own transitions as located in a necropolitical context. Eschewing etic categorization of narrators as "transsexual" or not based on medical and legal parameters, each narrator describes hir own self-defined transition from the gender assigned at birth to hir current expression. This chapter is structured around themes relevant to Mbembe's necropolitics that emerge as distinctly South African ways of understanding gender liminality. These themes include visions of freedom and somatic ideals, states of liminality and injury, changing and challenging imposed definitions, boundary policing, confrontations with death, and stealth in relation to the parameters of reality as woven together in postcolonial and necropolitical contexts. Taken together, these narratives allow us new understandings of gender liminality grounded in narrators own words and perspectives.

II. Envisioning Freedom

The focus of this chapter is on markedly South African narratives and those that challenge simple ideas of "transition." A logical starting point for this analysis thus rests in the decisions that lead to narrators' transitions and their ramifications. Narrators themselves often linked their decisions about whether or not to transition to time periods in South Africa's history and to the projected outcomes of their transitions. For all of these narrators, what Mbembe terms a "vision of the freedom not yet come" (2003: 39)—a future-oriented view of the freedoms they seek—guides their decision making.[11]

Oppression of those who identified as "gay" under apartheid influenced some narrators' decisions to transition from their assigned gender. Weighing the benefits and drawbacks of transitioning and living a new and different life in a self-defined gender was part of what some narrators discussed as a choice between identifying as gay or going through a medical sex reassignment as a transsexual. For instance, Carmella addressed the violence against gay men that characterized the time period in which she transitioned.

> I lived in Durban. And I was having an affair with a guy, he's dead today. He actually wanted me to be a woman. I didn't want to be a woman. And I agreed upon it. I didn't have the money for the operation, so I wrote a letter to the government. That time P. W. Botha was our President—"the crocodile?"[12] I wrote him a letter and he gave me a subsidy. [A public hospital] sent money to Durban. By the time the letter came to Durban my boyfriend was dead, he had passed away. And being a gay, a man, it's not very nice. You drink, you sleep around with any man that comes your way, you're so scared you're going get licked out [beat up]. Okay? And that's not in my line. (Riekert 2000)

In this narrative, Carmella described the violence that faced gay men in the time period in which she transitioned, as well as the coercive influence of her boyfriend in her decision-making process. She also alluded to the role of Prime Minister/President P. W. Botha in funding and legitimizing her sex reassignment surgery, a point to which I will return below. And, most relevant here, Carmella believed that gay men in the 1980s were faced with significant stress and threats of physical violence, which influenced her decision to go through sex reassignment surgery and live as a woman.

Alternately, Nicole Steenkamp's views of sex reassignment and homosexuality pushed her in a different direction. In describing factors influencing her decision to transition, she asserted:

I can tell you, there will not be so many sex changes in the future because people can live their lives, end of the story. They can dress up when they feel like it. They don't have to, [but] they can. . . . They don't have to become women to be happy. They can live an easy life as a gay person. They know they can live in a dress or they can work feminine, if they have the right job, and people accept them. . . . And then at night he can wear a dress. So they will grow up knowing they can live a gay life. But if you don't know what life you can live, you will look for a way out. And the only way out for a lot of us, like I say, years ago was this way. [Living as a woman] makes your life easier. The only way out was become a woman or what I did. But I know very few like me, they live and work as women, very few. They go for the whole tootie. . . . If I had the guts I would have, but knowing so many of them and seeing what they go through, I thought no. I like my life. I don't want to come out sideways. (Steenkamp 2000)

Much of the political shift Nicole identified related to the acceptance of gay people in South Africa is directly linked to the decriminalization of homosexuality and cross-dressing and the advent of the transition period. Elsewhere in her narrative Nicole spoke of difficulties of entering clandestine gay clubs under apartheid. She described the combined social and political forms of discrimination that targeted gender liminality and suggested transitioning as a way to avoid this. However, Nicole also undermined medical notions of transsexuals' transitions as their only option, as she didn't want to come out "sideways" postsurgery and instead put aside medical models or guidance in her transition, which included facial electrolysis and hormones.

Going through sex reassignment was not a panacea under apartheid. The psychological strength needed to endure the process itself was just one intense part of the procedure. Fears of the transition itself prevented many from going through surgery. Nicole alluded to this above saying that she didn't have the "guts" to go through "the whole tootie" of medical reassignment—usually penectomy and orchiectomy, followed by vaginoplasty. By contrast, Vita Edmunds, the oldest transsexual I interviewed, went through her first surgery in 1969. It is not surprising, given the strict gender restrictions that faced transsexuals and legal restrictions on cross-dressing, described in Chapter 1, well-known under apartheid, that her fear of arrest was palpable. That threat, combined with the life-altering significance of the decision and the pressure to "pass" post-operatively, meant that:

> [Going through the transition] took a tremendous amount
> of courage! Not only the surgical, of course the surgical is a
> great step, but it's living, knowing that from tomorrow this
> is your life. There is no turning back. You know you have
> to make a go of it, come [hell] or high water, you have to
> make a go of it. And you have to be successful, and that's
> the frightening thing 'cause you don't know. You don't know.
> That period you keep very quiet, and you dress and walk
> in the streets, and wear sunglasses. You're very, very sort-of
> aware of the situation. And then you realize that, gosh, in six
> months, seven months time, this is reality. And I think that's
> more frightening than the actual surgery. [I was] . . . afraid,
> afraid of the transformation. You know? (Edmunds 1997)

The transition and transformation period itself was tenuous and was facilitated by doctors' documentation, usually in the form of letters that transsexuals carried with them at all times. Most doctors' protocols relied (and often still rely) on transsexuals undergoing a requisite time period where they lived in their "new" genders. This period lasts from a few months to even years, depending on doctors' use of U.S. surgeon Harry Benjamin's Standards of Care.[13] In contexts like apartheid where one could be arrested for cross-dressing, this requirement increased the danger facing transsexuals. Concerns like those that Vita expressed about this period, as well as the permanence of the decision to transition, were echoed by many narrators.

Some in gender liminal positions also expressed fears about sexual function after their transitions as an important factor in their decisions. Genital surgery sparks many concerns, and Nicole spoke to this emotively:

> You see, what's the use of lying to yourself and lying to people
> knowing that you're not happy? . . . I mean some of them
> [transsexuals] are so beautiful, outside they look like film
> stars. They are so beautiful. But inside and down there, they
> can't even have sex. What's the use of having a fanny [vagina]
> if you can't have sex, you know what I mean? If you really
> go through all that, that's what you want, the main thing.
> (Steenkamp 2000)

The ability to orgasm postoperatively poses a concern for many trans-sexuals. And for some, knowledge of the experimentation that faced "spe-cials," conscripts, and others who were left without functioning genitals just exacerbated these concerns. Even ideal circumstances can result in postoperative physical problems. However for others, being accepted in their daily lives in their gender expressions and appearances superseded this anxiety in their decisions. As Vita put it:

> I said to myself, unless I, the person, can get away with it
> 100 percent, I wouldn't have gone through with it because
> it's a great step to take. You know? And you want to be
> accepted. That's the most important thing in life. You want
> to be accepted. And [in] those years it was striving, striving
> for a goal. To be what I felt I had to be. (Edmunds 1997)

The desire for this acceptance, and the ways Vita echoed textbook defi-nitions of gender dysphoria in her feelings—such as literally stating, "I was in the wrong body"—led her to go through medical transition. On the other hand, those like Nicole who expressed gender ambiguity made different decisions that did not potentially sacrifice sexual function, but sometimes meant that they could not "pass" and "get away with it 100%."

Those undertaking female-to-male transitions and seeking phallo-plasties and similar procedures add another complication to this con-sideration through the acknowledged inadequacies of these procedures' medical efficacy and their limited availability. A number of techniques have been attempted, with little success until very recently. One South African physician I interviewed, Dr. Jooste, explained a few of these:

> If they take a piece from the upper leg it looks like a shark has
> gotten hold of it. In the beginning they did the construction
> of the roll on the stomach, where it usually gained fat and
> went gangrene, and that was a major flop. Once Dr. Frank
> used a muscle from the stomach, taking some of the skin from
> the stomach, and we had to get electrolysis done first or else
> you would get a hairy penis, though today it would be easier
> with the laser. We did only one, and I didn't think it was
> successful. The procedure in which you take a piece from the
> arm looks bad—it's extremely mutilating—and I didn't want
> something that was not usable. The majority said that yes,

they were satisfied without the penis. I used to show them photos of the surgeries which were monstrous. I said that I didn't want it if it didn't work; the ones who went for it went without my knowing. This would have been a maximum of five out of at least 50 (probably less). Some would use the labia and created a scrotum, but rarely. (Jooste 2000)

The lack of success in these surgeries has led to a pattern of failed penis construction that both doctors and patients often avoid. In South Africa, the most common procedure does not use tissues from the patient's leg or stomach, but constructs a flap from the patient's arm and leaves a very noticeable scar. As a social worker explained,

I know that they used to take a flap from the thigh or from the stomach, and now the latest thing is to take it from here on the arm. I don't know how successful that is, I mean they're left with a huge scar on their arm. (Baker 1997)

The psychological effect of this procedure came in part from distress about having a large scar on one's forearm. Beginning in the late 1990s, South African television programs publicized this scar as part of sex reassignment surgeries. The attention given to such scars has made it less possible for trans men to conceal their transsexual status postoperatively, as the scars themselves now may identify them as transsexuals.[14]

With the delays in public health care that are an integral part of sex reassignment procedures in South Africa, the difficulties of phalloplasties can be exacerbated. Terrick provided a particularly candid account of his experience:

When they put in the expander they made a small slit near my wrist. They put in a pair of blunt scissors to separate the skin from the muscle and they pushed in the expander. There's a little part under the skin into which fluid is injected. In 1999, however, the government decided to halt all gender reassignment surgery, which meant I had the expander in my arm for a while. A few months later, when they decided to continue with the surgery, my expander had deflated as a result of a small hole and they had to take it out and put in another one. Because I have relatively thin arms, they should either have done it slowly, or perhaps used two expanders. The skin was too thin and broke through, which meant they had to take that expander out, let it heal and then try again. Then they made the urethra but, because of a hospital acquired infection, they had to take the urethra out again. And that's the last surgery I had. (Terrick in Morgan et al. 2009: 207)

Terrick's experience of phalloplasty and the complications that were part of it were physically and psychologically stressful. He expresses mixed feelings about the functionality of his postoperative penis and medical decisions about procedures related to his phalloplasty, over which he did not have control. However, Terrick notes that phalloplasty was essential to his transition; he feels he had the best medical team in South Africa and is "happy up to a point" with the phalloplasty (ibid.).

Taking a broader view, one psychologist I interviewed cautioned, "I haven't actually come across one female-to-male successfully bottom surgery managed. . . . There's that kind of shame attached to it. It's very hidden, it's very shameful." (Ryland 2007).[15] Most narrators expressed fear and caution about phalloplasties and the surgical difficulties associated with them. But as Terrick points out, "I think when you are going for this kind of major surgery, before the doctors even start the process, you first have to really look at what the doctors can do, what they are willing to do, how far they can take you, and what the final results will be" (Terrick in Morgan et al. 2009: 207).[16]

Narrators expressed similar concerns but with more success when obtaining mastectomies. Due in part to the prevalence of breast cancer, chest surgeries are considered much more commonplace than phalloplasties by surgeons, who are more confident about performing these procedures because of their wide use to treat breast cancer. Parallel concerns to those discussed above are expressed by narrators about how often surgeries are performed, and access to experts, particularly plastic surgeons, is often limited. As Giles Davids explained,

I had managed to find out that the surgeon that was going to be operating, doing the top surgery, was a general surgeon as opposed to a plastic surgeon. It was decided that a general surgeon is not the most ideal person to be reconstructing a chest. . . . It was actually a more complicated surgery than just a regular mastectomy. . . . I will go and speak to the professor and find out exactly what she actually does, what method they use. . . . I somehow doubt that a professor of gynecology who specializes in cancer patients is going to have sufficient knowledge in order to do correct gender reassignment surgery, or bottom surgery for a trans man. (Davids 2007)

Giles expressed a common concern among South Africans; even with surgeries that are performed more regularly, access is often limited, especially in the public health care system. The differences in public and private health care are debated by patients and carefully considered.[17] However, hysterectomies were relatively easy for narrators to attain. Overall, narrators consistently discussed their hopes for their ideal bodies and tried to reconcile them with available practices. In these and the other cases recounted here, individuals' visions for their futures and freedom shaped their analyses and decisions.

III. Beyond Liminality and "States of Injury"

For some narrators doctors facilitated change, while others were dissuaded by the medical establishment. The factors influencing these differences in admission to medical programs included class, race, time period, and location (in particular cities, as well as rural/urban areas). Some were able to access private health care or even travel outside of South Africa for sex reassignment, while others were restricted to the raced idiosyncrasies and limitations of public health care. And racial hierarchies were a consistent theme often determining the availability of and access to sex reassignment, at its most extreme resulting in forced sex reassignment surgeries described in Chapter 2. Occasionally this access seemed arbitrary for narrators, and effects of individuals' persistence are notable. However, for most people access followed lines constituting the boundaries of gender, class, and race in particular times and places.

Even in the best case scenarios, apartheid politics and nascent and experimental medical procedures intersected in South African narrators' stories. Contrasting three narrators' experiences of transition will be instructive here, focused on Vita Edmunds, Carmella Riekert, and Nicole Steenkamp and their historical, intersectional, and perceived worthiness. Vita's 1969 surgery was the earliest I documented and, as expressed above, she was extremely enthusiastic about going through the surgery. However, Vita also faced physical and emotional strains as a result of her sex reassignment, as her vagina was not fully functioning until ten years after she began her transition following repeated surgeries. Her procedure was historically early and of great interest to doctors seeking to define the boundaries of sex and its mutability, as described in Chapter 1. She recounted:

> The next morning [after surgery] I was [scared] because it was very new, because, I mean, because it was chaotic. Something I'll never forget. They gave me twenty drips without anesthetic beforehand. So they were plopping needles into each arm and legs and everything. And this was all done in the ward before they took you to surgery. And when I got to surgery, must have been, without exaggeration, it must have been forty, fifty people around. 'Cause you know [the surgical procedure] was new. . . . And they started a new process whereas before they used to amputate [the penis]. . . . Then they discovered that with inverting everything, you have all the feeling, all your central desires, all your orgasms, everything as before. So that this was quite a new process that was done five, maybe six years before I was done. The first batch [was] in the fifties. [And now] I mean down below there's no difference between you and me or anybody, there's nothing, there's no difference. Nothing. Exactly, exactly [the same]. . . . (Edmunds 1997)

Vita took a huge risk in undertaking surgery: the procedure she went through was new, and she was subjected to great scrutiny. But as she stated here, initially she was very pleased with the results in terms of the appearance and function of her body. Histories of South African sex reassignment procedures in specific locations are difficult to trace because accusations of inappropriate funding and medical experimentation explored in Chapter 2 make some medical practitioners who were involved in these processes reluctant to be interviewed. However, Vita's surgery was performed in a teaching hospital and was one of the first in the region, particularly as her penis was inverted and placed in the abdominal cavity to form her new vaginal canal, a technique more common in that context. She continued,

> I went through a lot of trouble, a tremendous amount of
> trouble with . . . [having a] functioning vagina. And then
> eventually, ten years after my original surgery, I found a
> wonderful doctor. . . . There was no follow-up [surgical
> procedure]. . . . One doctor in Pretoria, after the one who
> did me, he decided that he would like a follow-up and they
> contacted me and asked me to come and see them. That was
> once or twice, then he died, he had a heart attack while he
> was in surgery. . . . [I was never required to take hormones.]
> For male-to-female the hormones aren't a great [necessity,
> but] . . . Vice-versa [female-to-male] the transformation's quite
> outstanding. (Edmunds 1997)

Vita made two particularly notable points here; first, she needed to seek
out a second doctor to be able to have a functional vagina (a problem
faced by multiple narrators). Vita's comments indicate the difficulties she
faced, which are not uncommon but can be grave. Second, Vita never
took estrogen or other feminizing hormones. She indicates differences
among South African narrators' views about hormones; in Vita's opinion,
hormones are unnecessary for male-to-female transsexuals.

Carmella's surgery also involved extensive physical complications but
occurred in a different time and place in apartheid history, and her problems have persisted until the present. Carmella offers insights into many
issues that face transsexuals treated publicly in South Africa, particularly
"specials"—those who were offered free but botched surgeries—addressed
at length in Chapter 2. Perhaps the most striking part of Carmella's life
history was her explicit discussion of her physical transition and medical
difficulties. For her, no part of the surgical transformation was without complication; in fact, she has been near death a number of times
because of medical problems resulting from her sex reassignment procedures, recalling Mbembe's necropolitics. Her surgeries left her without a
functioning penis or vagina, and indeed made her dependent on medical
technology for basic life functions for a number of years. At the time of
this narration, Carmella was deciding if she would go through further
risky and painful medical procedures so that she could potentially resume
sexual intercourse twenty years following her initial surgery:

> At first, [the effects of the hormones were] terrible. I developed
> my breasts, it was very painful. I had to wear something very
> loose that it doesn't touch onto my skin. And, it had me very

dizzy and [gave] me fits. . . . So I started smoking buttons.[18] That they brought it down, at least, thank God, I lost all that weight that I was carrying around . . . And then the first operation was done, my breasts. I paid 12 Rands for it.[19] . . . And the second operation was when they took the male intestines out. That was the worst part of the operation, because there was a big hole above my penis. So big. So, I mean you could look inside my stomach, and it was very septic and sore and you know? It was terrible. And . . . after six months they did my vagina. But it wasn't very easy, because the vagina and the anus are close to one another. And that went fine for awhile, and then I developed a fistula. And I carried a [colostomy] bag on me for four years because it just couldn't get healed. I suppose it was through sex that [the fistula was formed] because it was a made vagina with skin grafts. And my penis was too small to make a big vagina. I had a small little toy, and I was circumcised also, so it made it even more worse. . . . And it was very bad, that part of the operation. Oh, God. I'll never forget it. I wished I was a man again. Just that period, I just didn't like that operation. Because they cut me open . . . they had to lift it up and tie it again. (Riekert 2000)

Carmella's narrative personifies the discussion of specials in the previous chapter and recalls Achille Mbembe's discussion of a "state of injury" for necropolitical subjects, defined as "a phantom-like world of horrors and intense cruelty and profanity" (2003: 21). The somatically liminal space she endures involves the formation of a fistula, likely a passage that developed between her vagina and rectum (a rectovaginal fistula), preventing normal bowel movements and allowing the introduction of bacteria into the healing vaginal canal.[20] Obstetric fistulas constitute an important site of activist and public health interventions in the global South; these fistulas often result from obstructed labor during childbirth and lead to death when emergency medical care is unavailable. In this case, not only are fistulas like this severe complications of sex reassignment, they also make postoperative sexual intercourse dangerous. Carmella explains:

The South African sex changes, the more they have sex, the more they get fistulas. You see like your vagina and your anus, they are very close. And that skin is very tender. Now that's why they made the mold so much bigger because your vagina is so small that it just gives you elasticity. But now you get the men that got a bigger penis and they force it in and they force it in. You, as the woman, you're laying on the bed, you're enjoying all this rubbish that's getting onto your body, and in the end, you don't want to suffer the consequences. . . . When a man pushed too deep in you, and then he tears your skin inside. And your poo comes from the back, and then it comes from the front and the back, both because it's now torn. And if you don't go and have it seen to, that hole can get bigger inside you. And then you can consider yourself front and back, you know what I mean? What comes from the back must come to the front. . . .

They tell you not to have sex. I didn't have sex for a very long time. It didn't worry me actually. And when they took the bag off me, they didn't open my vagina, because they were scared I might develop a fistula again. . . . Then they told me I must go home and I must have sex again. Then I thought to myself, "Why should I do it? They don't want to open me, they want a man to penetrate in me to open me. And it's gonna be now like being a virgin again. It's going be so sore, maybe this guy will tear me right through and then, back to square one." You know what I mean? So I didn't go back to the hospital. They phoned me, they sent me their tests, but I won't go. But I will go, because I know I have to have my vagina opened. . . . [They do it] surgically and [with] a mold. I asked them how do they make my vagina, and they told me they use the drill. Ooh God! I couldn't believe it. Thank God I was under anesthetic. Sssh, imagine if I wasn't. Oh my word! . . .

But otherwise being a woman is beautiful for me. . . . I was the first non-white that [my doctor] worked on. And it was very beautiful for me. Just until the fistula developed. Then the complications started. Up till this day, it's now three years now I haven't had my vagina opened again. I still got an opening passage, but I can't sleep with a man. A man can't penetrate in me 'cause I'm closed. So I have to go back and have it opened and they'll give [me] a mold. A mold looks like a penis, the size of your vagina. . . . Now you got to

push that thing in you, and it stretches your vagina. You see?
Gives your vagina elasticity. And I'm telling you, that pain,
oh my God, it's like an iron. It's like an iron going up you.
(Riekert 2000)

While the vaginoplasty Carmella described is healing, most doctors
require that their patients wear a plastic mold or dilator postoperatively
to maintain the shape and depth of the newly constructed vaginal canal.
In her case, doctors also advised that intercourse and insertion of a
penis would aid in maintaining and stretching her new vagina. But the
fistula forced Carmella's body to heal in a way that couldn't maintain her
vagina's size and depth, and she became unable to have intercourse with
a man and stated that she felt like a virgin. The intensity of Carmella's
physical transition illustrates the suffering and fear she has confronted
with the medical complications following her sex reassignment. She mentioned her pride as the first "non-white" to receive surgery but otherwise
expressed disappointment. Carmella demonstrates the forced liminality
of necropolitical regimes like apartheid; her physical problems are not
uniquely South African, but the complex of circumstances that created
them for her, as a "special" dealing with this manifestation of exploitative
public healthcare, are critical.

I was able to interview Carmella again in 2007, seven years after
our initial meeting. Her surgery was performed hundreds of miles from
her home, so during the intervening years she had seen various local
doctors. She described a new set of problems she faced:

[My] doctor, he also does sex changes. I just went to him after
all my operations and all the stresses and all this rubbish that
was going on. I went to him for a second opinion, you know,
just to see what does he think of it. And he thinks that I'm
beautiful and on my [vaginal] lips at the bottom it's lively, it's
not dead, it's not dead. But when my water breaks [urination],
it's not how it used to be when I'm a man. It's now very, very
little. Sometimes, it's just, not even, it's just a drop. . . . You
see, they don't actually cut your penis off, they tuck it in
you. But they can't reverse the operation. That's what I can't
understand. If your penis is still in you, why can't they bring
it out again? . . . It doesn't grow in. Like they can't cut off
every testicle in your body. They've got to leave some parts

> for the woman parts now, you see? And, I've only got feelings
> outside, but not inside my vagina. But it's very interesting.
> Very, very interesting. It's a lovely operation, I promise you.
> Afterwards, I'll do it again. . . . (Riekert 2007)

Inconsistent urination and confusion about the operation itself are a few
of the problems Carmella shared with me. She often discussed mixed
happiness and regret about the decision that she made.

Many of Carmella's feelings about her transition seemed to hinge
on her relationships with the doctors themselves, who formed a focus
for Carmella, as she is otherwise extremely isolated in the community
where she lives. She explained details of her interactions with her doctors, relevant here to understanding not only the details of Carmella's
narrative but also for illuminating the authoritative and even sexualized
relationships that underlie the necropolitical implementation of South
African gendered medicine. Such commentaries provide an important
intervention into much published scholarship on sex reassignment by
adding to the growing documentation of the role of transsexuals in their
own medical treatment and in shaping medical protocols and necropolitics in relation to the state.

Specifically, during both of our interviews, Carmella described
South African doctors' familiarity and paternalistic closeness with their
transsexual patients in great detail. For her, invitations to doctors' homes
and dancing with them at parties organized for transsexuals were affirmations of her femininity and her success as a woman. She joked with
her doctors in jabs with multiple meanings, too:

> I firmly and strongly believe that [my doctor] is so satisfied with
> me, because he has invited me to his home many a times, and
> I haven't gone. And another [doctor] . . . he's also invited me
> to his home. But I haven't gone. Because I'm very open, you
> see, I don't hold nothing back. If I felt like asking something,
> I will ask. If I'm in a bad mood, a very, very bad mood, then
> I come to the hospital, and I'm very angry now, then I ask
> the [doctor], "Where the hell is my cock?" <laughing> That
> was the most cleanest part of my body that they took away,
> because I never ever used it! <laughter>
>
> I only went to the party once that the hospital gave [for
> transsexuals]. . . . I bought a mini-skirt and a nice top and

my hair was long. Just like any other woman would go out, you know, and but now the others was dressed like Cinderella at the ball. . . . So the [doctor] came to ask me for a dance first. You know what I mean? And I'm feeling now to myself, "God I'm black. And he comes to me first?" And I danced with him three times! (Riekert 2000)

Carmella felt affirmed by her interactions with her doctor at "the ball," whom she implicitly portrays as the prince in her Cinderella tale. Also, Carmella's racial comparison of herself to the doctors' other patients (and feminine beauty standards more broadly) mirrors her views of racial hierarchies of gender in which those who are white are seen as the most successful women and transsexuals. Carmella's description of this party and dance fits the pattern of paternalism, sexualization, and objectification of patients expressed by doctors in interviews. During my interviews with physicians, for example, one had pornographic photographs of his former patients posted in his office in suggestive poses of which he was very proud, showing them off to visitors. When I interviewed Carmella seven years later, she again brought up her relationship with her doctor, talking about another recent party at the doctor's home and even showing me snapshots of him and his family that he had given to her.

Following a nonmedical path in her gender liminality, Nicole's transition eschewed medical convention and offers a useful point of comparison to those of Vita and Carmella in the ways that her narrative moves beyond simple liminality and "states of injury" in intentional ways. Nicole lived as a woman in private and public arenas, disrupting rigid categories and making decisions that do not follow medical or legal dictates. Relationships were perhaps the most tenuous part of her transition, as Nicole faced many rejections because of her liminality. She risked danger when revealing her body to straight male partners who might otherwise consider her female before seeing her penis and confronted condemnation for her femininity with gay male partners. Because of her choices, Nicole considered herself necessarily living alone, stating, "I can live without being loved by someone." She complicated the boundaries between gay and transsexual identifications, which are not as clear-cut as medical practitioners claim and are carefully linked to the social, political, and economic factors Nicole herself described.

Nicole was reflective about her position and her rationales for her choices. She was concerned about the physical risks of sex reassignment procedures, as well as the perceived high rates of suicide and prostitution found among postoperative South African transsexuals. But she also acknowledged the complicated ways conditions of discrimination shaped her decisions about how to embody womanhood and live in the world. Though her reasons for transitioning were complex, the incentive for the first alteration of her body, removal of her beard, came in part from an offhand comment from a child, and the physical abuse and danger she faced as a gay man were additional factors in her decision to transition. Nicole worked outside of a normative narrative that rendered transition without surgery inconceivable for many people.

> They had ads all over the show for hair removal. And . . . we were looking after someone's child at the time, me and my boyfriend. . . . And [this child] said to my boyfriend, "You know she would be a beautiful woman, it's just a pity she's got a beard." I overheard this and it hurt me so. And then I looked in the paper, I thought I have seen this ad and I'm gonna ask this woman [an electrologist] if she can do something about this beard. You know? So I went to her, I told her my story, and, praise the Lord, she was gay-friendly. And she said, "Well, I can see why you want to have it done, this is the story. It will cost so much, more or less, this is what you have to do, this is how long it's going to take, and this is what it's gonna be like. Painful, this and that." And I was desperate.
>
> When you're desperate, you go to extremes, so I was willing to do it. I worked overtime like nobody's business, because it cost a lot of money, but it was worth every cent. After three years, I said, "Well fine. Now I don't have to wear pancake make-up during the day. I don't have to worry about taking my hair away from my face. There's no more shadow at twelve o'clock at night. I don't have to get up running to the loo [bathroom] to shave. I don't have to do that anymore." . . .
>
> Then I decided, well I've gotta do something to live the way I want to. So I started letting my hair grow, I had my beard removed, taking hormones, and that was it. By doing that, I became more female and living a better life because people let me alone. I was just another woman. They didn't look at me and say, "Now, there's no boobs but it looks femme." I

didn't get blue eyes anymore.[21] You know what I mean? And my whole life changed because I was much more at ease. I could concentrate on my work, on my studies, because I wasn't an outcast.

Then I decided to go for a sex change, but when I spoke to the surgeon he said, "Look, you know what we will do to you. We will mutilate the body and stuff up the mind, basically. You've got to be a strong person, and the rate is 90% suicide or they become gay or prostitutes." So when I went [for a sex change and the doctor] told me this, I decided what's the use of going through all that and having all that drama, on top of what I'm going through? . . .

A lot of drag queens were beaten. I know, I've been there. The minute they see there's something not kosher here they just go for you and that's it. You go home with a blue eye. A lot of gay bashing, I mean they still do it here and there, but years ago it was very bad. And because people couldn't come out about being gay, they kept quiet. So they were beaten, but they couldn't report it because [the police would ask,] "Why did they beat you? What were you doing at Emmerentia Dam at 1:00 in the morning?" . . . You know, you just couldn't get away with that. No, there was a lot of gay bashing.[22] . . .

Fortunately I work with a lot of gay doctors. For my hormones I could get from them, and then when I came to Pretoria, I said to the people I knew at the time, "Listen, I need a doctor, preferably gay." And they said, "Oh yah, so and so, here's his address." And the next day I went to him and I said, "Look, I'm now here, and this is who and what I am, I need hormones, my usual prescription." And he said, "Fine. Just come and see me every six months." He examines me and I'm still okay, and that's it. I'm happy. (Steenkamp 1997)

In the narrative shared here, we see the varied options available to Nicole and the ways she transitioned within those options and implicitly critiqued a narrative of "true transsexualism." Whereas Vita and Carmella were encouraged to go through sex reassignment by their doctors, Nicole was dissuaded. In these three narratives, medical repression is juxtaposed with the agency and navigation of liminality.

IV. Changing Definitions and "Fantasized Objects"

Narrators directly confront descriptive and categorical terminology and definitions through their self-advocacy and education of those around them. These definitions and redefinitions challenge apartheid and transitional attempts to codify gender categories. Mbembe suggests that under necropolitics, "The truth of sex and its deadly attributes reside in the experience of loss of the boundaries separating reality, events, and *fantasized objects*" (2003: 15, emphasis added). In this context, we might think of the unattainable definitions of "true transsexuals" put forward by doctors as medicine's "fantasized objects" without a solid basis and undermined in South Africans' narratives, while a fantasized object also serves as a counterhegemonic norm itself, a fetishized or objectified norm sought by liberal and charitable doctors.

Transition itself is more complicated than is commonly believed, as it is often not an obvious and temporally chronological movement from one gender to another and it is increasingly common to transition in and out of genders and sexualities. Upholding falsehoods of gender rigidity, most medical and legal literature ignores the specificity and importance of transsexuals' own theoretical interventions. As demonstrated in Chapters 1 and 2, doctors' searches for "true transsexuals" (in their terminology) who fit specific definitions of Gender Identity Disorder rely on chronological narratives and on aspirations for hormonal and surgical procedures that may not be affordable, uniformly desirable, or medically successful. Nor do legal definitions of men and women and resulting legal documents such as birth certificates and passbooks give us simple truth about binary gender; the subjective means through which such documents are formed and changed are a clear indication of the instability of all gendered "reality."

Many narrators speak critically of the expectation of "true transsexual" narratives that they have faced with doctors who rely on a linear narrative of discovery within a rigid medical model of gender dysphoria. Giles, interviewed in 2007, provided a poignant account of the effects of offering a narrative of Gender Identity Disorder that varied from doctors' expectations of foci and chronology.

> So I went to go and speak to [the doctor]. One of the first things he wanted me to tell him was, he wanted me to give him a life history in five, ten minutes. So my logic was that,

because I had quite a hectic psychiatric past, of which he had my folder, that I would just give him a brief history. And then once I'd done that, then I could go in depth into all the gender stuff. Because I thought one of my main reasons for being there is because of the gender. I had been scared that my psychiatric past would disqualify me from being able to get gender reassignment through the hospital. But both [of my other doctors] had said that there's absolutely no way my past is going to influence what their decision will be. He said, "Anyone in their right mind will be able to see that you were just a troubled teenager, and that your past was due to the conclusion that you've now come to." So I gave this guy, the psychiatrist, his brief history, only mentioning the gender once or twice.

After that, he said something that I was not a "true transsexual," due to the fact that if I was, I would have spent the whole time talking about the gender, as opposed to actually giving him a life history. "But you asked me for a life history." Then he wanted to know, if I were to be in a relationship, would I be in a relationship with a female or a male. So I said with a male. I was then told that that again proved that I wasn't a transsexual, because in order to transition from female-to-male, I need to be sexually attracted to females. So then I said to him, "No, gender identity, sexual orientation are not the same thing. They're different." The more he told me that, "No, they're exactly the same thing, and they're intertwined," the more I tried to tell him that they weren't.

Then it went as far as him saying that he put me on the waiting list, and I'd be number 26 on the waiting list. They do one surgery per year, which means I'd be eligible for surgery when I was roughly somewhere between the ages of 46 and 48. He said to me he's going to put me on the waiting list, but no surgeon in their right mind is going to operate on someone with such a strong psychiatric past, because they prefer to take patients into their transgender program that have got clean psychiatric histories, and not ones that have got complicated ones. . . . Then he went and told me that he'd refer me to his colleague, at the hospital, but he feels that his colleagues are going to have the same

> response that he has. So then my logic was, why make me pay to fly to [another city] to be evaluated only to have the same answer? Which in his mind proved to him that I wasn't serious enough about it, because I was unwilling to pay to go to [another city]. So I said to him, "I'm coming to you guys because I don't have money to go private. If I had money to fly to [this city], then I'd have money to go private." I think that's where I started to lose my temper, and he kind of ended the appointment. (Davids 2007)

Giles' narrative clearly demonstrates his agency in defining his own narrative as a trans man as well as his role in educating his own doctors. Not only did he know what medically constitutes a "true transsexual," but he confronted his doctor's heterosexism and explained his differentiation between sexual orientation and gender identity. He anticipated retribution, and his confrontation of his doctor proved a point of contention that counted against Giles in this subjective process, especially when attempting to obtain highly desirable free sex reassignment surgeries in today's public health system in South Africa, which has particularly high stakes at this hospital where presently only one surgery is purportedly performed per year. Giles also provided important commentary on life histories themselves, conceptions of chronology and time, and expectations in medical settings such as this one. Despite the rejection he described here, Giles was able to network with a supportive local organization and his own psychologist to find a doctor who could support him and provide him with the surgery he was seeking without succumbing to the narrative expectations he confronted.

Living in the same neighborhood at this time and also struggling with a psychiatric history, we can contrast Giles' medical experience with that of Herman Maart, another female-to-male transsexual who has been largely unable to get similar surgeries. With the exception of the treatment of "specials" in the 1990s, anecdotal evidence suggests that it has been more difficult for coloured and black transsexuals to obtain surgery in the public system. In 1992, Herman had a hysterectomy and ovarectomy done "semi-privately" with a gynecologist at a state hospital which cost him 4,000 Rand, and the doctor "allowed me to pay his fees bit by bit." Herman waited to have a mastectomy done at a public hospital for years and finally was able to have this surgery in 2009. He told me he could never afford phalloplasty but was also saving for a surgical attachment of a dual prosthesis he planned to buy online from Australia.[23] Based on his experiences, he spoke to the current situation for sex reassignment in South Africa and to important priorities:

> I think, for most trans people, [the most pressing issues are] the accessibility to surgical procedures. It's out of the reach of most of us. [One of the only hospitals performing surgeries in South Africa] has got a waiting list of 20 and they're doing one or two a year. So, I mean, if I still have to go onto that waiting list, I'll be 70 by the time they get to me. So I think that is the one big thing. Not healthcare, healthcare is quite fine. It's the surgery and also the fact that the medical aid doesn't pay for it. It's regarded as cosmetic and so they don't. And yet you can argue that it's not cosmetic, that it's crucial to your wellbeing. But as of now they don't consider it as such. (Maart 2007)

Again and again, access to medical transitions proves inconsistent and mediated through the problematic interstices of race, class, and location. In more recent times during the political transition to democracy, doctors' understandings of sex reassignments have made medical transitions more widely known, though paradoxically even less commonly available.

However, even when doctors and patients shared understandings of "transsexual" as a category, access to hormonal and especially surgical assistance in transitioning was much more challenging. Donna's experience was characteristic of the kinds of challenges and dead ends that faced many South Africans under apartheid and during the transitional period. She described this in detail:

> When I first started looking at the whole transition thing and possibility of surgery, I started doing some investigation to find out where I could get it done in South Africa and how much it would cost me. And the first place that I found out about was [a particular hospital] and I managed to get a number of somebody there that I could contact and I contacted them and asked them, "Okay, now, what is the procedure and how do I go about it?" And they just told me straight, they said, "We no longer have the program running any more. The only people who are on the program still are those who were already in

the program before we stopped it." And the reason why they stopped it is that because the government decided that it isn't primary healthcare and therefore they were no longer prepared to finance the treatment. . . . It was somewhere in 1995.

And so I asked them, "Can you refer me to anybody else in private practice?" They referred me to a doctor who used to be part of the program and he had left and he was now private. I contacted him and he said to me, "Well, it's two years since [I] last did any gender surgery," and, as a result of it, he's not willing to do any right now because he doesn't feel that he's up to date with the latest procedures. So, with that, I found out that there was nobody in [the city where I was living] doing it. I then contacted [another location], where I was told that they also had a program there [but] . . . they had discontinued it as well because they no longer were receiving funding for it, either. Subsequent to that, I discovered that there were girls who were still getting onto the program and I was very disappointed that [the doctor] had told me categorically that there was no way they were ever going to do it again, and yet I heard of people that were going onto it. (Hendricks 2007)

This kind of years-long search for treatment and surgery is common, as others indicate in their narratives. The rationales they are given for their denial by medical practitioners are often confusing and contradictory. Other narrators were able to get surgery during this time period; it was not uniformly limited. Timing, fit with "true transsexual" criteria, and racial views of men and women expressed by doctors all form part of rationales as to why some people were denied treatment, despite doctors' claims of objectivity and rationality. Again, a combination of social factors and South African politics seems to have intervened in shaping the options available. Doctors' fantasies of "true transsexuals" and the challenges posed by those who confront these narrative expectations press and unsettle gendered boundaries.

V. Bureaucratic Boundaries and Forced Liminality

Legal struggles for those transitioning indicate both the loss of clear boundaries of gender and race and the simultaneous violent policing of these boundaries. While Chapter 1 describes maneuvers and enforcement of gendered spaces in terms of medical and legal discrepancies in South African history, this chapter revisits legal transitions and their facilitation or prohibition through specific narratives. These demonstrate political conjunctions with gendered identification numbers and inconsistent and slow bureaucratic structures, as well as the growing role of activist organizations in facilitating change. Here we see how these interrelated bureaucracies enforce particular racialized and sexed biopolitics.

Doctors, police, courts, and the South African Department of Home Affairs (which controls identity, immigration, and birth/marriage/death documents, among others) have been some of the most significant forces in constituting the documented boundaries of raced gender. During transitions, this documentation usually takes the form of doctors' permission letters, provided to transsexuals to protect them from harassment and prosecution, which also serve to police those bodies that are allowed to bridge the chasm between maleness and femaleness. For example, Vita faced legal threats when dressing as a woman before her surgery in the late 1960s because cross-dressing in South Africa was illegal. This illegality, coupled with the strict enforcement of apartheid pass laws, left her in a tenuous situation: she had to live as a woman to complete psychological tests required to attain surgery, but her legal documents could not be changed until her surgery was complete. She lived in poverty on "water and dry biscuits" while transitioning because she could not get a job in this liminal space and because she did not want to rely on her family for support.

> I was growing my hair. . . . I had been to see the doctors and they told me I've only now got to live as a woman. And I had no papers, I just had a handwritten note, almost like a doctor's prescription, saying that I am going through treatment, 'cause you could have been arrested in those days. Do you understand? But, it never happened, of course, thank God. (Edmunds 1997)

The collusion between legal and medical opinion that serves to maintain gender boundaries, even when there are discrepancies, frames Vita's dilemma. Laws are intertwined with and reliant upon doctors' mandates about those who count as women or men, as these mandates work hand in hand with the notes provided.

Nicole complicated the relationships among these entities in her description of the process of changing identification documents without doctors' permissions. She recounted both the public shame of advertising her intended name change in the government paper, which was required by law, and the slow bureaucracies of apartheid and their effects on those left in legally liminal spaces over periods of months and years, especially given apartheid's heavy reliance on documentation and legitimized proof of race (and gender).

> Years ago you used to change your name. It was difficult. Today it's a bit better, you still have to pay something, but then you have to advertise in the [government paper] . . . for a few weeks that you are changing your name. So that whoever wants to say something can now say it or forever hold your peace. And you must have a legal reason, you must say, "Well look, this is why I want to change it." You know? And then, with the sex changes, when they've had it done, my friend now had to wait nearly two years before everything was done. Nearly two years. She only got hers the other day and she had her [sex change] done two years ago. I mean, this is just how long it takes. You go for a passport, it takes about two, three months. You go for an ID book, they take four to six months. Now you want to come and change your name, which is worse than an ID book, you know? So it does take a long time. (Steenkamp 1997)

The process of changing documents and the time it takes was painstakingly slow or impossible in South African contexts during apartheid and even more so from 1993 to 2003, given the shift in the law described in Chapter 1. The effects of this change have been described in previous chapters, effectively preventing those transitioning from functioning as subjects and citizens—not being able to move freely, work, drive, vote, and obtain bank accounts, among other difficulties—and making everyday life almost impossible.[24]

Further, as Carmella's narrative points out, the subjectivity of gendered documentation changes in the Department of Home Affairs was mediated through racism and classism in which white and upper-class South Africans' transitioning, and those with medical approval, had greater access to such changes.

> Where you would have laughed [is] when I went to go and change my ID. I walked into Home Affairs in Cape Town. I

thought, "Ooh God, I can't just talk to anybody here now. They're gonna start talking here!" I said, "Can I please see your boss?" They asked me, "For what?" I said, "Because I'm looking for work." "No, there's no vacancies." "No, just tell your boss I want to see him or her." "It's a him." Ooh, when I heard him, I thought, "Oh my God, now must I tell what I am now!" I said, "Yes, just please tell him it's urgent, I just want to have five minutes with him." Okay, he wasn't busy and I went in to see him. He said, "Yes lady, take a seat. What can I do for you?" And there I came out with it. That man, I tell you, ne? He was sitting so nicely. He pushed his chair out and he stood up and he looked at me and he looked at my shoes and he looked at me up and down. <laughing> But he couldn't ask me to take off my clothes to prove it, because I had all the letters from the hospital. (Riekert 2000)

Despite the resistance she encountered and her need to use the strategy of feigning a job application, Carmella was able to parlay her doctors' approval into the legal change she needed. But those who exist in spaces that complicate and undermine medical expectations of "transition" such as Herman have struggled with the subjective restrictions of sexed bodies (who counts as a male or a female). Not only are types of surgeries and the resulting bodies policed by the state in making legal changes, the temporal expectations of a linear, consecutive, and quick transition have worked against those transitioning in different ways or those choosing to remain in liminal spaces. Herman had been in his process of transition since the 1970s:

I think things have been made easier through the Constitution. The strange thing is I've been starting now to get my ID, but I changed my name with the old regime. I've got a new ID book with the old regime with my name change. The lady who did it for me didn't bat an eyelid, and I did ask what the possibilities were of changing my ID number and, at that stage, she said I still had to have another op, at least. That was then [1992]. This is a new ID [from] 1999 but I had my name changed in '92 and then she said to me, at that time, you had to have at least two operations. She said two operations. The one operation, I mean, like, a lot of the trans guys now decide they're not having hysterectomies, but,

at that time, in order to have your ID changed, you had to
have no reproductive organs. So it was that and then one
other operation . . . there [are] only two other operations, a
mastectomy and then the phalloplasty, although, you know,
one trans, he had a vaginectomy and he was like that for
like three or four years before he had the next operation,
phalloplasty. So he was completely sexless. But I don't think
I want to do that. I think that's a bit drastic and also I want
to still enjoy what [I have.] . . . He says he's content leading a
celibate life. I'm not . . . I have a girlfriend. Actually, the law
said that anything that was done prior to '92 was acceptable.
(Maart 2009)

Herman's powerful comments point to the restrictions of gender boundaries, as well as the choices many are forced to make because of these
restrictions. Here, Herman contrasts his own decision not to undertake
the vaginectomy and phalloplasty (required for legal transition) with his
perception of his friend's forced celibacy, recalling the feared sacrifice of
orgasmic sexuality addressed earlier in this chapter. His transition has, so
far, been a decades-long process. However, as a result, Herman has been
forced into a legally liminal space much like the physically liminal space
facing "specials" and conscripts. Mbembe's discussion of forced liminality in colonial contexts as indicative of necropolitical states is recalled
here; changing documents is prevented, despite liminal bodies, and the
differences between male and female are so deeply engrained that even
identity numbers themselves are gendered.

Clearly, the process of gender enforcement is psychologically and
physically violent. Police enforcement and monitoring is a fear of those
who transition worldwide. In South African contexts, police violence
has historically been brutal and crime rates high, and apartheid laws
meant that racial and gender binaries were explicitly scrutinized. Nicole
explained some of the effects of this enforcement in her own life:

In my ID book, I have my male name, and [when thieves]
broke into my car in Jo'burg and I had to go to the police
station to report it and get my number for the insurance, the
policeman looked at a me, he looked at my ID book and said,
"Why did your parents give you these [masculine] names?"
And yet it says there, male. But they see what they want to

see—this is how we are. He didn't question [my sex], he just said, "Why did your parents give you these names?" I said, "Oh, you know, traditional names, what can I do?" <laughing> I mean, unfortunately, you learn to become such a good liar, you know? You have to! You have to. (Steenkamp 2000)

Even when Nicole had been a victim of a crime, she still had to justify her gender when questioned by the police and described the co-constitution of silence and violence. This narrative not only demonstrates her fear, it also shows Nicole's agency in working within a contradictory system: she knows what the police expect and how to manage their rigid and dichotomous ideas of gender.

The reasons legal changes are critical to defining citizenship and maintaining necropolitics have been described previously. The contrast of when such shifts are allowed and when they are not are expressly stated by Carmella, who claimed:

I was the first sex change to have an ID in South Africa. The first. And I'm very proud of it. . . . Oh, then I was so excited for that ID. Now I could go and open up an account at Woolworth's and Edgar's and Foschini's. <laughter> No one could . . . the people couldn't believe it. [When] I got my ID. Ooh, I opened it, I couldn't believe it. I said, "God, am I really a woman? Here's the ID now!" . . . I know a couple [of transsexuals] in Durban that still got no IDs. And then somebody else had to open up an account for them, because they can't do it because they're now female, but they are male. There was one who was a white [transsexual named] . . . Christine. Shame, shame. She just couldn't get her ID. And because she couldn't get her ID, they kept on calling her Christopher on her mail and . . . and it make things very bad for her. And it made her lose her sanity, just because of that. So I'm actually, I'm actually grateful that I was the first to get it. (Riekert 2000)

For Carmella, the junctures of her identification number with the class privileges she sought, shopping on credit at expensive department stores in downtown Cape Town that she mentions (Woolworth's, Edgar's, and Foschini's), are notable. Her new identity document provided her with what she conceptualized as confirmation and legitimization of her womanhood. She also speaks to the verification process she faces, which begins to feel Kafkaesque for many in liminal spaces.

Class mobility and literal movement are hindered or made easier by obtaining legal documents deemed necessary and policed by the state. Donna's narrative similarly points to the multiple, related, and inseparable problems of forced liminality that disallowing legal transition causes. Missing identity documents with accurate gender designators can facilitate poverty and unemployment, suspicion of fraud, arrest, and other legal problems. Lack of such documents denies basic rights, as well, such as voting. At time of this writing, decisions by Home Affairs about changes to such documentation are still made on a case-by-case basis and often require the intervention of activists and organizations for resolution.

Donna began her legal transition following her sex reassignment surgery in Thailand, and I share a lengthy segment of her narrative here because of the many related issues it raises:

> I didn't try and do any of the legal changes before the surgery. I tried after the surgery. [The doctor] . . . gave me a letter explaining about the procedure and what he had done. Then I went to my endocrinologist and he did a cursory inspection, just to see that yes, I had the surgery and he gave me a letter. And yeah, basically that was it. With those two letters, I then applied to Home Affairs to have my name changed, my birth certificate updated, and get the sheet with a new ID book [in 2005]. . . . I applied for the changes and it was six months later, and I'd heard nothing from them. So I contacted them to find out what was going on, and they said to me, they had a look on the system and they said yes, they can see that all the forms were received in Pretoria but since they were received and assigned to somebody in Pretoria, nothing had been done. So I said, "Well can you please try and find out what is going on?" So the lady phoned Pretoria and then they told me there's another form that I need to fill in, which I was never given the first time when I went and asked for what forms I had to fill out. So anyway, I got the forms and I filled them in, and I handed them in, and they said to me, "Okay, come back in three months time." So I went back in three months time and they said, "I've got your forms," but nothing

was being done. So I said, "Well, can you please try and ask somebody to do something?" So they said okay, they'll see what they can do. They said, come back in two weeks time. Two weeks time I went back and still nothing had been done. They said come back in two weeks time again. So every two weeks for almost six months I went back again, and again, and again, and I was getting so frustrated.

Eventually I spoke to [a friend and gender activist who] was going to Pretoria for some other meeting or conference. She said okay, she'll follow up because she has to go to Home Affairs as well for some other people. She went there and she started, like, throwing her weight around a bit and making a big fuss, and I think it was within three weeks I had my new birth certificate with my new ID, and my new name, and my new ID number, and the new gender on the birth certificate. So I had the new birth certificate. So I thought, okay, well, I'm going to apply for a new ID book now. I'd already applied previously and I thought, I'm just going to redo it now because now I've got my new birth certificate. They can base your ID on the birth certificate. Applied for the new ID book and the new passport at the same time. The passport I got within six weeks. The ID I got . . . almost two years later. So I get my new ID book and I go to all of the banks and all of the institutions that I have to go to, to get my details updated, and I went there, and I took my old ID book and my new ID book. And I went to them and said, "Right, here's my old. Here's my new. Can you please change it?" So they started doing all the changes on the computer and they issued me with new credit cards and what have you, and I went into the banks to get my new credit cards, and they gave them to me. And when we had to activate them, they said, "No, these cards have been cancelled, or they've been blocked." So I asked them, "So what's the problem?" They said, "Okay, we'll find the card division and find out what the problem is." Get hold of the card division. The card division says, "No, they can't make any changes until they get a letter from Home Affairs confirming the changes." Home Affairs never issued me with a letter. They're supposed to give you the letter with your new ID book. They never did it. . . .

So anyway, I go to Home Affairs, ask them, "So where's the letter?" "Oh no, the letter was never issued." I said, "So now what [am I] supposed to do?" "Now, you must apply for a duplicate." So I said, "Why must I apply for a duplicate if I haven't ever received an original, and an original was never even created?" No, I must apply for a duplicate. So I said, "Okay, what forms must I fill in?" They give it to me, fill in the forms, hand it in. "That'll be 45 Rand please." I said, "What for?" They said, "Because you're applying for a duplicate." I said, "But I'm applying for a duplicate because I never received an original, and an original was never, ever created." So they said, "No, that's the way it works." So I just thought, okay, I'm not going to fight with these people. I'm really so fed up already, I'll just pay for the duplicate. And I asked them, "So how long will this take?" "Oh, it'll take three months." So I said, "What?" Said, "Yes, no, that's how long it takes." I said, "Is there any way you can speed it up." "No, that's already priority." . . .

I eventually got all my banking stuff and all of my investments, and all of that stuff sorted out. [It took] almost two years for them to sort out all my stuff. . . . Okay, I think it had an impact on my ability to find a job, because so often I went for interviews and applied for positions, and I couldn't exactly go looking like a man. So I was applying for positions and whenever they asked for my identity number, obviously my ID number was in my old ID. . . . Yeah, and as a result, I don't know whether it was the reason I was discriminated, I don't know if I was discriminated against, or whether it's that I wasn't just as qualified as the other people were. But I couldn't find a job. [I've been without work for] three years, and I've been living full time for five years now. . . . Home Affairs need to get their act together. They really, really need to apply the law correctly and they need to handle these situations with the utmost urgency. (Hendricks 2007)

In her detailed description, Donna showed how painstaking and circular the steps of making gendered legal changes can be, as well as illustrating the extent of the skills required to deal with government bureaucracies. Her story replicates that of many others.[25] Donna had to be persistent over many years and, even then, was reliant on an activist to make the changes effective. Organizations have played an increasingly critical role in facilitating changes with Home Affairs in South Africa. Gender DynamiX, in particular, has taken on the role of assisting those transitioning in negotiating what has often been a very frustrating and isolating system.[26]

VI. The Postcolony and Transnational Connections

Transnational connections comprise one of the most striking components of South Africans' experiences of gender liminality, as they connect and bind locales. Such processes and relationships are not more significant in South Africa than anywhere else; however, South African narrators are extremely conscious and aware of these connections and articulate their importance in their own descriptions of their lives and transitions and their position in what Mbembe refers to as "the postcolony" (2001). Mbembe's postcolony is a way of describing the current period in and location of Africa, connecting and differentiating it from colonialism, and explaining how Africa is tied to fears and fantasies based in the global North.

The relationship of colonialism to the present is inseparable from the forces of globalization, technology, and movement that underlie the narratives of South Africans in gender liminal positions. I use the term "transnational" here in the way that Richa Nagar and I deploy it to explain our perceptions of transnational feminisms as a set of tools and practices that can:

(a) attend to a racialized, classed, masculinized, and heteronormative logics and practices of globalization and capitalist patriarchies, and the multiple ways in which they (re)structure colonial and neocolonial relations of domination and subordination;

(b) grapple with the complex and contradictory ways in which these processes both inform and are shaped by a range of subjectivites and understandings of individual and collective agency; and

(c) interweave critiques, actions, and self-reflexivity so as to resist a priori predictions of what might constitute feminist politics in a given place and time. (Nagar and Swarr 2010: 5)

Building on this interpretation of the potential use of the concept of transitional, the ways that transnational relationships manifest most markedly in these narratives are (1) through connections, especially between the United States/Europe and South Africa, in setting medical and legal precedents, (2) through international travel to obtain medical procedures, and (3) through information exchanges about liminal positions and transitions. The first of these three points, institutional connections in setting medical standards and legal decisions, is explored in Chapters 1 and 2. Analyses of travel and information exchanges in the postcolony broaden our discussion here.

Consistent concerns were expressed by narrators about the quality of locally-based surgeons in South Africa, many of whom perform sex reassignment procedures quite rarely, and difficulty obtaining information about their services. This is particularly true for female-to-male transsexuals who are seeking technically sophisticated phalloplasties mentioned previously. Anxieties are exacerbated by stealth and secrecy, as well as patients' needs for privacy and embarrassment about surgeries that may not have lived up to their expectations. As Giles explained,

> I'm aware of one or two guys that have had [bottom surgery] done. The one guy, I've been told that there's no point in asking him unless I go to him and tell him that I'm going to have the surgery and I want to find out about it. Then he'll be prepared to tell me. The other guy I was supposed to meet when I was up in Jo'burg, but he had a work emergency so I didn't end up speaking to him. But also, I think the problem, the difference in that is, I think they had it done—they paid to have it done. . . . I don't even know where they had it done. That's part of the problem. I don't actually know if there is a surgeon in South Africa that is capable of doing this. If there is a surgeon in South Africa, to be perfectly honest, I don't know if I would trust a South African surgeon. (Davids 2007)

Concerns like those Giles expresses about South African surgeons reflect on these surgeons' medical experience or inexperience, but they also indicate a broader concern based in South Africa's history. Under apartheid and continuing to the present, South Africa's public health care system has been inconsistent at its best and exploitative at its worst. Trust of

South African surgeons, given South Africa's medical histories and the experiences of those who have been increasingly speaking out about medical abuse, is often tenuous among those in gender liminal positions with concerns about both competency and motives regularly expressed. Not only is there interest in which surgeons provide the best quality and least expensive surgeries, but most narrators also compared public and privately available procedures and medical practitioners within South Africa. Carmella spoke to this common unease:

> Private, they don't care how you look, they will just do it for the money. Because [the cost] is now thousands, you know what I mean. And the state . . . they worry about you. If you don't come in, they phone you or they come up and check up on you. But not a private hospital. But I would really like one day to go to Singapore. Just so that they can have a look at me, my vagina, and even my breasts. (Riekert 2000)

Here, Carmella discusses what she sees as motivations for state versus private surgery. She feels well-taken-care-of in the local public system and has needed extensive follow-up care for decades, but she feels that private hospitals are more materially focused and do less gatekeeping.

Travel and the promises of travel for obtaining cheaper and quicker sex reassignment surgeries are a topic of regular discussion in narratives, and the regularity of such surgeries has increased in the years of South Africa's political transition. Both decreased availability of local South African sex reassignment surgeries and increased access to travel and information outside of South Africa following the end of apartheid have influenced this shift. The Internet has facilitated comparisons of the quality and prices of surgery in various contexts among those who seek it, providing increasing options and access to those who were previously isolated, a point to which I return below. Donna, for instance, compared surgeons and the prices of both surgeries and travel to these locales:

> I started looking at what are the other options available, and I went on the Internet and I started asking other girls on the Internet, post-op girls, where had they been, what had they done, how had they got it done and a lot of them referred me to the doctors in Thailand. As a result of that, I also realized that it's probably better to go to somewhere

like Thailand because the doctors there have so much more experience. From an experience point of view, obviously, the U.S. and the U.K. and Europe and Thailand, the doctors have all got a lot of experience. The only thing is, if I had to go to the U.S. or U.K. or Europe, it would have been very, very expensive, especially with our Rand/dollar, Rand/pound, Rand/Euro exchange rate. There was no way I would have been able to afford to go to any of those countries. Thailand, as far as the cost was concerned, it would have been almost the same as if I had it done in South Africa but I was then getting it done by somebody who had experience of doing 800 to 2,000 of these surgeries. So the experience point of view, the doctors in Thailand were by far the most experienced of all the doctors. (Hendricks 2007)

As Donna's comments indicate, conversations among transsexuals online allow for shared information about costs, availability, and the quality and experience of surgeons in various locations. This is a critical concern, especially for those considering surgery in a place like Thailand so culturally different from South Africa and where narrators indicate that communication between patients and medical staff can be hindered by language differences. Further, there are no universal standards by which to evaluate doctors and their skills, so narrators often relied on their virtual connections to others who have obtained sex reassignment surgeries in their assessments.

While Asian and European surgeons are often considered as viable options for those seeking surgery, outside of South Africa, most narrators were specifically focused on Thailand. Thai sex reassignment procedures are gaining great popularity and garnering serious consideration, especially as increasing numbers of transsexuals have surgery there and return to South Africa where they share their experiences. Such procedures are still quite expensive, and many South African transsexuals have literally sold their homes to afford surgeries.[27] But the inconsistent and long waits for treatment in South Africa, the relatively lower private cost in Thailand, and the expertise Thai surgeons have in sex reassignment procedures make it a desirable locale for many seeking surgery.[28]

Donna spoke to this most directly, as she researched Thai surgeons, when she accompanied a friend to Thailand where her friend went through sex reassignment. Donna eventually decided to pursue surgery there herself. Her discussion articulated many of the nuances of the decision process as well as the transnational relationships and class-based differences that underlie such considerations:

> Thing is, Thailand has a very large transgender community. There is also a lot of, what do they call it, the girly boys? Or the she-males? But [there are a] very, very high number of trans [people] there that have transitioned and have had the full surgery. So obviously they had lots and lots of experience. So many overseas people from all over the world were all going to Thailand. Australia, New Zealand, all those Eastern countries, all of the people were going to Thailand and so many girls from the U.S. were going to Thailand, from the U.K. were going to Thailand. So, yeah, and even when I got to Thailand, my doctor told me, "Oh, yeah, we've had quite a few girls from South Africa here."
>
> [The total cost] depends on who you go to. The doctor that I went to is probably one of the cheapest because I didn't have a lot of money. I had three surgeries. I had the gender reassignment surgery. I had breast augmentation and I had the Adam's apple shave. And those three surgeries, together, cost me 78,000 Rand. I had to pay for my airfare, which was 8,000 and something Rand and for a return and my accommodation cost me about 7,000 Rand while I was there. First, the first week, you stay in hospital and that's covered by that 78,000.[29] And then your second two weeks, you have to stay in a hotel. And you have to pay the hotel costs yourself. Fortunately, the hotel was, like, 500 meters down the road from where the hospital was so, when you needed to go for checkups, it was literally just a walk down the road.
>
> Initially, I went on my own and [my friend] came, I arrived there on the Saturday. The surgery was on the Monday morning and the Tuesday morning when I woke up, I was in Thailand. . . . It was just so nice and just to see somebody that I knew and that I can talk to, because the hospital, the nurses that day couldn't communicate in English very well. So fortunately [my friend] was there, and she could go and try and please explain when I was in pain that I need an injection or something. So that is very, very nice, having her there.

She only stayed for a week because she had to come back to work but it was really, really good having here there. [I had all three surgeries] at the same time. I was there for . . . just over three weeks. They normally say that if there are going to be any complications or any problems, they would normally show within the first three weeks of surgery. So fortunately, I had no complications and while I was still in the hospital the first week, I had, not an infection, but I had a fever. I was going through these hot and cold spells the first week, and they say that it's pretty normal, because your body has gone through a major shock, and it's really often that you do end up having a fever of some sort. But otherwise, I had no problems. The biggest thing that most of the girls struggle with is when they take all the bandaging off, and they take the catheter out, and you have to go and pee by yourself the first time. A lot of the girls really, really struggle, and I was very fortunate because the first time I went, everything worked fine, no problems. I was so pleased.

Really often some of the girls, they take the catheter out and they have to go and put it back in again, and they have to stay for another day or two in the hospital until their bladder can work normal or by itself. . . . They give you what they call a dilator or a stint. It's like a dildo which you then, every day, my procedure, I had to do it for 15 minutes, four times a day. With [my friend's surgery], she has to do it twice a day for two hours, but then she had a different procedure done to what I had done. I had the normal, what they call the penile inversion. [She] had a completely different procedure . . . basically they take the two halves of the penis and they make those your lips. Then they take all the skin from the scrotum, they take that skin and they form it into a tube, which they then insert into you, which then becomes your vagina cavity, which is the latest procedure that they're doing but it's a lot more expensive. Just that surgery alone I think cost [her] between $130,000 and $150,000 range. That's just for that surgery. [Mine] was about $56,000. So hers is a lot more expensive but it is the better surgery . . . because of the two halves of the penis, what happens is when you get sexually aroused, the same as a woman's labia. . . . So it's definitely got its advantages. It's more realistic. . . . Apparently this doctor is doing a very, very good job. Apparently it's very good and the results are fantastic, and the actual appearance once the swelling and everything has gone down is so good, you wouldn't know that it had been. . . . Obviously if I'd had complications, I would have had to try and find somebody either here that could help me, or I would have had to pay for a flight back to Thailand. And they do guarantee their work. If you have any complications within the first two years of having had your surgery, they will fix it for you free of charge. So it would just cost you whatever your airfare is. (Hendricks 2007)

Donna's narrative raised a number of important considerations specific to South African narrators. First, she spoke to the complicated relationships among Thais who choose to live in gender liminal spaces (she refers to them as she-males or girly boys—but there are various locally based terms in Thailand that do not map perfectly onto medical conceptions of transgender and transsexual) and those who transition medically (she refers to them as trans).[30] She also elucidated the transnational connections among those from Australia, New Zealand, the United States, and the United Kingdom in comparison to surgeries in Thailand.[31] Donna addressed how class affected surgical options for those in South Africa who are able to afford them and in terms of the differing effects of variously priced surgeries in Thailand. She spoke to the kinds, qualities, and timing of surgeries she and her friend were able to afford, strongly showing the effects of class, space, and temporality on the construction of bodies, even among white South Africans.[32]

Efforts to make transnational connections to obtain information about transitions, especially medical information, are common among South Africans. Such connections happen primarily through books, news and popular media, and the Internet. Sometimes these media provide a way to seek information about oneself, at other times they provide a way to connect and avoid isolation, and in some contexts connections facilitate surgeries like those described above. For example, Carmella described the comparisons she made between South Africa and Singapore and the importance of books in her self-evaluation:

What I also can't understand is in Singapore they don't do it like that. Singapore, you just have your operation and it's finished. You don't need all these things done to you, keeping

> this mold in you and you know. It's just the operation, one
> time, overnight, and it's done and it's finished. . . . I read a
> lot of books. And I went to the library and I studied such
> things, you know, before I went through with it. I knew I
> was gonna have marks under my breasts and I knew there
> is going to be something that somebody will see. . . . But I
> like it. I'm very happy. (Riekert 2000)

This discussion is complemented by her statement, shared previously, about how hard her breasts are, as compared to those who had such surgery in Singapore. For Carmella, the comparison she described between her own experiences and her vision of what her body could be was disappointing and satisfactory at the same time. Her evaluation of the Singaporean process was somewhat idealized, as well. But she exercised her agency in studying and reading about the procedures and their effects and envisioning her ideal body.

For Donna, both books and the Internet were useful in her transition, especially as she tried to understand her spirituality and what she saw as religious edicts against sex reassignment. She talked about how the Internet countered what she had learned in the church:

> Very soon after [my spouse and I] separated was when I first
> started getting access to the Internet and, at first, I really
> started getting desperate about, "What is this thing with me?"
> Having grown up in a church all the time, it had always been
> a thing that this is sin and what I'm doing is wrong and I
> need to stop doing it. So I never really thought that it might
> be something else. Once I got access to the Internet, I put
> a search in there about men dressing as women and I got
> all of these search results coming back and I started going
> through all of them and suddenly I discovered that I'm not
> the only one doing this. There are hundreds and thousands
> if not millions of other guys in exactly the same situation.
> (Hendricks 2007)

In Donna's narrative, online community and resources provided connections and space for her experience, making her feelings recognizable and undermining the isolation she felt from those who saw her as sinful. Donna was able to take this virtual connection and support a step further, obtain books on recommendation, and reconfigure the way that she understood gender dysphoria altogether.

> It was about 1998, '99. And I started corresponding with a woman in America and she suggested that I get two books from an author in the States, a psychologist who deals purely with transgendered people. . . . I read these two books and, for the very first time, I realized that this condition of mine is not a sexual condition, it's not a psychological condition, it's not a sociological condition, it's a physiological condition. And suddenly, for the first time, I realized that this isn't a spiritual thing that I'm dealing with. I'm not living in sin. I'm born with a physical defect, if you're going to put it that way. And nobody should judge me because of the fact that I had a physical defect. I didn't choose it. It's not that I'm choosing to be transgendered, I'm transgendered because that is what I am. It's like somebody is born with a cleft palate. They didn't choose to be born that way. . . . [It's] like a person with a cleft palate, they can go and have surgery done where they can correct it. I can't go for surgery and have them fix something in my brain because they don't have the medical knowhow to do that, but I can go for physical surgery to have my body changed to be in line with what my brain is like. There's a verse in the Bible . . . it says, "You will know the truth and the truth will set you free." And suddenly it was like I now understood what was wrong with me and it was like such a liberating experience to suddenly know that this is what I'm actually dealing with. And as soon as I realized that, I started trying to find out, now, what can I do to actually change my whole body? (Hendricks 2007)

In some ways, Donna used books and the Internet to juxtapose religion and medicine. She had been raised with religious ideas of gender transition as sinful, but she then turned to medical ways of conceptualizing gender she initially found online. Then she saw herself as having a physiological condition, a "physical defect" over which she has no control, and for her, surgery was the way to correct this physical problem to align her body with her brain. Donna experienced this revelation as extremely libratory and it had transformative effects for her.[33]

For Donna and other narrators, the media can also provide information as well as a way to begin to conceptualize medical sex reassignment as an option. Giles was introduced to gender transitions and sex reassignment procedures through an Oprah Winfrey[34] talk show.

> At one point towards the middle of [2006], I read an article, it wasn't a really an article, it was like a little snippet in one of the TV newspapers about a show that Oprah had done on sex changes. But, I didn't watch the show, I had missed it. But, I think I was probably reading that little tiny few sentences, that sort of like sparked things off. . . . So, I ended up speaking to my psychologist, and I wasn't aware of any terminology. I just basically said to her, "I want a sex change." And then she referred me to [an organization]. She said [that] I must phone them, which I did after I had told my dad. (Davids 2007)

Many times, as in Giles' narration, a simple awareness of physical transitions can spark a series of events. This is particularly true in less publicized surgical procedures for female-to-male transsexuals. For example, as mentioned previously, Herman was able to learn about an Australian phallic prosthetic implant online, information that he shared with his doctor. Giles explained another related arena of information about phalloplasty:

> I just read a book, *Both Sides Now*[35] . . . about the first surgery [the author] had and how they had to stop it halfway because of the immense blood loss. Then how he got infections within the testicular implants and then how there was too much scar tissue and he couldn't urinate properly.[36] All the complications, I just thought, "Damn!" . . . Then the second surgery turned out to be a success. That was a different type with a different surgeon in a different country. I kind of wish that they had gone into a little bit more detail on the successful one. That didn't really say much. They kind of mentioned in some part of the book, towards the end, that he'd spoken to people that had had the surgery done, everything was fully functioning, but I would have preferred to have known a little bit more. The trans men that have had bottom surgery, that I can access that have had bottom surgery done, aren't willing to discuss

it. The only time they're willing to discuss it is if you go and tell them that you have decided that you want to have it done, and that you're 100 percent certain you want it done. But I can't tell anyone that I'm 100 percent certain I want it done if I don't know what I'm getting myself into, if I don't know what the risks are. And it's much easier to find out the risks from speaking to someone, but the problem is actually finding people that are willing to talk to you. (Davids 2007)

Again and again, as in this narrative, we see themes of self-education and patients' education of doctors about complex medical procedures facilitated through these multiple connections. This self-education proves particularly useful to those who are not only marginalized for their gender liminality but within discussions of gender liminality. Issues of informed consent are also raised here, as well as uncertain medical projections of the future.

As alluded to in many of these narrative excerpts, transnational connections to the global North have proved an invaluable way to inform South African medical practitioners and patients of successful procedures and treatment protocols elsewhere.

The funny thing is that a lot of the material that I had read on the Internet, there is just so much available, you can almost self-treat yourself because of all the information that's available. In fact, some of the people were saying that a lot of the trans people, they may eventually end up seeing a psychologist, they know more than what most of the psychologists do about their condition. [Most of the material was from] . . . the British and the Americans, most of the material. It was quite a bit from Australia as well and predominantly U.S., obviously, the vast majority of information was from there. (Hendricks 2007)

Transnational medical connections, while useful in some contexts, have been used to justify medical experimentation in South Africa in different times and places, as discussed in Chapter 1. But being aware of the transnational relationships that underlie gender liminality more broadly can and has helped narrators and those in similar positions seek the bodies and treatment they desire. It is also important to note that not all South Africans have access to the Internet or books, though media is more widely available, and this access is primarily mediated through class and location. Those in rural areas and those who are poor are least likely to be able to access the resources that can be so helpful and transformative. Further, as Kristin Lord (2006) explains, the transparency that comes with increased access to information holds both promise and peril. In her broad analysis of global information flows, she observes that access to resources is assumed to be beneficial. But layers of complex analysis are still essential to understand the tempered nature of information as "consumers of information rely on organizations with goals such as profit, entertainment, or the promotion of a particular political agenda that takes precedence over their role as public educators" (2006: 10). Evaluating the quality, motives, and goals of the sources of information available is essential.

VII. Becoming a Subject through Confronting Death

> When you have the choice of death taken away from you, you have nothing left, nothing else, there is no lower you can go. You can't even choose your death. There is nowhere else you can go . . . The choice was taken from me so I had nowhere else to go but claw my way up again. Post transition. (Anonymous narrator in Morgan et al. 2009: 230)

When medical options are not available, many who want to transition take matters into their own hands. This can include self-medication through off-label uses of hormones, obtaining drugs illegally, or attempting to change their own bodies physically, sometimes through self-harm. Such decisions are never made lightly, and their seriousness indicates the space between life and death that they navigate. Again, Mbembe's framework of necropolitics helps to frame the specificity of South African gender liminal experiences. He explained how the human being becomes a subject, "in the struggle and the work through which he or she confronts death . . ." (2003: 14), central to the risk that often characterizes physical transitions.[37]

Without viable medical options, and even when these options may be available, individuals in gender liminal positions may create and seek their own alternative means of transition. For some this included choosing some surgeries and procedures and not others. Different kinds of nonsurgical transitions often provide desirable alternatives, and some of these choices involve eschewing established medical practitioners altogether. For instance, Donna described how those who couldn't access or afford hormonal treatments sometimes self-medicated:

> Obviously, you can't get hormone replacement without referral from a psychologist and you can't get the hormones without a prescription from a doctor. I know a lot of the girls tried to go the contraceptive route. They'd take contraceptives because a lot of them can get those a lot cheaper than I can get hormones and also some of them can organize it without having a prescription and they do self-medicate but it generally isn't recommended. (Hendricks 2007)

This kind of self-determined treatment—taking estrogen in the form of birth control pills—is creative but can be dangerous and constitutes a confrontation of risk and even death.[38] Donna also discussed specific problems she's had with her own health that interact with her use of hormones. She needed to take additional medication to prevent health problems including heart attacks and strokes and is concerned that these are, "[t]he kinds of things that people don't know about if they go onto hormone replacement without having proper medical care."

William Molobi's narrative doesn't fit the standard expectations for medical definitions of Gender Identity Disorder nor the chronologies of most published trans autobiographies and confronts death more directly. Sex reassignment surgery was never an option for William; instead, hir narration showed the interplay of sexuality and gender identification with racialized poverty and geographic location, resulting in a different conception of transitioning than those expressed in other narrations. S/he discussed hir thoughts on sexuality and gender working together in hir own body:

> So my gay thing, okay, the story, it's when I was six, or five this day . . . I was still at crèche [daycare], but I finish my crèche and I was supposed to go to grade one. I took a needle, you know, these big ones . . . and I tried to cut my penis, and I wounded myself. I wanted to be like the rest of the people that I wanted to be. I wanted to be a girl by then, you know? To look more girlish, you see. And this thing is just stopping

> me. Because every time when they want to wee-wee, they sit
> down. I want to sit down as well. Why should I stand, when
> everybody's sitting down? Okay, let's go to that one. But my
> mother was told that I'm going to be gay once. She must put
> an eye on me. . . . She took me to her physician. . . . Yeah,
> I'm fine! I'm fine! It didn't make any damage, because it was
> a light scratching. . . . (Molobi 1997)

William's attempt to remove hir own penis at a young age illustrates a desire to transition and the isolation faced in this process.

Self-injuring is not uncommon among those who don't have surgical options to change their bodies. The powerful narrative of U.S.-based trans woman Linda Thompson in the documentary film "Cruel and Unusual" (2006), a prisoner who physically cut off her penis in her prison cell and flushed it down the toilet after being consistently denied medical treatment for gender dysphoria, provides an unforgettable complement to William's description. South African accounts from Lyndsay, a trans woman who shot herself in the penis (Morgan et al. 2009: 42), and Robert, who speaks of the shame associated with self-mutilation, despite its commonality (Morgan et al. 2009: 230–231), further put William's actions in context in South African communities.

HIV both complicates and adds to this consideration, as those who are HIV positive are rarely, if ever, able to get sex reassignment surgeries, which can lead to a feeling of desperation. Yet those in such positions try to think of ways around these restrictions. For instance, one narrator shares the following account:

> Vanya talked of a friend of hers who is a trans women who is
> HIV positive—the head of the endocrinology unit at a major
> government hospital told her that they do not do sexual
> reassignment surgery on anyone who is HIV positive. Vanya's
> friend is now saying, "It is better if I castrate myself at home
> and they take me to hospital and they will be forced to do
> something about it." (Morgan et al. 2009: 218)

HIV adds an additional barrier to the complex of "true transsexual" definitions that those seeking medical interventions must navigate. Travel bans for those living with HIV can further restrict mobility. Like the other narrators described here, Vanya's friend thinks of creative, if violent and potentially fatal, solutions to eventually attain the body she desires.

More broadly, as a mental health practitioner explains, the relationship between HIV/AIDS and gender liminality in South Africa "hasn't been explored. We are in a vacuum. Remember, we don't even know how many queer men are HIV positive, right?" (Swanepoel 2007). The complications of sex, sexuality, and HIV are often ignored. Based on his years of experience working in outreach services, Andre Swanepoel describes how he sees this overlap on a daily basis with this memorable example of the physicality of being a woman:

> How do we work around [safer sex] where somebody identifies as male [and] likes getting fucked so he actually bleeds anally? "I'm a woman, I'm menstruating," in terms of HIV. In certain areas we work more with trans groups. [But] in the Cape Flats and we don't call them trans, we call them drag queens, because they're not identifying as trans. (Swanepoel 2007)

Here, the potential risks of sexual encounters are subsumed by the affirmation of femininity that they offer in a somatically powerful form (e.g., in the form of blood and menstruation). The lack of attention to the risks facing those who are expressing gender liminality by health practitioners increases the risk of transmission. In an interview, one psychologist suggested to me that, "HIV is kind of out there . . . far away" (Ryland 2007) for transsexuals because they are often assumed to be asexual, but this is amended by the kinds of affirmation Swanepoel identifies and the other raced and classed risk factors for HIV gender liminal people may face disproportionately. Often, a wide range of varied perceptions of medical practitioners seem to be fueled by particular definitions of transition and what kind of person qualifies as transsexual.

Given the time and place where William transitioned, as well as hir race and class, s/he did not feel that "trans" or "transsexual" categories were viable medical options or part of the activist lexicon s/he expressed. When William did find peers outside of gender binaries like hirself, these role models were self-identified gay men and lesbians working against apartheid homophobia and isolation, especially Simon Nkoli and others involved in Gays and Lesbians of the Witwatersrand (GLOW) in the 1990s. William explains that hir gender expression excluded hir from gay male spaces and community like the Skyline bar in Johannesburg.[39] Again, William's narrative does not match a traditional medically sexed "transition" but helps us to expand gender liminality, showing how individuals can create a space outside of gender expectations, including gender outside of ideals common among gay men.[40]

William also speaks directly about hir own suicide attempt, closely linked to hir own gender and sexuality, another common theme among South Africans who go through gender transitions. This instance again recalls Mbembe's necropolitical context, where suicidality must not be reduced to psychological analysis of the individual but necessitates careful consideration of political and cultural meaning. The suicide attempt William describes here followed rejection from a man s/he was interested in romantically:

> [After that] I tried to kill myself. I drank a cleaner, happy powder, for cleaning the toilet. Happy powder, to clean the toilet. It's got essence in it to clean and clean the germs. . . . I thought I'm alone. People are calling me names and a lot of things. They would say, "You're bisexual," but, you know, Zulu name is so wrong, like *stabane*, and *stabane* is like a big horrible name that we grew up knowing, you see, from our point, talking about it. We used not to have conversation with our own mothers. You know, when you talk about deep, bad conversations, not good, and you'd never talk about it—you only talk about it with your friends, and your friends would tell you what it means. [*Stabane* is a] person who's got two things. I said, "No, I must die." Because me, I love being with boys. Then I started to date a girl. It was so horrible! <feigns crying> Horrible. Then I stopped it, then I tried to kill myself. . . . I thought I was alone. How could I live when I'm so misbehaving? And I'm happy with [being attracted to boys], and it's wrong. I felt it's wrong. Then the one day, I wrote a letter to another girl. It was so innocent then, and I wanted her to be my girlfriend. It's because my friends always say, "You don't have a girlfriend, blah, blah, blah. We're having girlfriends." . . . One day, I drink that happy powder <whispering>. I said, "I want to die." (Molobi 1997)

Both William's isolation and community accusations of *stabane* contributed to hir suicide attempt. Linguistically *stabane* refers to intersexuality, but it is commonly known as a derogatory term leveled against gays and lesbians in South African contexts. William's use of it here shows how accusations of gender liminality can be devastating; I return to the concept of *stabane* and its usage and application in Chapter 4.

William's suicide attempt is best understood in the context of South African necropolitical and cultural trends of understanding death. The anecdotal commonality of suicide attempts among South African gays and lesbians was discussed in previous chapters. Here, as a number of South African narrators suggest, it is important to reconceptualize suicide attempts outside of medical models, especially for those who face gender liminality. Joy Rosemary Wellbeloved puts it this way: "Suicide attempts are not dead ends. [Attempted] suicide opened a door for me because I realised that I had got to a point in my life where it was either suicide or changing my gender" (Morgan et al. 2009: 230). Wellbeloved's model of suicide allows her space for a crucial gendered decision and even inspires this decision.

For William, this suicide attempt can be seen as part of hir transition. Alex similarly describes the role of suicide as a part of and a "cry for help" in his transition.

> At this time my mom took me to see a psychologist because, she said, I didn't want to be a girl and it worried her. I did not think it was working for me because I was still suicidal. The first and only time that I tried to commit suicide was at the age of 13, because I was so confused about why my physical body was not in line with my gender identity. Also, the other kids had started teasing me. I was called a tomboy, but it went so much deeper than that. It was a feeling of absolute confusion and just being so miserable and unhappy about the fact that, with the onset of puberty, I would biologically become a woman: something I could never be. I took an overdose of pills. It was not so much that I wanted to end my life right then. It was more like a cry for help. (Alex in Morgan et al. 2009: 87–88)

In some ways, all of these examples point to suicide as not only a confrontation of death but an expression of the seriousness of narrators' desire to transition. In considering these instances of suicide, we see how, as Mbembe predicts, within the parameters of biopower and necropower the boundary between resistance and suicide is blurred (2003: 40) and how suicide has been viewed as a form of action.

VIII. Stealth and Reality

In part because of the liminality of those who are transitioning and the lack of space for between male and female (e.g., for publically self-defined transsexuals), "stealth"—not sharing details about one's life from before transition—is a consistent concern and topic of conversation among those who transition in South Africa.[41] Stealth, sometimes thought of as similar to "passing," is a matter of life or death. Racial and gender "passing" are fairly well-known and problematized concepts in which an individual is accepted in a category incongruous with that to which they have been previously assigned or assumed.[42] While "passing" might be a temporary or changing state, stealth involves individuals passing all of the time and making a break with their previous gender history. Both concepts further help us to reconstitute "reality," in the Mbembian sense, as having loose and mutable boundaries. Post-transition stealth is sometimes part of the rationale those who transition provide to explain their perspectives. Two narrators in very different situations shared the reasoning behind their decisions to go into stealth.

At the time of this interview in 1997, Vita was living her life as an upper-class, white "gay girl" but expressed some conflict in her narrative about her openness identifying as a transsexual woman, especially in her previous relationships with men. When speaking about this conundrum during her narration, which occurred at a guesthouse where Vita was working, a woman who she employed to clean the guesthouse came in and out of the room a few times. At this point, Vita whispered to me that she is "out of the closet" but was not open about her history of sex reassignment to this employee, whose presence inspired her whispers. I am not passing judgment on her whispering, just noting the difficulty of speaking openly and being "out" consistently in all contexts. Vita explains:

> As I said to you, for a long time now I've been out of the closet . . . I speak to people quite openly, and I don't try to pretend to be what I'm not . . . And strange thing is, in the very beginning of the transformation <whispering> as a woman, after surgery . . . when I was still going to bars

and restaurants and having boyfriends, I think I was quite obvious. Because you just can't go through surgery and say ooh, like I am today. You know, if you saw me today on the street you wouldn't look or think twice. I've never-ever told a man [about being a transsexual], ever, ever, ever. . . . Never-ever. He suspected, that's his problem. And I must really thank God above my head, I've never had one problem with one man . . . and I've had lots of men. You know I had to, surgically I was told to fuck my ass off. . . . You have to, to keep everything functioning . . . I wasn't to go one day without sex. 'Cause you know the vagina has to stay open, it has to be used in the first two years . . . and that's how they spoke to me as well. . . . Like I told you, nothing's so exciting as people think . . . people always expect my life to be a roller-coaster. It was only that short while it was a roller-coaster. Otherwise . . . you meet people, and I never-ever once mentioned it [my transsexualism] to either of my husbands. It was never discussed. . . . I'd say [the marriages lasted] two years, a year and a half. . . . (Edmunds 1997)

Vita's narrative shows the ways that stealth is not simply mapped onto ideas of being in or out of the closet or "passing," as they might be conceptualized in the global North. For her, stealth is a navigation of expectations, assumptions, and safety based in what her doctors told her and visions of her own future, suggesting an alternate phenomenology and temporality. Stealth is much more encompassing than these concepts and is not merely "playing" with gender but can have serious consequences if undermined. Vita explains that she never spoke to either of her husbands about her sex reassignment surgeries, but for her this was not in contradiction with her being "out." Instead, she addressed the space between openness and stealth in navigating a world of gender-based discrimination and violence.

This analysis of stealth can extend Andrew Tucker's important critique of the concept of "the closet" in his analysis of race and gay male communities in contemporary Cape Town. For Tucker, assumptions about the closet as a location from which to "come out" depend on knowledge of a singular identity and can imply that those who do not come out are "in denial and suffering from an outdated and secretive mode of sexual identity" (Tucker 2009: 10). Furthermore, binaries can actually be reinforced through concepts such as the closet, which assume a heterosexual/homosexual dichotomy. Concepts of stealth or realness can similarly rely on a simplistic cisgender/transgender binary, assume a normative and stable gender identity, and expect a "teleological and developmentalist progression" (Tucker 2009: 12) from one gender to another. Further, as Martin Manalansan IV points out, public visibility and "the public avowal of gay identity" are not always seen as universally necessary; in his own work in Filipino immigrant communities in New York, such identifications as gay are often seen as "superfluous" (2003: 33–34). In applying these ideas to South African notions of stealth, "the need to be accepted unconditionally and without prejudice, and the need to protect oneself in the workplace" (Morgan et al. 2009: 236) are just two of the reasons stealth can be important.

The potential repercussions for Herman's openness about his past were perhaps even more severe, necessitating his living in stealth. He lives as a man in an institutional space that is sex-segregated and could lose his home or be subjected to physical violence were his male housemates to discover that he identifies as a transsexual. He explains the intersections of prejudicial perceptions, job discrimination, religion, sexual orientation, and his own tenuous health in his decision to embrace stealth and what it means to him:

> For me, [stealth is] being accepted for the man I know I am. I shouldn't have to tell somebody I'm a female-to-male transsexual. I want someone to look at me and say, "That's a man." And that is what it means to me. By me saying to them anything else would be admitting that I'm not a man. . . . The thing is, if I'm not in stealth, if I'm out, you are then always looked on as a freak. I mean, I've gone for job interviews where right to the last, I've got the job and the minute I mention this to them, I don't have the job. They'll come up with a lot of excuses for me not getting the job, and I will know it's none of the above. It's dangerous because, you know, you'd have the guy, and this has happened to me, "You want to be a man? We'll show you're not a man." That kind of thing. So it's more dangerous for a trans man out there than for a butch lesbian. I think a lot of it also has to do with my religion, my Christianity. I want to be a heterosexual man, not a homosexual woman. . . .

I mean, I don't even really know how the guys in this house would feel about me because it's just never come up . . . I always just worry that something might happen to me. That they might actually come and have to help me . . . I've had seizures in the house, and . . . last week, we had to talk about procedures in case of a seizure because [the staff] decided that they're a little bit concerned about me . . . in the light of the two seizures that I've had since I've been here. And especially the bathroom. I'm not allowed to bathe; I can only shower, in case I have a seizure. Then I can't drown. Whereas if I shower, I might just fall and knock my head but that's not bad. That's all the kinds of things I have to think about when I think about being in stealth. Obviously, if the guys don't want me here, I'll have to move out but I can't go live with girls. Yeah. I would have to go back to the family and that's what I don't want to do. (Maart 2009)

Herman describes his decision not as shame or embarrassment, but as a powerful recasting of gender that again blurs the lines between "sacrifice and redemption, martyrdom and freedom" (Mbembe 2003: 40). Herman falls into all four of these oppositional categories at different times, and sometimes simultaneously. He gives up a lot for his family though he feels conflicted about their approval, but Herman also defies simple categorization through the sacrifices he makes and the simultaneous freedoms he has achieved. All narrators in some ways and contexts are both in and out of stealth; while total in its vision, in practice it is not a simple and complete decision but a series of decisions constantly made by individuals in institutionalized and discriminatory spaces. Stealth is perhaps best understood as a continual process embedded in managing discontinuities. Narratives of "the closet" often idealize disclosure, but stealth and its implications unsettle this assumption. Stealth can also be seen as an expression of gender liminality, benefitting communities by opening a discursive possibility of safety.

Some activists oppose the conception of stealth, such as trans man Tebogo who states, "I don't encourage people to go into stealth. We want rights and we want to change our documents but we don't want to tell people we are trans. So how are they going to know we exist?" (Morgan et al. 2009: 238). This issue is especially poignant for Tebogo, who speaks elsewhere in this same text about his efforts to bring visibility to black trans experiences to counter assumptions of gender liminality as un-African. For Tebogo and other activists, the space between stealth and openness holds political potential.

The South African state's role in encouraging people to go into stealth and constituting "realness" proves intricate and critical to understanding the complications of gender boundaries in this context. This is another useful place to recall Mbmebe's notion of necropolitics and ideas of reality explored in the introduction to this chapter. What is reality and how is it dissolved and reconfigured by colonialism? Perhaps the most remarkable articulation of politics and reality is found in Carmella's narrative through her connection to the state, epitomized in her description of the role the government played in her transition. In the first narrative I collected in 1997, Carmella explained that former South African Prime Minister/President, Pieter Willem Botha, paid for her surgery and visited her in the hospital—claims which have multiple meanings.

> I promise you, [the hospital I went to] is the best. Especially when it comes to the plastic surgery department. The best. They treat you the best. And I had P. W., Pik Botha come to visit me, and his wife. I told him what I wanted to do with the money. It wasn't for me; they said the money is going to [the hospital], you see? [I wrote a letter to the President of South Africa, to the government and asked for the money for the sex change.] . . . And he didn't send me a nasty letter back. I got a letter from [the] hospital stating that the President has given me a subsidy of 97,000 Rands and boy, I thought, oh gosh, this is lovely.[43]
>
> [When P. W. Botha visited me in the hospital] I liked it. I didn't actually like him, I didn't like him. But when you get to know somebody, you know what they are. I didn't actually like him, 'cause he was a crocodile here in South Africa. But I'm very grateful to him. Very grateful. He felt sorry for me. As I told him, I'm a coloured, and you know? How can I put it now? I was working as a hairdresser, but I was earning 800 [Rands] in a month.[44] I didn't have the money for the operation. [I wrote], "Can't you please help me with a sex change 'cause I need to have the operation?" If he has to see me face to face, he will realize, he will see it. And I didn't see him. Only when I had the second stage of my operation.

> But he saw me when I was in a lot of pain and misery. But while this happened, you know, I got talking: they gave me tranquilizers to come right, so that, you know, so that I can talk. And I tell you, when they heard the President was visiting Carmella at the hospital, ooh! They was scrubbing the floors and my room was beautiful, they redecorated it. And he wasn't even worried about what they did, you know, 'cause he just wanted to see, to meet me. And he met me. (Riekert 2000)

To contextualize this narrative, it is important to note some inconsistencies. Carmella referred to P. W. or Pik Botha alternately, different and unrelated South African politicians; P. W. Botha was Prime Minister (1978–1984) and President (1984–1989) of South Africa, while Pik Botha was Minister of Foreign Affairs under apartheid and then Minister of Energy Affairs (after 1994). Regardless of its accuracy, this component of Carmella's narrative is critical to her perception of herself because it shows how she sees herself as a beneficiary of the state, specifically receiving financial support in the context of immense racism. The failures of her surgeries discussed previously seem irrelevant to her perception of this situation. Whether or not either of the two Bothas visited Carmella in the hospital, her commentary illustrates her sense of the South African government's affirmation and validation of her sex reassignment. But in a broader context, given her particular medical history, it can also indicate apartheid support of experimentation and liminality, as detailed in Chapter 2.

Politicians were not the only well-known figures central to Carmella's narrative; she spoke extensively about her relationships to other famous people, such Felicia Mabuza-Suttle, a famous television talk-show host in South Africa at the time, sometimes referred to as the South African Oprah Winfrey. She recounted the details of the interest the host had in her life:

> This woman, Felicia [Mabuza-Suttle] . . . went to [the] hospital, and while everybody knows who she is, and she went to the [doctor who is] now in charge. And she asked the professor can she put a few sex changes onto the show. And the professor said, "Yes, who would you like?" and gave her all the files. And [because of my surname I am] . . . very far in the alphabetical order. And she picked my file up! She

was offering me 30,000 Rands[45] to tell my history on tv. And I said, "Okay, she must give me fifteen minutes and she must phone me back." I phoned my parents first. My parents come first in my life because they accept me for what I am. And they said I mustn't accept, even if she offered me a half a million, I mustn't do it. And I turned her down. And she was very heart sore. Very, very heart sore. I would have liked to have met her in person . . . and then maybe we could have just spoken to one another. Then she could have picked up . . . a little bit of knowledge what she doesn't know and how to speak to other people on the shows. But unfortunately, I didn't get the chance to meet her.

Now I'm not ready to expose my history to South Africa. . . . My sister works for [a famous women's magazine]. And she told them about me. And they don't do such stories. But because she worked for them, they were gonna do an article on me. For 40,000 Rand.[46] And I turned them down. I mean, I could make a lot of money, just talking or showing my body off. . . . I'm not scared or ashamed or embarrassed what the people are gonna think of me. It's just that I think . . . I've had my share of going out. I've had my full share. And a lot of people know me, and I want to come out of the limelight, man, I want to come out of the limelight. I don't want people to talk about me anymore. Because I know the discussions they had about me, I know. And of course it does embarrass me a little bit. It does. But I don't give two hoots about them. Because . . . I don't think that they love themselves more than what I love myself. (Riekert 2000)

The exploitation of transsexuals in the media is not unique to South Africa; tabloid print and visual media have objectified and sensationalized those in gender liminal positions all over the world and throughout South Africa's documented history (e.g., Gevisser 1994). However, Carmella's narrative highlights her agency and excitement about connecting with and learning from Felicia, her pride in being selected over other transsexuals from the files provided by the doctor, the potential financial windfall of appearing on the television show, and her negotiations with her family.

Over the next seven years, these feelings only seemed to intensify. By 2007 when I spoke to her again, Carmella was feeling very isolated because she didn't have a cell phone or Internet access. She told me that her surgeon had called her because he wanted her to be interviewed by Oprah Winfrey, by then well-known in South Africa not only for her television show but for her philanthropic project starting a girls' school outside of Johannesburg. Carmella told me she got dressed up and went to the hospital, and this surgeon introduced her to Oprah saying, "This is the best sex change that I ever did." Carmella said that Oprah replied, "You were a man? I can't even tell!" She recounted her conversation with Oprah at some length, telling me that Oprah wanted her to come to the United States to be interviewed but that she didn't want anyone in the United States to know that she was a transsexual. Carmella also talked again about speaking to Felicia Mabuza-Suttle and said she was offered one million Rands to tell her story on television.

These descriptions of Carmella's relationships to famous people in South African politics and in the media and her recounting of them signify the ways she chooses to represent herself. The objective truth of these statements is not of particular interest, nor can these accounts be proven or disproven. As Luise White et al. (2001) point out,

> [I]t is not the historical veracity of a statement or memory that gives the statement or memory its constitutive power. The thing that happened, and the ideas transmitted by its distorted reporting, silencing, or even and most especially invention, reveal a space of colonial and postcolonial conflict. (16)

White et al. suggest that rather than querying events for their accuracy, oral materials are a way to uncover important ideas and sites of conflict, rather than facts. Carmella's narratives—including descriptions of her relationships with famous people such as P. W. Botha, Felicia Mabu-za-Suttle, and Oprah Winfrey—form her commentary on the political economy of South African sex reassignment and illustrate her connections between South African history and gender transition on multiple levels. As Mbembe reminds us, varying perceptions and roles of the state form an indicator of the ways that "colonial terror constantly intertwines with colonially generated fantasies of wilderness and death and fictions to create the effect of the real" (2003: 25). The effect of the real is slippery and both resists and compels representation (Butler 1993), especially in the midst of colonial fantasies of experimental sex reassignment that can result in terror and medical violence.

Despite her idealism about politicians and media figures, Carmella is ultimately unhappy with her postoperative body—she believes that her breasts are too hard and her vaginal canal was closed, which has prevented her from having intercourse. She blames some of these physical difficulties on "black magic" inflicted on her by members of her community, a perspective suggested to her by a Nigerian doctor. This is yet another version of reality offered here that needs to be valued. As Adam Ashforth puts it, "No one can understand life in Africa without understanding witchcraft and the related aspects of spiritual insecurity" (2005: xii). According to Carmella, jealousy led members of her township to curse her with black magic, which she credits with her loss of status in the community and her medical problems. For her, black magic is part of the reason that she is both invisible and ostracized in her community and simultaneously targeted for harassment and objectification. It also explains what the doctors could not, causes for the extensive life-threatening pain and physical complications she has faced since undergoing sex reassignment procedures.

> When I had the [vaginorectal] fistula and they removed the [colostomy] bag I met an African doctor . . . from Nigeria. [He was very familiar with sex changes and he looked at my files.] . . . And then he says to me, "I don't think you should come back here. There is nothing wrong with you." So I says to him, "Are you blind? Can't you read there?" He said to me, where he comes from people are very dirty, they use black magic. . . . I was very, very sick that even the professor's surgeons, nobody knew what's wrong with me. I kept on going into the [operating] theater, sometimes three times a week for three months. I couldn't use the toilet, I couldn't eat, I couldn't pee, I couldn't walk. I just lay over there with drips in my thighs and in my arms and one here in my neck. So I asked [the Nigerian doctor], "You are the professor, what is wrong with me?" He . . . discuss[ed] it with the people that were working on me and then [came] back to me. . . .
>
> He told me I was done with black magic. And I couldn't believe it. I first talked to one of my sex change friends that is jealous of me. But when the truth came out, it wasn't either of them. It was people here in [this township], people that I know that did it to me. They did it to me . . . it makes me

blank, blank, it makes you blank. Nobody looks at you. Or if people do, they must mock you. You lose your positions that you've got. You lose things, you don't know how, but it's just happening. Bad things [are] happening. And that's what happened to me.

I prayed very hard, very hard. And I'm on those stairs [the church altar] and I know God is helping me. Because I'm not a person that will go to dirt on people and dirt onto other people [gossip], because I firmly believe it's through God that I went through this operation so successfully. If God didn't want me to be a woman, I would have never made it. It would have been a complication from the word go. Right? If you haven't got the belief in you. But I had it in me, that's why it went so [smoothly]. But the [black magic] people did to me, may God help them now. I always pray, you'll always see a Bible in my house, I always pray. [I belong to] . . . the Roman Catholic Church. They're not actually against sex changes because if you watch a lot of tv or video movies, there's a hell of a lot of gays in the Catholic society. . . . Nuns, priests, people that are still learning, they're all gay, the whole lot. But this priest told me the day I die, he can't bury me. . . . I can't receive communion. I don't receive communion. (Riekert 2000)

This narrative again unsettles medical explanations of reality related to Carmella's physical problems—this time through cultural and spiritual interpretations. Carmella's perceptions of black magic and her strong Catholicism are not contradictory; they form complementary parts of her own spiritual understandings of her transition and place in her community. Ashforth, living in a different but similar South African township context in 1990s Soweto, explains that for most South Africans, "witchcraft is a matter of action leading to real, material consequences for living human beings—action, moreover, that creates injustice. Life in a world with witches, then, raises problems that are not easily sequestered in the institutional categories—particularly those of politics, law, medicine, and religion—that are taken for granted in liberal democratic thought" (2005–12).

Ashforth also points to "jealousy" as the reason regularly cited for causing harm to another through witchcraft. He states that the nuances of jealousy in this context may be similar to elsewhere:

> But people talk of jealousy more in Soweto than in other places
> I have lived, and its consequences are taken very seriously.
> They use the term to refer to matters of love and material
> possessions, to all those signs of achievement and success that
> they also term "progress." In many ways jealousy is the flip
> side of the coin that is egalitarianism. (Ashforth 1996: 1200)[47]

In some ways, the Nigerian doctor's diagnosis of witchcraft links Car-mella's physical problems to her neighbors' jealousy of her successes and her superiority over others in the township where she lives. Car-mella's discussion of jealousy should also not be interpreted through an individualistic frame, or a pathologizing one that positions her as vain or narcissistic. In this sense, even the feeling and concept of jealousy itself is culturally and historically specific. Furthermore, for Carmella, the connections between Nigerian ideas of black magic and her own unique interpretation of Catholicism help her better understand and indeed heal the problems she faces. Commonly, medical problems that surpass the expertise of medical doctors tend to facilitate fears of witchcraft. These explanations also bridge the gap between social and physical ailments, as Carmella links her social problems in the township where she lives—the ostracism and taunting she faces—with her physical complications fol-lowing her sex reassignment procedures.

Transition itself also positions Carmella as particularly vulnerable to witchcraft. Studies as early as Evans-Pritchard's (1937) well-known work have discussed the importance of moments of passage in life to the powers of witchcraft. Ashforth suggests, "The moments of life and death, when persons are in the process of transition from one form of being to another, are particularly vulnerable to attack by malicious agents using invisible forces. Discretion is of the utmost importance at such times in order to secure the mother and child from hostile interference or to allow safe passage for the deceased into the afterlife" (2005: 73). No studies to date have applied these ideas to transitions under consideration in this chapter; most have focused on birth and death. But considering the importance of Carmella's transition, the physical and emotional vulnerability it created, and the problems she consequently faced, point to the relevance of under-standing African witchcraft in analyzing sexed transitions.

Narratives such as Carmella's offered differing accounts of "truth" and blurred lines between the visible and invisible world. Ashforth's description of what he deems "spiritual insecurity" in Soweto during his many years living there proves a particularly apt point of comparison:

> I could never have imagined the degree of fear which people endure on a daily basis regarding the risk of witchcraft and sorcery, the constant threat of evil forces being unleashed by jealous neighbors, relatives, and acquaintances to cause them harm. I was completely unaware of the scale of the commerce in magical remedies, occult divinations, and spiritual solace that takes place in Soweto, nor had I learnt in my university studies to note the political consequences of the ways people protect themselves from such evil, and of the ways in which they interpret signs in a world full of unseen powers. Such powers, I slowly came to realize, lie at the very heart of the relationships constituting politics in that place, from the household to the state. It was as if I had been inducted into a world both secret and commonplace, a world where uncertainty, ambiguity, mystery, ignorance, and secrecy lie at the heart of power; an everyday world in which questions of power were not what I had expected. Nor, from the perspective of Social Science, were they what they are supposed to be. My life in Soweto forced me to take seriously the commonplace dialogue between beings and forces seen and unseen. (Ashforth 1996: 1184–5)

The kinds of rethinking that Ashforth describes undermine the relationships between truth and fiction he assumed prior to his research. Further, they unsettle categories and provide new dimensions to analyses of power dynamics within communities and on a larger hegemonic scale. Carmella's narrative expresses the loss of boundaries and assumed reality as the necessarily violent processes that Mbembe predicts in necropolitical contexts. Her narrative pushes us to rethink rationality and truth as simple premises. Foucault, in the context of his views of truth as a societal regime produced by multiple strategies and constraints, asked, "How much does it cost the subject to be able to tell the truth about itself?" (1996); we might frame answers to that question to consider the costs and benefits of stealth and the creation and recreation of reality more specifically.

IX. Inferences: "Visions of the Freedom Not Yet Come"

This chapter drew on narratives to complicate gender boundaries, unsettle medical definitions of transition, and understand the junctures of race and gender liminality. Narrators' descriptions of their lives and theories complement and challenge contemporary theorizations of the state, of gender, of intersectionality, and of the role and importance of transition. Visions of the future, and both constraint and agency in determining this future, are a consistent theme to narrations.

The specificities of South African narrators' theorizations here can also be linked to Jasbir Puar's ideas of "queer necropolitics." Mbembe's necropolitics attend to "the increasingly anatomic, sensorial, and tactile subjugation of bodies" (Puar 2007: 35) that we find in gender liminal South Africans' narrations in this chapter. Puar applies this concept to queer contexts in her own work on terrorism and queer liberalism that she deems homonationalism, pointing to the importance of simultaneously moving "beyond identitarian and visibility frames of queerness" within these queer necropolitics (ibid.). Among other questions, Puar asks: "How do queers reproduce life, and . . . how is life weighted, disciplined into subjecthood, narrated into population, and fostered for living? Does this secularization of queers entail deferred death or dying for others, and if so, for whom?" (Puar 36). These are the kinds of questions that have been under consideration in this chapter through comparative evaluation of the racialization and politicization of South Africans' narrations.

This consideration speaks to the range of opportunities and challenges faced by narrators, primarily along racial and historical lines in the context of apartheid and transitional South African politics. Those in liminal spaces navigate space between life and death constantly, albeit in unconventional ways; for Puar, "it is precisely within the interstices of life and death that we find the differences between queer subjects who are being folded (back) into life and the racialized queernesses that emerge through the naming of populations, thus fueling the oscillation between the disciplining of subjects and the control of populations" (Puar 2007: 35). This codified naming and categorization is precisely what most gender liminal narrators in South Africa resist, at the same time they negotiate discipline and control.

The presumed simplicity of identity categories has also been unpacked in this and the preceding chapters, tracing the development of transsexuality as an etiological category of medical diagnosis and legal transition, and sometimes a self-chosen and redefined category. Foci on the distinctions between public and private treatment and funding for medical procedures form one critical consideration in narrations. Medical complications are also common, as some narrators describe experimental and coerced procedures, closely linked to narrators' geographic locations. Generation plays a critical role in these narrations of transition inseparable from South African politics and history. Narrators further problematize the tripartite of gender, race, and class and the assumptions that a simplification of Crenshaw's original intention in defining intersectionality means an equal weighting of all social categories simultaneously. The narrations shared here undermine reduction to these three oft-cited categorizations through their gender, race, and class liminality, as well as the ways that other factors (including location, ability, sexuality, age, and ethnicity) may be, at times, more important than this trinity.

All of these narrators, in some way, envision the future after their transition. My use of Mbembe's work connects their visions to notions of time and political history that we see throughout this chapter. He puts it this way:

> What connects terror, death, and freedom is an ecstatic notion of temporality and politics. The future, here, can be authentically anticipated, but not in the present. The present itself is but a moment of vision—vision of the freedom not yet come. (Mbembe 2003: 39)

The potential terror and death of transitions elucidated in this chapter come in many forms: there are grounded fears that cross into terror—fears of physical violence, of medical experimentation, of somatic and legal liminality, and of community ostracism that are directly linked to transition. There is fear of death ranging from unsuccessful medical sex reassignments that have resulted in lives lost as well as fear of suicidal deaths. Instead of focusing on these connected fears, the anticipated freedom following transition provides a focus, vision, and optimism for gender liminal narrators. This is a place where Mbembe's vision might be put into conversation with José Esteban Muñoz's ideas of "queer futurity." While Mbembe points to the negation of futurity, for Muñoz, queerness is an ideality; "we must dream and enact new and better pleasures, other ways of being in the world, and ultimately new worlds" (2009: 1). Mbembe's refusal to pathologize suicide and Muñoz's strategic optimism can be read together in these contexts. The visions of the future dreamed by those describing their transitions in this chapter point to the potential of new worlds—both in specific political contexts and in their own lives and bodies. This vision, while clouded by the realities of temporality and the aging and changing body, relies on a sense of hope, critical to Muñoz, as "the emotional modality that permits us to access futurity, par excellence" (98). This hope and the promise of revisioning understandings of transition central to the narratives contained here temper and even reframe the violence and challenges that South African narrators face.

Four

Stabane, Raced Intersexuality and Same-Sex Relationships in Soweto

How does one prove the "realness" of a body? What kinds of evidence create this reality? And how do such realities, in the sense that narrators and Mbembe articulate in the previous chapter, shift and change over time? This chapter examines cocreated visions of the realities and meanings of gendered bodies—how they look, function, and are experienced—through a consideration of the relationships between intersexuality and same-sex sexualities and their violent enforcement. Transitions articulate gender liminality differently in different communities. This chapter extends the concept of gender transition, detaching it from self-chosen identities (such as "transsexual") and redefining transition as a space moved in and out of in the context of state politics, community expectations, and sexual encounters. It also challenges the temporality of transition in a different way than the chapter before it, considering how bodies can be differently sexed at different moments based on self-representation, community perception, or sexual orientation.

Theorists of sexuality and the body have led us to the point where we can confidently assert that the relationships among sexuality, gender, and sex are not fixed and stable but are the contingent outcomes of located and historical practices. Not only are these ways of theorizing the constitution of these categories important, but such distinctions must also be regularly applied to interpretations and theorizations of bodies and relationships. As the previous chapters demonstrated, corporeal expectations of both sex and race have been violently policed and used to justify imperialism. Such concepts have concrete effects because they establish norms about possible ways to be—in a body or in a sexual relationship. And, beyond simple analogy, gendered norms create violent hierarchies of located and raced bodies.

However, despite the destabilization and contingencies of these interconnections and despite persuasive analyses to the contrary, assumptions that all people are strictly "in" female or male bodies have remained central in feminist scholarship. In an effort to unsettle the persistent salience of sex and draw attention to the bases of its disruptions, *Sex in Transition* asks, in different ways, what circumstances challenge norms of sex, how do sexed expectations create racially normative bodies, and how and by whom are such challenges negotiated? These questions motivate this chapter's examination of a particular articulation of intersexuality and homosexuality with race and location.[1]

The concept of *stabane* is used in Zulu vernacular to describe an intersexual person—that is, to be called *stabane* is to be seen as having both a penis and a vagina.[2] However, those identified and referred to as *stabane* rarely have intersexed bodies; instead, in contemporary Soweto and elsewhere there is a widespread assumption and cocreated understanding that those who identify as lesbian or gay or engage in particular same-sex practices may be intersexed. This radical situation of *stabane* exposes the complications and violence the concept evokes in the lives of those labeled as such, as well as highlighting the instabilities of sex—femaleness and maleness—in South Africa and more broadly. Feminist theorists have refigured notions of sex from a biological fact to iterative performativity, "a regularized and constrained repetition of norms" with sex as the effect of "a process of materialization that stabilizes over time to produce the effect of boundary, fixity, and surface that we call matter" (Butler 1993: 9, 95).[3]

But how do these theories travel in Edward Said's sense? Considerations of *stabane* extend notions developed in the previous chapters to show us how the "matter" of sex is slippery, as sex is constantly re-created and negotiated in ways that are co-produced with culture, race, and location. And *stabane* highlights the false distinction between sex and gender, suggesting the necessary explication of the gendered body. Heterosexuality and gender "normativity" rely on same-sex sexuality and, in this case, intersexuality, to maintain the perception of their naturalness.

How can we bring Africanists' perspectives to the fore while foregrounding theories like Butler's? This chapter suggests that accusations of *stabane* as intersexuality strengthen the boundaries of femaleness and maleness at the same time that they highlight their inconsistencies; that is to say, *stabane* and its application both reinforce gender binaries while undermining them by allowing for the conceptual and physical possibility of intersexuality. Chapter 3 articulates the parameters of gendered reality, considering the borders of gender as articulated by narrators and the state within the framework of transition and necropolitics. This chapter extends and builds on these ideas in its arguments about "realness" and sex in Sowetan contexts. *Stabane* poses an important challenge to the gendered body as an oppositional proposition. Corporeally gendered disruptions are not exceptional; instead *stabane* points to the inadequately examined regularities and their raced and located specificities of such disruptions. It demonstrates the temporality and relationality of sex.

This consideration of *stabane* rests particularly on the work of South Africanist scholars of sexuality discussed throughout *Sex in Transition* who have disrupted assumptions of heteronormativity. I am particularly engaged with the work of Africanists such as Sylvester Charles Rankhotha (2005), Hugh McLean and Linda Ngcobo (1994), and Donald Donham (1998), who theorize the complexities of *stabane* and analyze their work in conversation here. Again, the metaphor of transition in both its political and gendered applications is integral to this chapter. The work of Rankhotha, McLean and Ngcobo, and Donham, explicating *stabane* in contemporary, transitional, and apartheid time periods, respectively, gives us a sense of how this concept has been connected to South African histories. And *stabane* itself indicates transition and liminality, both in terms of sexuality and gender in particular times and places. It can point to forced transitions and the evidence expected of the body, as well as transitions in and out of "real" categories.

In this chapter, I build on the nuances of gender liminality in the previous chapter and extend them through a specific consideration of the composition of the gendered body and its racialized interpretation in South African history, but with a focus on the period of South Africa's transition to democracy. An historical analysis of South African scientific and medical discourses and practices under colonialism and apartheid reveals racialized understandings of intersexuality and the body; clearly, colonial racism marked black bodies as essentially different from white ones, while it simultaneously marked female as different from male. Not only did this mean that essentialist dualisms were produced and integrated into dominant ideologies, but "mixed" or "third" categories of race and gender—such as coloured and intersexual—that would become important windows into the politics and cracks of such systems were marked as abject but not abstract. Remaking gender and race under apartheid and during the transition happened through medical enforcement and social control; this chapter shows how categorized boundaries are created and enforced not only through remarkable moments but also in everyday interactions.

I. Contextualizing and Racing Intersexuality

In considering race and sex, it is useful to revisit the intricacies of scientific racism in South Africa through a gendered lens.[4] As established in previous chapters, colonialism was predicated on creating the real through discursive and material violent enforcement. Beginning in the mid-nineteenth century, methods of describing and anthropologizing the body, such as craniometry and serology, were used as scientific means to suggest that black people were less evolved than whites (Davison 1993; Dubow 1995). Such racist practices may have emphasized skulls and blood, but they also relied upon analyses of sex organs as a marker of difference. Thus, in the colonial taxonomy, so-called hermaphroditism, like blackness, was seen as "primitive." Ideas about which bodies were normal were codified through science, law, and popular culture.

Perhaps the best-known demonstration of this relationship is found in the life of South African Saartjie (Sarah) Baartman, the so-called "Hottentot Venus," who was exhibited from 1810 to 1815 in Paris and London with particular attention paid to her buttocks ("steatopygia") and genitals (the "Hottentot apron").[5] Justified by the tradition of comparative anatomy, her objectification served to educate colonial observers in London and Paris to locate the boundaries of race in African women's bodies and provide scientists with gendered justification for racist hierarchies.

However, as South African scholars Ciraj Rassool and Patricia Hayes (2002) point out, Baartman's case is just one example of a larger project of scientific and popular endeavors to race sex and render Africans' bodies "abnormal" and "primitive."[6] Rassool and Hayes's discussion of the relationship between sex and race in South Africa rests on the life story of a woman named /Khanako who lived in the southern Kalahari in the early twentieth century. Like Baartman, /Khanako was seen as representative of indigenous "Bushmen" people, and she was photographed and exhibited with great attention paid to and casts made of her genitals. Rassool and Hayes's careful historical work also highlights /Khanako's agency in making careful decisions about her participation in such projects and acting as a spokesperson for other ≠/Khomani (N/u) speakers. Although there are some clues as to /Khanako's perspectives, written records demonstrate the interplay of racism and the objectification of /Khanako and other women's bodies in ways that exceed their control, exemplified in a postcard made of /Khanako's image in which a swastika was imprinted on her buttocks. Rassool and Hayes speculate that this postcard was most likely produced by an anti-German photographer between 1939 and 1941 and represents an attempt to mock Nazi aspirations of controlling South West Africa; in the process, the photographer colonizes /Khanako's buttocks, perhaps seen as representative of the land and its people.[7]

These two examples demonstrate how both popular culture and science in colonialism relied on representations of Africans' genitals and buttocks to create racial difference. Alexander Butchart, in his analysis of colonialism and the creation of the medicalized African body, writes, "[a]s pathological anatomy opened [the African body] . . . to invent and compare its configuration to that of the European body, certain organs, bones and systems of the African body attracted more intensive scrutiny than others" (Butchart 1998: 156). In addition to discussions of attention given to the liver and the heart, Butchart suggests, "[a] means of explaining the 'strange difference' between European women and African women in 'the obstetrical sphere,' . . . the pelvis of the Bantu female would also become the epicenter of more intensive study" (ibid.).

With this attention, building on the work of Rassool and Hayes (2002), Patricia Davison (1993), Pippa Skotnes (1996), and others, I suggest interpretations of both Saartjie Baartman and /Khanako that emphasize not only their sexualization and objectification but also their implicit intersexuality.[8] It could be argued that colonial scientists and exhibitors saw Baartman and /Khanako's genitals and steatopygia not only as excessive but as also locating them between femaleness and maleness. Scientists who studied /Khanako and other African women interpreted their genitals as simultaneously infantile, overtly sexual, and excessively masculine. James Drury and Matthew Drennan's 1926 "The Pudendal Parts of the South African Bush Race," for instance, evaluates the genitals and buttocks of the "Bushmen" and "Hottentots," finding that "Cape Bushwomen's" labia

> hung down together from the inside and in front of the vulva as two fleshy fingerlike pendants. They could have very readily been mistaken for a single organ. (Drury and Drennan 1926: 113)

Drury and Drennan's implicit comparison of women's labia to penises is strengthened by the authors' later assertion that these labia are "erectile," even sharing anecdotal comments from a magistrate and others indicating that "the labia stand out rigid in the state of desire" (ibid.).

The genitals of male Africans were also represented as excessive in colonial taxonomies; the supposed size of African men's penises symbolized their masculine virility in ways that were threatening to European men (Dart 1937). Kopano Ratele provides an important analysis of the racism of "phalloplenthysmography" (2005: 147)—the pseudoscience of penis-measuring. As Ratele points out, the racial comparisons inherent to these kinds of efforts left white men coming up short and erotically positioned black men as animals. They also demonstrated the colonial quest for order and related fears of virility as uncontrollable and black men as sadistic sexual predators (Butchart 1998).

By contrast, the genitals and buttocks of African women like Baartman posited them as lascivious but also outside of the bounds of appropriate femininity as unsuccessful women. For Drury and Drennan, for instance, "[o]n asking a woman of these tribes [so-called Bushmen and Hottentots] to remove her loin cloth or apron, one could not, at first, detect any difference between her and an *ordinary woman* . . ." (113, emphasis added). African women's objectification offers insight into the ways that intersexuality has served to delineate racial difference.

By considering the implications of scientific and popular colonial objectifications of African women's bodies through the lens of intersexuality, we can better understand the parameters of sex, as the "racial difference of the African body . . . was located in its literal excess, a specifically sexual excess that placed [African women's bodies] outside the boundaries of a 'normal' female" (Somerville 1997: 41). In this sense, African women's bodies were interpreted as exhibiting a combination of female and male qualities conceptualized as less evolved than white women's bodies and forced into liminality, recalling Mbembe.

In addition to scientific and popular renderings, medical assertions of intersexuality have relatedly served as a means by which whites established their racial superiority. This can be linked to prior chapters' discussions of raced and classed qualifications for "true transsexualism." During colonialism "true" intersexuality was seen as an aberration by medical practitioners, but by the late 1940s it was considered a treatable medical condition in South Africa.[9] Developments in surgery and endocrinology, as well as doctors' quests to prove that science could accomplish anything, made natal sex ambiguity medically unacceptable, and doctors began to physically enforce sex boundaries by changing intersexed bodies surgically over the next thirty years.

Beginning in the 1970s, various South African medical professionals claimed that "the incidence of hermaphroditism in the South African Bantu is about 1 in 10,000 live births. The incidence in White South Africans is, however, infinitesimal" (Grace and Edge 1973: 1554). Most published studies reference a master's thesis from the University of Natal entitled "Intersex in Four South African Racial Groups in Durban" (1970) that provides little evidence as to the actual incidence of intersexuality among black South Africans.[10] This racial juxtaposition, and its longevity in South African medicine, extends earlier connections between racist science and intersexuality by using claims of the common occurrence of intersexed bodies among black South Africans to reinforce assertions of racial difference and white superiority.[11] Again, we can recall Mbembe's articulations of forced liminality in other necropolitical contexts, demonstrated here through raced intersexuality.

Under apartheid, the uniform collection of medical statistics concerning black people was discontinued, a practice physicians like Baldwin-Ragaven et al. feel was intended to facilitate the impression of control over disease among blacks and to mask the fact that withholding medical services was a means of population control (1999). Consequently, medical statistics, such as those that reflect on the prevalence of transsexuals in the previous chapters or that racialize intersexuality here, are extremely suspect. The effects of medical claims about intersexuality were part of apartheid discourses that pathologized black South Africans by exaggerating sexual difference.

Since the end of apartheid, a small group of intersex activists has publically addressed medical abuses, and in 2000 they formed Intersex South Africa (formerly the Intersex Society of South Africa).[12] However, intersexuality is still seen as marginal in most contexts, and in medical communities, intellectual assumptions about and reliance on spotty research based on suspect racial differentiation continues. Since the official end of apartheid, in some ways black and coloured South Africans have had more control over their bodies and representations. But although those at the borders of gender and sexuality are speaking, writing, and organizing with growing visibility, in this and the previous chapters we see ways in which those in liminally gendered positions have faced increased difficulties in recent years.[13]

II. *Stabane* in Soweto

> We grew up knowing that a *stabane* is someone with two
> things. And if you are a woman going out with another woman
> that means you've got two things. (Zindzi Mthembu 2000)

In Soweto and other South African rural and township areas, slippage
among bodies, sexual practices, and identification is notable among those
who are labeled as *stabane*. Within this framework, individuals discovered
to have homoerotic sexual desires may, in some locations, be stripped
and examined for evidence of physical intersexuality by members of their
communities. Reports of these forced examinations are widely known
but anecdotal,[14] and the etiology and history of indigenous ideas of
intersexuality in South Africa are undocumented, as are the histories of
the confluence of intersexuality and same-sex desire. Without significant written texts to provide clues as to the archaeology of *stabane* as
a concept, I investigate *stabane* as a discourse informed by colonialism,
apartheid, and indigenous African practices. An empirical consideration
allows us to unpack articulations of *stabane* not just regarding scientific
understandings of sex and gender but in terms of its materialization in
the lives of contemporary South Africans as well, where this closeness
and dependence make tensions over sex and sexuality dangerous.

Accusations of *stabane* conflate and blur global Northern distinctions between gender and sexuality and, like Chapter 3, demonstrate
contexts in which "truth" is less important than its impact. An excerpt
from an interview with Vera Vimbela, the founder of a lesbian and gay
support group in Umtata, explicitly illustrates the relationships among
accusations of intersexuality, community norms, and sexual attraction.

> I shocked the whole village in Standard 6, when a rumour
> spread that I had proposed to another girl. It's true, I was
> madly in love with this girl, and I would follow her everywhere,
> from the river to her home. My grandparents and I were
> called to the village chief and his council of elders. The whole
> village turned up to the hearing, to insult me and make nasty
> comments. They assumed that because I had proposed to the
> girl I must be a *stabane*, a hermaphrodite, with both male and
> female genitals. I was taken to a hut where a woman forced
> me to undress and examined me. When they discovered I was
> "normal" the chief ordered that I be lashed. I don't remember

how many *sjambok* [whip] lashings I received; all I remember is crying and screaming with pain as the whole village jeered at me. I was warned never to repeat such behavior again. (Vimbela 1994: 194)

In describing the pain and humiliation that she experienced, Vimbela shows us how, without somatic cause, she was punished for her desire. Physical examinations such as this have at least three effects. First, they iterate the assumption that same-sex sexuality must have a physical explanation; second, they facilitate the impression that sexual acts require both a penis and a vagina; and third, they serve as a public and violent reminder of the possible consequences of defying compulsory heterosexuality.

Accusations of *stabane* also facilitate misunderstandings about what it means to identify as lesbian and gay. Buyisile Mfazo explains the impact of this concept in her community.

The general understanding is that when you say, "I'm a lesbian," you're probably having a penis. When you say, "I'm a gay man," people kind of think maybe you have some pussy down there. So we still need to work on that to clarify that "I'm a lesbian, I'm a woman who sleeps with a woman." That's the simplest definition. So now our people [lesbians and gays] experience things like people undressing them because they want to really see, is there a penis or a cunt? (2000)

Mfazo explains some of the physical and conceptual consequences of *stabane* and points to a priority among Sowetan lesbians and gays— educating their communities about distinctions between same-sex desire and gendered bodies. Young Sowetan lesbians and gays such as Mfazo promote identity-based understandings of sexual orientation that they feel will depathologize and normalize their desires.[15]

In the meantime, pathologization runs deep. Sylvester Charles Rankhotha's (2005) analysis of black South African masculinities among gay men suggests that terms such as *isitabane*, which he defines as "a Zulu word for the question *Usistela banti?* or 'you are a sister who?'" and *sister-bhuti*, "sister-brother," indicate additional nuances. He suggests that the terms not only indicate gender liminality but also connote a "perversion of kinship ties" through their incestuous roots, a further reinforcement of the layers of the perceived perversion of *stabane* (2005: 170).

The effects of *stabane* and the perceptions it facilitates extend to lesbians' and gays' self-perceptions. Some South Africans who feel same-sex desire face difficulties coming out because they are not physically intersexual. Thandazo Alice Kunene, Sowetan lesbian and member of the Lesbian Forum of the Gay and Lesbian Organization of the Witwatersrand (GLOW), reflects:

> My family does not talk about homosexuality, and if they do, they talk about *stabane* and all that. So maybe I was scared to face up and say I like girls because they would call me *stabane*. I knew that logically I couldn't be *stabane* because that is a hermaphrodite, someone with both male and female genitals. Yet I was afraid of the stigma and sadness of *stabane*. I laugh when I think of how confused I was as a teenager; I even went to the dictionaries and looked up the word *stabane* and learned the word "hermaphrodite." It fascinated me and yet I couldn't understand why. (Kunene in Chan Sam 1994: 188)

Kunene elucidates the extent of her internalization of community ideals and resulting confusion about distinctions between designations of homo-sexuality and intersexuality. Her self-discoveries are marked by secrecy and shame, yet Kunene feels a simultaneous sense of identification with the idea of *stabane*. And her reliance on the dictionary shows the lived effects of words and their meanings.

Many Sowetans use the term *stabane* derogatorily—intending to insult, demean, and intimidate lesbians and gays. For example, Buyani Dhlomo, a young Sowetan lesbian, explains how she is taunted by the men in her community:

> You know, in Soweto there is . . . this word that they are calling us, *stabane*. . . . The word *stabane*, it's so painful when someone is calling you like that because *stabane* is someone who has two things, you know, like penis and vagina, you know. So, we [lesbians] are not like that. We are women. It's just that we are different because of feelings, you know. We feel like we can have another woman next to [us]. (Dholomo 2000)

According to Dhlomo, being a lesbian is based on her desires and emo-tions, not her genitalia, a misunderstanding that she finds hurtful as it prevents her from being recognized in the same way that she sees herself. She and other Sowetan lesbians are often verbally and physically abused by the young men in their communities, and, for Dhlomo, *stabane* is the most offensive term that they call her.

Dhlomo is not simply negatively affected by these taunts, but she reflects and theorizes about their origins and ways to counter them. In response to a question about why people label lesbians *stabane*, she replies:

> Because they see the way I act and the way I am. They are like, "A woman falling in love with another woman—[how can] that happen?" You know, sometimes they go straight to sex position, like, "What do they do when they're together?" . . . I mean it's a question that is always in their minds, that "I just wonder what they are doing in the bed." (ibid.)

Based on her experiences, Dhlomo theorizes that accusations of *stabane* are based in most Sowetans' reluctance to conceptualize sex as anything other than heterosexual intercourse. In Soweto, femininity and masculinity are often violently oppositional, and sexual behavior is usually focused on the pleasure men derive from it; when this heterosexist focus dominates, pleasurable sexual encounters that do not involve a penis are difficult to imagine. Here, the accessibility of such bodies to inquiry constitutes the body's existence.

III. *Stabane* and Sexual Interactions

The concept of *stabane* and assumptions of the necessity of coupling penises with vaginas complicate expectations in relationships. For instance, many Sowetan lesbians, most of whom label themselves as "butch," have relationships with women referred to and self-identified as "straight"—those who do not identify as lesbians and who eventually marry men.[16] The term "butch" here indicates Sowetans' self-chosen identity labels; Sowetan butches describe butchness as encompassing appearance, behavior, and attitude. Zindzi Mthembu explains:

> So I've always been this butch woman. I'm not saying I'm a man, I'm not a man—I'm a woman, attracted to another

woman. But I've got this mannish thing in me, that people out there, even if I don't have to tell them that I am a lesbian or I'm a girl or what, they always have this question of "You look like a boy." . . . So all my actions, the things that I do, the way I act, the way I dress identifies me as a lesbian, and as a butch lesbian. (2000)

For Zindzi, butchness is not only her way of claiming masculinity as falsely exclusive to males; it also provides visibility. Published accounts also prove relevant; Zozo, similarly, articulates her butchness: "It is because of my physical structure and this is why people sometimes are confused if I am a woman or a man. My attitude is manly; sometimes I tell myself that in my relationship, I am the man" (Kheswa 2005: 212). And for Stallion, "I'm not a man and I'm not a woman. I'm a lesbian and I'm butch" (Nkabinde 2005: 250).[17]

Butchness means different things in different times and places. Historically, Joan Nestle (1992), Carla Trujillo (1991), and Elizabeth Kennedy and Madeline Davis (1994), for instance, spoke to the specificities of butch/femme in working-class and communities of color in the United States, and, focused outside of the United States, authors such as Megan J. Sinnot (2004) and Ara Wilson (2004) address the differences between tom/dee relationships in Thailand and butch/femme relationships, for example. Evelyn Blackwood and Saskia E. Wieringa's work, *Same-Sex Relations and Female Desires: Transgender Practices Across the* Cultures (1999), is one of the most well-known documentations of female masculinities—including "butchness"—while critical of the universal application of such terminology cross-culturally. Within African Studies, the critical research and analyses of those involved in the African Women's Life Story Project into butch/femme in southern and eastern Africa, compiled in *Tommy Boys, Lesbian Men, and Ancestral Wives: Female Same-Sex Practices in Africa* (Morgan and Wieringa 2005), provides a critical archive of masculinities and butchness linked to transnational and especially locally-based practices in contemporary contexts. In short, the composition of "butchness" clearly has temporal and geographical elements.

In South Africa, although straight women who have relationships with butch lesbians and straight men who have sex with gay men might be considered bisexual in practice, I use the term "straight" here in accordance with how they self-identify and are identified in their communities.[18] In Soweto, as is true in many contexts, having sex with someone of the same sex does not necessarily change your sexual orientation; lesbian and gay identifications are usually based on gender identification as well as sexual practices. Thus, both feminine women who have sex with women and masculine men who have sex with men commonly identify as straight.

These ideas have corporeal effects. Because of understandings of *stabane*, many straight women expect penetration by a penis during sex with butch lesbians. Some butch lesbians prevent straight women from seeing or touching their bodies and facilitate the perception that they have penises by penetrating their partners in other ways. Phakamile Ndana explains how straight women's expectations inevitably lead to disappointment for both people in the relationship.

> There are slim chances for you to satisfy her. . . . Because in her mind when you start undressing, she'll be expecting a very long, big dick. . . . And then, maybe she'll come and [say], "You have breasts, as well." And one day she'll start a silly, confusing conversation, "Do you have a penis as well?" A woman can be shy like that. Thirdly, she'll maybe want you to just penetrate her, not to play around. You know this foreplay thing. And then if you don't do that as quick as she wants, she expects it, and then you are a failure in bed. (2000)

Straight women's expectations about butches' bodies often lead butches to describe feelings of inadequacy in relationships, which are typically quite short. Butch lesbians, while affirmed in their masculinity by these relationships, often reflect bitterly on the betrayal they feel when straight women eventually leave them for men. The serious social effects of these failed relationships are reflected anecdotally in high rates of suicide among Sowetan lesbians.

Sowetan gay men have similar difficulties in relationships and create new realities of sexed bodies. Like butch lesbians' relationships with straight women, many effeminate Sowetan gay men, sometimes referred to as *skesana*, have relationships with masculine men or *pantsula*. In a published interview, the late Linda Ngcobo reflected on his experiences:

> In the township they used to think I was a hermaphrodite. They think I was cursed in life to have two organs. Sometimes

> you can get a nice *pantsula* and you will find him looking for
> two organs. You don't give him the freedom to touch you.
> He might discover that your dick is bigger than his. Then he
> might be embarrassed, or even worse, he might be attracted
> to your dick. (McLean and Ngcobo 1994: 168)

Here, as in lesbians' experiences discussed previously, the presence or
absence of a penis in constituting sex is paramount. Ngcobo created an
impression of his body as female by hiding his penis. In another notable
instance, Ngcobo discussed how during a sexual encounter he used fish
to convince a *pantsula* that he has a vagina:

> Sardines is one of the tricks the *skesanas* use. We know
> that some *pantsulas* like dirty pussy, for those you must
> use pilchards. . . . So before I went to bed I smeared some
> pilchards around my anus and thighs. When he smelled the
> smell and found the hole, he was quite happy. We became
> lovers for some months after that. He never knew that I
> was a man and he never needed the smell again because he
> was satisfied after the first time. (McLean and Ngcobo 1994:
> 172–173)

Here I am interested in the ways Ngcobo represented his body to his
lover and the way this suggests certain assumptions about "femaleness."
In some ways, Ngcobo created the impression ("reality?") of a vagina
through the use of pilchards.

According to Hugh McLean and Ngcobo, the *pantsula* is an " 'accidental' homosexual . . . who sleeps with what he believes to be a hermaphrodite or with someone who pretends, and who he pretends, is
female" (1994: 166).[19] The complexities of these interactions are great.
In these examples, although Ngcobo presented himself as a woman, his
body was gendered male (that is, he had a penis and no breasts), and the
pantsula, who defines himself as straight, either assumed that Ngcobo is
a "hermaphrodite" or pretends or is convinced that Ngcobo is a woman.
In a similar instance documented elsewhere, a gay man involved in such
negotiations refers to straight men's interest in him as "a lady with a
dick" (Rankhotha 2005: 172).

Ngcobo's remarks also illustrate an important difference between
skesanas, or gay men, and butch lesbians. Whereas butches may facili-

tate the illusion that they are men, reconfiguring Mbembian "reality," ultimately many want to be accepted and known for who they are in relationships. Some butches also indicate a preference for equality in sexual encounters, a preference that may outweigh their butch identifications. Dhlomo explains:

> You know in sex—no, let me say, in making love— . . . if you are a lesbian, a real lesbian, everything has to be 50/50 in bed . . . because you can't just do and not be done. You have to be done. The main thing is that you are a woman and you really need that thing. . . . How can you get the satisfaction if you don't want to be done? (2000)

This preference for "50/50" in sexual relations, although not shared by all butches, sometimes leads butch lesbians to be honest with their straight partners about their sex and sexual orientation. By contrast, according to Ngcobo, a *skesana* fears that a *pantsula* might discover his penis or "even worse" be attracted to it (1994: 168). For Ngcobo, who seemed to both conceive of himself as outside of the female/male binary but also considered himself a gay man, attraction was dependent on both the illusion of difference and the repudiation of gay identification.

However, like lesbians, gay men also face the stigma of *stabane* when developing sexual relationships. The late activist Simon Nkoli offered the following advice:

> [If] you discover that you are absolutely attracted to men, you'd better keep quiet in the township. Don't ever tell somebody he's beautiful, because he will tell you, "Why are you saying this? Don't think I am a *sitabane*. Go away!" (Nkoli 1995: 22)

The perception and denigration of *stabane* prevents the formation of relationships. This can be alienating and dangerous for gay men in the process of coming out. Many lesbians and gay men are the targets of homophobic violence and murders, and this violence is exacerbated by (mis)understandings of *stabane*.[20]

The complexities of these interactions are great, and there are constant negotiations of the parameters of gender reliant on the presence or absence of a penis or vagina. *Pantsulas* and straight women offer contradictory responses concerning their expectations of lesbians' and gay men's bodies—at best, ambiguity and confusion are paramount—but *stabane* is also seen as providing an excuse, a rationale given by both straight women and men for homoerotic relationships. Partners in such relationships tend to establish common understandings of how each wants the relationship and their bodies to be perceived. But when these cocreated understandings of reality break down, the potential for violence, especially rape and murder exacerbated by conceptions of *stabane*, are substantial.

The concept of transition is unsettled and revisited in this chapter with a renewed focus on temporality. For those facing expectations of *stabane* in sexual relationships, their bodies may transition from female (lesbian) to male (through a co-constituted penis) and back again—or vice versa—within a short period of time and relationally. These conceptions of transition challenge the permanence of gender liminality and transition, as well as the necessity of chronological progress.

IV. Interpretations of *Stabane* in Varied Contexts

Although *stabane* tells us something about self-perceptions and relationships in the communities in which it is used, it also has implications for broader understandings of gender and sexuality in relation to transnational processes and race. This is particularly clear in the ways the term has been appropriated by those asserting commonality with it or defining themselves against it. The term *stabane* (or, less commonly, *sitabane*) has been romanticized and claimed by those in the global North invested in disrupting gender binaries.

For instance, a number of U.S.-based Web sites that contain long lists of words intended as alternate self-descriptors for "masculine women" or for "genderbending or genderbreaking people," include versions of the following:

> WOR SITABANE: (South African, from Sesotho lit. "having two sex organs, a penis and a vagina"): hermaphrodite, a feminine gay male. (Bowen 1999)

> Wor sitabane (South African for "possessing both a penis and a vagina"; also often used to refer to feminine gay men), (www. queerbychoice.com 2004)

Although intended to show possibilities for living outside of rigid ideas of "woman" and "man," such Web sites idealize and homogenize culturally specific concepts. *Sitabane* is not a term specific to feminine gay men, and "South African" is not a language. Interpretations like these erase the experiences of those labeled *sitabane* and *stabane* in South Africa and appropriate them in the service of creating global queer identities.

As we have seen, *stabane* is not a self-chosen identifier; in fact, its usage is derogatory and upsetting to black lesbian and gay South Africans. Were a "genderbending" person in the United States, for instance, to claim to be *sitabane*, most South Africans labeled as such against their wishes would be offended. On *Behind the Mask*, a Web site focused on "lesbian and gay affairs in Africa," South African visitors to the site comment on their preferred terms of identification:

> Call me anything just not *isitabane*, it is very offensive.

> They call us names . . . [including] *Isitabane*. . . . These names just marginalize gay people as if they are not part of the society.

> I prefer to be called by my name Tsakane, I do not want to be called names such as he/she, *stabane*, *moffie* and more. (Mabena 2005)

These comments clarify South Africans' perspectives on this issue. Attempts to create transnational queer solidarities illustrate that *stabane* cannot be mapped perfectly onto Northern ideas of "transgendered" or "gender queer" identifications; it is a distinctly South African juncture of sex, sexuality, and culture that must not be decontextualized. Neville Hoad, writing more broadly about same-sex sexualities but with critiques of paternalistic assistance often offered to those in the global South puts it this way: "The Euro-American politics of moral outrage that only lingers long enough to establish shared 'gayness' and does not care enough to learn about the worldings of those it purports to help does little more than shore up the moral credentials of the outraged" (Hoad 2007: xiii). Attempts to discover commonalities often result in cultural insensitivity.

Interpretations of *stabane* range to the opposite extreme, as well. Some white South Africans I interviewed cited the concept of *stabane* as illustrative of black South Africans' ignorance and remarked incredulously on what they perceived as a regressive conflation, the inability to separate bodies from same-sex desire. White lesbians and gays frequently attempt to position black township ideas about gender (for example, butch/femme) as "primitive." As Ian Barnard (2001) points out, whiteness and gayness are often mutually reinforcing means by which gay white South Africans emphasize their normality. Many white South Africans are invested in promoting themselves on a global level as cosmopolitan; indeed, soliciting global gay tourism relies intrinsically on the construction of an exotic and inferior "other." White lesbian and gay South Africans' comments and the imperialism of Northern appropriations of queer identifications, such as *stabane*, reflect the interplay of location and race in the materialization of intersexed categories.

Although *stabane* is not transgressive or primitive, neither is it anomalous. As addressed earlier, this concept can be related to historical precedents locating racial and sexual differences in intersexuality under the auspices of scientific racism in South Africa under colonialism and apartheid. Relatedly, same-sex sexual desire has been perceived as having physical and psychological causes in many times and places. Historian George Chauncey (1994), for example, traces medical literature that located homosexuality as a form of somatic or psychic hermaphroditism in various historical periods, and this pattern is found in varied South African medical literature, as well. The pathologization of same-sex desire continues through genetic, biological, and psychological research that attempts to relate same-sex desire to, for instance, the "masculinization" of lesbians' inner ears (McFadden and Pasanen 1998) or to predict it by the fact that "homosexual" women and men have higher rates of non-right-handedness for which possible explanations posed include cerebral laterality and prenatal exposure to sex hormones, maternal immunological reactions to the fetus, and developmental instability (Lalumiere et al. 2000). The implications of these studies are that same-sex desire, if understood, can be cured. Further, as Siobhan Somerville points out:

> [R]ecent scientific research into sexuality has reflected a determination to discover a biological key to the origins of homosexuality. Highly publicized new studies have purported to locate indicators of sexual orientation in discrete niches of the human body, ranging from a particular gene on the X chromosome to the hypothalamus, a structure of the brain. In an updated and more technologically sophisticated form, comparative anatomy is being granted a peculiar cultural authority in the study of sexuality. (1997: 48)

Somerville's analysis highlights the long-term influences of racist colonial comparative anatomy in contemporary medical ideologies and the psychoanalytic model of sexuality. Thus, we see both the pervasiveness of ideologies that pathologize (and create) difference, as well as the common ways that difference is embodied. These examples of the relationships of same-sex desire and racial/locational identifications as part of historical and contemporary comparative anatomy are two more instances whereby genitals have been the means for establishing difference and hierarchies.

In addition to interpretations that celebrate or condemn *stabane* as a concept, a few studies attempt to articulate its relation to same-sex sexuality more directly. McLean and Ngcobo's explanation credits accusations of *stabane* with an attempt to ground same-sex sexuality in the corporeality of the body:

> A belief in hermaphroditism is a logical consequence of the polarity of gender in broader society. . . . This "deformity" safely locates homosexuality within the catalogue of clinical disorders, thereby making it at least explicable and, to a degree, acceptable. That someone would choose to be a homosexual simply because he likes other men is unacceptable to most people because it questions the most basic patriarchal assumptions about men and women. (1994: 169)

According to McLean and Ngcobo, somatically based attraction, reliant on physical possibilities for penile/vaginal intercourse instead of affection or desire, poses a lesser threat to gender binaries than psychologically based homosexuality. Basing his article on McLean and Ngcobo's work, anthropologist Donald Donham similarly argues: "In sum, [people in] black townships during the apartheid era found it easier to understand gender-deviant boys as girls or as a biologically mixed third sex" (1998: 9). According to these theorists, sexual attraction can be more easily understood and accepted when it has a physical basis and pardoned when same-sex sexuality can be explained through an intersexed body.[21]

Intersexuality is not only regarded as the explanation for the feminine behavior of *skesanas* McLean and Ngcobo interview, but shared understandings of *stabane* are also commonly considered plausible justification for why and how some men sleep with them (1994: 168). Intersexuality, construed as *stabane*, can be seen not only as an explanation for homosexuality and as a cause for gender liminal behavior but also as a rationale for "straight" men sleeping with other cisgender males. Dhlomo suggests that *stabane* is a logically constructed rationale that attempts to explain how lesbians and gays could have sex (when defined as heterosexual intercourse) by conceptually providing a penis and a vagina.

V. Implications of *Stabane*

As McLean and Ngcobo, Donham, and Dhlomo all argue, *stabane* serves as a means of explaining same-sex attraction. But I do not believe that it avoids questioning patriarchal assumptions or simply enforces gender polarity as McLean and Ngcobo claim; in short, *stabane* is not an easy way to avoid the complications of sexuality and gendered bodies. Indeed, it returns us in a different way to the Mbembian concepts of "reality" addressed through examination of gendered transitions and necropolitics discussed in Chapter 3.

The examination of *stabane* here points us to a contradictory analysis. The perceived abnormality of intersexed bodies reinforces the solidity and normality of female/male sexed bodies. However, the recognition of intersexed bodies as inhabiting a category outside of female or male simultaneously challenges gender binaries. Scholars and activists who have explored *stabane*'s meanings suggest that sexual desire can be more easily understood and accepted when it has a physical and essentialist basis. But *stabane* does not simply enforce gender polarity; it both reinforces gender binaries while it undermines them by allowing for and even encouraging the conceptual and physical possibility of intersexuality. Liminality, thus, cannot occur outside of dichotomies but simultaneously splinters them.

Butler's "heterosexual matrix" describes the dominant Northern paradigm by which the relationships among sex, gender, and sexuality are understood. How does this concept travel, in Said's sense? She uses the phrase:

> [T]o characterize a hegemonic discursive/epistemic model of gender intelligibility that assumes that for bodies to cohere and make sense there must be a stable sex expressed through a stable gender (masculine expresses male, feminine

expresses female) that is oppositionally and hierarchically, defined through the compulsory practice of heterosexuality. (1990: 151n6)

Within a heterosexual matrix what constitutes a "man" includes sex (maleness), gender (masculinity), and heterosexuality (attraction to women); conversely, "women" are female, feminine, and attracted to men. In South Africa and elsewhere, gender orientation supersedes choice of sexual partner, and congruency between gender and sex (feminine females and masculine males) becomes the prerequisite for heterosexuality. Put differently, in order to be a lesbian a woman may be masculine; feminine women who have sex with other women may be straight. This disruption is not limited to South Africa, of course, as the conditions of lesbian and gay identifications vary widely. For example, Don Kulick's ethnography of *travestis* in Brazil (who, born male, change their names, femininize their appearances through clothing and hairstyles, and modify their bodies using female hormones and injections of industrial silicone) points out that *travestis* may not "fall outside" of the gender binary but instead "suggest that the binary is configured in radically different ways than we are conditioned to expect" (1998: 230).[22]

Sex in Transition, and this analysis of *stabane*, contributes to a substantive and temporal rethinking of the constitution of sex. What it means to be female or male, and the ways that these identifications intersect with sexual desire, is constantly reified in the relationships described here through the presence or absence of a penis and the ability to penetrate and be penetrated. Sex is thus revealed as a cocreated set of practices that are constantly renegotiated, and the negotiation of the composition of the body unsettles the consistency of gendered categories. This reiterates and refigures an important question central to Transgender Studies, "What does it mean to suggest that the body itself comes into being through desire? This [question] underscores the degree to which our embodiment is intersubjective, a project that can only be undertaken in the presence and with the recognition of other embodied beings" (Salamon 2010: 46). In this case, Ngcobo was, for a time, female, in relationships when believed to be so, and in shifting his sex constantly uncovered the expectations and ruptures in what sex means. Similarly, Ndana's penis, in sexual encounters with straight women, constitutes her as male in particular times and places.

In Soweto, then, *stabane* highlights contestations over the authenticity or reality of gendered bodies and its effects for those at the junctures of gender and sexuality. It points to the temporality of bodies and sex. Its application reinforces the idea that sexuality can be equated to heterosexual intercourse and that same-sex desire cannot exist without gendered implications. Physical examinations violently impose community norms and reinscribe the idea that non-normative bodies must be examined and scrutinized. But by allowing for the conceptual presence of intersexuality, *stabane* also poses a potential challenge to the male/female binary as an "either/or" proposition.

VI. Why This Matters

> On the evening of 2 June 2008, five close friends, four proudly identifying as Drag Queens, went for an outing in Yeoville [Johannesburg]. Confronted by homophobic hate speech, they challenged three men to stop calling them "izitabane." Shortly after 9 pm, one of the three men, sitting in a white Corolla, handed a gun to the other friend to "shoot izitabane." Twenty five year old Desmond Dube, fondly known as Daisy, died on the scene. ("Shoot the Drag Queen! . . . and Daisy Died," Queer Life Web site)

Most importantly, these theoretical contestations play out on the bodies of those who are caught at the fractures of the heterosexual matrix. Since the end of apartheid, the promise of the Constitution for creating a framework for gender and sex equality and protection from discrimination on the basis of sexual orientation has not been actualized for those commonly labeled as *stabane*. But perhaps our focus on material realities unsettles the suggestion that this promise was ever a realistic possibility. Despite speculations that the advent of Northern lesbian and gay identifications in black township communities would bring the end of *stabane* and similar designators, evidence exists to the contrary. Donham suggests that the end of apartheid brought about a shift that meant, "Now, *both* partners in a same-sex relationship were potentially classified as the same (male) gender—and as 'gay'" (1998: 11, emphasis in original). However, in the townships these two seemingly contradictory ways of thinking—lesbian/gay identifications and *stabane*—exist in simultaneity with differing degrees of difficulty and acceptance, regardless of laws and constitutions.

The challenges posed by *stabane* point to the fear and violence that can be inspired by gender liminality and transitions. They also expose the implicit temporality of gender that poses a challenge to those who fear its borders. Rejecting linear movement from one gender to another recalls Victor Turner's notions of "permanent liminality" addressed in the Introduction. For Turner, speaking of religion among the Ndembe, "a set of transitional qualities 'betwixt and between' defined states of culture and society has become itself an institutionalized state . . . Transition has here become a permanent condition" (1969: 107). Turner creates an important analytic space with his analysis. But in this context, perhaps the confrontation of same-sex sexualities is less an opportunity for permanent liminality than a creation of new ways of thinking about sexed bodies outside of the presence or absence of a penis.

The transition to democracy has proven to be a difficult time for gender liminal South Africans. Upheaval has been characteristic of a period that was initially marked by hope. Multiple and emerging studies confirm that homophobic and gender-based murders are increasing in South Africa and that masculinity is being contested through public sexual violence (Swarr 2012; Mkhike et al. 2010; Reid and Dirsuweit, 2002; Morrell 2001). South Africa currently has one of the highest rates of rape in the world, and rapes and murders of lesbians and gays have increased dramatically since the end of apartheid. Much of this rape is punitive and rape of lesbians has been labeled by activists as "corrective," intended to correct homosexuality and enforce heterosexism. In this context, sex is being unsettled by the disruption of sexed bodies, and violence is articulating its borders.[23]

Transitional concerns related to *stabane* illustrate temporally-based and constantly shifting ideas of gender and sexuality in South Africa. Activists and scholars responding to violence like that faced by Daisy Dube are redefining what it means to be a woman or a man, as well as claiming sexual identification as separate from conceptions of *stabane*. For the time being, the contradictions of *stabane* will continue to reflect the inconsistencies and juxtapositions of extreme repression and freedom in South Africa. And within this framework, sex will continue to be unsettled and renegotiated through everyday practices both individually and through growing social movements.

Five

Performing Hierarchies and Kinky Politics

Drag in South Africa's Transition

In January of 1997, three years after the official end of apartheid, the Top of the Times/J&B Met contest for "Most Elegant Couple" in South Africa progressed as usual with twenty-three couples competing for prizes including money and exclusive fashion creations. However, the *Cape Argus* newspaper reported,

> The judges blushed at first—then laughed it off, when they heard they had chosen two men as the . . . Most Elegant Couple 1997 award. "That's one of those things that happen these days," one judge said in accepting they had crowned a man at the weekend as one of the best dressed women at the horse racing event of the year in the Cape. (Vongai and Templeton 1997)

In this moment, one of the most well-known white drag performers in Cape Town, Keiron Legacy (Martin van Staden), became the most elegant woman at the horse racing event of the year.

By contrast, in 2004 the Johannesburg Metro Police announced that they would arrest drag queens at the annual Gay and Lesbian Pride March because their wigs and makeup (construed as a "disguise") would contravene the Regulation of Gatherings Act, an apartheid legal intervention. During a huge public outcry, it was determined that the source of the opposition to drag queens came from a conservative white gay and lesbian group, the Gay and Lesbian Alliance. The group's founder and leader, David Baxter, told reporters,

> We are totally against such parades because they are unlawful and harm the image of lesbians and gays. They incorrectly

207

>   imply that being gay and lesbian means jumping into the
>   clothing of the opposite sex. (Baxter in Khangale 2004)

Even after police changed their position and agreed not to arrest drag
queens, Gay and Lesbian Alliance members "vowed to make sure drag
queens in particular are arrested for contravening the apartheid-era act"
(Khangale 2004).[1]

What do these two public discussions about drag during the transitional period tell us about the materialization of sex and gender with race
and class? Gendered transitions and liminality have been foci of conflicts
regarding drag during South Africa's transition and have occurred along
raced and classed lines in public and private fora. Gender binaries and
the realities of gendered bodies discussed in the previous chapters have
been consistently reinforced and challenged through drag performances.
Drag performances took complex forms in apartheid and transitional
South Africa. They could be intentionally humorous, intensely glamorous,
or shockingly political. Drag was performed widely in elite white clubs,
gay township shebeens,[2] and as part of mainstream community celebra-
tions. During the upheaval of the transition South Africans continued to
live in a society fraught with enormous social, economic, and political
contradictions, as well as gendered hierarchies among those in liminal
positions. Understanding the disparities inherent in this transitional context is fundamental to understanding South African drag and allows us
to see not only how social differences influence drag, but also how drag
cyclically produces race and gender.

The transitional period has been marked by its promise and its
disappointments. Within the context of continuing and shifting inconsistencies, race and class have retained critical salience. One methodological
note complements the examples given above and indicates some additional hierarchical tensions found in the transitional period. In 1997, Sam
Bullington and I attended a concert at a gay-owned establishment fre-
quented by white South Africans. Though the two of us arrived alone, we
were invited to sit at a table with a recent acquaintance, Vita Edmunds,
the self-defined upper-class white transsexual narrator notable in Chapter 3. Soon afterward, a so-called coloured male drag performer dressed
in full feminine drag who we also knew, Chris Daniels, sat at the table
behind us, and began to speak loudly. Chris's arrival was considered
disruptive by Vita, and consequently, an altercation between Vita and
Chris broke out. Each disputed the other's claims to successful "passing."

Vita accused Chris of being a "common drag queen," and threats soon escalated to physical violence.

This incident and the two others described thus far in this chapter demonstrate how the terrain of gender liminality is not smooth or consistent. Hierarchies are constantly reinforced in concert with contests over permanent and temporary gendered transitions. The temporality of transition is paramount again in a different way as we see the hierarchies related to race, class, and the extent/time of transition reflected here. Legacy undermined the attention to her transition in the competition, Baxter revealed his discomfort with even temporary transition in the parade, and Edmunds and Daniels articulated interpersonal fears and anger about transition. Within these considerations, raced and classed distinctions are drawn among drag queens, drag artists, and transsexuals, among others. This chapter refocuses on the temporality of transitions in and out of gender through drag expressions, as well as the ways that such transitions constitute the parameters of raced genders as part of transitional South Africa and the context of social pressures on the nation. It analyzes how these transitions are not merely moments of difference but reflect the composition (and junctures) of race and gender.

In this chapter, I consider historical and contemporary drag in the urban centers and surrounding townships of Cape Town, Johannesburg, and Pretoria from the perspectives of its participants, focusing on the period of 1996–2000 as a different way to articulate the potential and restrictions of biopolitics and necropolitics in the transition. Here, I argue that urban and township drag produce whiteness and femininity through raced and classed juxtapositions. I contend that hierarchies and relational oppositions are critical components of contests over gender liminality. I also suggest that the temporality, motion, and instability of "drag" in South Africa detaches this concept from common representations of it in academia. Like those that precede it, this chapter unsettles assumptions about categorical definitions to complicate the co-constitution of race and gender beyond simple binaries and chronologies.

I. Conceptual Frameworks of Drag

Gender and race, although inherently unstable as social categories, are politically important; however, although these categories may seem to be fixed, their meanings are never fully consistent and must constantly be

reworked and negotiated. My use of articulation as a method for conceptualizing these intersections works alongside and extends Butler's notion
of *performativity* described previously through South African drag queens'
notions of *performing*.[3] Performativity allows us to avoid oversimplifying
race and gender as natural or as socially constructed by giving space
for staged "performances" while moving beyond this definition. Iterative
performativity, "a regularized and constrained repetition of norms" (Butler
1993: 95), creates the effect of matter or fixity over time. In looking at
performances here, and differentiating them from performativity, it is
important to note that performativity is not simply about individuals'
practices and will; through citationality—the invocation of norms and
conventions—norms are reiterated that "preceed, constrain, and exceed
the performer" (1993: 234). This chapter reiterates, in different ways,
how race and gender are imitations for which there are no originals that
we constantly create and recreate through our everyday practices and
repeated performances.[4] But how does performativity travel, in Said's
sense? For South African drag queens, performing has an additional
meaning—to act outrageously and dramatically in a public setting to
gain attention. Among black and coloured drag queens this concept challenges assumptions of the necessity of paid audiences for performance.

Contemporary theorists and activists have increasingly imagined
ways to avoid the false separation of race, gender, class, and sexuality to conceptualize junctions referred to as, for example, kinky politics (Ratele 2004), intersectionality (Crenshaw 1993), or borderlands
(Anzaldúa 1987).[5] Central to this chapter are the ways that scholars
ranging from queer theorist José Esteban Muñoz (1999) to geographer
Andrew Tucker (2009) have reconceptualized the relationships among
queerness and race in contemporary drag in very different contexts. Analyses of gender performances that pose race and class as supplementary
are always incomplete, as there is no generic "woman" or "man" represented in drag—there are only particular raced, classed, and historically-
and geographically-specific genders. It is impossible to generalize about
drag without exploring the various ways that each drag performance
temporally articulates the simultaneity of social categories. This chapter
attends to contradictory articulations of race and gender in communities
that are at once similar and vastly different by drawing on the work of
multiple scholars who dwell in these complexities, centrally considering
individuals who both adopt and confront dominant ideals by combining
contingent social identifications.

In this chapter we see how both gender and race operated oppositionally under apartheid and continue to do so in the political transition. In South African Studies, many scholars have demonstrated how heterosexuality is conceptualized at the borders of queerness (e.g., Epprecht 2008), femininity and femaleness operate in opposition to masculinity and maleness (e.g., Elder 2003), and blackness functions as the negative antithesis of whiteness (e.g., Ratele 2004). None of these categories are monolithic, and close examination reveals that though commonly conceived of as binaries, they mask multiple human differences and similarities, as well as hierarchies like those described in the opening vignettes to this chapter. Such categories function socially as oppositions, and examining their relationality reveals how drag is produced by and produces a range of social factors. This chapter is the final means through which I delineate this oppositional simultaneity by analyzing the constitution of whiteness/blackness, masculinity/femininity, and heterosexuality/homosexuality and the cracks within and transitions among these dichotomies. Through drag, these cracks often occur in what Andrew Tucker refers to as "queer visibilities," his way of conceptualizing heteronormativity and its contradictory effects on "passing."

Finally, as described in the Introduction to *Sex in Transition*, Kopano Ratele uses a notion of kinky politics to explain the uniquely South African workings of race, gender, and sexuality articulated here, as well as their motion and instability. The refetishization of race he identifies can inform our comparative analysis of drag. Kinky politics elucidates the ways that "difference is held *permanently constant* and becomes an explanation of what the idea of race or the policy of racial domination generates in the first place" (Ratele 2004: 143, emphasis added). In this analysis of the production of race through transitional drag in South Africa, we see how the politics of apartheid embed race into South African politics of gender liminality and sexuality. If we take seriously Elizabeth Freeman's recommendation to reconsider drag as an historical signifier and temporal phenomenon (2010) and read it against Ratele's kinky politics as indicative of the temporality/constancy of difference, Ratele's concept also extends our considerations of the temporality of transition. In this chapter, we see that the transitions of drag performances can be moments or lifetimes long. Kinky politics allows us to explore the movement and volatility of drag, further pushing the boundaries of gender liminality.

II. Racing South African Drag

Although since the end of apartheid South Africans have created a nation based on rhetoric of freedom from oppression, the legacy of apartheid and the racial and economic division enforced remain central components of South Africans' daily lives. These divisions became poignantly apparent during the transition in contrast to hopes of equality. Gay men of all races in South Africa drag, but drag venues, forms, and opportunities have been decidedly shaped by race and class. During the transition, performances by white gay men occurred in urban bars and clubs in front of largely white audiences. As part of troupes, they did not receive tips but were paid by venue owners and were usually part of choreographed shows. While some urban troupes included black and coloured performers, most black and coloured gay men dragged primarily in pageants and competitions for titles, and unlike most white gay men, many also dragged publicly and expressed gender liminality in their daily lives.

Differences among drag performances are rooted in racialized genders. Distinguishing among sex (male or female bodies), gender (masculinity and femininity), and sexuality (sexual practices and orientation), while running the risk of codifying problematic concepts, is useful to understanding South African drag. During the transition, white South African drag performers linked sex and gender in particular ways. Generally, most white gay men who identify as gay are conventionally masculine. Indeed, while "playing" with gender in social settings is accepted, gender liminality is looked down upon within many white gay communities. White South African drag paralleled this construction. For most South African urban whites, drag was an aestheticized and spatialized form of self-expression confined to bars and clubs—it was a bounded spectacle authorized by its content, not an everyday practice, performed by "drag artists."

During the transition, the period under consideration in this chapter, drag was an integral part of urban white gay communities but did not necessarily reflect the gender of the person who was dragging. Within urban white communities, same-sex desire usually indicates homosexual identification; males who have sex with other males label themselves "gay." In coloured and black township communities, masculine males who have sex with feminine males are often considered "straight." Here, as discussed in Chapter 4, gay identifications are defined not only through same-sex desire, but through feminine gender. Thus, in some township contexts, gender is disconnected from sex and instead coupled with sexuality, sometimes problematically seen as insufficiently modern or illiberal in the global North.

In recent years—as I discuss in the previous chapter regarding conceptions of *stabane*, and as scholars including Tucker (2009), Leap (2002, 2005), Barnard (2001), Reid (1999), and Donham (1998) have pointed out—white and Northern definitions of "gayness" have influenced how urban black and coloured gay men identify themselves in South Africa. Among gay men who are upwardly mobile and move out of the townships, increasing numbers of black and coloured masculine men who have same-sex relationships identify as gay. However, according to approximately 150 interviews with those who dragged, which I conducted during my research in the Western Cape and Gauteng during South Africa's transitional period, these men were the exception to township ideologies. In fact, feminine gay men in the townships fell outside of the man/woman binary into their own categories as, for example, *moffies* (in coloured townships) as *skesana* and *stabane* (in some black townships), among other designators.[6] In South Africa's transitional townships, drag performances were not simply personal expressions; they had implications for relationships and for community visibility. Dragging in pageants and to attract masculine males' attention was also an important way that township "drag queens" affirmed their feminine genders. In these contexts, drag performances produced particular raced and classed genders.

These two means of conceptualizing the relationships among sex, gender, and sexuality and the ways they were articulated during South Africa's transition cannot be separated from the national and regional histories of South Africa. South Africa is well-known for its brutal and contradictory system of legalized racial segregation. But this chapter shows again, in a different way, how like most colonial states, the apartheid regime legitimated itself by affirming gender rigidity or gender subversion in various times, spaces, and among different individuals. Slippages in the treatment of gender and sexuality affected the specific ways drag developed in South Africa.

Historically, drag has not simply been an aesthetic practice for black and coloured gay men, but a component of everyday life. Here, drag and trans* are not discrete categories. Under apartheid, in the coloured townships outside of Cape Town, *moffies* dragged in their jobs, often as hairdressers or caterers, and in sport on gay netball teams in women's leagues (Gevisser 1994).[7] The annual Coon Carnival has also been a site for drag performances since at least the 1930s. Although the name of the carnival itself is contentious to outsiders,[8] it is the highlight of the year for many working-class coloured people of the former District 6 and the coloured townships surrounding Cape Town.[9] While historically women have not participated, femininity is represented in the Coon Carnival through *moffies* in drag, an integral part of the festivities since their inception. Although some historians have claimed that *moffies* reversed or subverted gender and sexuality through their roles in the Coon Carnival in ways similar to carnivals in other parts of the world (Jeppie 1990; Chetty 1994), the *moffie* might alternately be seen as a crucial part of understanding gender unique to coloured township culture. Drag could be seen as both outside of gendered categories or exemplary of them.

As apartheid undermined the Coon Carnival by restricting the movement of those designated as coloured through the 1966 Group Areas Act and similar legislation, troupe captains increasingly viewed *moffies* as symbolic of autonomy and freedom (Martin 1999: 16). However, despite Coons' defiant attitudes, apartheid officials simultaneously manipulated the Coon Carnival to demonstrate the supposed inferiority and primitiveness of coloured people (Martin 1999: 127, 130). Further, the Coon Carnival reminds us that it is important not to homogenize racial communities but to attend to differences within them, often based in class or location. The perceived outrageousness of Coons, who sing and dance in satin costumes with painted faces, and *moffies* was a source of entertainment for whites, and often a source of embarrassment for aspirant coloureds (Jeppie 1990). As Andrew Tucker points out, "[t]he cross-dressing queer at the Coon Carnival in effect went to air what the middle class saw as the 'dirty laundry' of the colored community" (Tucker 2009: 79), a perspective similar to the position of the Gay and Lesbian Alliance mentioned at the start of this chapter and their disavowal of drag. Some middle-class coloured men who chose not to drag link this decision to their aspirations toward a more favorable economic position (Tucker 2009: 90). Tucker explains gendered and raced shame and hierarchies expressed: "For many middle-class queer colored men, cross-dressers were and continue to be a sign of both pre-modern sexual identities associated with cross-dressing and racially inferior social identities" (Tucker 2009: 28). And the same intraracial tension expressed among coloured South Africans regarding the Coon Carnival was replicated in print media, such as the pages of tabloid magazines *Drum* and *Golden City Post* (Chetty 1994).[10]

The entrenchment of specifically "coloured culture" through events like the Coon Carnival also increasingly distinguished coloured from black South Africans and reinforced apartheid rhetoric.[11] Drag among black South Africans was also accepted by apartheid officials when it served the interests of the state and capital. Historically, same-sex relationships between black men have been common, though not always indicating "homosexual" identifications. For instance, as described previously, gendered "mine marriages" among black men who lived in the compounds of South Africa's diamond and gold mines were a site of relationships beneficial to "husbands" as a source of sex, companionship, and domestic service. "Wives" participated, according to Philemon, a Tsonga miner, "for the sake of security, for the acquisition of property, and for the fun itself" (Wa Sibuye 1993: 62). Under colonialism and apartheid, these same-sex relationships included both a feminine and masculine partner and were accepted among miners. The feminine partner, who was usually younger, would often drag to attract partners, receive protection and privileges, or establish roles in the relationship (Moodie 1989; Murray and Roscoe 1998; Epprecht 2004). Philemon explains the processes through which "wives" would drag:

> They would get pieces of clothing material and they would sew it together so that it appeared like real breasts. They would then attach it to other strings that made it look almost like a bra so that at the evening dancing "she" would dance with the husband. It would appear very real. . . . That was a norm on the mines. (Wa Sibuye 1993: 54)

Miners' same-sex relationships were common enough to be acknowledged, and indeed encouraged, by the state. Black same-sex sexuality and, by association, drag, was supported by the apartheid government and capitalist interests to the extent that it facilitated control over black labor.

Among most white gay South Africans, historically dragging was less common as an everyday practice but instead provided a form of entertainment and gendered self-expression. As with black and coloured drag, the South African state attempted to use white drag to reinforce its own power. For example, drag performer and author Matthew Krouse describes how drag shows in the South African Defense Force during 1984 were sometimes organized by the military, which paid for costumes and wigs. Shows were attended by "a couple of thousand soldiers" (Krouse 1994: 216) and intentionally posited male homosexuality as abnormal by linking it to femininity. Drag performers were objectified by the largely straight audience; in Krouse's words, "[d]uring the performance there was an enormous din of catcalls and mocking masturbatory behavior" (ibid.). These shows reinforced the inferiority of drag artists and the masculinity of their straight audiences in ways he found degrading. Krouse writes, "I can only imagine that the upper echelons of the camp must have felt a tremendous sense of strength on those nights [of drag performances]" (218), as they reaffirmed the state's control over white drag's subversive potential. This extends and complicates accounts of medical experimentation and aversion therapy in the SADF affecting gays and lesbians during the same period detailed in Chapter 2.

Apartheid was a system fraught with raced and gendered contradictions, however, and the South African state also struggled to restrict drag and enforce heterosexuality through laws and police violence (Retief 1994). Although access to private spaces and the privileges of whiteness often protected upper-class white homosexuals from detection, policing of white males' gender and sexuality was especially vigorous under apartheid (Elder 1995). Uncontrolled threats posed by drag and homosexuality were often not accepted under Afrikaner nationalism, since supposedly normative gender and sexuality were essential components of the racial categories of apartheid—such as white Afrikaner masculinity. As mentioned previously, beginning in the 1960s Parliament enacted a variety of laws intended to suppress certain kinds of gendered behaviors, including the Prohibition of Disguises Act 16 of 1969 that criminalized males dressing in feminine clothing, and like those categorized as "transsexuals," gay men of all races who dressed in drag or "cross dressed" were increasingly charged with "masquerading as women in public" (Gevisser 1994; Cameron 1994).[12]

Drag, as a public marker of disruption to apartheid conceptions of sex, gender, and sexuality, was outlawed when outside of the control of the state. Not surprisingly, drag still flourished in spaces like private parties and gay bars, but it was driven further underground by restrictive legislation. During the transition, drag was still characterized by contradiction, but white drag continued to be largely confined to urban gay bars and clubs, while black and coloured men continued to incorporate drag into their daily lives.

In more recent years, as Andrew Tucker's research (conducted from 2003–2007 in the Cape Town area) describes, transnational influences became increasingly salient. Tucker points out that drag as manifested in Capetonian contexts undermines the global/local divide.

> There are no simple binaries of "the West and the rest" but instead communities with remarkably different histories that partly depend on each other today to exist at all. These groups can draw inspiration from "the West" *and* from communities in Africa (or South East Asia). (2009: 5, emphasis in original)

Straightforward transnational movement of concepts and priorities from one location to another, particularly impositions from the global North, are not multifaceted enough to explain the complications of drag, within transitions and more broadly. What's more, as Tucker emphasizes, interactions among and within communities, especially along racial and class lines, *within* South Africa are paramount to understanding drag.

III. Urban Whiteness and Drag

In June 1997, Lili Slapstilli, a member of the drag troupe Mince, was favorably reviewed in the mainstream *Cape Times* newspaper as "one of the most convincing impersonations of Tina Turner on the market" (Devenish 1997). Slapstilli gyrated to a live recording of "Proud Mary," her mime perfectly matching the difficult lyrics, and, as the tempo of the song increased, she danced flawlessly like Turner in concert.[13] Slapstilli herself did not try to perfectly mimic the women she impersonates, stating, "At 6'2" there's no way I'll look exactly like them" (Slapstilli 1997).[14] However, the fissure in Slapstilli's authenticity came not through her height, her skill, or her costume, but through her race. Lili Slapstilli defines herself as white. How is it that she could be considered to be an "authentic" Tina Turner in the hyperracialized context of Cape Town?

Despite outward differences between Slapstilli and Tina Turner, during the transition white South African performers enjoyed great autonomy and were perceived as authentic in their performances of blackness. In some ways, Slapstilli's authenticity as Tina Turner might be interpreted as undermining racial expectations and revealing the fiction of race; Slapstilli's clothes, miming, and mannerisms superseded phenotypical differences in the eyes of the audience and reviewers. Impersonations of Eartha Kitt, Millie Jackson, Jennifer Holiday, and Aretha Franklin by white drag performers in South Africa's urban clubs and bars garnered similar praise. However, this was not because whiteness was unimportant to white audiences; instead, drag produced whiteness as an unmarked category, a space in which to create characters, while black and coloured performers were largely restricted to impersonating women of color.

Whiteness in South Africa is anxiously policed, and the new post-apartheid "non-racialism" of the transition threatened this category that still retains enormous social and economic privileges. In South Africa, as elsewhere, whiteness hinges on an implicit comparison to "non-white," a catch-all category that elides difference. Race is an unstable complex of social meanings, "a concept which signifies and symbolizes social conflicts and interests by referring to different types of human bodies" (Omi and Winant 1994: 55) and takes on meanings and significance that far surpass these origins. Here, we return to Deborah Posel's analyses of race addressed in the Introduction as self-evident, hierarchical, and tautological. Posel shows us how race in South Africa has combined science and culture, sometimes reliant on violent policing and at other times intentionally flexible and elastic (2001a, 2001b). In this chapter, considerations of drag demonstrate that embodiment of race is similar and linked to the embodiment of gender and sex; both are without significant biological basis but articulated through repeated nebulous practices, beliefs, and behaviors. Like gender, its cracks and fissures illustrate the insubstantial and falsely essential nature of race itself.

Like in apartheid, transitional conceptions of race continued to be predicated on the hierarchical conception that whiteness is not only fundamentally different from, but also superior to blackness. Although South African racial articulations include categories beyond black and white—and coloureds were singled out by the apartheid government at various points in history for political purposes—the apartheid regime nevertheless conceived of itself in terms of whiteness, with other categories implicitly falling into the inferior "non-white."[15] Drag is one means through which the instability of whiteness was fixed and its meaning produced under apartheid.

During the transition, drag among South African urban, white, gay men was socially accepted if confined to commercial performances, and gay male drag was found in almost all gay-owned bars and clubs in Cape Town and Pretoria. Some urban drag was glamorous, while other performances were comedic, ironic, and/or parodic. These comic performances were one site for producing racial juxtapositions, explored through interviews with Warren Coetzee (1997).[16] Coetzee was not only the owner of a prominent urban gay bar; he hired performers, choreographed all of their numbers, and even chose costumes, stage names, and musical pieces. When describing how he envisioned performers' roles, Coetzee stated that coloured and black performers must be comic in order to entertain a white crowd. Most white South Africans, accustomed to interacting with "non-whites" in inferior positions, found it difficult to take black and coloured people seriously. In urban drag, white audiences were comfortable seeing black and coloured performers in the roles of entertaining and silly clowns.

However, it is important to note that Coetzee's comment was undermined by the sensual acts of the few coloured and black members of his drag troupe. Their performances reinforced the contradictions of racial production, as well as the autonomy of the artists themselves. Black sexuality was simultaneously desired while repressed as immoral. Given white fears of black sexuality, glamorous and sensual performances by black and coloured artists were potentially both titillating and disruptive to largely white audiences.

White drag artists also differentiated among and complicated forms of whiteness.[17] And within this context, our considerations of white drag need to be contextualized in terms of spatial and class-based divisions among white South Africans. One such performer is Sonja Koekemoer, who during 1996–1997 performed as a *boeremeisie*, literally "farm girl," a favorite trope of Afrikaans drag artists in Cape Town and Pretoria. The *boeremeisie* embodied on stage is an example of intentionally unsuccessful femininity. Koekemoer as a *boeremeisie* wore bright, clashing colors and garish styles as well as giant plastic flowers or bright ribbons in her teased blonde wig. She moved awkwardly and used props such as bedroom slippers to emphasize her working-class aesthetic. Koekemoer's drag included silver and blue makeup with sparkles that contrasted with her intentionally hairy arms, and she mimed in Afrikaans to traditional songs in an overdramatized, tragic style. Her performances were immensely popular; she was featured in mainstream newspapers in Cape Town and was the headline performer in a national drag tour.[18] Koekemoer's parody articulated contemporary ambivalence about the place of Afrikaner culture following the end of apartheid in South Africa. She also performed a class-based and negative judgment of a *boeremeisie*. During the political transition upwardly mobile Afrikaners, in particular, often distanced themselves from their working-class, rural roots. However, Koekemoer's popularity also reflected white gay men's increasing rejection of traditional South African values in favor of an emerging global urban gay sensibility.

Racial tension is produced by drag performances. For instance, when Brenda Gordon, a coloured drag artist, performed comically to the "Click Song (Qongqothwane)" by Miriam Makeba, the legendary black South African singer, she reinforced white/black dichotomies and stereotypes of black inferiority. Gordon's traditional African costume and padded buttocks, exaggerated miming and ridicule of the clicks of the Xhosa language, and overtly sexualized dancing during which she intentionally opened her legs to expose her crotch left her largely white audiences laughing hysterically.[19] Further, Gordon's performances occurred in the context of Cape Town's coloured/black racial tensions, exacerbated by political maneuvers such as divisive labor policies and voting privileges afforded to coloured people under apartheid. As a coloured performer stereotyping a black woman, her performances affirmed a coloured/black distinction and her superiority in South Africa's racial hierarchy as a coloured person. But Gordon's tenuous position and her strict supervision by a white bar owner in this urban context also allowed for the reinscription of an overarching white/black binary.

Drag is an important way that gay whiteness is constituted in South Africa. Most urban white gay men value masculine genders, and many middle-class white gays have been concerned with respectability and social approval. As Tucker describes, some of these men were able to afford a lifestyle and culture based around a particular kind of identity to which they were quite attached (2009: 62–3). This kind of elitist identity politics rests on racial and gendered divisions. Despite the acceptance of drag in commercial performances, those in gender liminal spaces have often been rejected and ridiculed. For example, in interviews with Jan Oosthuizen (2000), a white middle-class gay man from an urban area, he expressed his belief that drag artists were "backwards," temporally and morally, especially those who cross-dress in their daily lives. He saw them as "unresolved" psychologically and claimed that in the gay and lesbian movement, "we don't want court jesters." Jan's comments were commonplace among white gays during the transition, and in South Africa such sentiments have distinctly racial overtones. Jan was disdainful of white drag artists' performances, but he was far more condemnatory of black and coloured drag queens with liminal gender expressions. Through statements like this, Oosthuizen implicitly established his own gender and race as superior and normative, while drag queens were represented as inferior and inappropriate.

Warren Coetzee's comments are similarly instructive for understanding how drag produced racial differences in urban contexts during the transition. In interviews, he distinguished between "drag artists" who performed in his bar and "common drag queens" (Coetzee 1997). This comparison, widely held beyond Coetzee and articulated in Simone's narrative in the Introduction and in the vignettes beginning this chapter, was loaded with racial and classed meanings and simultaneously constituted hierarchies of race, gender, and sexuality. White drag was considered superior in this context because it was a conscious performance, an upper-class theatric art form (hence the preferred term, "drag artist") that was economically valuable. Such drag may not explicitly challenge the unity of sex and gender, as most performers did not express gender liminality in their daily identifications—they dragged as actors, as characters in a play. Black and coloured queens' drag, in comparison, formed part of their gender expressions.

Gendered differences among forms of drag allowed some white gay men to make judgments that subtly (or overtly) established their racial and economic superiority. Despite their strong racialized generalizations, these opinions contrast sharply with the gender liminality expressed by white South Africans who live in transitional spaces found in the narratives in the previous chapter. William Leap's attention to spatialized racial divisions (2005) reminds us of this integral part of the divisions and hierarchies we find in such drag that have continued into the transitional period. Leatt and Hendricks give one explanation of this pattern, suggesting that "[e]lements of gay life that were part of the Western Cape cultural milieu such as drag queens or transvestites, are increasingly marginalized or commercialised" (2005: 304). This commercialization, and the broader role of global capital, is another integral piece of the constitution of raced genders produced by drag.

IV. Femininity and Township Drag

Township histories are also inseparable from gender, race, and sexuality. As Leap demonstrates in his work on gay men and lesbians and their racialized locations in Cape Town during the time period under consideration,

> legacies of colonial rule and apartheid were still shaping the everyday experience of South African lesbians and gay men, and . . . certain components of those experiences, in turn, were reproducing and re-validating those legacies even as Cape Town entered the post-apartheid moment. (Leap 2005: 260)

This historical context, as well as urban-township social and spatial relationships, proves integral to expressions of township drag. An examination of coloured and black South African township drag enables the binary construction of masculinity and femininity as opposites while simultaneously positioning "gayness" as its own gender category. Three components of this articulation in black and coloured township contexts—drag pageants, drag and sexual relationships, and the vulnerabilities drag facilitates—prove instructive, as do these categories' overlap and intersections.

Black and coloured drag illustrate the performativity of femininity, as José Esteban Muñoz puts it, "simultaneously identifying with and rejecting a dominant form" (1999:108). During South Africa's political transition, drag pageants followed formats of beauty contests, featuring various dress competitions and interviews.[20] And, as historian Peter Alegi notes, citing a 1993 *New York Times* article on the advent of democracy, "[f]ew countries take beauty pageants as seriously as South Africa" (2008: 31). In township drag pageants, participants sometimes paid to enter contests, instead of being paid, as in urban drag, although pageant winners could obtain cash and prizes. They entered competitions as individuals and answered questions based on their opinions, not as "artists" in a show. For example, the Miss GLOW 1999 pageant final (Gays and Lesbians of the Witwatersrand) was held in a gay *shebeen* (township bar) in Sebokeng and attended by gay and straight members of black township communities surrounding Johannesburg. The seven finalists showcased both casual and evening dress, and each answered two questions on topics ranging from trivia about local gay icons to their own positions on coming out. Participants in Miss GLOW 1999 did not wear prosthetic breasts or wigs to make their bodies appear female but performed femininity through their dress, makeup, and movements.

In the eyes of the audience and judges, contestants embodied a particular form of black and coloured township drag in which juxtapositions between male bodies and feminine performances are the norm.[21] Drag produces gender (femininity) as more important than sex (maleness). In his discussion of the 1993 funeral of the late Linda Ngcobo, the well-known black gay activist whose theorizations of *stabane* are discussed at length in Chapter 4, journalist Mark Gevisser describes some mourners wearing "that peculiar androgyny of township drag borne of scant resources and much imagination, nodding at gender—inversion with no more than a frilly shirt, a pair of garish earrings, a touch of rouge, a pair of low-heeled pumps, a third-hand wig" (1994: 14–15). In township contexts, the raced and classed ways that femininity is articulated, while perhaps slight or even indecipherable to outsiders, provide signposts to indicate the parameters of the performance to those who can read them. This form of drag produces gender, as Gevisser says, of "scant resources and much imagination." "Imagination" is the key word here. It suggests how drag queens and their audiences (per)form something not entirely real—gender—and in so doing make it real by sustaining the collective notion of gender fixity.

Drag queens prepare their physical bodies with their audiences, especially masculine men, in mind. To prepare for the Miss Gay Universe 2000 pageant, Nasreen Isaacs, a self-defined coloured drag queen from an urban township, described having her eyebrows shaped and growing her hair, in addition to making her own gowns. She superseded her male body and performed a femininity considered beautiful and prizeworthy. Isaacs believed that "passing" as a woman and being sexually desired while dragging were the greatest affirmations of her femininity. Dragging also provided her with family and community approval. She described how a neighbor told her mother about seeing Nasreen in a pageant: "You know, I saw your son, but I didn't know he was your son. I thought he was a real lady." Her success as a woman despite her male body led her family to be, in Isaacs' words, "not proud, but supportive" (Isaacs 2000). While Isaacs fit within acceptable notions of gender linked to sexuality in her township community as a *moffie*, she would rather be a woman and said that she dragged to "pass." Township drag produced contradictions within sex and gender. Township gender and sexuality interplay was inclusive of *moffies*, *stabane*, and *skesanas*, but the man/woman binary retained significant social relevance. Drag queens like Nasreen Isaacs articulated gender and sex in ways that could fit the category of "woman," while they concurrently cracked its coherence.

Drag was also an important component of black and coloured drag queens' sexual relationships, and, during the transition, these relationships actively produced gay femininity through contrast with its supposed opposite, the "real man." Relationships with masculine and especially straight men reinscribed gender binaries and thus affirmed drag queens' genders. The more masculine their partner, the more feminine they were by association.[22] Many drag queens, like Rashid Abrahams and Kenneth Blouws, went solely to "straight" bars because they were only interested in "real men" as partners (2000). Their sexual relationships, frequently characterized in townships as "butch/femme," rendered same-sex sexuality culturally intelligible within their communities. They made it easy for families to understand gay relationships because they paired masculinity and femininity. Further, what communities described as butch/femme roles, articulated publicly through drag, clarified sexual expectations in relationships. Isaacs explained this popular sentiment among both coloured and black drag queens:

> [Butch/femme relationships are] very, very, very good . . . you'll see it's like boyfriend and girlfriend, the one is passive and the one and active. You know which one is the girl and which one is the boy. . . . I enjoy being a drag queen, because I know who I am. (Isaacs 2000)

Sexual roles and drag were important in constituting credible femininity and masculinity for both partners, and the binaries within which they function secured these identifications. Gender and sex were not simply produced through drag performance but, as discussed in Chapter 4, through sexual encounters in which partners articulated their respective genders as masculine and feminine.

Although embodying a convincing femininity was a goal of most drag queens during this time period, and the ability to "pass" was idealized, "passing" also leads to one of the ambiguities of township drag. That drag queens were also *moffies*, *skesana*, or *stabane*—categories neither entirely man or woman—made individuals constantly unsure whether or not they were being read as women, which can be quite dangerous. Brandy Roeland, a coloured drag queen who was extremely successful in drag competitions in the Western Cape in her youth who was discussed in depth in Chapter 2, described the difficulties she faced:

> I was even shot for my beauty. I didn't know that this man was stalking me all the time in Mitchell's Plain at a night club, and eventually the man found out I was gay and the man shot me right here in this spot. (Roeland 2000)

The dangers that Roeland and other drag queens confront represent contradictory acceptance and hatred of gays in township contexts, some of which can be differentiated along racial and class lines. One member of this community, Farid Mohammed, suggested that "people adore gays" in the coloured townships, but this approval was not uniform (Moham-med 2000). Mohammed explained that, despite the tolerance of many community members, drag queens were targeted by *tsotsis* or *skollies* (gangsters) to be terrorized and even murdered. He stated, "That's why I basically had to stop [dragging] because it just got too dangerous for me. . . . I just felt that this was not the life for me" (ibid.). During and since the transition documented incidents of such violence have increased dramatically as the murder of Daisy Dube and others indicate. In the wake of social upheavals and frustrations following the end of apartheid, South African gays and lesbians are subjected to extreme levels of sexual violence, and drag queens are frequently raped and murdered.[23]

The correlations among drag, sexual relationships, and violence also highlight differences between black and coloured drag concerning visibility and safety. Andrew Tucker's (2009) work on "queer visibilities" in Cape Town—his means to examine the opportunities, manifestations, and detrimental effects of sexual and gendered visibility—complicates assumptions of uniformity among racial groups. Tucker's research finds that in coloured township communities feminine gender expressions among gay men facilitate sexual relationships with straight men. How-ever, during this time period (2003–2007):

> The very "obviousness" of many queer men in drag, tied to the femininity inherent in such acts, permits these men a degree of social safety when socialising with the "straight" community. The long association coloured communities have with cross-dressing as a normalised expression of queer sexuality further limits the possibility of violence against them. (Tucker 2009: 86)

Tucker connects this safety with the commonality of same-sex sexuality among black and especially coloured men in prison and gangs in Cape Town and to the importance of (feminine) gender to "gay" identifications. His research illustrates, for example, the extent to which gang members' normalized sexual relationships with other men in no way threaten their heterosexuality; such relationships are, instead, integral parts of some heterosexual prison and gang cultures. In these contexts, it might be argued that the visibility of coloured drag has allowed those who drag a measure of safety through both their relationships with straight men and through their legitimacy in coloured township communities (Tucker 2009: 95–7). Furthermore, some of Tucker's interviews suggest that in the cramped living quarters of the townships, it is difficult to maintain privacy about one's sexuality. Rather than hide oneself: "A solution to this problem is to become overtly visible" (Tucker 2009: 90) through drag, thus intentionally occupying a legitimatized and safer gender category.

By contrast, black men in Tucker's study—specifically Xhosa men in Cape Town's townships—have faced significant violence when dragging. Tucker contends that in these communities, Xhosa traditions place a great emphasis on overt masculinity and notes that primarily younger men drag, which is sometimes viewed as a temporal "developmental stage" (2009: 123). He speculates on manifold reasons for less common incidence of drag in black gay male communities, the most significant being that drag puts gay men at high risk for severe violence:

> While there is evidence that points towards homophobic violence in all three of the racially-defined communities under study, it is among black African township men that this violence is most forceful. Cases of gang rape against black African queer men, along with premeditated beatings and frequent verbal attacks were often documented during the research period. Sporadic and seemingly unprovoked incidents were also noted, including spitting and throwing of objects such as house bricks at queer men walking along streets. (Tucker 2009: 128–9)

While in some coloured communities during the recent period of the transition, drag may provide community acceptance and even safety, Tucker's work suggests that the opposite may be true in some black communities where gender transgressions are met with extreme violence. These trends are not uniform, but this difference between coloured and black communities provides an important point of comparison to the earlier period of transition documented in my own research.

In short, drag clearly has contradictory draws and consequences for black and coloured South Africans. Those who drag produce femininity through pageants and relationships, but their gender expressions can facilitate safety and visibility and/or put them at risk for violent attacks. Notwithstanding the differences between and within racial groups, and the complexities and changes emerging within the transition, drag continues to position gay identifications as a particular gendered category. In public contests, sexual relationships, and violent exchanges in varied

township contexts, gender performance proves equally if not more important than sexual orientation and relationships.

V. "Performing" in South Africa:
Extending Performativity with Kinky Politics

What does it mean to perform in South Africa? Drag offers one means of
examining the performativity of gender and race; however, the specificity
of drag performances simply calls attention to this quality. Performativity
is a means of creating social categories through regularized and repetitive
citations of norms evident in everyday practices and, for our purposes,
a traveling theory. As Judith Butler explained in an interview with South
African scholar Vasu Reddy, "The first point to understand about performativity is what it is not: identities are *not* made in a single moment
in time. They are made again and again" (Butler in Reddy with Butler
2004: 116, emphasis in original).

The differences between performativity and performance have been
explored at length elsewhere (e.g., Lloyd 1999). Conflating the two is
one of the most common misreadings of Judith Butler's work, which
she addresses herself in *Bodies that Matter: On the Discursive Limits of Sex*
(1993). But in township gay vernacular, "performance" has another meaning. To perform is to try to gain attention, to act outrageously, to cause
a scene. For example, a *moffie* who gets drunk and acts flamboyantly in
a public place may be accused of "performing," the essence of which is
drama.[24] When a drag queen "performs" in this sense, she is making a
scene and acting without a stage.

In most published scholarship, gay male drag is defined as that
which is performed on stage in front of an audience cognizant of performers' male bodies. The role of "audience," and especially the collusion between audience and performer in maintaining or disrupting the
linkage between sex and gender, has long been critical to scholarship
analyzing drag (e.g., Baker 1994). But how is the notion of audience
constituted? In most scholarly considerations, classed assumptions that
drag necessitates a paying audience have often been overlooked. These
junctures are critical to understanding South African drag. Few black
and coloured South Africans have the opportunity to drag on stage, as
white performers do. The audiences to drag queens' performances are
community members, and township streets are their stages, thus calling

into question the racial, class, national, and cultural assumptions that underlie perceptions of audience.

South African township drag also blurs and races distinctions between "drag" and "cross-dressing," as well as transsexual, transvestite, and homosexual categorizations. South African drag is not simply about maintaining illusion or crossing from one gender to another; such assumptions reinscribe gendered binaries and simple chronologies. Transitional township drag relied on daily self-expressions, as drag queens articulated gender in ways that matched, instead of contradicting, their self-defined genders. The differentiation between drag queens and drag artists by white gay men and the hierarchies articulated in the vignettes that began this chapter, which often had roots in racism and pathologization, were called into question by the specifics of township drag. Just as South African drag illuminated the performativity of race and gender, it also raised new possibilities about what kinds of performances can be redefined as drag.

In South Africa's transition, urban drag artists were paid to drag in gay bars and clubs, while township drag queens performed for community recognition in competitions and their daily lives. As both of these forms of drag emerged from the racially segregated history of South African apartheid, they reflect the gender and sexuality linkages salient in their communities. But drag does not merely mirror the societies in which it occurs. Rather, drag produces race and gender through artists and queens' performances and "resists the binary of identification and counteridentification" (Muñoz 1999: 97). Freeman suggests that performativity has a temporal component as a referent to the past, asking: what is "the time of queer performativity?" (2010: 62). If we consider performativity with historical and temporal attention to South African performance, we can begin to attend to the conceptual potential of township drag.

Returning to the idea of "kinky politics" provides a point of conclusion here. As Kopano Ratele describes it, kinky politics denotes the juncture of race with a "sexual warping of identity politics" (2004: 142). The interplay of sexual relationships and identity politics are clear in the ways that gender expressions articulate "gayness" along racial lines. The assumption of necessary linkages between sexual desire and sexual identification is undermined by black and coloured township drag and relationships. Kinky politics thus provides a way to extend the ideas Butler articulates about performativity and performance with attention to Freeman's cautions about time within a specific South African context.

For both Ratele and Butler, the perversion and connections between race and sexuality are exposed in their inconsistencies. By analyzing some of the complexities of South African transitional drag, we can ascertain not only the motivations of individual performers, we can also begin to better understand the contexts in which their performances and performing are created.

Like those before it, this chapter challenges Northern conceptions of "transition" through its rearticulation of drag through the self-descriptions of South Africans and attention to the temporality of gender. Some may want to read medicalized concepts such as transvestite and transsexual into and onto South African drag queens. Those who interpret South African gender liminality through such lenses often implicitly seek to determine *permanent transition* as an indicator of gender liminal identification. The drag queens described in this chapter usually embody genders not assigned at birth in their daily experiences. But I argue that rather than fitting into these compartmentalizations, those in this chapter unsettle both easy categorization and transition. Transitioning from stable to unstable category to unstable category results in a complex liminal process.

Reconceptualizing the temporal qualities of transition, and the expectations of chronology and progress, forms an important contribution of this chapter to the questions under consideration in *Sex in Transition*. Like Mbembe's necropolitics in its unsettling of colonial realities and temporality, Ratele's conception stresses that "Kinky politics is personal and institutional practices, politics, programmes, cultures that naturalise, objectify, and stabilise difference, *refusing to allow for its characteristic of movement and change*" (Ratele 2004: 143, emphasis added). Allowing and encouraging this categorical movement and change, by contrast, pushes the boundaries of gender liminality beyond the distortion of categorical hegemony.

Conclusion

"Extra-Transsexual" Meanings and Transgender Politics

In the 1990s and early 2000s, the word "transgender" was rarely spoken in South Africa. Gender liminality was largely medicalized and criminalized, and it fell outside the purview of activism. In interviews, doctors told me stories of celebratory parties thrown for their postoperative patients, while self-identified transsexuals shared concerns about their inabilities to attain legal documentation and their forced and botched surgeries. Over the following ten years of transition, concerns and connections shifted; increasingly, transsexuals who could afford to do so traveled outside of South Africa (especially to Asia) to attain surgeries, while activists advocated for South Africans at the margins of gender as part of a nascent self-defined transgender sociopolitical movement. Simultaneously those at the borders of gender and sexuality have faced escalations in sexual violence as their legal rights have increased during the transition to democracy. How and why have issues facing gender liminal South Africans shifted since the end of apartheid? What does it mean for South Africans to define their gendered identifications both in collaboration with and opposition to those in the global North? And how are activists advocating for the raced and classed concerns of those who do not clearly fall within gendered binaries?

Sex in Transition concludes by discussing these questions, as well as the ways that the paradoxes of gender, sex, and race illuminate what South African legal scholar Angelo Pantazis terms "extra-transsexual meanings—meanings for people who are not transsexuals" (1997: 468). Pantazis highlights how South African opposition to legal recognition of transsexuals was based in fears of the radical implications of such meanings: "the law has been against the recognition of transsexualism precisely because it perceives the extra-transsexual meanings and seeks to control them" (ibid.). He suggests that legal approaches have largely endeavored

231

"to pathologize, to minoritize, and only then to sympathize and legal-ize" (470). As this text has demonstrated, extra-transsexual meanings are those with significance for both gender liminal communities and for cisgender people, as well as for broader understandings of gender.[1] Here, I ask about the potentials and pitfalls of "extra-transsexual mean-ings" through an analysis of the burgeoning transgender movement in South Africa. "Transgender" is a term with growing significance in the global South that can function paradoxically as a community-building tool and Northern imposition simultaneously. This Conclusion queries the implications and importance of bringing attention to gendered dis-crimination, and the possibilities of such work to effect change in all South Africans' lives.

I also return to the concept of transition articulated throughout this text here. As the range of conundrums explored in the chapters of *Sex in Transition* indicate, gender liminality takes many forms. David Valentine's *Imagining Transgender: An Ethnography of a Category* (2007) describes the nuances of this concept, based on his work in New York City:

> "Transition" is a complicated idea, one which often refers to someone's physical transition, through sex reassignment surgery, from one gender position to another. But transition does not necessarily require or imply surgery. One can begin transition by taking hormones, or transition by adopting one's desired gender in one's workplace or at home through more mundane technologies of clothing. The paths to transition are as varied and complex as the lives that undergo this shift. (Valentine 2007: 258n5)

As chapters have focused centrally on paradoxes and questions, not par-ticular subjects or communities, the range of "transitioning" in South Africa emerged here. Gendered transitions linked to South African histo-ries, and especially the transition from apartheid to democracy, have been shown through changing concepts of "sex" and "transsexual"; through the parameters of medical experimentation; through necropolitical narratives of those who plan their own gender transitions; through the imposition of concepts of *stabane*; and through the production of race through drag. Taken together, these interventions help us think about "sex in transition" in both senses—both sex as it changes for individuals and sex during the political transition.

Sex in Transition has addressed and put into conversation theories from the global North and South, testing the ways that well-known theorists such as Foucault, Butler, and Mbembe have produced work that travels spatially and temporally in concepts such as biopower, performativity, and necropolitics. But perhaps the most crucial parts of the theoretical pastiche woven together in this text are the complexity and multifaceted contributions of lesser-known Africanists. Glen Elder's ideas of heteropatriarchy (2003), Marc Epprecht's history of the idea of heterosexuality (2008), Andrew Tucker's formulation of queer visibilities (2009), and Kopano Ratele's theorization of kinky politics (2004), among others, have formed critical components of this analysis of the junctures of gender and race. The theories and terminology discussed through *Sex in Transition* need to be understood and contextualized in terms of South African's daily struggles. One service provider explains his perspective on "transgender" issues this way:

> I mean many guys living in Khayelitsha[2] are trying to survive this week without being stoned, being harassed. Can you hear what I'm saying? So the room for this kind of abstraction is just—I try to make do with what I've got and as long as I can survive today, fine, and if you want to struggle with theories and labels then I can't quite go there. (Swanepoel 2007)

My discussions of theories in *Sex in Transition* have been cognizant of Swanepoel's perspective, recognizing that theories offer us useful tools that need to be actualized in people's lives. Without this application they run the risk of being empty rhetorical exercises. However, these same theories also provide conceptual frameworks, funding, and outreach which beg for interrogation.

I. Simone Heradien: September 15, 2007

The Introduction to *Sex in Transition* highlighted reflections by Simone Heradien from 1997, shared during the transition to democracy and relating her own gendered transition to the political economy of South Africa. Ten years later, I was able to interview Simone again, illustrating the changes in her own thinking. This time her concerns had shifted from her own transition to broader legal, political, and social transformation. She details the emergence and recent successes of the burgeoning transgender movement and points to the meanings of this work and its ideal goals. Like the narrators represented previously, Simone's narrative is not exceptional or emblematic but provides new assessments of community and reflects on ten years of South Africa's political and gendered transition.

[When you interviewed me in 1997,] I was about three years into complete full womanhood. And now it's ten years later. . . . I think probably the most important milestone for me in this past ten years was in . . . September–October, 2003. In South Africa, we established the transsexual, transgender support group via the Triangle Project in Cape Town, myself and a few other . . . pre-op transsexuals or transgenders. And the fact that we've been a democracy for nearly ten years since, and it was still not legal, or completely legal, or they were black points as to if one has gender reassignment surgery whether one could actually change one's ID. And apparently, according to the law at that stage, it was not legal at all. And then it was debated by Parliament at that time and through the transsexual and transgender support group we gave our input in at Parliament, sat at Parliamentary sessions for probably about three weeks in and out, I think. We made a submission on behalf of the transsexual and transgender support group and I also made a submission about myself. . . .

Eventually what transpired from that and what I'm really proud of is that I made a positive contribution to changing the laws in South Africa in the fact that when you have gender reassignment surgery you are now allowed to change your gender on your ID book plus your ID, and also you actually do not have to have full gender reassignment surgery, especially in the case of biological female to becoming a gender male, because of the success rate.[3] So in South Africa you are allowed certain criteria. You don't actually have to have the physical genitalia of the sex as perceived by the majority of the population or what defines one as being male or female. So I think that's a big milestone for South Africa as a democracy, and it was a milestone for me as well. That I could personally have partaken in that process and I could personally have made a contribution and made probably one of the biggest changes to gender classification in South Africa and probably one of the very few countries in the world that has got that kind of laws. So as far as the gender issues are concerned that's been one of the most important milestones.

When you met me in 1997, I had become the woman that I was destined to be, but I still saw myself as a woman and as a postoperative transsexual. Now I just see myself as a woman. I almost feel that I never was a transsexual, I was always a woman. And I just had to be referred to in that way to make sense for people who don't understand what a woman is with male genitalia. So I just feel that I've always been a woman. I feel today I don't regret any single thing that I've ever done. And if I should ever be reborn or reincarnated à la some cultures in the Southeast Asia region I would want to be reincarnated as Simone again and go through exactly the same. And hope it turns out a success as it was in the past. I don't regret a single thing. I'm more established. I've got much more self esteem about myself. I would never hide the fact about my past, but I don't blatantly blurt it out, "Hi, I'm Simone and I was a TS" because straight people do not blurt out, "Hi, I'm John and I'm straight." <laughing> . . .

[During the transition when legal changes were not allowed] . . . I had an operation and used all the threats and went to the Attorney General and the Director of the Home Affairs and whatever and they changed my ID for me. Because I don't know if the [United] States' IDs are the same, but there's four digits within our ID that indicates one's gender. . . . So the first six would be one's birth dates—year, month and date—and the next four between 0001 and 4999 indicates that one is female, and from 5000 to 9999 indicates one is male. So they changed that for me, actually, before the law and I actually stated that anomaly to them when we were changing the laws as to having one reclassified. They were obviously all dumbfounded, and they said it couldn't be, it can't be. And I had to produce all the documentation. Then it was determined that actually I'm probably the only official postoperative transsexual registered as a female in South Africa. But at that time it was not a case of wanting to get all the glory and publicity about Simone having had the first change long before this became legal. . . . That wasn't important to me. It was important to me that the law had to be changed, redressed, and it had to be available for those who wanted to change their IDs and their gender. That was the main aim. And I mean there wasn't anything that they could do about me. They couldn't tell me that I had to go back to my first ID then. They couldn't, because it was done in a legal way.

I think the battle as far as that is concerned is actually to make . . . transgender [communities] . . . aware that they actually have recourse to this, because I think most transgender people, transsexuals in South Africa, are not even aware of this at all. I'm in contact with one in Cape Town at the moment, just email contact, I've never met her, and sent her one or two emails. And I could see that she's quite ignorant about all her rights. I think that is the next hurdle that needs to be crossed. As in most cases in South Africa, we've *got this fabulous Constitution and this fabulous Bill of Rights and this fabulous Charter, whatever, but it's not being translated to the person in the street . . .*

Ten years ago I would have made the distinction between transgender, transsexual, homosexual, intersex . . . but I think also having been in the transgendered support group opened my own eyes to the fact that one doesn't necessarily have to be transsexual to actually want to be the other gender. It's intricate. It's delicate. I must honestly say something that I'm still grappling with myself to understand, for example, how one would be a female in a man's body, have gender reassignment, but still remain a lesbian. It was difficult for me to understand that, because having been brought up in a sense that you're either male or you're female and if you want to be a female you have to be attracted to a male, and if you want to be a male you have to be . . . vice versa. Having been exposed to the different degrees from transsexualism to transgenderism, it made me realize that, basically, who am I to judge? And if that is whatever you feel you're comfortable with, that is what you're comfortable with. . . .

So, yeah, listening to myself I'm thinking if I'm still grappling with that, how are we going to get to Joe Public eventually? I think in South Africa itself, well in Cape Town itself, Cape Town has always been an open society as far as I would say transsexualism is concerned. It wasn't seen as transsexualism. It was seen as being overtly gay. . . . Cape Town, within the so-called coloured community, apparently has the highest percentage of transsexuals or transgenders per population . . . ratio, than any other community in the world except Malaysia. . . .

There's quite a few [trans and intersexed organizations in South Africa today]. I'm not up to speed as to all the organizations but there are quite a few. They've become more vocal. They've become more prolific. And I think some of the organizations are finding niche markets, to put it in that sense. The one would concentrate just on legal issues, the other one will concentrate on social issues, the other one on socio-economic issues, stuff like that, but I've been a bit out of touch.

My sister, she's deceased now, she was what one would term pre-operative transsexual, so she laid the foundations for me. . . . I think she was 12, 13 years older than what I am. . . . Unfortunately she never had gender reassignment surgery, and she was in the unfortunate category of transsexuals who lived a street life. It's a case of, at that time, a TS, it was just impossible to get a so-called conventional job, so most of them turned to street life and prostitution, et cetera. I always say that it may sound silly, but I actually do thank my sister in a sense, but I always see her as my sister. I could never refer to her as my brother. I can't. I just can't. In a way that when I saw her life, I said to myself that, "I'm a woman, but that is not the life that I want to be. I'm going to show the world and to myself that I'm a woman and I'm going to live a normal, conventional, probably off the beaten track, but a woman's life and not be relegated to that . . . that's not going to be." But if I wanted to live the streets and become a prostitute, it would have been out of choice and not because I was going to be forced in that, and I fought against that all the time. And I mean when I went for interviews before my gender reassignment surgery, I went for a few interviews right at the beginning and they said to me, "You know we would consider giving you the job but then you must come to work dressed as a man." And I said, "I'm wasting my time here. Thank you very much, goodbye." In the same sense that I would rather eat dry toast and black coffee, I mean the decision that I made now, same thing. . . .

Unfortunately in South Africa, access to gender reassignment is actually very strange. There was much better access to gender reassignment surgery in South Africa in the apartheid era, especially in the '70s and '80s and, in fact, I'm not sure if you're aware of it at that stage it was compulsory for the so-called whites, white males to do military service for two years and the military service actually paid for gender reassignment surgery for TSs and for gay males. Unfortunately, a lot of mistakes were made, because they sort of coerced gay males to have gender reassignment, the overtly effeminate gay males, to have gender reassignment surgery, so a lot of mistakes were made. I think in the '80s, for example, one had access in Cape Town, Pretoria, as well as—I speak under correction—either two of the military hospitals or one, but they must have been up to four hospitals within South Africa that wanted access for gender reassignment surgery. And they would perform up to four to five per year at each, so I mean that was the turnover that they had. By the time I had mine which was in 1994, [it] was also the year of reconstruction development in South Africa, so I'm honored that I was reconstructed during South Africa's RDP years. At that stage, due to lack of funding and it was the entire reallocation of expenditures as far as health is concerned, the government said that, "We cannot be spending R60,000 on gender reassignment when people are dying of TB," for example.[4] So, of course, funds were cut . . .

I think the most important issue is for pre-op TSs or transgendered is to empower themselves. I haven't thought about this at length. I don't know how because one also has to take into consideration that there are TSs out there who are not educated in the sense or [weren't] exposed to education so they are naïve and ignorant. But I think to me that is probably the greatest issue empowerment within the community or as to the entire broad spectrum of who one is, what

*you are, what you can be, and what you want to be, and to take it forward
because we are living in a new democratic, open society. We're not living in the
apartheid years or in a dictatorship. So to me that is the most important. And
probably being where I am now is to sustain that and also in whatever small
way one can to try and make a positive, meaningful change and contribution as
far as empowerment of TSs and gender issues in general are concerned.*

In this second narrative, Simone addresses some of the most important
changes and milestones of the transitional period for those in gender liminal positions. She speaks to the significance of the legal changes for which
she advocated and their implications not only for her, but for other gender
liminal people. Historical notes, such as changing access to sex reassignment procedures and experimentation on gay and lesbian conscripts, are
important to Simone, as are her connections between the Reconstruction
and Development Programme (RDP) and her own transition.

Simone compares her own knowledge of and access to sex reassignment to that of her sister, poignantly contrasting their differing opportunities available under apartheid and during the transition. She represents
herself as a manifestation of the transition and part of the changes of
democracy. For many South Africans like Simone, politics are not something external and distant. In a nation where suggestions about the 1996
Constitution were solicited via call-in phone hotlines, for example, most
citizens consider themselves integral to and agents in political change.
Simone references the growing transgender movement and her changing views of the variability of gendered categories, indeed the growing
continuum of gender liminality she perceives, as well as her perspectives
on lessening distinctions between gender and sexual identifications (gay
and transsexual). For Simone, the most important future initiatives for
gender liminal individuals and communities in South Africa relate to
(etic) awareness and (emic) empowerment, as she defines them.

II. Histories through Transitions

Simone and the other narrators in *Sex in Transition* contribute significantly
to a theorization of the materialization of gender and sex as co-produced
with South African history and politics. South African scholars and activists have carefully documented histories of same-sex sexuality, though
disruptions to gender binaries have generally been subtle aspects of this

work or excluded entirely. And outside of South Africa, some of the most complex analyses of transsexual history published to date speak to the importance of considering gender liminal narratives in terms of medical histories, both shaping and shaped by the perspectives of doctors and medical institutions. However, few of these texts have contextualized accounts of gender liminal experiences in both national and transnational histories. This is an intervention of *Sex in Transition*.

The context for this intervention must be explained. We are all familiar with accounts of "homosexuality around the world" that attempt to provide a country-by-country reclaiming of a singular gay identity which has never existed. Transnationally-focused organizations that create a sense of relief and superiority for global Northerners "saving" queers in the global South are problematic in their oversimplification and reliance on funding that dictates agendas and identity categories with little attention to local perspectives. Similarly, academic accounts of sexual histories often create conditions in which "colonial ethnographic and anthropological materials are revisited and mined for their endorsements and descriptions of homosexuality" (Arondekar 2009: 8). Replicating these troublesome perspectives in analyses of gender liminality are activist texts that serve a U.S.-based activist movement, but can also force contemporary "transgender" identities on communities based outside of the United States.

Instead of representing gender liminality as insignificantly related to geographic locations and histories thus promoting a generic transsexualism, as many scholars and narrators in the United States and Europe have done, or presenting it in isolation, taken together these narratives point to the importance of the role of national history in both defining and understanding gender liminality, as well as the role gender liminal people play in undermining, reinforcing, and ultimately producing gender. Rather than presenting a linear chronology, in *Sex in Transition* colonialism, apartheid, and the democratic transition are revisited and considered in relation to specific questions and paradoxes. The account in this conclusion, offered largely for its potential for South African activists working for social change, is intended to trace historical expressions of gender liminality in South Africa not as an extractive interaction with archive but as an historically and geographically specific discussion of the interplay of gender with apartheid and transitional medicine, law, and state politics.

The first sex reassignment surgeries in South Africa occurred roughly at the same time as the inception of apartheid, a period of great repression on the basis of race, sexuality, and gender. In the 1950s and 1960s during the administration of President Verwoerd, "People didn't even . . . mention the word homosexual in those days, let alone transsexual" (Edmunds 1997). This period in South African history was characterized by political repression and the formulation of a white supremacist Afrikaner patriarchy.[5] As Leonard Thompson explains, beginning in 1950, "security legislation [gave] the government vast powers over people and organizations" (1995: xvii). The 1960 ban of African political organizations and murder of 67 anti-pass law demonstrators at Sharpeville and the 1964 sentencing of Nelson Mandela to life imprisonment are just a few examples of the sociopolitical extremism that shaped South African society.

In this period transsexuals confronted troublesome circumstances and few options for liminally gendered self-expression. As Vita explains of her own transition, those cross-dressing "could have been arrested in those days." This led her to surmise, "Unless I, the person, can get away with it 100 percent, I wouldn't have gone through with it. . . ." Vita, deciding that she wanted to transition, underwent sex reassignment surgery in the early years of its availability and thus became the subject of great attention in the hospital (as she notes, during her procedure "it must have been forty, fifty people around"). In this period Vita chose not to disclose her transition to either of her two husbands; this was a personal decision, but one likely informed by the gendered expectations she faced as a white woman in this era.

Between at least 1963 and 1976, transsexuals were able to change the sex indicated on their birth certificates, provided they could "prove" their medical reassignment by utilizing experts from South African institutions, employers, and other authoritative figures. This was the time when apartheid was solidified; restrictive laws created in the 1950s were met with resistance, and during the 1960s African National Congress (ANC) and Pan Africanist Congress (PAC) leaders were imprisoned and repression strengthened. South Africa was built on raced and gendered documentation and doctors facilitated access to rights to such documentation in this constrained period. But as scholars as varied as Mark Hunter (2010), Nan Hunter (2004), Jasbir Puar (2007), Dean Spade (2011), and many others have pointed out in very different U.S. and South African contexts, queer and gendered rights frameworks often have contradictory effects. These include subjecting those trying to access rights to increased scrutiny thus creating conditions in which state power is used against ideally-protected classes of people, facilitating privilege hierarchies among those able to access rights, and opposing rights to "tradition," whereby local and indigenous knowledges are understood as temporally and morally backwards. Throughout *Sex in Transition* it is evident that even during this period when legal sex reassignments were allowed, they were accompanied by significant restrictions and subjective decisions about who counted as a "true transsexual." Further, as Simone explains, "in the '70s you could have your ID changed . . . but you couldn't have your ID number changed. So if it was still in the computer, it would still come up as male." This legal option was not ideal, even though gender changes were perceived to be advantageous to most transsexuals.

During this same period, medical treatment of gender liminality was highly racialized. The master's thesis entitled "Intersex in Four Racial Groups" (Grace 1970) mirrored the racialization of genitals documented in the treatment of Baartman and /Khanako under apartheid. It was to be cited authoritatively for decades as an explanation for and record of black abnormality and objectification. However, beginning in 1976 following *W vs. W* and the imposition of the "Ormrod Test" for "true" sex described in Chapter 1, transsexuals were increasingly denied legal access to changing identity documents. 1976 is a significant year in South African history, as June 16th brought student uprisings against forced Afrikaans language education that were met with violence and showed the brutality of apartheid to the world. This year also brought new legal precedents that were to shape transsexuals' and intersexuals' statuses for almost three decades. Decisions about legal reassignments were made on a case-by-case basis during this time. Arbitrary factors, such as which government officials one spoke to, as well as subjective and often raced individual perceptions of successful "womanhood" and "manhood" by authority figures, shaped whether or not legal sex changes were granted then, as they continue to do now. Further, when such changes were allowed, they regularly took up to ten years to be fully processed.

At the same time, medical reassignments were unevenly available to gender liminal people in different provinces and with different doctors and similarly took many years to complete. It is complicated to ascertain the time periods in which programs operated at certain hospitals and the eligibility criteria employed by different doctors, in part because of the secrecy that has surrounded them. Instead of a logical and standardized treatment of transsexuals, we find a patchwork of treatment clinics and individual doctors with dedication to performing surgeries for their own reasons. We also get a sense of the origins of transsexuals' well-justified suspicions of institutions they were forced to navigate and the economic affects on and effects of choosing public or private treatment.[6]

The late 1970s in South Africa brought the intensification of apartheid in efforts to stem the tide of political resistance. *The Aversion Project* exemplifies the conjunction of sexuality and gender and its violent enforcement. Beginning in this period, some white conscripts with same-sex desire were tortured into heterosexuality. If shock and chemical therapies were unsuccessful, forced and coerced sex reassignments changed "unsuccessful" men's and women's bodies. For white South Africans in these circumstances, heterosexuality was paramount and superseded concerns about the medical mutability of sex. Sex could, and should, in this view, change to facilitate heteronormativity. We also see the increasing racialization of liminality, with sexed non-normativity working in concert with racism.

In the 1980s, extremely different decisions about gender expressions exploded simple adherence to medical categories. For instance, Nicole began electrolysis to remove her beard in 1981 in Gauteng and completed the process in three years. In 1984 she pursued surgery, and, as she explains,

> When I wanted to go it was 1984 when things were still very bad in South Africa. Not that it's much better now, but it's reasonably well now. But in 1984, it was sort-of the only way out, look, go and have [a sex change] done, live a normal life. But when I heard [from the doctor about the mental and physical instabilities that can result] and when I met people that had it done, I thought, no, this is not what I want.

Nicole, like other narrators, made somatic decisions consciously influenced by political economies of South Africa. From 1984–1986, prolonged resistance to governmental repression was met with violent state responses, including declarations of states of emergency in many parts of the country. Emergency regulations "gave every police officer broad powers of arrest, detention, and interrogation, without a warrant," allowed public meetings to be banned, and prohibited media coverage of anti-apartheid resistance: "[t]he government had resorted to legalized tyranny" (Thompson 1995: 235). This is the political context for Nicole's decision about this physically and psychologically risky procedure, and she chose not to undertake surgery. But this decision came at the expense of sexual relationships with men and the possibility of changing her sex legally. Nicole postulates, "[a]t the time there were no other options to live a normal life. This was the only one, and I have no regrets because I'm happy" (2000).

By contrast, Carmella's perceptions of her options in this time were different; she was classified as coloured and Nicole as white, and in the late 1970s she lived in a township outside of Durban and Nicole lived in Gauteng, factors that are enmeshed with and shaped by the political and racial climates in which they made their decisions. Carmella saw sex reassignment as her best alternative to "gay life" and an avenue to "normalcy." She describes her life as a gay man in Durban as unhappy and explains in Chapter 3, "being a gay, a man, it's not very nice. You drink, you sleep around with any man that comes your way, you're so scared you're going get licked out" (2000). Consequently, even though, as she states, "I didn't want to be a woman," she decided to write a letter to the President of South Africa, in her words, to ask the government—specifically P. W. Botha—to pay for her sex reassignment (she paid a nominal fee of approximately $6). In this period it seems that the state, represented in her narrative by Botha, and medical institutions were similarly invested in facilitating the congruence of sex and gender, making gender liminal South Africans clearly male or female. Financial subsidization of treatment supported government perceptions of dual gender binaries. The political climate in South Africa in the early 1980s was one of extreme repression coupled with fear from apartheid's leaders about its efficacy. Botha and his administration attempted to reform apartheid while retaining Afrikaner power, moves which had effects for transsexuals, by both supporting their medical reassignments and rendering them expendable through experimental procedures.[7] While Carmella speaks openly of the extensive medical complications and the social and religious ostracism she has faced, she also feels affirmed by the state and the media through their personal interest and financial investments in her.

The effects of institutional and state support of poor transsexuals were to enforce gender binaries while also allowing for medical experimentation on black and coloured bodies. Carmella claims that she was the first coloured transsexual on whom her doctor performed sex reassignment procedures. Her surgeries went horribly wrong, as they did for other "specials" during the 1990s described in Chapter 2. The racist culture of medical experimentation during this time (Baldwin-Ragavan et al. 1999), and disregard for the consequences of such medical procedures, are embodied by those like Carmella. Surgical sex reassignments left Carmella consistently near death for a number of years and ultimately, at the time of this writing, without functioning genitals. From Nicole's narrative it is not possible to decisively ascertain the motivations of the doctor who advised her against surgery, but the suggestions made to Nicole, as a white transsexual woman, can be read against Carmella's experience of botched medical procedures.

Simone also pursued sex realignment in this period, becoming involved with a treatment clinic around 1985. But, as she explains, financial costs prevented her from undertaking medical treatment.

> What happened to me was twelve years ago I was going to have my surgery, but at that time I wasn't working. So the only criteria was that I had to work for a year to show them that I'm now totally stable and then come back. And when I had worked for a year, I came back and [the sex reassignment program] was suspended, due to lack of funds, and then I had to wait ten years. (1997)

The lack of funds for desired surgeries described here has had corporeal and material effects for many transsexuals. The mid-1980s brought the height of black resistance and resulting violent state repression. Speculatively, state funds that could have been spent on sex reassignment surgeries may have been diverted to shoring up apartheid and combating its internal and external enemies. Apartheid leaders initiated regional wars intended to destabilize southern Africa and increased bureaucracy (e.g., through the 1983 creation of coloured and Indian branches of government in an effort splinter the liberation movement); combined with worldwide economic sanctions, these factors severely threatened apartheid's economic viability.

Undermining the notion that chronology can be simply linked to surgical availability, as well as expected chronologies of transition, are accounts like Herman's. Seeking medical transitions from the 1970s to the present in different ways, he had both successes and thwarted attempts to engage medicine and its restrictions. These efforts were mediated through his race and class, as well as his ability to access the public health care system. The social stigmas facing those who threatened the stability of gender and sexuality persisted throughout apartheid. Accusations of *stabane* confronted those expressing same-sex desire with violent effects. Drag performances and drag outside of performance venues were encouraged in some situations and denigrated in others, usually along racial lines. All of these different instances exemplify the instability of gender and the inadequacy of existing categories to explain and understand the interplays of gender binaries with location, race, sexuality, class, and political economy. And they show that gender liminality cannot be simply reduced to categories labeled as transsexualism or intersexuality.

As described above, uneven availability of and funding for sex reassignment procedures has led to incomplete documentation of gender identity clinics, and geographic locations of these gender liminal individuals undoubtedly shaped their perspectives and decisions. Historical material suggests, for instance, that gender liminality was more accepted in Cape Town than in Johannesburg and Pretoria, factors that likely shaped transsexuals' choices and the availability of procedures. Narrators described in Chapter 3 from different areas of South Africa share varied and mappable stories of surgical availability.

For Simone, her dedication to obtaining surgical realignment led her to pursue possible avenues of treatment all over the country until ten years later, when she finally was able to begin her medical transition. As she points out, "if I wasn't that determined or that tenacious type of person then maybe . . . it still would have passed me by." But this initial unavailability of surgery in the 1980s during the chaos surrounding the South African state may have been beneficial to Simone, as when she did begin her surgical realignment in 1994, the success of sex reassignment procedures had increased as doctors gained experience and knowledge (often at the expense of patients such as Carmella).

Also significant was the 1992 repeal of the Births, Deaths, and Marriages Act, which increased difficulties for transsexuals attempting to change the sex on their birth certificates. This decision may have been based in a backlash against equal rights campaigns that accompanied the political transition to democracy in South Africa, but, as I explain in Chapter 1, it did not indicate a significant ideologically progressive or repressive shift. Conservative perceptions of sex and gender have remained similar since the end of apartheid, though officially sex, not gender, was conceptualized rigidly, making transsexuals legally nonexistent during the transition.

A few individuals saw opportunities for legal changes despite the law, based in the new and progressive South African Constitution. Simone shows us how legal restrictions cannot be taken at face value. There are ways that transsexuals attempted to change their identity documents legally, but few knew about and had the resources to access these rights. Simone's quest to change her identification was a successful exception. Because of her social location as an educated middle-class woman and the historical period in which she attempted her re-registration (in the mid 1990s), Simone was uniquely positioned to undertake perhaps the most complete legal shift of sex documented in South Africa to date. She changed both her identity documents and her identification number, and "except for one lousy thing on microform somewhere up in Pretoria," all evidence of her "maleness" had been erased. Simone's transition coincided with the political transition from apartheid to democracy in South African history, which she finds analogous to her own situation. In the Introduction to *Sex in Transition*, I note how Simone's comparison of the Reconstruction and Development Programme (RDP) to her own surgical "reconstruction" is an important example of narrators' deployment of national history and personal history concurrently. At least in part, South Africa's political transition allowed for Simone's successful personal transition, and she links the two conceptually.

The transition has also facilitated the visibility and popularity of different nonmedical alternatives for those in gender liminal positions. Broadening social categories outside of medical contexts has highlighted narrators' decisions to transition in and out of gender like William does. And growing awareness of and access to international travel have facilitated choices like Donna's to pursue sex reassignment surgeries in Thailand.

The combination of legal, social, and political factors that the transition to democracy brought allowed some in gender liminal positions more possibilities to live the lives that they envision for themselves without fear of repercussions. Yet throughout the transition they also continued to operate within a system of inconsistent legal and medical treatments of transsexuals that persists in South Africa and elsewhere. Giles's narrative concerning his current transition points to perhaps the most ideal and idealistic picture of this vision, while Herman reminds us how the complexities of access have limited and shaped the parameters of transition.

III. Transitioning from the Transition

A number of organizations have offered assistance, support, and community to gender liminal, transgender, transvestite, transsexual, and intersexual South Africans over the past fifty years.[8] The Phoenix Society is the oldest organization that served those between genders in South Africa, and its members were primarily male-to-female transvestites (self-defined) in Cape Town. Activist and writer Charl Marais describes himself as the only coloured member and the only trans man (as he identifies now) in the group during the apartheid era (Morgan et al. 2009: 30). Budding Roses currently serves a similar role in Gauteng, meeting monthly for social objectives. Both of these groups had and have a primarily white membership, with one member of Budding Roses describing the group to me as "99.97% white."[9] The Triangle Project, while initially conceptualized as a mental and physical health-focused nonprofit organization serving gays and lesbians, has also historically served gender liminal clients in Cape Town. With a name recalling Nazi oppression of same-sex sexuality, The Triangle Project has organized support groups for transgendered and transsexual clients and their families since the late 1990s and offers psychological support, counseling, and referrals. Intersex South Africa, founded in 2000 as the Intersex Society of South Africa, has coordinated legal efforts on behalf of intersexuals' rights and more broadly. Its founder, Sally Gross, is well-known as an important advocate for gender rights in South Africa. Most recently since 2005, Gender DynamiX has served "Transgender, Transsexual and gender non-conforming people" (Gender DynamiX 2011), especially in the Western Cape and Gauteng, through community education, social and informational meetings for members, and advocacy for individuals in medical and legal settings.[10] All five of these organizations have been sources of information for those seeking to make medical and legal transitions. They have also provided spaces in which individuals come together to overcome the isolation of gender liminality. Most have transnational connections both ideologically and as sources of funding.[11]

As described in Chapter 3, the advent of the Internet during the transition has been a boon for gender liminal people, as well, serving similar functions to these organizations on a virtual level. Gender DynamiX, in particular, itself has a significant and influential presence online, combining virtual community with in-person meetings and interventions.

And the online resource *Behind the Mask* has provided LGBT news and information since 2000. In addition to these organizations there are numerous ways the Internet has been helpful and utilized: as a way to meet people with similar romantic and sexual interests (there are Web sites serving just this purpose in South Africa), to find out about similar social movements in other parts of the world, to order books or read about medical transitions, and to research and arrange medical services, including those outside of South Africa (particularly in Thailand).

Significantly, founders of both the Phoenix Society and Gender DynamiX have written and spoken about the transnational connections that underpinned their decisions to start organizations in South Africa. Doctors' narratives and ideas travel transnationally, but so do activist organizations and objectives. Marlene describes the origins of the Phoenix Society:

> One day I read an advert in *Scope* magazine for the Beaumont Society [established in 1966] in England for cross-dressers or transvestites. I thought, "My goodness! There are other people like me in the world." I wrote to them, joined the Beaumont Society and was told that there was one other South African member. We eventually met . . . Between the two of us . . . we managed to start the Phoenix Society. . . . Eventually, [in 1984] we brought out our little magazine called *Fanfare* and made contact with more and more clubs overseas, in the United States, Australia, and even in Latvia. We simply grew from there. (In Morgan et al. 2009: 58)

More than twenty years later, Liesl Theron's description of the origins of Gender DynamiX follows a similar path, making connections by traveling to England and touring organizations based there. From this, she founded Gender DynamiX focused specifically on designated "transgender" concerns. Since then the organizations' efforts have extended to relevant communities throughout southern Africa.

One of the most pressing problems activists are addressing through their work has been mentioned by numerous narrators—the inconsistency between new laws that allow for change of sex status and their application. Most specifically, working through the Department of Home Affairs has presented huge problems to those seeking changes to their identity documents. This is not without precedent. Legislation on race was similarly administered by the Departments of Native Affairs and Home Affairs under apartheid. Then, as now, bureaucratic decisions made as "discretionary judgments" (Posel 2001a: 91) about the parameters of race had life-changing consequences.

In contemporary times, those working for the Department of Home Affairs are not only arbitrary in their decisions, they often do not even seem to be aware of current law. This will likely lead to legal consequences. Anthropologist Thamar Klein suggests,

> [t]he Department of Home Affairs is caught in a rather awkward position: it violates both the Equality Clause in the Bill of Rights and The Alteration of Sex Description and Sex Status Act. This must lead sooner or later to a court case if the Department does not abandon its current practice of demanding documents of completed genital surgery. (2008: 9)

These inconsistencies are manifold and represented in narrators' stories; narrators in Chapter 3 describe some of their own struggles with changing identity documents through Home Affairs. Donna, for instance, describes waiting for years through confusion and mistakes of staff and getting no results in changing her identity documents until an activist advocate intervened on her behalf. *Trans: Transgender Life Stories from South Africa* similarly documents these struggles; for instance, Leo writes:

> An alarming fact is that when I asked a home affairs official what forms I needed to complete if I wanted to change my gender, I got resistance from her. She asked me why I wanted to do that. She told me I couldn't just change my gender, and that home affairs didn't have any available forms for that. She couldn't really give me the correct information and seemed not to know about the new act that had been passed regarding gender changes. (In Morgan et al. 2009: 24)

Inconsistencies in the Department of Home Affairs's capacity to make the changes legally mandated presents a serious difficulty those wishing to transition. Their efforts prevent legal citizenship for those involved, affecting voting rights, passports, driver's licenses, bank accounts, and employment. Even when identity documents are changed, gender identification numbers continue to present problems. As Vayna explains:

My ID number says I'm a man. I do have problems, especially with the banks. I went to the bank one day to withdraw some money and they called forensics to verify my signature. It was such an embarrassing moment because they thought I was there to defraud somebody. I was admitted into the hospital for depression and my mother did the paperwork. A guy came to take me into the ward, looked at me, then passed. He asked where Mr Zwane was. They pointed at me; he looked at me and said they made a mistake on the application. They have male and female wards and because I didn't want to complicate things, I said I had a sex-change. I was a boy but I'm a girl now. They put me in the female ward and everything was sorted. (Vanya in Morgan et al. 2009: 69)

In locations as varied as banks and hospitals, gendered identity numbers produce effects including prosecution for fraud and violence in gender-segregated spaces. And in South Africa, unlike some other places in the world, even the delivery of mail and accounts are predicated on gender pronouns. One narrator recounted being unable to receive hand-delivered packages because his chosen pronoun (Mister) didn't match his identification (Miss). In hypergendered contexts like this, and given growing global fears and policing of identity documents related to terrorism, even when names are accurate, pronouns impart persistent problems.

In all of the organizations documented here, language, constituencies, and coalitions have been consistent themes and challenges. Not only are there eleven national languages in South Africa, but speaking of gender liminality itself has disciplinary, geographic, and temporal components. During most of the transitional period, medicalized or indigenous terminologies dominated discussions and descriptions of those between genders, sometimes in direct opposition to each other. In the past five years, with the increasing influences of globalization in positive and negative ways, the term "transgender" has entered common parlance and has become increasingly popular. Marlene, founder of the Phoenix Society, suggests that she and Joy Rosemary Wellbeloved coined the term "transgender" earlier:

I was born a transgender person. Of course, at that time, nobody knew the word. It didn't exist. Joy and I actually coined the word "transgender" because we felt we didn't fit into the only two available categories in the early days. We weren't transvestites because we wanted more but we weren't transsexuals because we didn't want the operation. (Marlene in Morgan et al. 2009: 57)

Marlene points to the ways that terms can develop in different places simultaneously and to the creativity of gender liminal communities in defining themselves outside of medical terminology. Marlene also address-es her own opposition to sex reassignment and her self-definition beyond these boundaries:

> I'm as close to a transsexual as you can get, but I have never had or even will have the sex reassignment surgery. I do not believe in and approve of it. I needed hormone therapy though because I would consider it almost normal for any transsexual to want to feminise as much as possible. (60)

This original exposition of new terminology and recreation of oneself out-side of medical models provides increasing space for gender liminality.[12]

Terminology can be reworked or it can problematic in its appli-cation and adoption. Swanpoel, an activist who works to prevent the spread of HIV/AIDS through his outreach, argues against the imposition of categorical language altogether:

> I think that many people around here are dealing with gender identity issues without the word "trans" even coming into the stratosphere. It just doesn't exist. Can you hear what I'm saying? So at a much more concrete level . . . the majority of the interfacing is with those kind of people. I don't think you can even call them questioning. That's the way it is. (Swanepoel 2007)

As a service provider focused on daily struggles, Swanepoel finds that the language of "trans" can be alienating to those who are gender liminal. And not only is the terminology questionable in who adapts and accepts it, but its promotion affects the kinds of services gender liminal people access, especially in efforts to prevent HIV. Swanepoel further explains that the language of "transgender" is not reaching people, especially poor and black and coloured people, and as a result:

> If you're looking at trans, and it sounds horrible, how many people are actually identifying as "trans" who pick up something that says, "Hello trans people, this is for you. Read me." (ibid.)

The exclusion of gender liminality from organizations focused on gender (read: women) and sexuality (read: gays and lesbians) leads to lack of understanding and inadequate services for those in these positions. Estian Smit sees the development of trans and intersexed organizations as a manifestation of this omission, articulating the effects of this conundrum:

> The result [of exclusion], more often than not, is the eventual emergence of independent trans and intersexed organisations. Such a trend can also be seen in South Africa. But one has to be aware that such divisions are far from absolute—there are many people who crisscross and blur all the boundaries between intersexed, transgender, transsexual, bisexual, lesbian, gay, straight and many more labels than the mind can conceive of. (Smit 2006: 286–7)

For both Smit and Swanepoel there are both positive and negative effects of recent linguistic and conceptual developments. Without common language, it is difficult to connect people with services they might be seeking, but when common language is imposed, it can pose a different set of problems about who sets terms and how they create new and sometimes problematic categories of existence and being.

Gender DynamiX is working to translate words and concepts among communities, which has proven to be an impactful project, despite its complexity. The founder of the organization, Liesl Theron, explains the complexity of these processes:

> For example, I can give you a few small incidents that happened why I say the word "transgender" is not necessarily the word that is right to use in South Africa, it's by lack of something else that we are using it right now. I went with OUT LGBT Wellbeing of Pretoria . . . to one of their rural areas, Mamelodi, where they have a satellite support group or office and once a week the outreach person is having like an LGBT get-together. So I went with that day and I've been

introduced as Liesl Theron from Gender DynamiX and she's working with transgender people, da-da-da. And everyone's sits and smiles nicely at me, and I say to them, "Okay, so do you know what is transgender?" And everyone sits and smiles at me. You know, I thought, "Okay, here we have to very quickly backtrack and forget about political correct." So I said to them, "I work with people who's having sex changes." And up come the hands with questions . . . and informed questions, you know? They didn't challenge me in funny ways. [They asked,] "Where can I get hormones? Where this? Where that?" They ask the same questions as every other person is asking, so they knew exactly what I spoke about when I said, "I work with sex changes," then they knew. . . .

At the end of the day [do you] go by the political correct word, or do you go by the word which makes some people cringe but at least we know what we're talking about? Which one? . . . The people who don't know that word trans whatever, once you explain to them the whole thing and incorporate their words or understanding into the example, yes, everyone is at that stage is comfortable with transgender as the umbrella. So I think that might stay quite clearly like that. But once we come to, "How do you express yourself?" Or, "What is your lived experience? What's the word you call yourself?" You can't say, "Oh well, sorry we think you are actually an MTF." Sorry, that person is not saying it, that person is not an MTF, even if they have the will to change their gender physically. (Theron 2007)

These issues are not merely semantic. The communication Theron describes here is both linguistic and cultural. It also demonstrates the importance of emic terminology (coming from within communities) rather than etic impositions. And it has effects on activists' abilities to share life-changing information about discrimination, services, laws, and rights. Activists like Theron draw on language such as "sex changes" that is often considered derogatory but can be self-descriptive and may be helpful to those who use these expressions to explain their experiences. Through our considerations of organizations active in the transition and reflections on gender liminality, language remains a critical and complex concern. As discussed in Chapter 4, regarding accusations and claiming of *stabane*, terminology cannot be unproblematically applied or imposed but must have origins and meanings in people's daily lives.

Transitioning within the political transition has also been complex and changing because of shifts in medical availability and the law. Treatment programs have decreased in size and number, and today activists sometimes protect those accessing these services by publicizing the services that are available only to those who need them.[13] The contradictions in expectations and treatment that face those seeking services have been documented in previous chapters. Two additional accounts add to the picture of inconsistent inclusions and exclusions. In the first account, Prier explains the effects of divergent opinions of medical practitioners like those described in Chapter 1 in his own life:

> When I first went to the psychiatric ward of Tygerberg Hospital, the psychiatrist and the psychologist there didn't know what this was about. I was wearing an oestrogen patch on my leg and the psychiatrist saw it, ripped it off, and threw it in the wastepaper basket. Later, when I was in Valkenberg Hospital, the nurse assumed that if you wanted to be a woman it meant that you were homosexual. I tried to explain that it wasn't the same thing. At Lentegeur Hospital, there was a psychologist who said he himself was a bit gender variant and that was the first place where they actually encouraged me to cross-dress. (Prier in Morgan et al. 2009: 37)

This kind of disparate treatment is not only conflicting, it determines the kinds of access to surgeries and medical treatment available and demonstrates how the hyperobjectivity of medicine loses sight of the patient. The second account supplementing previous discussions of the parameters of treatment in public and private medical settings is found in Joy Rosemary Wellbeloved's narrative. Wellbeloved navigated the interplay of both the South African Law Commission's boundaries around standards of care described in Chapter 1 and the expectations of "true transsexualism" addressed in Chapter 3. She explains:

> In those days you had two choices. The one was to go privately, in which case they wanted virtually two years of psychotherapy and a recommendation from a psychiatrist. And if you could

pay the doctor's bills there was a reasonable chance you
could have it done. The second was through Groote Schuur
Hospital. The evaluation methods done for both were a little
bit screwed, to put it plainly. If you had the money and you
could get somebody to give you a letter saying you were okay,
the chances were you got it. At Groote Schuur, when I was
trying to go there, there was on old fogey who was probably
85 in the shade. He had this idea that unless you were ultra,
ultra fem you didn't qualify. He took one look at me, and
threw me out as I had children. I tried getting the medical
aids involved but they were not interested. It was just terrible!
(In Morgan et al. 2009: 133)

As Wellbeloved articulates here, gender was strongly policed in public
settings and the ability to pay for private treatment was not an option
for many people, including her. Taken together, these two accounts show
contradictions within and among medical systems and strict effects of
the category of Gender Identity Disorder.

Problems facing those seeking medical treatment like Prier and
Wellbeloved included high costs, small programs with a reliance on a
few gatekeepers with significant power, the subjectivity of medical definitions for "true transsexuals," difficulty in finding and accessing programs,
decades-long waiting periods, and geographic limitations both within
and outside of South Africa. Financial stability is required for medical
treatment, both in the form of supplementary payments for public care
and full payments for private care, combined with costs for transportation to and lodging at a narrow range of medical sites. Further, doctors'
expectations that transsexuals are financially stable in their jobs prior to
surgery prove problematic because of rates of unemployment, geography,
and discrimination facing those transitioning. Under these circumstances,
mounting numbers of transsexuals who can afford to do so are traveling to Thailand and elsewhere to obtain surgery with less gatekeeping,
quicker timeframes, and lower costs.

Secrecy has protected both those engaging in medical experimentation and doctors earnestly seeking to protect programs and funding from
popular opinion and backlash. Like elsewhere, South African individuals undergoing physical transitions as transsexuals have historically been
actively advised or even required to break ties with family and friends and
to move to new regions of the country where they don't know anyone.

This advocacy of stealth has clearly been a double-edged sword. The culture of secrecy around medical experimentation, around apartheid practices more generally, and around transsexuals' medical treatments has led to a lack of documented gender liminal histories in South Africa. The Internet, growing organizations, and published writing by gender liminal people and their allies are working to challenge and fill this lacuna.

IV. "Extra-Transsexual" Transitions

The concerns raised in *Sex in Transition* have repeatedly been referred to in the context of Pantazis' conception of extra-transsexual meanings and thus in South African histories, but their influence and implications go far beyond the small communities in which they are based. Extra-transsexual meanings provide one answer to the question of "why is this work important?" However, this work also foregrounds gender liminality and its effects on specific individuals and communities. In so doing, it takes seriously cautions from those who point out the ways that transgendered people have been used, erased, and objectified in academic accounts when considered only for the ways their choices contribute to gender theory (e.g., Namaste 2000; Valentine and Wilchins 1997). In short, I am not interesting in unpacking extra-transsexual meanings at the expense of the exploitation of transsexuals nor appropriating gender liminalilty for the sake of gender theory or a global transgender movement.[14]

Thus, while the focus of *Sex in Transition* is on gender liminality, its intent is to remind us that *all* genders are conflicting and mutable but with careful attention to the specific kinds of struggles faced by those in gender liminal positions. Theories that posit gender liminality as inherently subversive analogously pose those who are cisgender as naturalized. The materialization of gender is much more complicated. Histories of South African gender liminality expose contradictions in the rigidity of apartheid ideas about gender as co-produced with race and class.

In addition to gender disjunctures and apartheid, the paradoxes of raced gender, and varied kinds of transitions explored throughout this book, the constitution of reality and its temporality has been under consideration in all chapters. In the first chapter, medical and legal experts argued about the composition and reality of sex and if and when it can change. Transsexuals were, in some times and places, perceived as fictions. In Chapter 2, reality was forcibly reconstituted through medical experimentation. The third chapter used gender liminal narratives, as well as Mbembe's conceptions of necropolitical realities, to argue for the shifting qualities of gender and transition. Chapter 4 contributed to a rethinking of the temporal reality of genitals in sexual encounters and to the raced relationships of intersexuality to same-sex sexuality. And in the fifth chapter, drag proves a way to create reality through a collective, if impermanent, production of gender and race. Through all of these considerations, notions of truth, both in seeking accuracy in narratives and in the creation of "true transsexuals," have been undermined as an ideal goal—conflicts around truths are much more telling.

Two final narrative excerpts concerned with unsettled reality in narrators' own gender expressions supplement this picture while raising additional questions. In the first, Prier, living then as a man in a heterosexual relationship, shares the following:

> I had a particularly memorable experience in 1972. While my second wife was away, I suddenly had the feeling that I actually was a woman. For a short time—it may have only been half an hour—I seemed to be a woman. My face felt different. It felt soft. For the next two days my breasts grew. It was one of those inexplicable experiences, but a very real one. I tried to talk to my wife about it when she came back but she didn't want to hear anything about it. It illustrated to me that something was going on with me. (In Morgan et al. 2009: 36)

For Prier, this articulation of the changes she felt in her body were both real and indicated her gender liminality to herself. These experiences were not tangible, but "very real." By comparison, in a different South African setting butch lesbian *sangoma* (traditional healer) Nkunzi Zandile Nkabinde uses her autobiography to explain her temporal gendered reality. Nkabinde is inhabited by her male ancestor, named Nkunzi, who makes his presence known during sex with women:

> Nkunzi loves women, especially young women. If I am with a woman of 21 or 22, Nkunzi will want to have sex with her. I will feel his presence as if someone is touching my shoulders and sometimes I see the legs and genitals of a man. This is one way he shows himself to me. I have more power when Nkunzi is in me, especially when we both desire the same

woman. When this happens, I change. I become so strong. He takes control of my body and even the sounds I make are different. The woman I am with will tell me, "your eyes are changing." Women I have slept with say my eyes become red or green and I become so wild and strong. Women tell me that my body becomes very heavy and when I come my partner will say, "In that moment you were not yourself. What was happening?" I will make a sound like a lion roaring. That is how I know that Nkunzi is satisfied. After sex I will hear someone saying, "Light a candle." That is how I know Nkunzi has got what he wants. (Nkabinde 2008: 68–9)

Nkunzi, through the words, experiences, and inhabitation of Nkabinde, expresses himself through these sexual encounters. For both Prier and Nkabinde, their transitions have corporeal and somatic aspects, creating new realities of sexed bodies, if only temporarily. These two different but overlapping creations of reality demonstrate the slippery and contested boundaries of gender that create both violence and possibilities in South Africa.

How do the discussions in *Sex in Transition* affect the daily lives of the South Africans with whom I worked during the course of this research project? Kamala Visweswaran writes that researchers' encounters with colonialism have taught us to question not how to better represent "subjects" of such research, but how to be accountable to their struggles for self-representation and self-determination (1990: 32). There are a number of activist and policy directions related to this directive. Medically, guidelines as to the treatment of transsexuals and intersexuals should be developed in conversation with members of these communities, particularly those who have experienced medical experimentation and forced and coerced procedures. Those who have intimate experience with South African medical institutions are best positioned to make recommendations as to future directions. Legally, significant change has taken place during the transition, due to the actions of activists; however, policies and laws must be put in place that allow South Africans to align their legal documents with their self-identifications so as to permit them to function economically and socially as members of South African society and without burdens of medical "proof." Finally, cautions about the limitations of legal rights for effecting change have been increasingly salient as contemporary rates of gender-based violence rise. Social solutions emerging from local communities and political organizing that changes how people feel and think may offer the most viable avenues for addressing these complex inequities.

South Africa's political transition has not been a smooth panacea, nor have most gender transitions undertaken by South Africans within it. But by examining the connections and relationships among them, especially in relation to the co-production of race and gender, we can learn from the extra-transsexual meanings that underpin this analysis. By doing so, we can attend to the daily struggles and visions of those who express gender liminality.

Notes

Introduction

1. Barring this one exception, at Simone's explicit request, I rely on pseudonyms to protect narrators' anonymity throughout this book in accordance with Human Subjects requirements.

2. Medical gendered transitions are referred to many ways—including sex or gender reassignment, sex or gender realignment, sex changes, or gender confirmation. These differences are not merely semantic but describe various theories of gender and its origin. For instance, some see a "sex change" as a transition from a birth sex to a new sex, while others see this term as derogatory, whereas "sex realignment" refers to changing the body to match unchanged birth gender. I discuss this in more depth later but write with awareness of these debates. In South Africa, "sex reassignment" is the most common way narrators describe their transitions.

3. Turner goes on to describe gendered components of liminality outside of binaries, suggesting, "[i]t is consistent to find that in liminal situations . . . neophytes are sometimes treated or symbolically represented as being neither male nor female. Alternatively, they may be assigned characteristics of both sexes, regardless of their biological sex" (1967: 98). Another pairing of gender liminality is found in Niko Besnier's work, "Polynesian Gender Liminality in Time and Space" (1994). Besnier uses the concept as a more accurate alternative to "transgender" and similar terminology, yet "much more than conveniently gender neutral labels" (287). Besnier's use of this concept differs from my own in his link to Turner's three specific meanings of liminal events and persons (specifically, "their 'betwixt and between' locus, outsider status and social inferiority"). I extend and broaden this concept, combining common usage of liminality with understandings of gender outside of anthropological application that allows space for social encouragement and valorization in some times and places.

4. David Valentine (2007) provides an excellent analysis of the term "transgender" and its raced and classed exclusions in the United States. See also Stryker and Whittle, *The Transgender Studies Reader* (2008), and Currah et

261

al., *Transgender Rights* (2006). I explore this term's application in South African contexts later.

5. Gender DynamiX is undertaking important public advocacy work in South Africa under the specific rubric of transgender rights; this group and additional organizations doing related political and social work of great importance are discussed in the Conclusion at length.

6. This is despite important exceptions recommending more careful attention to the composition of categories of gender and woman (e.g., Walker 1990; Manicom 1992).

7. While Van Zyl cites Reddy, Reddy relies on Africanists' work in *Rethinking Sexualities in Africa* (2004) that preceded his own, indicating intertwined geneaologies. He points out, "Recently Arnfred (2004: 7) has suggested that rethinking sexualities in Africa entails 'a double move of de-construction and re-construction' beyond the 'conceptual structure of colonial, and even post-colonial European imaginations.' This issue of *Agenda* articulates a similar concern, demonstrating that the meanings of contemporary discourses on 'African sexualities' have much to tell us about the discursive aspects of sexuality in Africa" (Reddy 2004: 5).

8. Hoad's process of reworking theory leads to the following generalizable conclusions: "Rubin's essay reminds us that theory is produced in and out of a space-time, with political allegiances to that space-time, and that while any theory of sexuality risks reifying and universalizing its space-time, it can be adapted, reworked, and embraced as it travels, and travel it will" (Hoad 2010: xx).

9. The scale of slavery was monumental; Harsch (1980) suggests that within approximately 150 years 25,000 Africans and Asians had been enslaved in the region.

10. The temporality of mine marriages has not been fully explored, as most analyses assume either situational same-sex sexuality (e.g., men having sex with wives because women were unavailable) or historical proof of gay identity. I'm interested in a more gendered interpretation of mine marriages attentive to the intricacies of queer temporalities in all contexts. I return to this concept in Chapter 5.

11. This relationship between South Africa and Britain was maintained until 1961 when South Africa withdrew from the British Commonwealth and became a Republic.

12. In Foucault's terms, apartheid was a biopolitics as it involved the politics of policing the population but also the politics of its populations' quotidian daily rituals.

13. *Moffies* is a term that was considered derogatory when referring to gays and lesbians, and sometimes gay men who are effeminate, with regional dominance in the Western Cape, but has been largely reclaimed in the past twenty years. See also Cage 2003 and Van der Merwe 2006.

14. I offer more detailed analyses of race and intersexuality in Chapter 4 and of Cape Town's Coon Carnival in Chapter 5.

15. As Mbembe (2002) argues, African discourses of the self unsettle colonial truth claims like those represented in accusations implicit and explicit in the Prohibition of Disguises Act.

16. Documentation of racialized same-sex sexuality before apartheid, while largely outside of the purview of this manuscript, is critical to this consideration. See, for example, the important historical work of Marc Epprecht (2004) and the groundbreaking films of Zackie Achmat and Jack Lewis (1999) on white homosexualities and interracial relationships in colonial and apartheid contexts in southern Africa.

17. As I discuss in Chapter 5, there was a potentially radical element to drag, as well, but I want to be cautious about positioning drag as either repressive or subversive. This can be related to Mbembe's analysis of "the postcolony," "we need to go beyond the binary categories used in standard interpretations of domination, such as resistance vs. passivity, autonomy vs. subjection, state vs. civil society, hegemony vs. counter-hegemony, totalization vs. detotalization. These oppositions are not helpful; rather they cloud our understanding of postcolonial relations" (2001: 103).

18. Groote Schuur is one of the most well-known hospitals in Africa and was the site of both the first open-heart surgery (performed by Dr. Christian Barnard, as Simone mentions) and likely the first sex reassignment in Africa. Simone refers to the medical process as "sex realignment," not the more common "sex reassignment," as she sees surgery as bringing the physical body—sex—in line with gender.

19. I use square brackets [ ] to insert words of my own to summarize or clarify narrators' ideas. Angle brackets < > designate sounds, such as laughter.

20. By "the test," Simone is referring to psychological tests for "true transsexualism" and resulting diagnoses of Gender Identity Disorder.

21. This amount was equivalent to $7.78–7.89 in July 1997 when this interview was conducted (Oanda FX History 2003).

22. Simone's abbreviations refer to transsexuals (TS), transvestites (TV), and transgendered people (TG).

23. The Bronx and Angels were considered "gay bars" in Cape Town at the time. Caesar's was a similar bar in Cape Town with a large coloured clientele that closed in the early 1990s and was a site for drag shows and pageants but was also boycotted by ABIGALE (the Association of Bisexuals, Gays, and Lesbians), a group dedicated to anti-racist action, for its racist exclusions. These were in the area Tucker (2009) and others refer to as the "gay village" in Cape Town.

24. I describe the class tensions and hierarchies Simone raises here at length in Chapter 5.

25. Kate Bornstein (1994) was one of the first authors to write about similar hierarchies in U.S. contexts.

26. Discussions about whether those who undergo transitions would commit suicide without medical treatment or whether those who get botched

operations more commonly kill themselves are common topics of conversation in Cape Town and elsewhere that I address in more detail later.

27. Susan Stryker defines cisgender and cissexual, writing: "The idea behind the terms is to resist the way that 'woman' or 'man' can mean 'nontransgendered woman' or 'nontransgendered man' by default, unless the person's transgender status is explicitly named; it's the same logic that would lead someone to prefer saying 'white woman' and 'black woman' rather than simply saying 'woman' to describe a white woman (thus presenting white as the norm) and 'black woman' to indicate a deviation from the norm" (2008: 22). See also Serano 2007.

28. David Valentine points out that some activists in the United States choose to spell "transexual" with one "s" to "resist the pathologizing implications of the medicalized two 's' 'transsexual'" (2007: 25). For Valentine his usage of "transexual" "marks the historical moment and context within which [he] worked" (ibid.). This activist spelling is not found in South Africa, so I retain the traditional spelling of transsexual here. I also choose the term "intersex" over the more recent term, "disorders of sex development (DSD)," as this new conceptualization has not gained popularity in South Africa.

29. "Trans*" is said to have origins in technological language, as an asterisk is sometimes referred to as a wildcard character or any unit in computing. While useful for the space it provides, I use it sparingly in this text as it is not deployed in South African contexts.

30. Susan Stryker describes these difficulties of language in U.S. contexts this way: "Most disturbingly, 'transgender' increasingly functions as the site in which to contain all gender trouble, thereby helping secure both homosexuality and heterosexuality as stable and normative categories of personhood. This has damaging, isolative political corollaries. It is the same developmental logic that transformed an antiassimilationist 'queer' politics into a more palatable LGBT civil rights movement, with T reduced to merely another (easily detached) genre of sexual identity rather than perceived, like race or class, as something that cuts across existing sexualities, revealing in often unexpected ways the means through which all identities achieve their specificities" (2004: 214).

31. The contributors throughout *Critical Transnational Feminist Praxis* discuss these concepts at length (Swarr and Nagar, 2010).

Chapter One

1. In this chapter, I again use the term "sex reassignment" in accordance with doctors' and patients' own usage, yet I also recognize its limitations and theoretical assumptions.

2. This chapter draws primarily on medical and legal literature, archival research, and interviews with surgeons and mental health professionals con-

ducted in South Africa from 1997 until 2009. Interviews were conducted in Cape Town, Durban, Pretoria, and Johannesburg—areas in South Africa where sex reassignment surgeries have been performed—and included medical experts in both public and private practice. While not exhaustive, these interviews reflect a cross section of medical and legal opinion in South Africa.

3. For further discussion see Feinberg 1996; Devor 1997; Nanda 1999; Kulick 1998; Kandiyoti 2002; Stryker 2008.

4. Male-to-female transsexualism was referred to as "male transsexualism" in this time period and continues to be referred to as such in many contexts; however, I use "male-to-female" and "female-to-male" (and the abbreviations MTF and FTM, as well as trans women and trans men) here for clarity and in line with narrators' self-identifications.

5. This surgery took place at The Johns Hopkins University Medical Center in Baltimore, Maryland, in the United States.

6. Intersex in South Africa is explored at length in Chapter 4. On this point in the United States, see also Preves (1999, 2003) and Karkazis (2008).

7. The most disturbing example of this of which I am aware was the well-publicized case of David Reimer, in which Money surgically reassigned one of two male twins as female following a circumcision accident in 1966. Reaching adulthood, the reassigned twin changed his identification back to male (and it was also suggested that both Reimer twin brothers had been forced to engage in sexual acts by Money). David's twin, Brian, died of a drug overdose in 2003, and David committed suicide in 2004. This tragedy has become increasingly publicized and well-known (see especially Colapinto 2000, 2004), demonstrating the pitfalls and implications of forced reassignments.

8. For instance, Harry Benjamin was charged with unethical and illegal conduct for his treatment of transsexuals, and at one point the courts threatened to revoke his medical license. The ideas and treatment practices of physicians who used such methods "provoked hostile reactions from psychoanalysts who charged that it is one thing to remove diseased tissue and quite another to amputate healthy organs because emotionally disturbed patients request it" (Billings and Urban 1996: 100).

9. I am cognizant of the important critiques of Dwight Billings and Thomas Urban and Bernice Hausman for their reduction of transsexuality to a medical invention (e.g., Prosser 1998; Namaste 2000), a perspective undermined by the historical work of Feinberg (1996) and others. Further, Hausman's dismissal of transsexuals as "dupes of gender" (Hausman 1995) notably biases her work. In this chapter, I draw on interviews with medical practitioners conducted by Billings and Urban (1996) and Hausman (1995) but temper their critiques with careful attention to transsexual subjectivities and agency.

10. Bernice Hausman writes: "Unwilling to settle for the patients who would come to them due to accidents, car wrecks, or congenital deformities, cosmetic surgeons decisively rewrote the code of normal appearance to enhance

their practices" (1995: 63). Sex reassignment procedures are not merely cosmetic; patients' encouragement by medical professionals can be linked to the economic context of this period.

11. Devor and Matte (2004, 2007), Califia (1997: 53), and Meyerowitz (2002: 210) suggest that the founder of this foundation, Reed Erickson, was the recipient of an early female-to-male sex reassignment surgery himself, which inspired these interventions. Erickson wrote the forward to Green and Money's foundational text (1969), but he does not address his motivations in this forum (Green and Money 1969: xi–xii).

12. The efforts of the Erickson Foundation also inspired great public sympathy around transsexuality by positioning transsexuals as victims of unjust policies and discrimination. Consequently, the foundation "created a National Transsexual Counseling Unit in conjunction with the San Francisco Police Department and issued identification papers to transsexuals otherwise subject to police harassment" (Billings and Urban 1996: 106). It provided funding for individual patients, established a national referral network, published a newsletter, and gave grants to researchers and gender clinics. The actions of the Erickson Foundation marked the beginning of a close relationship between medical professionals and public policy/legal scholars around gender and sex that continues today. See also Devor and Matte (2004, 2007).

13. See also Amanda Lock Swarr, Jaye Sablan, and Kai Kohlsdorf, "Transnational Transgender Medical Discourses" presented at *Hypatia*'s 25th anniversary conference at the Simpson Center at the University of Washington (2009).

14. Some transgender and intersex activists in the United States oppose the diagnosis of gender dysphoria as pathologizing, while others embrace it as a means of achieving the bodies they desire from the medical establishment with the possibility of medical insurance coverage. Doctors may also reference the *International Classification of Diseases* (ICD), a publication of the World Health Organization with similar perspectives; South African Estian Smit (2006) provides a detailed discussion of the differing perspectives on Gender Identity Disorder in these two texts from a regional perspective.

15. By comparison, cross-dressing with erotic feelings is defined as transvestitism in this context.

16. Specifically, Don explains the processes paramount to this study in the following way. "A medical and psychiatric history was obtained and a full general and neurological examination was performed on admission. The sex of the individual was determined as comprehensively as possible by the assessment of the nuclear pattern of the buccal mucosal cells; study of the endocrine status, physical examination with special reference to the gonads, external genitalia and secondary sex characteristics, and finally by psychological reactions and social behavior" (Don 1963: 479). This examination of patients' skulls for evidence

of intersexuality is reminiscent of the racist science of craniometry discussed in Chapter 4.

17. When I first heard the word "stealth" in South African contexts in the 1990s, I thought it was only regional. Since then, its usage has been explored more widely, as in Kristen Schilt's (2010) discussion of the differences between "passing" and stealth:

> as *passing* suggests acting rather than embodying, I adopt the term many transgender people I encountered in my fieldwork used, *going stealth*, to discuss transmen who choose not to disclose their gender transitions at work. *Stealth* might seem like a strange choice of word, as its definition includes "furtive," "sly," and "underhanded." However, its meaning also encompasses "covert" and "clandestine," synonyms that are in closer keeping with a view that transitions are of a private history that may be disclosed in some circumstances and not in others. *Stealth* also avoids the assumption of fraud of deceit implied by *passing* (2010: 15).

I use the terms "pass" and "passing" in quotations here, as this concept relies on an idea of sex (or the body) as the authentic determiner of a person's gender identity and does not allow for ambiguity beyond a man/woman distinction. I discuss this concept, and the analogous notion of "stealth" addressed among South African transsexuals, in depth in Chapters 3 and 5.

18. "Phenomenology, psychoanalysis, and queer and transgender theory each approach the question of what it means to assume a body by asserting the primacy of a 'felt sense' of the body, and the different means by which each discipline does so, when examined in conjunction, can begin to delimit the contours of this body whose felt sense is usually questioned. Phenomenologists think of this felt sense as *proprioception*, psychoanalysis thinks of it as *bodily ego*, and it sometimes has emerged in transgender theory as the grounds for claims about identity and 'realness'" (Salamon 2010: 2).

19. Louise Vincent and Bianca Camminga refer to Elize van der Merwe as South Africa's first "media transsexual." Van der Merwe had surgery in 1975 and her story was publicized in 1982: "Of all the newspaper and magazine reports on the story only one refers to her as a transsexual, the rest refer to a woman *in the wrong body*. The reports are at pains to extol her womanly interests including baking, house-keeping and her life-long search for a husband" (Vincent and Camminga 2009: 689, emphasis added).

20. Published in 1994/1995, this composite report draws on and cites only three articles, two of which are by Harry Benjamin and published thirty years prior in 1953 and 1969 (SALC 1994: 7, fn 25).

21. I return to concerns about the categories and the criminalization of drag in Chapter 5.

22. I consciously choose to refer to Frederica/Frederic X using male pronouns and his chosen name to reflect how he referred to himself, in contrast to the physicians cited here who retain feminine pronouns in their references.

23. While this lack of stringent criteria made surgery accessible to those who wanted it, it also allowed those who did not fully understand the process to undertake surgeries and their potential effects and costs. I discuss the complications of consent under apartheid in the following chapter.

24. I address sex reassignment and racialized medical experimentation at length in relation to particular groups of South Africans in Chapter 2.

25. See Chapter 5 for further discussion of this Act in relation to drag and its connections to apartheid and racism.

26. Deborah Posel provides a careful articulation of the subjective decisions of police officers under apartheid regarding racial designations (2001a).

27. One narrator anecdotally recalls how her sister, a transsexual like herself, was arrested three or four times (Heradien 1997).

28. The racial dynamics of this legislation have not yet been explored by South African historians. Strauss writes, "Registration of births is governed by the Births, Marriages and Deaths Registration Act 81 of 1963 which (in its application to Whites) is administered by the Minister of the Interior" (Strauss 1974: 27, emphasis added). It is unclear whether the Registration Act applied only to whites or whether only whites applied to the Minister of the Interior (and people of other races applied elsewhere or could not apply at all).

29. Despite the ways that this law facilitated easier changes in documentation, South African transsexuals point out that the identity number itself (akin to a social security number in the United States) is gendered male or female. Only a few transsexuals I interviewed were successful in changing this number when they changed their birth certificates and other documents during the transition.

30. In this time period, the political uprisings and state control that characterized the 1976 Soweto uprisings and murder of protesting school children were to set the stage for the international condemnation of apartheid.

31. In 1993 an amendment was added to the 1992 Births and Deaths Registration Act to "grandfather" in those who had begun their transitions before its passage. It reads: "A person who was in the process of undergoing a change of sex before the commencement of this Act, may on completion of the said process apply in terms of section 7B of the Births, Marriages, and Deaths Registration Act, 1963, for the alteration of the sex description in his birth register" (in SALC 1994: 20).

32. As discussed in later chapters, there were exceptions to this legislation when legal changes were facilitated by advocates and based on the intersections of other social and temporal factors.

33. A "Nat" refers to a member of the National Party, the conservative Afrikaner party which instituted apartheid and ruled in South Africa from 1948–1994. "DP" refers to the Democratic Party, formerly the Progressive Federal Party, which consisted primarily of white liberals. In 1999 these two parties merged in an attempt to build a viable opposition to the now dominant African National Congress.

34. Thanks to Lynn Thomas for her suggestions in these interpretations.

35. As detailed in the Introduction to this text, Simone Heradien provides a striking exception to this law, as she effectively threatened constitutional court action in order to get her documents changed. However, hers is the only case of this sort that I documented, and it seems that the majority of South African transsexuals were unable to pursue such changes.

36. As Carrie Shelver, then Director of the South African National Coalition for Gay and Lesbian Equality, put it, "It is odd that [the Department of] Home Affairs could change documents back then to reflect the outcome of the surgery, but we often have to fight to have them perform the same procedure now" (Shelver in Kirk 2000c: 10).

37. See, for example, Reid and Dirsuweit (2002) and Mkhize et al. (2010).

38. Taitz was recognized as one of the leading experts on transsexuality and law in South Africa at this time.

39. In Chapter 2, we see one horrific manifestation of state control of sex reassignment among conscripts in the SADF and explore medical experimentation at length.

40. For example, a 1970 South African medical report indicates that when "J.B.," aged 17 and living as a woman, came to see physicians because she was not menstruating, physicians determined that she did not have a uterus and had a number of XX chromosomes. Her mother repeatedly refused to allow physicians to perform exploratory surgery to determine if she was intersexual despite their persistent attempts (Jackson 1970).

41. I suggest alternative means of viewing gender through an analysis of varied "transitions" in Chapter 3 and through a discussion of drag and race in Chapter 5.

42. For example, when the new South African Constitution was introduced with much fanfare about its protection of citizens from discrimination on the basis of sexual orientation, for a number of years this Constitution existed simultaneously with anti-sodomy laws that had not been changed.

43. The work of these contemporary trans and intersex activists is addressed in the Conclusion in more detail. See also Klein (2008) and Gross (2009).

44. The quotidian effects of these discrepancies are explored in Chapter 3 and the Conclusion.

45. For further discussion of the objections to this new Bill, see the "Oral Presentation for the South African Home Affairs Portfolio Committee Hearings" (Cape Town Transsexual/Transgender Support Group 2003).

46. Although clear patterns did not emerge through this research, the ease with which transsexuals have changed identity documents has varied immensely in different time periods and regions of the country, paralleling inconsistencies in state power common under apartheid. Other factors, such as race and individual transsexuals' persistence and agency, seem to have played a role in shaping decisions about and the ease with which documents were changed. Further systemic research into the records of medical institutions would offer important insights in these arenas.

47. See, for instance, Sally Gross "Intersex and the Law" (2009).

48. See also Gross (2009), Swarr with Gross and Theron (2009), and Klein (2008).

49. Deborah Posel (2001b) provides an analysis of the lingering power of racial reasoning in South Africa, including discussion of a relevant survey conducted by the Institute for Justice and Reconciliation.

Chapter Two

1. As an aside to this chapter, it is important to note that medical abuses and questionable practices, including genital surgeries (e.g., on the intersexed; as part of rituals including circumcision; reductions of clitorises deemed "too large"), continue to be commonplace in the United States today. Similar practices in the global South are often sensationalized in media and academic discourse and used to bolster racist ideologies.

2. Homosexuality also overlapped with the contagions listed by Lalu as colonialism transformed into apartheid, as those engaging in same-sex practices were seen, for instance, as lunatics, criminals, and prostitutes in many contexts beginning in the 1950s.

3. The Public Health Act 36 of 1919 constituted the official origins of the system of public health care in South Africa (Culver 1958: 337).

4. The *Bantustans* were the rural areas where black South Africans were forced to live under apartheid as a result of the Group Areas Act (1950). These regions were declared "independent" by the South African government, but they had extremely limited political rights, resources, and infrastructure.

5. See Klausen (2004a, 2004b) for related historical examinations of birth control and illegal abortion in South Africa.

6. The precise numbers of patients who sought these surgeries are unavailable. I follow activists' requests not to name hospitals here, for fear such naming could undermine their attempts to obtain surgeries for transsexuals in the future. As mentioned in the Introduction, both doctors and patients in South Africa express a high level of secrecy about when and where sex reassignment programs have operated.

7. A "fistula," in this context, is usually an opening between the vaginal canal and the bladder or the vaginal canal and the rectum that does not allow urination and bowel movements to take place naturally. Left unattended they can be fatal, and even with treatment the development of fistulas usually necessitates that the vaginal canal be closed (Stedman 2000).

8. None of the medical practitioners I interviewed would share the costs of these procedures. As a rough guideline, South African narrators estimate that their procedures cost between R97,000 (approximately equivalent in dollars—$97,000—in the early 1980s, Riekert 2000) and R12,000 (approximately $4,000 in the 1990s, Jansen 1997). Estimates compiled from a number of clinics' Web sites range from around $7,000 (in Thailand) to $60,000 (in the United States).

9. I explore additional narratives' disruptions of "transition" through eschewing surgery in Chapter 3.

10. Smit prefers the gender neutral pronoun "e."

11. Due to medical confidentiality and lack of relevant publications, I was unable to precisely document demographics of the patients treated.

12. Furthermore, in the past ten years transsexuals have increasingly sought inexpensive surgeries outside of South Africa, particularly in Thailand. This subject, though largely outside the scope of this project, necessitates further research. See, for example, Swarr, Sablan, and Kohlsdorf 2009.

13. One patient who was refused surgery was reportedly psychotic and the other developmentally delayed (Vorster 2000).

14. Standard protocol is usually a life-long regiment of hormone therapy.

15. An "anastomosis" is an opening created or a natural space between two tubular structures or between two separate spaces or organs and "peritonitis" is an inflammation of the peritoneum, membrane and tissue that line the abdominal cavity (Stedman 2000). It is worth noting that, even in death, this physician does not describe the patient using her chosen gender pronouns.

16. The implications of this shooting on Roeland's position as a drag queen are explored in Chapter 5.

17. I share extensive excerpts of a narrative of a transsexual who went through this experimental program (a "special") in the next chapter.

18. See Kirk 2000b; 2000d; 2000e.

19. By the 1980s, South Africa was a largely militarized society with its people living in war-like conditions. Notably, from 1977–1987 enforced conscription required that young white South African men enlist in the SADF for two years; in 1988 this term was reduced to one year (Van Zyl et al., 1999: 37).

20. This abuse occurred as part of the South African Medical Services, the medical branch of the South African Defense Force, established in 1979 to consolidate medical services in the military, also responsible for chemical and biological weapons and warfare under apartheid.

21. Though outside the scope of this project, these patterns of homophobic harassment and abuse coexisted with very accepted gay subcultures in the SADF and even the encouragement of drag in some contexts, which I explore in Chapter 5. Future research might explore the divergent experiences of conscripts and when, where, and why gays and lesbians were seen as threatening, vulnerable, and/or entertaining.

22. See " 'I am First a Solider and then a Psychiatrist': The Abuse of Psychiatry in the SADF" (1986/1987).

23. The public records of these interviews are anonymous; references used to identify individuals have been changed and pseudonyms are used. Interview transcripts and related texts are housed at Gay and Lesbian Memory in Action (GALA, formerly the Gay and Lesbian Archive) in the historical papers section of the William Cullen Library at the University of the Witwatersrand.

24. Villesky, protected in this report by a pseudonym, is claimed to be the same individual publically identified in newspapers and through the TRC as Dr. Aubrey Levin, who I discuss below.

25. I initially conducted analyses of these interview transcripts for the National Coalition for Gay and Lesbian Equality (later renamed the Equality Project) in October 2000 as part of their legal effort to prosecute those involved in these medical crimes (Swarr 2000). This group and other organizations are working to bring justice to those involved in this situation.

26. The details and evidence for these demographic claims are not fully substantiated in Kirk's work; only a few examples are given and no dates or locations complete the partial picture. Some activists have privately questioned parts of Kirk's research, but the majority of it fits well with the work of the thoroughly documented Aversion Project and other interviews (e.g., Morgan et al. 2009).

27. As mentioned in the Introduction, I use gender neutral pronouns such as "hir" to indicate gender ambiguity and avoid imposing gender expectations.

28. Lyndsay later traveled to Bangkok to have sex reassignment surgery.

29. It is unclear if the choice of a masculine pseudonym for a postoperative male-to-female transsexual, Jonathan, and a feminine one for a female-to-male narrator, Mary, reflect the preferences of the narrators or of Kirk. When appropriate, I again use gender-neutral pronouns "ze" (instead of "he" and "she") and "hir" (instead of "him" or "her").

30. Kirk's articles sometimes sensationalize the experiences of transsexuals. For example he chooses to describe medical procedures used to treat trans men as "bizarre" (2000d) and victims of the program as "crippled and disfigured" (2000c). Thus, while Kirk's interviews and exposé of Levin/Villesky are useful, they are couched in his condemnation and objectification of transsexuality.

31. See especially McGreal 2010; Gibson 2010; and van Rassel 2010.

Chapter Three

1. Mbembe's epistemological critique extends discussions of institution-alization in Chapter 2 and Foucault's notions of governmentality.

2. This point is one Butler raises repeatedly, not only in *Bodies that Matter* (1993), but also in her articulation of the relevance of her work to South African academics and political activists. In an interview published in the South African journal *Agenda*, she states that: "It comes down to the question of whose lives are regarded as worthy lives, and whose illness is worthy of treatment, and whose dying and death is worthy of acknowledgement and grief" (Butler in Reddy with Butler 2004: 120). Jasbir Puar's discussion of the tension between biopolitics and necropolitics (2007: 35) helps us think about how the conjunction of Foucault's biopolitics, Mbembe's necropolitics, and (implicitly) Butler's analyses of them move beyond identitarianism and viability and allow us to address the questions of ontology and affect that are at the center of this chapter.

3. The long-range impact of these autobiographical works has been sig-nificant and documented elsewhere (e.g., Prosser 1998; Surkan 2003).

4. These transnational connections extend beyond doctors; for instance, Marlene explains the influence of the famous American transvestite Virginia Prince on her own gender presentation, "I always go out dressed as Madam without excep-tion. I don't try to feminise my voice but even when I speak people address me as Madam without exception. There are women with some pretty deep voices out there. I picked up on an idea from a transvestite called Virginia Prince. . . . She said it's not what you look like—you don't have to be beautiful because biological females are not all beautiful. The beautiful ones are actually the exceptions. Most women are pretty ordinary" (Marlene in Morgan et al. 2009: 61).

5. Morgan and Wieringa carefully articulate the relationships between the local and global in this way: "Global queer theorists . . . tend to stress the determining influence from above that global gay or queer movements have on local gay and lesbian groups. . . . The communities of women engaging in same-sex practices . . . [in southern Africa], however, do not conform to that pattern. We rather view the communities described here as relatively autonomous subcultures who are rooted in past practices, even though only the echoes of those practices remain" (Morgan and Wieringa 2005: 310).

6. "Transnational feminist conversations . . . cannot be productive unless feminist academics based in Western/Northern institutions produce research agendas and knowledges that do not merely address what is theoretically excit-ing or trendy *here*, but also what is considered politically imperative by the communities we work with or are committed to over *there*. . . . In other words, widening the notion of what constitutes theory should form the core of trans-national feminist praxis" (Nagar 2002: 184, emphasis in original).

7. I make a conscious choice to use the first name pseudonyms of narrators in this chapter. This is not intended to convey any less respect than those in other chapters who I refer to by chosen surnames but to reflect the chosen genders of their first names.

8. *Huisgenoot* (Afrikaans for "house companion") is a weekly magazine with the highest circulation of any circular in South Africa and was begun in 1916. Its English-language equivalent, *You*, has the second highest circulation (Weideman 2006).

9. Gender-neutral pronouns honor Smit and William's choices to be both and neither male and female in self-descriptions in this chapter.

10. For Freeman, specifically, "unbinding time and/from history means recognizing how erotic relations and the bodily acts that sustain them gum up the works of the normative structures we call family and nation, gender, race, class, and sexual identity, by changing tempos, by remixing memory and desire, by recapturing excess" (2010: 173).

11. This queer futurity also recalls Muñoz's (2009) work, to which I return in the conclusion to this chapter.

12. Prime Minister/President P. W. Botha was referred to as "the crocodile" because of his dictatorial and oppressive policies under apartheid.

13. These standards, originally penned in 1979 and revised many times, articulate U.S.-based "professional consensus about the psychiatric, psychologic, medical, and surgical management of gender identity disorders," issued by the organization now referred to as the World Professional Association for Transgender Health (Benjamin 2001). Although these Standards of Care are not monolithic, they are the only ones I encountered during this research. Alternative standards of care exist that are considered more lenient in their parameters of diagnosing and treating Gender Identity Disorder, especially in Europe, Latin America, and Asia where diagnostic and treatment emphases are less based on Northern psychological models.

14. Such sensationalism at the expense of individuals is not unusual.

15. Genital surgeries are often referred to as "bottom" surgeries.

16. Related surgeries including metiodioplasty, scrotoplasty, and vaginoectomy were rarely discussed.

17. Another trans man, Alex, explains his views and decisions on chest surgeries and the public/private system: "In most cases they do the bilateral mastectomy for trans males, they remove the aerolas, make them a bit smaller, or they even remove part of the nipple if they are too long, and then sew it back onto the skin itself. I have chosen to go the private route because I don't really want to feel like I am someone's experiment. I know that for some that is not an option because they are not financially in a position to have it done privately. In my case, I had planned well ahead" (In Morgan et al. 2009: 93).

18. Buttons, otherwise known as mandrax, are tranquilizers (methaqualone or quaaludes) that are crushed and smoked with marijuana. Mandrax is a sedative that suppresses the central nervous system, often leading to intoxication followed by sleepiness, enhancing the effects of marijuana. Mandrax is a highly addictive drug used widely in South Africa and has side effects that include hallucinations, respiratory problems, and neurological damage ("Mandrax" 2003; "Fact File on Drugs" 2000).

19. This amount was equivalent to around $6 in the early to mid 1980s (World Currency Yearbook 1993).

20. Amy Hunter (2010) explains the specific anatomical and logistical conditions that complicate such surgery for MTF transsexuals. See especially Kotula (2002) on FTM experiences of surgery.

21. "Blue eyes" are what people in the United States usually refer to as "black eyes," that is, eyes that are bruised.

22. Emmerentia Dam is a cruising area outside of Johannesburg where many gay men nationwide have experienced homophobic violence. High rates of violence facing gay men have gained increasing attention since 1997 when this interview was conducted; see, for instance, Reid and Dirsuweit 2002.

23. A dual prosthesis for FTM transsexuals is one that is implanted or applied using a medical adhesive. A Web site for this very realistic alternative to phalloplasty that the narrator references describes it like this: "The internal implant allows the wearer to manually bend the prosthesis 'down' in the flaccid position or 'up' into the erect position. Careful planning led us to use a non-metal implant, so no problems would be encountered at airports etc." (http://www.ftmprosthetics.com/dual.htm).

24. Dean Spade explains similar functions of identity documents in U.S. contexts: "People whose identity documents do not match their self-understanding or appearance also face heightened vulnerability in interactions with police and other public officials, when traveling, or even when attempting to do basic things like enter age-barred venues or buy age-barred products, or confirm identity for purposes of cashing a check or using a credit card or a public benefits card" (2011: 146).

25. See, for instance, Candice's narrative in Morgan et al. 2009.

26. I examine Gender DynamiX and other organizations in more detail in the Conclusion.

27. One psychologist described the extent of the costs facing transsexuals who try to transition privately this way: "People mortgage their houses, for example. They take out a second mortgage. They go into big debt around it. You can save and save, but how long is it going to take? Twenty years and you're already like thirty [years old]. People do what they must do in their youthful state" (Ryland 2007).

28. The transnational connections among transsexuals and among medical practitioners are important avenues of future research; see, for example, Swarr, Sablan, and Kohlsdorf (2009).

29. The rate of exchange in August 2005 was around 6.5 Rands to the dollar, which would make the total cost of Donna's surgery approximately $12,000. In addition, she paid just over $1,200 for airfare and around $1,000 for accommodations.

30. These terms may be considered derogatory. On Thai gender liminality and local concepts and terminology see, for instance, the work of Megan Sinnot (2004) and Ara Wilson (2004).

31. See Swarr and Nagar (2010) on related global hierarchies.

32. See also discussions of other South African narrators who sought sex reassignment surgery in Thailand in Morgan et al. (2009) such as Lyndsay.

33. Many narrators I interviewed and those represented in Morgan et al. (2009) talk about the importance of such online connections. One narrator explains how he heard about the term "sex-change" and, "I just did a Google search on sex-changes and looked at what came up" (Leo in Morgan et al. 2009: 22).

34. As shown later in this chapter, Oprah Winfrey is a salient cultural figure in South Africa. In Morgan et al., Tebogo describes his introduction to the idea of sex reassignment through a program on the show (Morgan et al. 2009: 123) and Terrick talks about the broad influence of talk shows, including Winfrey's.

35. *Both Sides Now: One Man's Journey through Womanhood* by Dhillon Khosla (2006).

36. The physical complications of FTM "bottom" surgeries can include extensive difficulties with penile construction and function.

37. Tim Dean's (2009) work on barebacking (sex without condoms) among gay men in the United States is a useful point of comparison in evaluating engagement with death risks and the concept of risk management as essential to health. As he puts it, "Embracing risk, including the risks associated with unprotected sex, offers one way around superegoistic health imperatives" (66). Dean continues, "Paradoxically, bareback subculture institutionalizes risk as a permanent condition of existence, embracing and eroticizing while promulgating the idea that seroconversion renders moot one particular risk" (69). Conceptualizing risk not as pathological but as inherent to engagement with life is critical to this assessment.

38. Self-direction in medical care among those who wish to transform their bodies is not unique to South Africa. For example, Don Kulick's well-known work found *travesti's* similar use of hormones, as well as injections of silicone, in Brazil (1998). And a recent *New York Times* article found similar practices with inventive but potentially fatal consequences in New York City (Murray 2011).

39. For broader contexnt, see Graeme Reid's work examining the space of the Skyline bar (1999, 2010).

40. I return to a discussion of South African gay male communities' ideals of gender in Chapter 5.

41. Morgan et al. define stealth in this way: "Being in stealth refers to the refusal to publicly identify with trans issues or to disclose the fact that one is a trans person" (2009: 236).

42. Recent work addressing the complications of passing in trans* and/or gender liminal communities in the United States includes Sycamore (2006) and Serano (2007).

43. The cost of surgery—R97,000—was approximately $72,750 at this time (World Currency Yearbook 1993).

44. In the early 1980s, Carmella's stated income would have been the equivalent of about $550 per month.

45. R30,000 was approximately $7,833 in the mid 1990s (Oanda FX History 2003).

46. R40,000 was approximately $10,445 in the same time period (Oanda FX History 2003).

47. Ashforth's later work provides further explanation of the specificities of jealousy: "In every instance the answer to the question, 'Why would they do witchcraft' is 'Because of jealousy.' In everyday usage in Soweto, the commonplace English word, 'jealousy' encompasses envy of others' goods and good fortune as well as well as fear of rivals' obtaining what one already has. Local African languages make no distinction between 'envy' and 'jealousy' . . . 'Jealousy' serves as the name of the primary motive for witchcraft. It is premised upon hatred, which itself is taken as a free-flowing accompaniment of everyday life (as omnipresent as its opposite love, comradeship, and fellow feeling) that flares into rage on account of jealousy" (2005: 70).

Chapter Four

1. I primarily use the contemporary term "intersexual" here to refer to those between sex categories, as it is preferred by most intersexed people today. I use "hermaphrodite" only when historically appropriate or when a narrator self-identifies as such. I do not use the newer terminology of "disorders of sex development" (DSD) as it has not been widely taken up in South Africa.

2. The concept referred to here as *stabane* is also described as *istabane, sitabane, isitabane* by narrators. There are similar conceptual usages in Zulu, Sotho, Xhosa, Afrikaans, and other languages spoken in South Africa's so-called black and coloured townships and rural areas.

3. I provide a more detailed discussion of performativity in Chapter 5.

4. I appreciate Neville Hoad's rethinking of the "lens" of race and homosexuality he uses in his work, "as much a kaleidoscope as it is a camera, microscope, or telescope" (Hoad 2005: xix).

5. For a further discussion of Baartman, see, for example: Gilman 1985; Collins 1991; Dubow 1995, Davison 1993; Strother 1999; Coombes 2003; Elbourne 2002; Crais and Scully 2009.

6. Rassool and Hayes explicate how as part of academia Saartjie Baartman has not been historicized within a larger analysis of the production of images of steatopygic women which has continued since colonial times (2002: 120). I also believe that the broad fetishization of Baartman among contemporary feminists in the global North deserves further attention and analysis.

7. Jack Stodel, who claimed to have produced the postcard, printed it in one of his memoirs with the caption: "She only answered me in German, so I painted a swastika on her (Namib Desert)." (1965). This comment conveys a popular sentiment of colonists of the period, although Rassool and Hayes believe Stodel may not have been the true photographer behind this postcard.

8. Patricia Hayes reminds us that "European ideas about African women focused on their supposedly excessive sexuality. Buttocks and private parts (particularly of Khoisan women) were represented as unusual" and were subjects of both science and pornography (Hayes 1996: 381).

9. A. P. Cawadias, *Hermaphroditos: The Human Intersex* (London: William Heinemann, 1946).

10. H. J. Grace, "Intersex in Four South African Racial Groups in Durban" (M.Sc, University of Natal, Durban, South Africa, 1970). Studies citing this work include J. J. L. DeSouza, P. Barnett, G. D. Kisner, and J. P. Murray, "True Hermaphroditism: A Case Report with Observations on its Bizarre Presentation" (1984), and Michele Ramsay, Rennee Bernstein, Esther Zwane, David C. Page, and Trefor Jenkins, "XX True Hermaphroditism in Southern African Blacks: An Enigma of Primary Sexual Differentiation" (1988).

11. See, for example, racialized assertions made in the documentary film. *The Third Sex*, directed by Jack Roberts (2000). Historian Marc Epprecht similarly suggests that the supposed frequency of intersexuality among black South Africans and the lack of medical services to these individuals "provides yet another example of how medical science and sexuality could be used both to rationalize white privilege and to create ever-clearer lines between the races" (2005: 148).

12. See www.intersex.org.za. I return to the legislative work of this group and its founder, Sally Gross, in the Conclusion. See also Gross (2009) and Swarr, Gross, and Theron (2009).

13. The recent case of South African athlete Caster Semenya has raised the issue of gender testing and verification in this context; see Swarr with Gross

and Theron, "Intersex Activism: Caster Semenya's Impact and Import" in *Feminist Studies*, fall 2009. See also Dworkin, Swarr, and Cooky, forthcoming in *Feminist Studies*.

14. See, for example, Gevisser and Cameron 1994 and Krouse 1993.

15. Many scholars trace the advent of specifically labeled "lesbian" and "gay" identification to the Delmas Treason Trial of gay anti-apartheid activist Simon Nkoli in 1984. See Simon Nkoli, "Wardrobes: Coming Out as a Black Gay Activist in South Africa," in *Defiant Desire*; and Donald L. Donham, "Freeing South Africa: The 'Modernization' of Male-Male Sexuality in Soweto," *Cultural Anthropology*.

16. I discuss the concept of butchness and relationships in relation to sexual violence at length in an article entitled "Paradoxes of Butchness: Lesbian Masculinities and Sexual Violence in Contemporary South Africa" (2012) in *Signs: Journal of Women in Culture and Society*.

17. Kheswa's important study also explores the composition of femme identifications among lesbians in the Johannesburg area (2005).

18. One exception is Rankhotha's 2005 interview indicating an unusual perception of bisexuals as *izitabane* who spread HIV. For further discussion of bisexuality, see also Epprecht (2006) and Stobie (2007).

19. A *pantsula* is also defined as "a township macho who dresses like a fifties mafioso" (McLean and Ngcobo 1994: 185). Thus, like *stabane*, this term has social significations that are tied to, but go beyond, sexuality.

20. The implications of these relationship dynamics for HIV transmission are beyond the scope of this chapter, but it is important to note that both Linda Ngcobo and Simon Nkoli died of AIDS-related complications. And intentional HIV infections of lesbians as part of what activists are calling "corrective rapes" add another element to this violence.

21. As a related point of comparison, see Epprecht's historical analysis of his interviews with *n'angas* (traditional healers) in Zimbabwe about same-sex sexual encounters:

> What we today would now term homosexual orientation or transgender identity was not necessarily an offense at all but a respected attribute if caused by certain types of spirit possession and manifested in certain ways. This would have included rare cases of physiological hermaphroditism as well as possession by benign spirits of the opposite sex. Such explanations of cause removed blame from an individual, and same-sex couples so possessed could live together as husband and wife without attracting opprobrium. (2005: 35)

22. As Kulick reminds us, Butler's work in *Gender Trouble* disrupts the oft-emphasized distinction between sex and gender.

If the immutable character of sex is contested, perhaps the construct called "sex" is as culturally constructed as gender; indeed,
perhaps it was always already gender, with the consequence that the
distinction between sex and gender turns out to be no distinction
at all. (1998: 6–7)

23. One early discussion of statistics on rape is provided in Yoon Jung Park,
Joanne Fedler, and Zubedá Dangor (2000), and such discussions have continued
to the present. Recent accounts unpack the specificity of survivors' same-sex
sexuality as a motivation for sexual violence: "Shoot the Drag Queen! . . . and
Daisy Died," (2008), Mufweba (2003); Ngubane (2003); Smith (2003); Fraser
(2008); Mkhize et al. (2010). As Deborah Posel (2005) points out, while male
sexuality is contentious and analysis of it is critical, nationhood and morality
in the transitional period are fundamental to understanding sexual violence in
South Africa. Further, Lahiri (2011) critically unsettles the language of "correction" and points to the ways that South African men have been represented as
primitive and exceptional for their attacks, perpetrating a "particularly invidious
racist mythology" (122). Both she and Moffett (2006) highlight racism inherent
in representations of such rapes as solely perpetrated by black men. I address
the parameters and causes for sexual violence targeting lesbians at length elsewhere (Swarr 2012).

Chapter Five

1. See also De Waal and Manion's *Pride: Protest and Celebration* (2006).
2. *Shebeens* are establishments in former townships outside of urban centers akin to locally-owned bars where community members gather and drink
alcohol.
3. In this chapter, I borrow from Stuart Hall's understanding of articulation as "the form of connection that can make a unity of two different elements,
under certain conditions . . . a linkage which is not necessary, determined, abso-
lute and essential for all time" (Slack 1996: 115).
4. Viviane Ki Namaste offers important critiques of the ways that Butler
and other feminist theorists have objectified gender liminal people for the sake
of advancing queer theory, what Namaste calls a "distortion of transgender realities" (1996: 188). While drawing on Butler's insights, I pay close attention to
the contexts of drag in this chapter.
5. In another complementary instance Butler, in her analysis of *Paris
is Burning*, suggests that drag performer Venus Xtravaganza cannot be simply
referred to as "marked by race and class, for gender is not the substance or

primary substrate and race and class the qualifying attributes. In this instance, gender is the vehicle for the phantasmatic transformation of that nexus of race and class, the site of its articulation" (1993: 130).

6. As addressed previously, within Afrikaans etymology, the term *moffie* may be derogatory or, more recently, a self-chosen label of pride, and connotes an *effeminate* gay man. The term has roots in intersexuality, as well, recalling the discussion of *stabane* in the previous chapter.

7. The origins of "coloured" identification in South Africa—used here again in accordance with individuals' self-designations—are in the Population Registration Act of 1950 which designated seven subgroups as coloured: Cape Coloured, Cape Malay, Griqua, Indian, Chinese, Other Asiatic, and Other Coloured.

8. Despite its racist connotations, "Coon" has been reclaimed by the carnival's participants. As a famous coloured Cape Town composer and coach of a Coon troupe puts it, "[t]he Americans come and they don't want us to use the word Coon because it is derogatory. Here Coon is not derogatory in our sense" (Martin 1999: 4).

9. District Six is a community that was destroyed in the 1950s under apartheid relocation schemes and is now a site of fierce contention (Jeppie 1990). District Six in many ways epitomizes how struggles around race, class, and gender are often intensely spatial.

10. Evidence of tabloid accounts recalls attempts to sensationalize gender liminality by "buying" Herman's story in Chapter 3.

11. For a discussion of the relationship between minstrelsy and transvestitism in the United States, see Garber (1992).

12. Though a comprehensive study of the application of these laws has yet to be published, geography, political climate, and race all seem to have influenced their enforcement.

13. "Miming" is how South African drag performers describe "lip synching" to the words of pre-recorded songs.

14. "Impersonation" indicates drag intended to imitate a particular singer.

15. Anti-apartheid activists in the 1980s redeployed this construction by adopting an inclusive "black" identity that included all racial groups—African, coloured, and Indian—that were systematically oppressed by the apartheid regime.

16. Pseudonyms protect narrators' anonymity again here, except when analyzing performances reviewed in newspapers.

17. As previously mentioned, whites commonly classify themselves into two cultural groups—English and Afrikaans—and there is a long history of cultural and political conflict between these two groups.

18. See especially "Boeremeisie" (1996). It is of note that Koekemoer also impersonated Tina Turner as a *boeremeisie*, reinforcing the point that multiple forms of whiteness can serve as mediums for impersonating women of color.

19. The use of this buttock padding recalls representations of Saartjie Baartman and /Khanako's "steatopygia" described in Chapter 4 and common representations of African women's bodies.

20. For nuanced discussions of beauty pageants in South Africa, see also Thomas (2006) and Clowes (2001).

21. Miss GLOW is not representative of all pageants—South African drag pageants and competitions vary and some outside of the townships feature white participants (e.g., Miss Gay SA).

22. Such a conceptualization of gender, sex, and sexuality is not unique to South Africa; anthropologists Don Kulick (1998) and Roger Lancaster (1992), for example, have written about similar ideologies and terminology in Brazil and Nicaragua, respectively.

23. The murder of Daisy Dube addressed in the previous chapter is one recent example of this violence. The rapes and murders of lesbians including famous soccer star Eudy Simelane and lesbian couple Sizakele Sigasa and Salome Masooa, whose attack incited the 07-07-07 Campaign (the date of their murders), have brought increasing attention to these atrocities, continuing in high numbers. Though statistics on the levels of sexual violence in South Africa are hotly contested, it is generally agreed that one sexual assault occurs approximately every 28 seconds in South Africa, which makes the incidence of rape of women in South Africa twice as high as in any other country for which statistics are currently available (e.g., Simpson and Kraak 1998: 2). Such violence is not really quantifiable, and I discuss contentious debates over rape statistics elsewhere (2012). See this work and Mkhize et al. (2010) for detailed discussions of additional instances of violence and their implications.

24. As a useful point of comparison, see Martin F. Manalansan IV's work on drag and multiple meanings of "drama" among Filipino drag performers in New York City in *Global Divas: Filipino Gay Men in the Diaspora* (2003). Manalansan explains how the multiple meanings of the concept of drama interweave in his ethnography to expose the dynamism of words, concepts, and transnational connections.

Conclusion

1. Unlike in U.S.-based feminist and trans studies, trans* bodies have not been appropriated and objectified to facilitate academic gendered analyses in South Africa. Trans activists in South Africa actively resist gender minoritization and seek to facilitate collaboration against the divisiveness of apartheid through coalition-building.

2. Khayelitsha is a former township outside of Cape Town located in the Cape Flats.

3. I document the poor medical outcomes of many phalloplasties in Chapter 3, one argument that inspired this legal shift.

4. This was approximately $17,142 in 1994.

5. The contours of this patriarchy have been increasingly explored by feminist scholars. For instance, in her study of incest in white Afrikaner families, sociologist Diana Russell (1997) draws important parallels between the brutality and sense of entitlement associated with white men's treatment of black South Africans and the extreme violence inflicted upon members of their own families.

6. Smit (2006) and Klein (2008) document some of the nuances of the network of services and treatments available in South Africa.

7. As South African historian Leonard Thompson explains, policies of Botha's administration "included efforts to neutralize South Africa's neighbors, to scrap apartheid laws that were not essential to the maintenance of white supremacy, to draw English-speaking citizens into the party, to win the cooperation of big business, to intensify the ethnic and class cleavages among the subject's peoples, and to suppress domestic dissidents" (1995: 224).

8. See, for instance, Swarr with Gross and Theron 2009 and Morgan, Marais, and Wellbeloved 2009. The Web sites of these organizations are also instructive: (Budding Roses) http://christelle03.50megs.com/photo2.html, (Triangle Project) http://www.triangle.org.za/, (Intersex South Africa) http://www.intersex.org.za/, (Gender DynamiX) http://www.genderdynamix.co.za/ (as of 2010).

9. No statistics on membership demographics are available.

10. Other organizations focused primarily on gays and lesbians like the Equality Project and OUT—LGBT Well-being or addressing other issues like the Sex Worker Education and Advocacy Task Force (SWEAT) have also served gender liminal, transsexual, and intersexual South Africans on issues ranging from immigration to safer sex.

11. Despite their research and efforts, numerically it is likely that the majority of those who are gender liminal in South Africa do not access these organizations' services.

12. I am not interested in tracing the historical origination of terminology here but in what it represents.

13. Joy Wellbeloved suggests, "We need a pool of information which includes doctors and psychologists, and we need to tell people that this pool is available. That is really what I think we should be focusing on in order to help" (In Morgan et al. 2009: 135).

14. David Valentine writes that his ethnographic work inspired him to address these concerns with three goals in mind: "First . . . to note the dangers in taking actual bodily modification as the exemplar of what we mean by the social construction of the body; second, to question what it means to consider such social constructions solely in terms of groups or individuals who are othered by their bodily practices or makeup; and third, to use the space opened

by such practices and bodies to consider a wider field in which to consider what the 'construction of bodies' means" (Valentine and Wilchins 1997: 221). The gendered and sexed inconsistencies of all bodies are critical to this analysis.

Bibliography

Abrahams, Rashid. Interview by Amanda Swarr and Sam Bullington. Cape Town, South Africa. 2000.

Abu-Lughod, Lila. "Can there be a Feminist Ethnography?" *Women and Performance: A Journal of Feminist Theory* 5, no.1 (1990): 7–27.

———. "The Romance of Resistance: Tracing Transformations of Power Through Bedouin Women." *American Ethnologist* 17, no. 1 (1990): 41–56.

———. "Writing Against Culture." *Recapturing Anthropology*, ed. R. G. Fox, 137–62. SAR Press, 1991.

Achmat, Taghmeda, and Theresa Raizenberg. "Midi and Theresa: Lesbian Activism in South Africa." *Feminist Studies* 29, no. 3 (fall 2003): 643–675.

Achmat, Zackie. "Apostles of Civilized Vice: Immoral Practices and Unnatural Vice in South African Prisons and Compounds, 1890–1920." *Social Dynamics* 19, no. 2 (1993): 92–110.

Agamben, Giorgio. *Homo Sacer*. Stanford, CA: Stanford University Press, 1998.

Alexander, M. Jacqui. "Imperial Desire/Sexual Utopias: White Gay Capital and Transnational Tourism." In *Talking Visions: Multicultural Feminism in a Transnational Age*, ed. Ella Shohat, 281–305. Cambridge, MA: MIT Press, 1998.

———. *Pedagogies of Crossing: Meditations on Feminism, Sexual Politics, Memory, and the Sacred*. Durham, NC: Duke University Press, 2005.

Alexander, M. Jacqui, and Chandra Talpade Mohanty, eds. *Feminist Genealogies: Colonial Legacies, Democratic Futures*. New York: Routledge, 1996.

Algei, Peter. "Rewriting Patriarchal Scripts: Women, Labor, and Popular Culture in South African Clothing Industry Beauty Contests, 1970s–2005." *Journal of Social History* (fall 2008): 31–55.

"Alteration of Sex Description and Status Act: No. 49 of 2003. No. 331." *Government Gazette*, vol. 465, no. 26148. Pretoria: Government Printer, March 2004.

Amadiume, Ifi. *Male Daughters, Female Husbands*. London: Zed Books, 1988.

Angier, Natalie. "New Debate Over Surgery on Ambiguous Genitals." *New York Times*, Tuesday, May 13, 1997. B7, B11.

Anzaldúa, Gloria. *Borderlands/La Frontera: The New Mestiza*. San Francisco, CA: Aunt Lute Press, 1987.

Apartheid and Health. Geneva, Switzerland: World Health Organization, 1983.

"Apostles of Civilised Vice." Directed by Zackie Achmat and Jack Lewis. Part One: Questions of a Queer Reading History and Part Two: A Natural Thing. 1999.

Arnfred, Signe, ed. *Re-thinking Sexualities in Africa.* Uppsala, Sweden: Almqvist and Wiksell Tryckeri AB, 2004.

Arondekar, Anjali. *For the Record: On Sexuality and the Colonial Archive in India.* Durham: Duke University Press, 2009.

Ashforth, Adam. "Of Secrecy and the Commonplace: Witchcraft and Power in Soweto." *Social Research* 63, no. 4 (winter 1996): 1183–1234.

—————. *Witchcraft, Violence, and Democracy in South Africa.* Chicago: University of Chicago Press, 2005.

Asscheman, Henk, and Louis J. G. Gooren. "Hormone Treatment in Transsexuals." In *Gender Dysphoria: Interdisciplinary Approaches in Clinical Management,* ed. Walter O. Bockting and Eli Colman, 39–52. New York: The Haworth Press, 1992.

Baard, Sandra. Interview by Amanda Swarr and Sam Bullington. Cape Town, South Africa. May 2000.

Baker, Elizabeth. Interview by Amanda Swarr and Sam Bullington. July 1997.

Baker, Roger. *Drag: A History of Female Impersonation in the Performing Arts.* Washington Square, NY: New York University Press, 1994.

Baldwin-Ragaven, Laurel, Jeanelle de Gruchy, and Leslie London. *An Ambulance of the Wrong Colour: Health Professionals, Human Rights, and Ethics in South Africa.* Cape Town: University of Cape Town Press, 1999.

Barnard, Ian. "The United States in South Africa: (Post)Colonial Queer Theory?" In *Postcolonial and Queer Theories: Intersections and Essays,* ed. John C. Hawley, 129–38. Westport, CT and London: Greenwood Press, 2001.

"Be Like Others" [Transsexual in Iran]. Directed by Tanaz Eshaghian. Necessary Illusions, 2008.

Behar, Ruth, and Deborah Gordon, eds. *Women Writing Culture.* Berkeley and Los Angeles, CA: University of California Press, 1995.

Behind the Mask Web site. www.behindthemask.org.za.

Bell, Diane, Pat Caplan, and Wazir Jahan Karim, eds. *Gendered Fields: Women, Men, and Ethnography.* New York and London: Routledge, 1995 [1993].

Bell, Vikki. "On Speech, Race, and Melancholia: An Interview with Judith Butler." In *Performativity and Belonging,* ed. Vikki Bell, 163–74. London: SAGE, 1999.

Benjamin, Harry. "The Standards of Care for Gender Identity Disorders." International Gender Dysphoria Association, http://gendercare.com/library/hbigda-sc6.html 2001 [1979].

—————. *The Transsexual Phenomenon.* New York: The Julian Press, Inc., 1966.

Bennun, Mervyn E. "Understanding the Nightmare: Politics and Violence in South Africa." In *Negotiating Justice: A New Constitution for South Africa*, ed. Mervyn Bennun and Malyn D. D. Newitt. 26–61. Exeter: University of Exeter Press, 1995.

Besnier, Niko. "Polynesian Gender Liminality through Time and Space." In *Third Sex, Third Gender: Beyond Sexual Dimorphism in Culture and History*, ed. Gilbert Herdt. 285–328. New York: Zone Books, 1994.

Billings, Dwight B., and Thomas Urban. "The Socio-Medical Construction of Transsexualism: An Interpretation and Critique." In *Blending Genders: Social Aspects of Cross-Dressing and Sex-Changing*, ed. Richard Ekins and Dave King. New York: Routledge, 1996.

Binnie, Jon. *The Globalization of Sexuality*. London: Sage, 2004.

Blackwood, Evelyn, ed. "Falling in Love with an-Other Lesbian." In *Taboo: Sex, Identity and Erotic Subjectivity in Anthropological Fieldwork*, ed. Don Kulick and Margaret Willson, 51–75. New York: Routledge, 1995.

———. *The Many Faces of Homosexuality: Anthropological Approaches to Homosexual Behavior*. New York: Harrington Park Press, 1986.

Blackwood, Evelyn, and Saskia E. Wieringa, eds. *Female Desires: Same-Sex Relations and Transgender Practices Across Cultures*. New York: Columbia University Press, 1999.

Block, Norman L., and Arthur N. Tessler. "Transsexualism and Surgical Procedures." *Surgery, Gynecology, and Obstetrics* (March 1971): 517–25.

Blouws, Kenneth. Interview by Amanda Swarr and Sam Bullington. Cape Town, South Africa. 2000.

Bockting, Walter O., and Eli Coleman. "A Comprehensive Approach to the Treatment of Gender Dysphoria." In *Gender Dysphoria: Interdisciplinary Approaches in Clinical Management*, ed. Walter O. Bockting and Eli Coleman, 131–55. New York: Haworth Press, 1992.

Boellstorff, Tom, and William L. Leap. "Introduction: Globalization." In *Speaking in Queer Tongues: Globalization and Gay Language*, ed. William L. Leap and Tom Boellstorff, 134–162. Urbana and Chicago: University of Illinois Press, 2004.

"Boeremeisie," *Cape Times* (Cape Town), Wednesday 22 May, 1996.

Bonner, Philip, and Lauren Segal. *Soweto: A History*. Cape Town: Maskew Miller Longman, 1998.

Bornstein, Kate. *Gender Outlaw: On Men, Women and the Rest of Us*. New York: Routledge, 1994.

Borstelmann, Thomas. *Apartheid's Reluctant Uncle: The United States and Southern Africa in the Early Cold War*. New York: Oxford University Press, 1993.

Bowen, Gary. "A Dictionary of Words for Masculine Women." http://www.amboyz.org/articles/f2mwords/f2mvwxyz.html. 1999 [January 29, 2004].

Bozzoli, Belinda, with Mmantho Nkotsoe. *Women of Phokeng: Consciousness, Life Strategy, and Migrancy in South Africa, 1900–1983.* Portsmouth, NH: Heinemann, 1991.

Brandzel, Amy L. "Queering Citizenship?: Same-Sex Marriage and the State." *GLQ: A Journal of Lesbian and Gay Studies* 11, no. 2 (2005): 171–204.

Breckenridge, Keith. "Verwoerd's Bureau of Proof: Total Information in the Making of Apartheid." *History Workshop Journal* 59, no. 1 (2005): 83–108.

Bridges, William. *Transitions: Making Sense of Life's Changes.* Cambridge, MA: Perseus Books, 1980.

Bruns, Karen, and Vallance Kannelly. "The Legal Definition of Marriage with Particular Reference to Sex Changes and the Prohibition of Discrimination on the Grounds of Sexual Orientation." *Responsa Meridiana* 6, no. 5 (1995): 487–504.

Bullington, Sam. "From the 'Rainbow Nation' to the 'New Apartheid': Sexual Orientation and HIV/AIDS in Contemporary South African Nation-Building." Dissertation, University of Minnesota, 2005.

Bullington, Sam, and Amanda Lock Swarr. "Conflicts and Collaborations: Building Trust in Transnational South Africa." In *Critical Transnational Feminist Praxis,* ed. Amanda Lock Swarr and Richa Nagar, 87–104. Albany: State University of New York Press, 2010.

Bullough, Vern L., and Bonnie Bullough. *Cross-Dressing, Sex, and Gender.* Philadelphia, PA: University of Pennsylvania Press, 1993.

Burana, Lily, Roxxie, and Linnea Due, eds. *Dagger: On Butch Women.* Pittsburgh and San Francisco: Cleis Press, 1994.

Butchart, Alexander. *The Anatomy of Power: European Constructions of the African Body.* New York: Zed Books, 1998.

Butler, Judith. "Gender is Burning: Questions of Appropriation and Subversion." *Bodies that Matter: On the Discursive Limits of "Sex,"* 121–40. New York: Routledge, 1993.

———. *Gender Trouble: Feminism and the Subversion of Identity.* New York: Routledge, 1990.

———. "Imitation and Gender Subordination." *Inside/Out: Lesbian Theories, Gay Theories,* ed. Diana Fuss, 13–31. New York: Routledge, 1991.

———. *Undoing Gender.* New York: Routledge, 2004.

Cage, Ken, in collaboration with Moyra Evans. *Gayle: The Language of Kinks and Queens, A History of Gay Language in South Africa.* Houghton, South Africa: Jacana Press, 2003.

Califia, Pat. *Sex Changes: The Politics of Transgenderism.* San Francisco, CA: Cleis Press, 1997.

Cameron, Edwin. "'Unapprehended Felons': Gays and Lesbians and the Law in South Africa." In *Defiant Desire: Gay and Lesbian Lives in South Africa,* ed.

Mark Gevisser and Edwin Cameron, 89–111. Johannesburg, South Africa: Ravan Press. 1994.

Cameron, Loren. *Body Alchemy: Transsexual Portraits*. Pittsburgh, PA and San Francisco, CA: Cleis Press, 1996.

Canaday, Margot. "Thinking Sex in the Transnational Turn: An Introduction." *American Historical Review* 24, no. 5 (December 2009): 1250–1257.

Cape Town Transsexual/Transgender Support Group. "Oral Presentation for the South African Home Affairs Portfolio Committee Hearings," 2003.

Cawadias, A. P. *Hermaphroditos: The Human Intersex*. London: William Heinemann, 1946.

Chan Sam, Tanya. "Five Women: Black Lesbian Life on the Reef." In *Defiant Desire: Gay and Lesbian Lives in South Africa*, ed. Mark Gevisser and Edwin Cameron, 186–97. Johannesburg, South Africa: Ravan Press, 1994.

Chatterjee, Partha. "Was there a Hegemonic Project of the Colonial State?" In *Contesting Colonial Hegemony: State and Society in Africa and India*, ed. Dagmar Engels and Shula Marks, 79–84. London: The German Historical Institute, British Academic Press, 1994.

Chauncey, George. *Gay New York: Gender, Urban Culture, and the Making of the Gay Male World, 1980–1940*. New York: Basic Books, 1994.

Chetty, Dhianaraj R. "A Drag at Madame Costello's: Cape Moffie Life and the Popular Press in the 1950s and 1960s." In *Defiant Desire: Gay and Lesbian Lives in South Africa*, ed. Mark Gevisser and Edwin Cameron, 115–27. Johannesburg, South Africa: Ravan Press, 1994.

Clowes, Lindsay. "'Are You Going to be MISS (or MR) Africa?': Contesting Masculinity in *Drum* Magazine 1951–1953." *Gender and History* 13, no. 1 (April 2001): 1–20.

Cock, Jacklyn. *Colonels and Cadres: War and Gender in South Africa*. Cape Town: Oxford University Press, 1991.

———. "Engendering Gay and Lesbian Rights: The Equality Clause in the South African Constitution." In *Sex and Politics in South Africa,* ed. Neville Hoad, Karen Martin and Graeme Reid, 188–209. Cape Town: Double Storey Books. 2005.

———. *Maids and Madams: Domestic Workers Under Apartheid*. London: Women's Press, 1989 [1980].

Coetzee, Warren. Interview by Amanda Swarr and Sam Bullington. 1997.

Colapinto, John. *As Nature Made Him: The Boy who was Raised as a Girl*. New York: Perennial, 2000.

———. "Gender Gap: What Were the Real Reasons Behind David Reimer's Suicide?" Slate, June 3, 2004. http://www.slate.com/id/2101678/

Collins, Patricia Hill. *Black Feminist Thought: Knowledge, Consciousness, and the Politics of Empowerment*. New York: Routledge, 1991.

Comaroff, Jean. "Beyond Bare Life: AIDS, (Bio)Politics, and the Neoliberal Order." *Public Culture* 19, no. 1 (2007): 197–219.

Comaroff, Jean, and John Comaroff. *Of Revelation and Revolution: Christiantity, Colonialism, and Consciousness in South Africa, Volume One.* Chicago: University of Chicago Press, 1991.

Constantine-Simms, Delroy, ed. *The Greatest Taboo: Homosexuality in Black Communities.* Los Angeles: Alyson, 2000.

Constitution of the Republic of South Africa. Pretoria: Government Printers, 1996.

Coombes, Annie E. *History After Apartheid: Visual Culture and Public Memory in a Democratic South Africa.* Durham and London: Duke University Press, 2003.

Cooper, Barbara M. *Marriage in Maradi: Gender and Culture in a Hausa Society in Niger, 1900–1989.* Portsmouth, NH: Heinneman, 1997.

Crais, Clifton, and Pamela Scully. *Sara Baartman and the Hottentot Venus: A Ghost Story and a Biography.* Princeton: Princeton University Press, 2009.

Crawhall, Nigel. "Balancing Freedom and Fear: Gay Men, Sex, and HIV in the Post-apartheid Era." In *Performing Queer: Shaping Sexualities, 1994–2004—Volume One*, ed. Mikki van Zyl and Melissa Steyn, 267–279. Roggebaai: Kwela Books. 2005.

Crenshaw, Kimberlé William. "Beyond Racism and Misogyny: Black Feminism and 2 Live Crew." In *Words that Wound: Critical Race Theory, Assaultive Speech, and the First Amendment*, ed. Mari J. Matsuda, Charles R. Lawrence III, Richard Delgado, and Kimberlé William Crenshaw, 111–32. Boulder, CO: Westview Press, 1993.

Crichton, Derk. "Gender Reassignment Surgery for Male Primary Transsexuals." *South African Medical Journal* 83, no. 5 (May 1993): 347–49.

"Cruel and Unusual: Transgender Women in Prison." Documentary film produced by Janet Baus, Dan Hunt, and Reid Williams. Outcast Films, 2006.

Cruz-Malavé, Arnaldo and Martin F. Manalansan IV, eds. *Queer Globalizations: Citizenship and the Afterlife of Colonialism.* New York: New York University Press, 2002.

Culver, E. H. "Health Legislation." *Public Health in South Africa*, 337–352. Cape Town: Central News Agency, 1958.

Currah, Paisley, Richard M. Juang, and Shannon Price Minter, eds. *Transgender Rights.* Minneapolis: University of Minnesota Press, 2006.

Darling, Hope. Personal Communication, 2009.

Dart, Raymond A. "The Physical Characters of the /?Auni-≠Khomani Bushmen." In *Bushmen of the Southern Kalahari*, ed. J. D. Rheinallt Jones and C. M. Doke, 118–188. Johannesburg, South Africa: The University of the Witwatersrand Press, 1937.

Davids, Giles. Interview by Amanda Swarr. Cape Town, August 2007

Davis, Angela. *Women, Race, and Class.* New York: Random House, 1981.

Davison, Jean. *Voices from Mutira: Change in the Lives of Gikuyu Women, 1910–1995*. Boulder, CO: Lynne Reinner Publishers, 1996.

Davison, Patricia. "Human Subjects as Museum Objects: A Project to Make Life-Casts of 'Bushmen' and 'Hottentots,' 1907–1924." *Annals of the South African Museum* 102, no. 5 (1993): 165–183.

Day, Lynda. "Mamatoma: 'The Chief's Namesake': Female Chiefs in Sierra Leone, and their Stranger from America." Paper presented at the annual meeting of the African Studies Association, San Francisco, CA, November 1996.

Daymond, M. J., ed. *South African Feminisms: Writing, Theory, and Criticism, 1990–1994*. New York and London: Garland Publishing, 1996.

De Beer, Cedric. *The South African Disease: Apartheid Health and Health Services*. Trenton, NJ: Africa World Press, 1986 [1984].

De la Chapelle, Albert. "Invited Editorial: The Complicated Issue of Human Sex Determination." *American Journal of Human Genetics* 43 (1988): 1–3.

DeSouza, J. J. L., P. Barnett, C. D. Kisner, and J. P. Murray. "True Hermaphroditism: A Case Report with Observations on its Bizarre Presentation." *South African Medical Journal* 66 (December 1, 1984): 855–858.

De Waal, Shaun, and Anthony Manion, eds. *Pride: Protest and Celebration*. Johannesburg, South Africa: Fanele/Jacana, 2006.

Dean, Tim. *Unlimited Imtimacy: Reflections on the Subculture of Barebacking*. Chicago: University of Chicago Press, 2009.

Devenish, Marc. "High-kicking Class Act is on the Cards from the Start," *Cape Times* (Cape Town), Thursday, 5 June, 1997.

Devor, Aaron, and Nicholas Matte. "Building a Better World for Transpeople: Reed Erickson and the Erickson Educational Foundation." *International Journal of Transgenderism* 10, no. 1 (2007): 47–68.

———. "ONE Inc. and Reed Erickson: The Uneasy Collaboration of Gay and Trans Activism, 1964–2003." *GLQ: A Journal of Lesbian and Gay Studies* 10, no. 2 (2004): 179–209.

Devor, Holly. *FTM: Female-to-Male Transsexuals in Society*. Bloomington and Indianapolis: Indiana University Press, 1997.

———. *Gender Blending: Confronting the Limits of Duality*. Bloomington and Indianapolis: Indiana University Press, 1989.

Dewaele, P. A. L. M., and B. van Iddekinge. "Absence of a Functional Vagina: A Report of Two Cases and a Review." *South African Medical Journal* 71, no. 12 (June 1987): 788–9.

Dhlomo, Buyani. Interview by Amanda Swarr and Sam Bullington. Gauteng, South Africa. July and October 2000.

Diamond, Morty, ed. *From the Inside Out: Radical Gender Transformation, FTM and Beyond*. San Francisco, CA: Manic D Press, 2004.

Dinner, M. "Intersex: A Review and Report of Experience at Baragwanath Hospital." *South African Journal of Surgery* 7, no. 2 (April–June 1969): 49–61.

Dirsuweit, Teresa. "The Problem of Identities: The Lesbian, Gay, Bisexual, Transgender and Intersex Social Movement in South Africa" In *Voices of Protest: Social Movements in Post-Apartheid South Africa*, ed. Richard Ballard, Adam Habib, and Imraan Valodia, 325–347. Scottsville, South Africa: University of KwaZulu-Natal Press, 2006.

Dladla, Mpho. Interview by Amanda Swarr and Sam Bullington. Cape Town, South Africa. October 2000.

Don, Alexander M. "Transvestism and Transsexualism: A Report of 4 Cases and Problems Associated with their Management." *South African Medical Journal* 37 (May 4, 1963): 479–85.

Donham, Donald L. "Freeing South Africa: The 'Modernization' of Male-Male Sexuality in Soweto." *Cultural Anthropology* 13, no. 1 (1998): 3–21.

Dreger, Alice Domurat, ed. *Intersex in the Age of Ethics*. Hagerstown, MD: University Publishing Group, 1999.

Drury, James, and Matthew Drennan. "The Pudendal Parts of the South African Bush Race." *Medical Journal of South Africa* 22 (November 1926): 113–17.

Du Preez, Amanda. "Technology and Transsexuality: Secret Alliances." In *Sex, Gender, Becoming: Post-Apartheid Reflections*, ed. Karin van Marle, 1–18. Pretoria: Pretoria University Law Press, 2006.

Dubow, Saul. *Scientific Racism in Modern South Africa*. New York: Cambridge University Press, 1995.

Durkheim, Emile. *Suicide*. Translated by John A. Spaulding and George Simpson. Glencoe, IL: The Free Press, 1951 [1897].

Dworkin, Shari L., Amanda Lock Swarr, and Cheryl Cooky. "Sex, Gender, and Racial (In)Justice in Sport: The Treatment of South African Track Star Caster Semenya." *Feminist Studies*, Spring 2013.

Edmunds, Vita. Interview by Amanda Swarr and Sam Bullington. Cape Town, South Africa. July and August 1997.

Ekins, Richard, and Dave King, eds. *Blending Genders: Social Aspects of Cross-Dressing and Sex-Changing*. New York: Routledge, 1996.

Elbourne, Elizabeth. "Domestic Disposessions: The Ideologies of Domesticity and 'Home' and the British Construction of the Primitive from the Eighteenth to the Early Nineteenth Century. In *Deep hiStories: Gender and Colonialism in Southern Africa*, ed. Wendy Woodward, Patricia Hayes, and Gary Minkley, 27–54. New York and Amsterdam: Rodopi, 2002.

Elder, Glen S. *Hostels, Sexuality, and the Apartheid Legacy: Malevolent Geographies*. Athens, OH: University of Ohio Press, 2003.

———. "Of Moffies, Kaffirs, and Perverts: Male Homosexuality and the Discourse of Moral Order in the Apartheid State." In *Mapping Desire: Geographies of Sexualities*, ed. David Bell and Gill Valentine, 56–65. New York: Routledge, 1995.

————. "The South African Body Politic." In *Places Through the Body*, ed. Heidi J. Nast and Steve Pile, 153–164. London: Routledge, 1998.

Eng, David L. *The Feeling of Kinship: Queer Liberalism and the Racialization of Intimacy*. Durham and London: Duke University Press, 2010.

————. *Racial Castration: Managing Masculinity in Asian America*. Durham, NC: Duke University Press, 2001.

————. "The White to be Angry: Vaginal Davis's Terrorist Drag." *Social Text* 52/53 15, no. 3/4 (1997): 78–103.

Enloe, Cynthia. *Making Feminist Sense of International Politics: Bananas, Beaches, and Bases*. Berkeley and Los Angeles, CA: University of California Press, 1990.

Epprecht, Marc. " 'Bisexuals' and the Politics of Normal in African Ethnography," *Anthropologica* 48, no. 2 (2006): 187–201.

————. *Heterosexual Africa?: The History of an Idea from the Age of Exploration to the Age of AIDS*. Athens, OH: University of Ohio Press, 2008.

————. *Hungochani: The History of a Dissident Sexuality in Southern Africa*. Montreal: McGill-Queen's University Press, 2004.

————. "Sexuality, Africa, History." *American Historical Review* 24, no. 5 (2009): 1258–73.

————. *Unspoken Facts: A History of Homosexualities in Africa*. Harare, Zimbabwe: Gays and Lesbians of Zimbabwe, 2008.

Epstein, Julia, and Kristina Straub. *Body Guards: The Cultural Politics of Gender Ambiguity*. New York: Routledge, 1991.

Evans-Pritchard, E. E. *Witchcraft, Oracles and Magic Among the Azande*. Oxford: Clarendon Press, 1937.

"FTM Prosthetics." http://www.ftmprosthetics.com/dual.htm. Accessed February 2011.

Fabian, Johannes. *Time and the Other: How Anthropology Makes its Object*. New York: Columbia University Press, 1983.

"Fact File on Drugs: Facts on Some Mood-Altering Drugs." *Mail and Guardian* (South Africa): June 5, 2000.

Fanon, Frantz. *Black Skin, White Masks*. New York: Grove, 1967 [1952].

Fausto-Sterling, Anne. "The Five Sexes: Why Male and Female Are Not Enough." *The Sciences* (March/April 1993): 18–23.

————. *Sexing the Body: Gender Politics and the Construction of Sexuality*. New York: Basic Books, 2000.

Fayman, M. S., and E. P. Frohlich. "Gender Reassignment Surgery for Female to Male Transsexuals." *African Sexology Journal* 3, no. 2 (May 1999): 4, 6, 8, 10, 34.

Feinberg, Leslie. *Stone Butch Blues*. Ithaca, NY: Firebrand Books, 1993.

————. *Trans Liberation: Beyond Pink or Blue*. Boston: Beacon Press, 1998.

———. *Transgender Warriors: From Joan of Arc to RuPaul.* Boston: Beacon Press, 1996.

Ferguson, Roderick A. *Aberrations in Black: Toward a Queer of Color Critique.* Minneapolis, University of Minnesota Press, 2004.

Fester, Gertrude. In *From Amazon to Zami: Towards a Global Lesbian Feminism,* ed. Monika Reinfelder, 98–108. New York: Cassell, 1996.

Findlay, Eileen. *Imposing Decency: The Politics of Sexuality and Race in Puerto Rico, 1870–1920.* Durham, NC: Duke University Press, 1999.

Flemming, Shauna. Interview by Amanda Swarr and Sam Bullington. Cape Town. July 1997.

Forbes, J. I. and B. Hammar. "Intersex Among Africans in Rhodesia." *Archive of Diseases of Childhood* 41 (1966): 102–7.

Forgey, Herma, Anthea Jeffrey, Elizabeth Sidiropoulos, Cheryl Smith, Terence Corrigan, Thabo Mophuting, Andrea Helman, Jean Redpath, and Tamara Dimant. *South African Survey 1999/2000 Millennium Edition.* Johannesburg: South African Institute of Race Relations, 1999.

Foucault, Michel. *The Birth of the Clinic: An Archaeology of Medical Perception.* New York: Vintage Books, 1994 [1973].

———. *Discipline and Punish: The Birth of the Prison.* Translated by Alan Sheridan. New York: Vintage Books, 1977.

———. *The History of Sexuality: Volume 1: An Introduction.* New York: Vintage Books, 1990 [1978].

Fraser, Bruce. "Eudy's Dream Denied." *The Sowetan* Web site, http://www.sowetan. co.za/News/Article.aspx?id=765812. May 14, 2008.

Fredrickson, George M. *White Supremacy: A Comparative Study in American and South African History.* New York: Oxford University Press, 1981.

Freed, L. F. "Homosexuality and the Bill: Correspondence." *South African Medical Journal* (8 June 1968): 567.

Freeman, Elizabeth. *Time Binds: Queer Temporalities, Queer Histories.* Durham, NC: Duke University Press, 2010.

Friedberg, S. H., and E. E. Rosenberg. "46/XX Chromosome Constitution of a True Hermaphrodite." *South African Medical Journal* 39, no. 1 (1965): 327–8.

Garber, Marjorie. *Vested Interests: Cross-Dressing and Cultural Anxiety.* New York: HarperPerennial, 1992.

Gay, Judith. "'Mummies and Babies' and Friends and Lovers in Lesotho." *Journal of Homosexuality* 11, no. 3–4 (1985): 97–116.

Gegenbach, Heidi. "Truth-telling and the Politics of Women's Life History Research in Africa: A Reply to Kirk Hoppe." *The International Journal of African Historical Studies* 27, no. 3 (1994): 619–27.

Geiger, Susan. *TANU Women: Gender and Culture in the Making of Tanganyikan Nationalism.* Portsmouth, NH: Heinneman, 1997.

————. "What's So Feminist about Women's Oral History?" *Journal of Women's History* 2, no. 1 (1990): 169–182.

————. "Women's Life Histories: Method and Content." *Signs: Journal of Women and Culture* 11, no. 2 (1986): 334–51.

Gender DynamiX website. www.genderdynamix.co.za. Accessed March 15, 2011.

George, G. C. W., and P. J. V. Beumont. "Transsexualism in a Fourteen-Year-Old Male." *South African Medical Journal* 46, no. 4 (1972): 1947–8.

Germond, Paul, and Steve de Gruchy, eds. *Aliens in the Household of God: Homosexuality and Christian Faith in South Africa.* Cape Town, Johannesburg, David Philip, 1997.

Gevisser, Mark. "A Different Fight for Freedom: A History of South African Lesbian and Gay Organisation from the 1950s to the 1990s." In *Defiant Desire: Gay and Lesbian Lives in South Africa*, ed. Mark Gevisser and Edwin Cameron, 14–86. Johannesburg, South Africa: Ravan Press, 1994.

Gevisser, Mark, and Edwin Cameron, eds. *Defiant Desire: Gay and Lesbian Lives in South Africa.* Johannesburg, South Africa: Ravan Press, 1994.

Gibson, Erika. "SA Psychiatrist Held in Canada." *Beeld* (South Africa), March 26, 2010.

Gibson, P. D. "Marriage and the Post-Operative Transsexual." *Obiter* (October 1987): 38–45.

Gilman, Sander L. *Difference and Pathology.* Ithaca, NY: Cornell University Press, 1985.

Gilson, Lucy, and Di McIntyre. "South Africa: Addressing the Legacy of Apartheid." In *Challenging Inequities in Health: From Ethics to Action*, ed. Timothy Evans, Margaret Whitehead, Finn Diderichsen, Abbas Bhuiya, and Meg Wirth, 190–220. New York: Oxford University Press, 2001.

Golde, Peggy. *Women in the Field: Anthropological Experiences.* Chicago: Aldine Publishing Company, 1970.

Goodwin, June. *Cry Amandla!: South African Women and the Question of Power.* New York: Africana Publishing Company, 1984.

Grace, H. J. "Intersex in Four South African Racial Groups in Durban." M.Sc. University of Natal, Durban, South Africa. 1970.

Grace, H. J., and W. E. B. Edge. "A White Hermaphrodite in South Africa." *South African Medical Journal* 47 (1973): 1553–4.

Gramsci, Antonio. *Selections from the Prison Notebooks of Antonio Gramsci*, eds. and translators Quintin Hoare and Geoffrey Nowell Smith. New York: International Publishers, 1971.

Green, Jamison. *Becoming a Visible Man.* Nashville, TN: Vanderbilt University Press, 2004.

Green, Richard. "Attitudes Toward Transsexualism and Sex-Reassignment Procedures." In *Transsexualism and Sex Reassignment*, ed. Richard Green and John Money, 235–42. Baltimore: The Johns Hopkins Press, 1969.

Green, Richard, and John Money, eds. *Transsexualism and Sex Reassignment*. Baltimore: The Johns Hopkins Press, 1969.

Grewal, Inderpal, and Caren Kaplan. "Global Identities: Theorizing Transnational Studies of Sexuality." *GLQ: A Journal of Lesbian and Gay Studies*. 7, no. 4 (2001): 663–679.

———. *Scattered Hegemonies: Postmodernity and Transnational Feminist Practices*. Minneapolis: University of Minnesota Press, 1994.

Gross, Sally. "Intersex and the Law." *Mail and Guardian* (South Africa). September 19, 2009.

Grosz, Elizabeth. *Volatile Bodies: Toward a Corporeal Feminism*. Bloomington, IN: Indiana University Press, 1994.

Hage, J. Joris, and Moshe S. Fayman. "Masculinizing Surgery for Male Intersexes and Female-to-Male Transsexuals." *Medical Sex Journal of South Africa* 6, no. 2 (1995): 5–13.

Halberstam, J. *Female Masculinity*. Durham, NC: Duke University Press, 1998.

———. *In a Queer Time and Place: Transgender Bodies, Subcultural Lives*. New York: New York University Press, 2005.

Hale, C. Jacob. "Leatherdyke Boys and their Daddies: How to have Sex without Women or Men." *Social Text* 52/53 15 no. 3–4 (1997): 223–236.

Hammonds, Evelyn. "Black (W)holes and the Geometry of Black Female Sexuality." *differences: A Journal of Feminist Cultural Studies* 6, no. 2/3 (1994): 126–145.

Haraway, Donna J. *Simians, Cyborgs, and Women: The Reinvention of Nature*. New York: Routledge, 1991.

———. "Race: Universal Donors in a Vampire Culture: It's All in the Family. Biological Kinship Categories in the Twentieth-Century United States." In *Modest_Witness@Second_Millennium.FemaleMan_Meets_OncoMouse: Feminism and Technoscience*, 213–65. New York: Routledge, 1997.

Harries, Patrick. "Symbols and Sexuality: Culture and Identity on the Early Witwatersrand Gold Mine." *Gender and History* 2, no. 3 (1990): 318–336.

Harsch, Ernest. *South Africa: White Rule, Black Revolt*. New York: Monad Press, 1980.

Hausman, Bernice L. *Changing Sex: Transsexualism, Technology, and the Idea of Gender*. Durham, NC: Duke University Press, 1995.

Hayes, Cressida J. "Feminist Solidarity After Queer Theory: The Case of Transgender." *Signs: Journal of Women in Culture and Society* 23, no. 4 (2003) 1093–1120.

Hayes, Patricia. "'Cocky' Hahn and the 'Black Venus': The Making of a Native Commissioner in South West Africa, 1915–46." *Gender and History* 8, no. 3 (1996): 364–92.

Hendricks, Donna. Interview by Amanda Swarr. Cape Town, August 2007.

Heradien, Simone. Interview by Amanda Swarr and Sam Bullington. Cape Town and Pretoria. July and August 1997. September 2007.

Herdt, Gilbert, ed. *Same Sex, Different Cultures: Gays and Lesbians Across Cultures.* Boulder, CO: Westville Press, 1997.

———. *Third Sex, Third Gender: Beyond Sexual Dimorphism in Culture and History.* New York: Zone Books, 1996.

Hermaphrodites with Attitude. Intersex Society of North America. Fall/Winter 1995–6.

Herskovits, Melville. "A Note on 'Woman Marriage' in Dahomey." *Africa* 10 (1937): 335–41.

Hirschowitz, Sidney. "Intersex: A Simplified Perspective." *South African Journal of Obstetrics and Gynaecology* 7, no. 1 (22 November 1969): 22–6.

Hoad, Neville. *African Intimacies: Race, Homosexuality, and Globalization.* Minneapolis: University of Minnesota Press. 2007.

———. "Introduction." In *Sex and Politics in South Africa,* ed. Neville Hoad, Karen Martin, and Graeme Reid, 14–24. Cape Town: Double Storey Books. 2005.

———. "Re: Thinking Sex from Global South Africa." *GLQ: A Journal of Lesbian and Gay Studies* 17, no.1 (2010): 119–124.

Hoad, Neville, Karen Martin, and Graeme Reid, eds. *Sex and Politics in South Africa.* Cape Town: Double Storey Books. 2005.

Holloway, John P. "Transsexuals—Some Further Legal Considerations." *Comparative and Legal Journal of Southern Africa* 5 (1972): 71–89.

Holmes, Rachel. "Winnie Mandela and the Moffies." *Social Text* 52/53, 15 no. 3–4 (1997): 161–180.

"Homosexuality and the Bill: Editorial." *South African Medical Journal* 42, no. 19 (May 11, 1968): 457–458.

hooks, bell. *Ain't I a Woman: Black Women and Feminism.* Boston: South End Press, 1981.

———. "Is Paris Burning?" In *Black Looks: Race and Representation,* 145–156. Boston: South End Press, 1992.

———. *Yearning: Race, Gender, and Cultural Politics.* Boston: South End Press, 1990.

Hoosain, Miriam, Rachel Jewkes, and Simphiwe Maphumulo. "Gender Audit of Health Research—10 Years of the *South African Medical Journal.*" *South African Medical Journal* 88, no. 8 (August 1998): 982–985.

Hunter, Amy. "Sex Reassignment Surgery: When Things Go Wrong." *Bilerico Project.* http://www.bilerico.com/2010/06/sex_reassignment_surgery_ when_things_go_wrong.php?utm_source=tbpfront&utm_medium= bestof&utm_campaign=best_of_box. June 6, 2010.

Hunter, Mark. *Love in the Time of AIDS: Inequality, Gender, and Rights in South Africa.* Bloomington and Indianapolis: Indiana University Press, 2010.

Hunter, Nan D. "Sexual Orientation and the Paradox of Heightened Scrutiny." *Michigan Law Review* 102, no. 7 (June 2004): 78–103.

"'I am First a Soldier and then a Psychiatrist': The Abuse of Psychiatry in the SADF." *Resister: Journal of the Committee on South African War Resistance* 47 (December 1986–January 1987).

Incite! Women of Color Against Violence. *The Revolution will Not be Funded: Beyond the Non-Profit Industrial Complex*. Cambridge, MA: South End Press, 2007.

Intersex Society of North America. *Recommendations for Treatment: Intersex Infants and Children*, 1995, 1–2

Isaacs, Gordon, and Brian McKendrick. *Male Homosexuality in South Africa: Identity Formation, Culture, and Crisis*. Cape Town: Oxford University Press, 1992.

Isaacs, Nasreen. Interview by Amanda Swarr and Sam Bullington. South Africa. 2000.

Jackson, W. P. U., and N. Marine. "Variability of the Human XX/YY Mosaic." *South African Medical Journal* 44, no. 1 (1970): 208–11.

Jacobs, Max. "The Treatment of Homosexuality." *South African Medical Journal* 43 (September 13, 1969): 1123–26.

Jacobs, Sue-Ellen, Wesley Thomas, and Sabine Lang, eds. *Two-Spirit People: Native American Gender Identity, Sexuality, and Spirituality*. Chicago: University of Illinois Press, 1997.

Jansen, Odessa. Interview by Amanda Swarr and Sam Bullington. Cape Town, South Africa. July and August 1997.

Jeeves, Alan. "Histories of Reproductive Health and the Control of Sexually Transmitted Disease in Southern Africa: A Century of Controversy." *South African Historical Journal* 45 (2001): 1–10.

———. "The State, the Cinema, and Health Propaganda for Africans in Pre-Apartheid South Africa." *South African Historical Journal* 48 (2003): 109–129.

Jeffrey, Anthea. *Bill of Rights Report: 1996/97*. Johannesburg, South Africa: South African Institute of Race Relations, 1997.

Jeppie, Shamil. "Popular Culture and Carnival in Cape Town: the 1940s and 1950s." In *The Struggle for District Six: Past and Present*, ed. Shamil Jeppie and Craig Soudien, A Project of the Hands Off District Six Committee, 67–87. Cape Town, South Africa: Buchu Books, 1990.

Jooste, Michael. Interview by Amanda Swarr. South Africa. October 2000.

Kaminsky, Amy. "Gender, Race, *Raza*." *Feminist Studies* 20, no. 1 (Spring 1994): 7–31.

Kandiyoti, Deniz. "Pink Card Blues: Trouble and Strife at the Crossroads of Gender." In *Fragments of Culture: The Everyday of Modern Turkey*, ed. Deniz Kandiyoti and Ayşe Saktenber, 277–293. New Brunswick, NJ: Rutgers University Press, 2002.

Kanfer, Stefan. *The Last Empire: De Beers, Diamonds, and the World*. New York: The Noonday Press, 1993.

Kaplan, R. M. "Treatment of Homosexuality During Apartheid." *BMJ (Clinical Research Ed.)*. 329, no. 7480 (2004): 1415–6.

Kaplan, Robert. "*The Aversion Project*—Psychiatric Abuses in the South African Defence Force During the Apartheid Era." *South African Medical Journal* 91 (2001): 216–217.

Karkazis, Katrina. *Fixing Sex: Intersex, Medical Authority, and Lived Experience.* Durham, NC: Duke University Press, 2008.

Kennedy, Elizabeth Lapovsky, and Madeline Davis. *Boots of Leather, Slippers of Gold: The History of a Lesbian Community.* New York: Penguin, 1994.

Kessler, Suzanne. *Lessons from the Intersexed.* New Brunswick, NJ: Rutgers University Press, 1998.

———. "The Medical Construction of Gender." *Signs: Journal of Women and Culture* 16, no. 1 (1990): 3–26.

Kessler, Suzanne, and Wendy McKenna. *Gender: An Ethnomethodological Approach.* New York: John Wiley and Sons, 1978.

Khangale, Ndivhuwo. "Rival Gay Group Out to get Drag Queens." *IOL.* September 21, 2004.

Khewsa, Busi, with Ruth Morgan. "'My Attitude is Manly . . . a Girl Needs to Walk on the Aisle': Butch-Femme Subculture in Johannesburg, South Africa." In *Tommy Boys, Lesbian Men and Ancestral Wives: Female Same-Sex Practices in Africa*, ed. Ruth Morgan and Saskia Wieringa, 199–229. Johannesburg: Jacana Media, 2005.

Khosla, Dhillon. *Both Sides Now: One Man's Journey through Womanhood.* New York: Penguin, 2006.

Khubeka, Bass John [no pseudonym for first name]. Interview by Amanda Swarr and Sam Bullington. Gauteng, South Africa. October 2000.

Khumalo, Mandisa. Interview by Amanda Swarr and Sam Bullington. Cape Town, South Africa. October 2000.

Kirk, Paul. "Doctor Seeks Action in Canadian Courts." *Mail and Guardian* (South Africa), August 11–17, 2000a, 4.

———. "'Freaks' Offered a Chance to Change." *Mail and Guardian* (South Africa), July 28–August 3, 2000b, 4.

———. "Military Mutilation: Another Victim Steps Forward." *Mail and Guardian* (South Africa), August 4–10, 2000c, 10.

———. "Mutilation by the Military." *Mail and Guardian* (South Africa), July 28–August 3, 2000d, 4–5.

———. "A Painful and Dangerous Op." *Mail and Guardian* (South Africa), July 28–August 3, 2000e, 5.

Kistner, Ulrike. *Commissioning and Contesting Post-Apartheid's Human Rights: HIV/AIDS—Racism—Truth and Reconcilation.* Munster: Lit Verlag, 2003.

Klausen, Susanne Maria. *Race, Maternity, and the Politics of Birth Control in South Africa, 1910–39.* Houndmills: Palgrave Macmillan, 2004a.

———. "Women's Resistance to Eugenic Birth Control in Johannesburg. 1930–39." *South African Historical Journal*, 50 (2004b): 152–169.

Klein, Thamar. "Querying medical and legal discourses of queer sexes and genders in South Africa." *Anthropology Matters* 10, no. 2 (2008): 1–17.

Kotolo, McKeed. "Three Held in 'Muti' Murder." *Sowetan* (South Africa), August 14, 2000, 1.

Kotula, Dean. *The Phallus Palace: Female to Male Transsexuals.* Los Angeles: Alyson Publications, 2002.

Kroker, Arthur, and Marilouise Kroker, eds. *The Last Sex: Feminism and Outlaw Bodies.* New York: St. Martin's Press, 1993.

Krouse, Matthew. "The Artista Sisters—September 1984: An Account of Army Drag." In *Defiant Desire: Gay and Lesbian Lives in South Africa,* ed. Mark Gevisser, and Edwin Cameron, 209–218. Johannesburg, South Africa: Ravan Press, 1994.

———, ed. *The Invisible Ghetto: Lesbian and Gay Writing from South Africa.* London: The Gay Men's Press, 1993.

Kuipers, Anne Jayne. *Anne's Metamorphosis.* Cape Town: Camelon Books, n.d.

Kulick, Don. *Travesti: Sex, Gender and Culture Among Brazilian Transgendered Prostitutes.* Chicago: University of Chicago Press, 1998.

Lahiri, Madhumita. "Crimes and Corrections: Bride Burners, Corrective Rapists, and Other Black Misogynists." *Feminist Africa* 15 (2011): 121–133.

Lalu, Premesh. "Medical Anthropology, Subaltern Traces, and the Making and Meaning of Western Medicine in South Africa: 1895–1899." *History in Africa* 25 (1998): 133–59.

Lalumiere, M. L., R. Blanchard, and K. J. Zucker. "Sexual Orientation and Handedness in Men and Women: A Meta-analysis." *Psychological Bulletin* 126, no. 4 (July 2000): 575–92.

Lancaster, Roger N. *Life is Hard: Machismo, Danger, and the Intimacy of Power in Nicaragua.* Berkeley and Los Angeles, CA: University of California Press, 1992.

Landau, Paul Stuart. *The Realm of the World: Language, Gender, and Christianity in a Southern African Kingdom.* Portsmouth, NH: Heinemann, 1995.

Leap, William L. "Finding the Centre: Claiming Gay Space in Cape Town." In *Performing Queer: Shaping Sexualities, 1994–2004—Volume One,* ed. Mikki van Zyl and Melissa Steyn, 235–264. Roggebaai: Kwela Books. 2005.

———. "Language, Belonging, and (Homo)sexual Citizenship in Cape Town, South Africa." In *Speaking in Queer Tongues: Globalization and Gay Language,* ed. William L. Leap, and Tom Boellstorff, 134–162. Urbana and Chicago: University of Illinois Press, 2004.

———. "'Strangers on a Train': Sexual Citizenship and the Politics of Public Transportation in Apartheid Cape Town." In *Queer Globalizations: Citizenship and the Afterlife of Colonialism,* ed. Arnaldo Cruz-Malavé, and Martin F. Manalansan IV, 219–235. New York: New York University Press, 2002.

———. *Word's Out: Gay Men's English.* Minneapolis: University of Minnesota Press, 1996.

Leatt, Annie, and Graeme Hendricks. "Beyond Identity Politics: Homosexuality and Gayness in South Africa." In *Performing Queer: Shaping Sexualities, 1994–2004—Volume One*, ed. Mikki van Zyl and Melissa Steyn, 303–357. Roggebaai: Kwela Books. 2005.

Levin, Adam. "The Secret Sex." *Style* (October 1996): 72–5.

Levy, Robert. "The Community Function of Tahitian Male Transvestitism: A Hypothesis." *Anthropological Quarterly* 44 (1971): 12–21.

Lewin, Ellen. "Writing Lesbian Ethnography." In *Women Writing Culture*, ed. Ruth Behar, and Deborah A. Gordon, 322–35. Berkeley and Los Angeles, CA: University of California Press, 1995.

———, ed. *Inventing Lesbian Cultures in America*. Boston: Beacon Press, 1996.

Lewin, Ellen, and William L. Leap. eds. *Out in the Field: Reflections of Lesbian and Gay Anthropologists*. Urbana and Chicago: University of Illinois Press, 1996.

———. *Out in Public: Reinventing Lesbian/Gay Anthropology in a Globalizing World*. Malden, MA: Wiley-Blackwell, 2009.

———. *Out in Theory: The Emergence of Lesbian and Gay Anthropology*. Chicago: University of Illinois Press, 2002.

Lewis, Jack, and Francois Loots. " 'Moffies en Manvroue': Gay and Lesbian Life Histories in Contemporary Cape Town." In *Defiant Desire: Gay and Lesbian Lives in South Africa*, ed. Mark Gevisser and Edwin Cameron, 140–57. Johannesburg, South Africa: Ravan Press, 1994.

Livingston, Julie. *Debility and the Moral Imagination in Botswana: African Systems of Thought*. Bloomington, IN: Indiana University Press, 2005.

Lloyd, Moya. "Performativity, Parody, Politics." In *Performativity and Belonging*, ed. Vikki Bell, 195–213. London: SAGE, 1999.

Lodge, Tom. *Black Politics in South Africa Since 1945*. London: Longman Group Limited, 1983.

Lord, Kristin M. *The Perils and Promise of Global Transparency: Why the Information Revolution May Not Lead to Security, Democracy, or Peace*. Albany, NY: SUNY Press, 2006.

Lorde, Audre. *Sister/Outsider*. Freedom, CA: The Crossing Press, 1984.

Louw, Ronald. "Gay and Lesbian Sexualities in South Africa: From Outlaw to Constitutionally Protected." In *Legal Queeries: Lesbian, Gay, and Transgender Legal Studies*, ed. Leslie J Moran, Daniel Monk, and Sarah Beresford, 139–154. London and New York: Cassell, 1998.

Louw, Stephen J., Jonathan G. Goldin, and Gina Joubert. " 'Racial' Categories in South African Health Research." *South African Medical Journal* 88, no. 2 (February 1998): 153.

Lowe, Lisa. "Heterogeneity, Hybridity, Multiplicity: Making Asian American Differences." *Diaspora* 1, no. 1 (spring 1991): 24–44.

Lucas, Mary Bisset. "Diamond Jubilee Medicine: The Medical World of 1897 and 1898 as Seen in the Pages of the South African Medical Journal." *South African Medical Journal* (20 October 1979): 688–94.

Maart, Herman. Interview by Amanda Swarr. Cape Town, February 10, 2009.

Mabandla, Brigette. "Women in South Africa and the Constitution-Making Process." In *Women's Rights, Human Rights: International Feminist Perspectives*, ed. Julie Peters, and Andrea Wolper, 67–71. New York: Routledge, 1995.

Mabena, Stanley. "Call Me Anything but Not Isitabane." Behind the Mask, www.behindthemask.co.za. Accessed 2004.

Magubane, Zine. *Bringing Empire Home: Race, Class, and Gender in Britain and Colonial South Africa.* Chicago: University of Chicago Press, 2004.

Manalansan IV, Martin F. *Global Divas: Filipino Gay Men in the Diaspora.* Durham: Duke University Press, 2003.

"Mandrax." http://www.drugwise.co.za. 2003.

Mangaliso, Zengie A. "Gender and Nation-Building in South Africa." In *Feminist Nationalism*, ed. Lois A. West, 130–46. New York: Routledge, 1997.

Manicom, Linzi. "Ruling Relations: Rethinking State and Gender in South African History." *Journal of African History* 33 (1992): 441–465.

Manuel, M. A., A. Allie, and W. P. U. Jackson. "A True Hermaphrodite with XX/YY Chromosome Mosaicism." *South African Medical Journal* 39, no. 1 (1965): 411–4.

Marcus, Tessa. "The Women's Question and National Liberation in South Africa." In *The National Question in South Africa*, ed. Maria van Diepen, 96–109. London: Zed Press, 1988.

Marks, Shula. *Divided Sisterhood: Race, Class and Gender in the South African Nursing Profession.* New York: St. Martin's Press, 1994.

———, ed. *Not Either an Experimental Doll: The Separate Worlds of Three South African Women.* Bloomington and Indianapolis: Indiana University Press, 1987.

Martin, Denis-Constant. *Coon Carnival: New Year in Cape Town, Past and Present.* Cape Town: David Philip, 1999.

Martin, Emily. "The Egg and the Sperm: How Science Has Constructed a Romance Based on Stereotypical Male-Female Roles." *Signs: Journal of Women and Culture in Society* 16, no. 1 (1991): 485–501.

Marx, Anthony W. *Lessons of Struggle: South African Internal Opposition, 1960–1990.* New York: Oxford University Press, 1992.

Mascia-Lees, Frances E., Patricia Sharpe, and Colleen Ballerino Cohen. "The Postmodern Turn in Anthropology: Cautions from a Feminist Perspective." *Signs: Journal of Women and Culture* 15, no. 1 (1989): 7–23.

Matshoba, Mtutuzeli. *Call Me Not a Man.* Johannesburg: Ravan Press, 1979.

Maynes, Mary Jo, Jennifer L. Pierce, and Barbara Laslett. *Telling Stories: The Use of Personal Narratives in the Social Sciences and History.* Ithaca: Cornell University Press, 2008.

Mbembe, Achille. "Necropolitics." *Public Culture* 15, no. 1 (2003): 11–40.

———. *On the Postcolony*. Berkeley, Los Angeles, London: University of California Press, 2001.

———. "On the Power of the False." *Public Culture* 14, no. 3 (Fall 2002): 629–641.

———. "Prosaics of Servitude and Authoritarian Cultures." *Public Culture* 5, no. 1 (Fall 1992): 123–145.

McCall, Michal M. and Judith Wittner. "The Good News about Life History." In *Symbolic Interaction and Cultural Studies*, ed. Howard Becker and Michal M. McCall, 46–89. Chicago: University of Chicago Press, 1990.

McClintock, Anne. *Imperial Leather: Race, Gender, and Sexuality in the Colonial Contest*. New York: Routledge, 1995.

McCloskey, Deidre. *Crossing: A Memoir*. Chicago: University of Chicago Press, 1999.

McFadden, D., and E. G. Pasanen. "Comparison of the Auditory Systems of Heterosexuals and Homosexuals: Click-evoked Otoacoustic Emissions." *Proceedings of the National Academy of Sciences of the United States of America* 95, no. 5 (March 3, 1998): 2709–13.

McGreal, Chris. "'Doctor Shock' Charged with Sexually Abusing Male Patient: Canadian Police Investigate Dozens of Allegations Against Psychiatrist Nicknamed for Use of Electricity to 'Cure' Gay Soldiers." *Guardian*, www.guardian.co.uk. March 28, 2010.

McKenna, Wendy, and Suzanne J. Kessler. "Retrospective Response." *Feminism and Psychology* 10, no. 1 (2000): 66–72.

McLean, Hugh, and Linda Ngcobo. "Abangibhamayo Bathi Ngimnandi (Those Who Fuck Me Say I'm Tasty): Gay Sexuality in Reef Townships." In *Defiant Desire: Gay and Lesbian Lives in South Africa*, ed. Mark Gevisser and Edwin Cameron, 158–85. Johannesburg, South Africa: Ravan Press, 1994.

Mead, Margaret. *Male and Female: A Study of the Sexes in a Changing World*. New York: The New American Library, 1959.

———. *Sex and Temperament in Three Primitive Societies*. New York: Morrow Quill, 1963 [1935].

Meena, Ruth. *Gender in Southern Africa: Conceptual and Theoretical Issues*. Harare, Zimbabwe: SAPES Books, 1992.

Meer, Shamim, ed. *Women Speak: Reflections in Our Struggles, 1982–1997*. Cape Town: Kwela Books, 1998.

Meintjes, Shelia. "Gender, Nationalism, and Transformation: Difference and Commonality in South Africa's Past and Present." In *Women, Ethnicity, and Nationalism: The Politics of Transition*, ed. Rick Wilford, and Robert L. Miller, 62–86. New York: Routledge, 1998.

Meintjes, Shelia, Anu Pillay, and Meredeth Turshen, eds. *The Aftermath: Women in Post-Conflict Transformation*. London and New York: Zed Books, 2001.

Mermelstein, David, ed. *The Anti-Apartheid Reader: South Africa and the Struggle Against White Racist Rule.* New York: Grove Press, 1987.

Meyerowitz, Joanne. *How Sex Changed: A History of Transsexuality in the United States.* Cambridge: Harvard University Press, 2002.

Mfazo, Buyisile. Group interview by Amanda Swarr and Sam Bullington. Gauteng, South Africa. October 2000.

Mirza, Sarah, and Margaret Strobel. *Three Swahili Women: Life Histories from Mombasa, Kenya.* Bloomington and Indianapolis, IN: Indiana University Press, 1989.

Mkhize, Nonhlanhla, Jane Bennett, Vasu Reddy, and Relebohile Moletsane. *The Country We Want to Live In: Hate Crimes and Homophobia in the Lives of Black South African Lesbians.* Cape Town: HSRC Press, 2010.

Mkhwanazi, Muzi. "Soweto Sangomas Face Trial for Muti Murder." *Sowetan* (South Africa), August 14, 2000.

Moffett, Helen. "'These Women, They Force Us to Rape Them': Rape as Narrative of Social Control in Post-Apartheid South Africa." *Journal of Southern African Studies* 32, no. 1 (2006): 129–44.

Mohammed, Farid. Interview by Amanda Swarr and Sam Bullington. Cape Town, South Africa. 2000.

Mohanty, Chandra Talpade. "Cartographies of Struggle: Third World Women and the Politics of Feminism." In *Third World Women and the Politics of Feminism,* ed. Chandra Talpade Mohanty, Ann Russo, and Lourdes Torres, 1–47. Bloomington, IN: Indiana University Press, 1991.

———. *Feminism without Borders: Decolonizing Theory, Practicing Solidarity.* Durham: Duke University Press, 2003.

———. "Under Western Eyes: Feminist Scholarship and Colonial Discourses." In *Third World Women and the Politics of Feminism,* ed. Chandra Talpade Mohanty, Ann Russo, and Lourdes Torres, 51–80. Bloomington, IN: Indiana University Press, 1991.

Molobi, William. Interview by Amanda Swarr. Soweto, October 11, 2000.

Money, John, and Anke A. Ehrhardt. *Man and Woman, Boy and Girl: The Differentiation and Dimorphism of Gender Identity from Conception to Maturity.* Baltimore: The Johns Hopkins University Press, 1972.

Money, John, and Florence Schwartz. "Public Opinion and Social Issues in Transsexualism: A Case Study in Medical Sociology." In *Transsexualism and Sex Reassignment,* ed. Richard Green, and John Money, 253–69. Baltimore: The Johns Hopkins Press, 1969.

Moodie, T. Dunbar, with Vivienne Ndatshe. *Going for Gold: Men, Mines, and Migration.* Berkeley and Los Angeles: University of California Press, 1994.

Moodie, T. Dunbar, with Vivienne Ndatshe and British Sibuyi. "Migrancy and Male Sexuality on the South African Gold Mines." In *Hidden from History: Reclaiming the Gay and Lesbian Past,* ed. Martin Duberman, Martha Vicinus, and George Chauncey, Jr., 411–25. New York: Meridian Press, 1989.

Moore, Henrietta L. *Feminism and Anthropology*. Minneapolis, MN: University of Minnesota Press, 1988.

Moraga, Cherríe. *Loving in the War Years: lo que nunca pasó por sus labios*. Boston, MA: South End Press, 1983.

Morgan, Ruth, Charl Marais, and Joy Rosemary Wellbeloved. *Trans: Transgender Life Stories from South Africa*. Auckland Park, South Africa: Jacana Media, 2009.

Morgan, Ruth, and Saskia Wieringa, eds. *Tommy Boys, Lesbian Men and Ancestral Wives: Female Same-Sex Practices in Africa*. Johannesburg: Jacana Media, 2005.

Morgan, Ruth, and Saskia Wieringa. "Introduction." In *Tommy Boys, Lesbian Men and Ancestral Wives: Female Same-Sex Practices in Africa*, ed. Ruth Morgan and Saskia Wieringa, 11–24. Johannesburg: Jacana Media, 2005.

———. "Present-day Same-Sex Practices in Africa: Conclusions from the African Women's Life History Project." In *Tommy Boys, Lesbian Men and Ancestral Wives: Female Same-Sex Practices in Africa*, ed. Ruth Morgan and Saskia Wieringa, 309–324. Johannesburg: Jacana Media, 2005.

Morrell, Robert, ed. *Changing Men in South Africa*. University of Natal Press and Zed Books: Scottsville, South Africa, London, and New York, 2001.

Morris, Jan. *Conundrum*. New York: Henry Holt and Company, 1986 [1974].

Mthembu, Zindzi. Interview by Amanda Swarr and Sam Bullington. Gauteng, South Africa. October 2000.

Mtintso, Thenjiwe. "Representivity: False Sisterhood or Universal Women's Interests? The South African Experience." *Feminist Studies* 29, no.3 (Fall 2003): 569–579.

Mufweba, Yolanda. "'Corrective Rape Makes You an African Woman." *Saturday Star* (Johannesburg, South Africa). November 7, 2003.

Muholi, Zanele. *Only Half the Picture*. Johannesburg: Michael Stevenson/STE Publishers, 2006.

Muñoz, José Esteban. *Cruising Utopia: The Then and There of Queer Futurity*. New York: New York University Press, 2009.

———. *Disidentifications: Queers of Color and the Performance of Politics*. Minneapolis: University of Minnesota Press, 1999.

Munt, Sally. *Butch/Femme: Inside Lesbian Gender*. London: Cassell, 1998.

Murray, Laura Rena. "The High Price of Looking Like a Woman." *New York Times* 21 August, 2011.

Murray, Stephen O., and Will Roscoe. *Boy-Wives and Female Husbands: Studies in African Homosexualities*. New York: Palgrave, 1998.

Nagar, Richa. "Exploring Methodological Borderlands through Oral Narratives." In *Thresholds in Feminist Geography*, ed. J. P. Jones, H. J. Nast, and S. M. Roberts, 203–24. Lanham: Rowman and Littlefield Publishers, 1997.

———. "Footloose Researchers, 'Traveling' Theories, and the Politics of Transnational Feminist Praxis." *Gender, Place and Culture* 9, no. 2 (2002): 179–186.

Nagar, Richa, and Amanda Lock Swarr. "Theorizing Transnational Feminist Praxis." In *Critical Transnational Feminist Praxis*, ed. Amanda Lock Swarr and
Richa Nagar. 1–20. Albany: State University of New York Press, 2010.

Najmabadi, Afsaneh. "Transing and Transpassing Across Sex-Gender Walls in
Iran." *WSQ: Women's Studies Quarterly* 36, no. 3–4 (Fall/Winter 2008):
24–42.

———. *Women with Mustaches and Men without Beards: Gender and Sexual Anxieties of Iranian Modernity*. Berkeley, Los Angeles, and London: University of
California Press, 2005.

Namaste, Viviane K. *Invisible Lives: The Erasure of Transsexual and Transgendered
People*. Chicago: University of Chicago Press. 2000.

———. "Tragic Misreadings: Queer Theory's Erasure of Transgender Subjectivity." In *Queer Studies: A Lesbian, Gay, Bisexual, and Transgender Anthology*,
ed. Brett Beemyn and Mickey Eliason, 183–203. New York: New York
University Press, 1996.

Nanda, Serena. "The Hijiras of India: Cultural and Individual Dimensions of an
Institutionalized Third Gender Role." In *The Many Faces of Homosexuality:
Anthropological Approaches to Homosexual Behavior*, ed. Evelyn Blackwood,
35–54. New York and London: Harrington Park Press, 1986.

———. *Neither Man Nor Woman: The Hijiras of India*. Revised edition. Belmont,
CA: Wadsworth, 1999.

Ndana, Phakamile. Interview by Amanda Swarr and Sam Bullington. Gauteng,
South Africa. October 2000.

Nel, Juan. "Moving from Rhetoric to Creating the Reality: Empowering South
Africa's Lesbian and Gay Community." In *Performing Queer: Shaping Sexualities, 1994–2004—Volume One*, ed. Mikki van Zyl and Melissa Steyn,
281–300. Roggebaai: Kwela Books. 2005.

Nestle, Joan, ed. *The Persistent Desire: A Butch/Femme Reader*. Boston: Alyson
Publications, 1992.

Newton, Esther. *Mother Camp: Female Impersonators in America*. Chicago: The
University of Chicago Press, 1972.

Ngubane, Musa. "Lesbians Under Attack in Khayelitsha." Behind the Mask Web
site, www.btm.org.za. November 5, 2003.

Nkabinde, Nkunzi Zandile. *Black Bull, Ancestors and Me: My Life as a Lesbian
Sangoma*. Sunnyside, South Africa: Fanele, Jacanda Press, 2008.

Nkabinde, Nkunzi, with Ruth Morgan. "This has Happened Since Ancient
Times . . . It's Something that You are Born with.': Ancestral Wives among
Same-Sex Sangomas in South Africa." In *Tommy Boys, Lesbian Men and
Ancestral Wives: Female Same-Sex Practices in Africa*, ed. Ruth Morgan and
Saskia Wieringa, 230–258. Johannesburg: Jacana Media, 2005.

Nkoli, Simon. "This Strange Feeling." In *The Invisible Ghetto: Lesbian and Gay
Writing from South Africa*, ed. Matthew Krouse, 19–26. Johannesburg:
COSAW Publishing, 1993.

————. "Wardrobes: Coming Out as a Black Gay Activist in South Africa." In *Defiant Desire: Gay and Lesbian Lives in South Africa*, ed. Mark Gevisser and Edwin Cameron, 249–257. Johannesburg, South Africa: Ravan Press, 1994.

Nzimande, R.M. "Sex Exchange Operations—Transsexualism: Are they Recognised by Law?" *African Law Review* 5, no. 3/4 (November 1994): 52–6.

O'Brien, Denise. "Female Husbands in Southern Bantu Societies." In *Sexual Stratification: A Cross-Cultural View*, ed. Alice Schlegel, 109–26. New York: Columbia University Press, 1977.

Oanda FX History. "Historical Currency Exchange." http://www.oanda.com/convert/fxhistory. April 2003.

Oboler, Regina. "Is the Female Husband a Man?: Woman/woman Marriage among the Nandi of Kenya." *Ethnology* 19, no. 1 (1980): 69–88.

Omi, Michael, and Howard Winant. *Racial Formation in the United States: From the 1960s to the 1990s*. New York: Routledge, 1994.

Oosthuizen, Jan. Interview by Amanda Swarr and Sam Bullington. Gauteng, South Africa. 2000.

Ortner, Sherry. "Is Female to Male as Nature is to Culture?" In *Woman, Culture, Society*, ed. Michelle Zimbalist Rosaldo and Louise Lamphere, 67–87. Stanford, CA: Stanford University Press, 1974.

Pantazis, Angelo. "Meanings of Transsexualism." *South African Journal on Human Rights* 13, no. 3 (1997): 468–75.

Park, Caron. "The Need for Reconsideration of Treatment Methods for Transsexual Patients." *Medical Sex Journal of South Africa* 1, no. 2 (1990): 34–40.

Park, Yoon Jung, Joanne Fedler, and Zubeda Dangor. *Reclaiming Women's Spaces: New Perspectives on Violence Against Women and Sheltering in South Africa*. Johannesburg: Nisaa Institute for Women's Development, 2000.

Patai, Daphne. "U.S. Academics and Third World Women: Is Ethical Research Possible?" In *Women's Words: The Feminist Practice of Oral History*, ed. Sherna Berger Gluck and Daphne Patai, 137–53. New York: Routledge, 1991.

Patton, Cindy. "From Nation to Family: Containing African AIDS." In *The Gender/Sexuality Reader: Culture, History, Political Economy*, ed. Roger Lancaster and Micaela de Leonardo, 279–290. New York and London: Routledge, 1997 [1993].

————. "Inventing African AIDS." *City Limits* 363 (September 1998): 15–22.

Pegge, John L. "The Role of NGOs: Managing AIDS in Our Midst." *Salus* 17, no. 5 (December 1994): 20–3.

Petersen, Maxine E., and Robert Dickey. "Surgical Sex Reassignment: A Comparative Survey of International Centers." *Archives of Sexual Behavior* 24, no. 2 (1995): 135–156.

Petzer, Shane A., and Gordon M. Isaacs. "SWEAT: The Development and Implementation of a Sex Worker Advocacy and Intervention Program in Post-Apartheid South Africa." In *Global Sex Workers: Rights, Resistance and*

Redefinition, ed. Kamala Kempadoo and Jo Doezema, 192–6. New York: Routledge, 1998.

Pharr, Suzanne. *Homophobia: A Weapon of Sexism*. Little Rock: Chardon Press, 1988.

Phillips, Oliver. "White Men Thirteen Years Later: The Changing Constitution of Masculinities in South Africa, 1987–2000." In *Performing Queer: Shaping Sexualities, 1994–2004—Volume One*, ed. Mikki van Zyl and Melissa Steyn, 137–163. Roggebaai: Kwela Books. 2005.

Potts, Andrea. Interview by Amanda Swarr and Sam Bullington. Gauteng, South Africa. October 2000.

Povinelli, Elizabeth A., and George Chauncey. "Thinking Sexuality Transnationally." *GLQ: A Journal of Lesbian and Gay Studies* 5, no. 4 (1999): 439–449.

Pratt, Minnie Bruce. "Identity: Skin Blood Heart." In *Yours in Struggle: Three Feminist Perspectives on Anti-Semitism and Racism*, ed. Elly Bulkin, Minnie Bruce Pratt, and Barbara Smith, 9–63. Ithaca, NY: Firebrand Books, 1984.

Preves, Sharon Elaine. *Intersex and Identity: The Contested Self*. New York: Rutgers, 2003.

———. "Sexing the Intersexed: Lived Experience in Socio-Cultural Context." Dissertation, University of Minnesota, 1999.

Prieur, Annick. *Mema's House, Mexico City: On Transvestites, Queens, and Machos*. Chicago: University of Chicago Press, 1998.

Portelli, Alessandro. *The Order has been Carried Out: History, Memory, and Meaning of a Nazi Massacre in Rome*. New York: Palgrave Macmillan, 2003.

Posel, Deborah. "Race As Common Sense: Racial Classification in Twentieth-Century South Africa." *African Studies Review* 44, no. 2 (2001a): 87

———. "The Scandal of Manhood: 'Baby Rape' and the Politicization of Sexual Violence in Post-Apartheid South Africa." *Culture, Health & Sexuality* 7, no. 3 (2005): 239–52.

———. "What's in a Name? Racial Categorisations Under Apartheid and Their Afterlife." *Transformation*, no. 47 (2001b): 50–74.

Prosser, Jay. *Second Skins: The Body Narratives of Transsexuality*. New York: Columbia University Press, 1998.

Puar, Jasbir. *Terrorist Assemblages: Homonationalism in Queer Times*. Durham, NC: Duke University Press, 2007.

Queer by Choice.com. "For Genderbending or Genderbreaking People." http://www.queerbychoice.com/genderbend.html. January 29, 2004.

Ramsay, Michele, Rennee Bernstein, Esther Zwane, David C. Page, and Trefor Jenkins. "XX True Hermaphroditism in Southern African Blacks: An Enigma of Primary Sexual Differentiation." *American Human Genetics* 43 (1988): 4–13.

Rankhotha, Sylvester Charles. "How Black Men Involved in Same-sex Relationships Construct their Masculinities." In *Performing Queer: Shaping Sexualities, 1994–2004—Volume One*, ed. Mikki van Zyl and Melissa Steyn, 165–175. Roggebaai: Kwela Books, 2005.

Rassool, Ciraj, and Patricia Hayes. "Science and the Spectacle: /Khanako's South Africa, 1936–1937." In *Deep hiStories: Gender and Colonialism in Southern Africa* ed. Wendy Woodward, Patricia Hayes, and Gary Minkley, 117–161. New York and Amsterdam: Rodopi, 2002.

Ratele, Kopano. "Kinky Politics." In *Re-thinking Sexualities in Africa*, ed. Signe Arnfred, 139–154. Uppsala, Sweden: Almqvist and Wiksell Tryckeri AB, 2004.

Raymond, Janice. *The Transsexual Empire: The Making of the She-Male*. Boston: Beacon Press, 1979.

Rebelo, Ethelwyn, Christopher Szabo, and Graeme Pitcher. "Gender Assignment Surgery on Children with Disorders of Sex Development: a Case Report and Discussion from South Africa." *Journal of Child Health Care* 12, no. 1 (2008): 49–59.

Reddy, Chandan. *Freedom with Violence: Race, Sexuality, and the U.S. State*. Durham and London: Duke University Press, 2011.

———. "Home, Houses, Non-Identity: Paris is Burning." In *Burning Down the House: Recycling Domesticity*, ed. Rosemary Marangoly George, 355–379. Boulder, CO: Westview Press, 1998.

Reddy, Vasu. "Sexuality in Africa: Some Trends, Transgressions and Tirades." *Agenda* 62 (2004): 3–11.

Reddy, Vasu, with Judith Butler. "Troubling Genders, Subverting Identities: Interview with Judith Butler." *Agenda* 63 (2004): 115–124.

Rees. Mark. *Dear Sir or Madam: The Autobiography of a Female-to-Male Transsexual*. New York: Cassell, 1996.

Reid, Graeme Charles. "Above the Skyline: Integrating African, Christian and Gay and Lesbian Identities in a South African Church Community." Master's thesis, University of the Witwatersrand, 1999.

———. *Above the Skyline: Reverend Tsietsi Thandekiso and the Founding of an African Gay Church*. Pretoria: UNISA Press, 2010.

Reid, Graeme, and Teresa Dirsuweit. "Understanding Systemic Violence: Homophobic Attacks in Johannesburg and Its Surrounds." *Urban Forum* 13, no. 3 (2002): 99–126.

Reiter, Rayna R. *Toward an Anthropology of Women*. New York: Monthly Review Press, 1975.

Retief, Glen. "Keeping Sodom out of the Laager: State Repression of Homosexuality in Apartheid South Africa." In *Defiant Desire: Gay and Lesbian Lives in South Africa*, ed. Mark Gevisser and Edwin Cameron, 99–111. Johannesburg: Ravan, 1994.

Rich, Adrienne. *Blood, Bread, and Poetry: Selected Prose, 1979–1985*. New York and London: W. W. Norton and Company, 1986.

Riekert, Carmella. Interview by Amanda Swarr and Sam Bullington. Western Cape, South Africa. May 1, 2000.

———. Interview by Amanda Swarr. Western Cape, South Africa. September 3, 2007.

Robert, Helen, ed. *Doing Feminist Research*. London: Routledge and Kegan Paul. 1981.

Robertson, Jennifer. *Takarazuka: Sexual Politics and Popular Culture in Modern Japan*. Berkeley and Los Angeles, CA: University of California Press, 1998.

Robinson, Jennifer. "White Women Researching/Representing 'Others': From Antiapartheid to Postcolonialism?" In *Writing Women and Space*, ed. Alison Blunt and Gillian Rose, 197–226. New York: Guilford, 1994.

Roeland, Brandy. Interview by Amanda Swarr and Sam Bullington. Cape Town, South Africa. May 2000.

Rosaldo, Michelle Zimbalist, and Louise Lamphere, eds. *Woman, Culture, Society*. Stanford, CA: Stanford University Press, 1974.

Roscoe, Will. ed., compiled by Gay American Indians. *Living the Spirit: A Gay American Indian Anthology*. New York: St. Martin's Press, 1988.

———. *The Zuni Man-Woman*. Albuquerque, NM: New Mexico Press, 1991.

Roth, Sir Martin. "Transsexualism and the Sex-Change Operation: A Contemporary Medico-Legal and Social Problem." *Medico-Legal Journal* 49, no. 5 (1981): 5–19.

Russell, Diana E. H. *Behind Closed Doors in White South Africa: Incest Survivors Tell Their Stories*. New York: St. Martin's Press, 1997.

———. *Lives of Courage: Women for a New South Africa*. Claremont, South Africa: BasicBooks, 1989.

Ryland, Karen. Interview by Amanda Swarr. August 2007.

Said, Edward W. *Orientalism*. New York: Vintage Books, 1978.

———. "Traveling Theory." In *The Edward Said Reader*, ed Moustafa Bayoumi and Andrew Rubin, 195–217. New York: Random House, 2000 [1982].

———. "Travelling Theory Reconsidered." In *Critical Reconstructions: The Relationships of Fiction and Life*, ed Robert M. Polhemus, and Roger B. Henkle, 251–265. Stanford, CA: Stanford University Press, 1994.

Salamon, Gayle. *Assuming a Body: Transgender and the Rhetorics of Materiality*. New York: Columbia University Press, 2010.

Samuelson, Meg. *Remembering the Nation, Dismembering the Women?: Stories of the South African Transition*. Scottsville: University of KwaZulu-Natal Press, 2007.

Sangtin Writers, and Richa Nagar. *Playing with Fire: Feminist Thought and Activism through Seven Lives in India*. Minneapolis: University of Minnesota Press, 2006.

Saunton, Irene, ed. *Mothers of the Revolution: The War Experiences of Thirty Zimbabwean Women*. Bloomington, IN: University of Indiana Press, 1990.

Scheman, Naomi. "Queering the Center by Centering the Queer: Reflections on Transsexuals and Secular Jews." In *Feminists Rethink the Self*, ed. Diana Tietjens Meyers. New York: Westview Press, 1997.

Schilt, Kristen. *Just One of the Guys?: Transgender Men and the Persistence of Gender Inequality*. Chicago: University of Chicago Press, 2010.

Schmidt, Elizabeth. *Peasants, Traders, and Wives: Shona Women in the History of Zimbabwe, 1870–1939*. Portsmouth, NH: Heinneman, 1992.

Scott, Joan W. "The Evidence of Experience." *Critical Inquiry* 17, no. 4 (1991): 773–797.

Seedat, Aziza. *Crippling a Nation: Health in Apartheid South Africa*. London: International Defence Fund for Southern Africa, 1994.

Serano, Julia. *Whipping Girl: A Transsexual Woman on Sexism and the Scapegoating of Femininity*. Emeryville, CA: Seal Press, 2007.

Shapiro, Judith. "Transsexualism: Reflections on the Persistence of Gender and the Mutability of Sex." In *Body Guards: The Cultural Poetics of Gender Ambiguity*, ed. Julia Epstein and Kristina Straub, 248–79. New York: Routledge, 1991.

"Shoot the Drag Queen! . . . and Daisy Died." *Queer Life* Web site. http://queer-life.co.za/test/content/view/1324/120/, December 10, 2008.

Simo, Ana. "South Africa: Apartheid Military Forced Gay Troops Into Sex-Change Operations." August 25, 2000. *theGully.com*. Accessed June 2003.

Simpson, Graeme, and Gerald Kraak. "The Illusions of Sanctuary and the Weight of the Past: Notes on Violence and Gender in South Africa." *Development Update* 2, no. 2 (1998): 1–10.

Sinnot, Megan J. *Toms and Dees: Transgender Identity and Female Same-Sex Relationships in Thailand*. Honolulu: University of Hawai'i Press, 2004.

Sithembe, Phumelele. Interview by Amanda Swarr and Sam Bullington. Cape Town, South Africa. October 2000.

Skotnes, Pippa, ed. *Miscast: Negotiating the Presence of the Bushmen*. Cape Town: University of Cape Town Press, 1996.

Slack, Jennifer Daryl. "The Theory and Method of Articulation in Cultural Studies." In *Stuart Hall: Critical Dialogues in Cultural Studies*, ed. David Morley and Kuan-Hsing Chen, 112–27. London: Routledge, 1996.

Slamah, Khartini. "Transgenders and Sex Work in Malaysia." In *Global Sex Workers: Rights, Resistance and Redefinition*, ed. Kamala Kempadoo and Jo Doezema, 210–24. New York: Routledge, 1998.

Slapstilli, Lili [stage name, not pseudonym]. Interview by Amanda Swarr and Sam Bullington. Cape Town, South Africa. July 7, 1997.

Smit, Estian. "Western Psychiatry and Gender Identity Disorder (GID): A Critical Perspective." In *The Gender of Psychology*, ed. Tamara Shefer, Floretta Boonzaier, and Peace Kiguwa, 250–292. Cape Town: University of Cape Town Press, 2006.

Smit, N. "A Comparative Perspective of Gender Discrimination in the Workplace (Including Discrimination Due to Pregnancy and Family Responsibilities)." *Journal of South African Law* 3 (1998): 494–515.

Smith, Gail. "Hating Girls who Love Girls." Behind the Mask Web site, www.btm.org.za, 2003.

Smith, Kathleen M. "Dr. James Barry: Military Man—or Woman?" *CMA Journal* 126 (April 1, 1982): 854–7.

Somerville, Siobhan. *Queering the Color Line: Race and the Invention of Homo-sexuality in American Culture*. Durham, NC: Duke University Press, 2000.

———. "Scientific Racism and the Invention of the Homosexual Body." In *The Gender/Sexuality Reader*, ed. Roger N. Lancaster and Micaela di Leonardo, 37–52. New York: Routledge, 1997.

South African Law Commission Website. wwwserver.law.wits.ac.za/salc/objects. html. Page updated 10 March 1997.

South African Law Commission. "Examination of the Legal Consequences of Sexual Realignment and Related Matters." Working paper 24, project 52, June 1994.

South African Law Commission. "Examination of the Legal Consequences of Sexual Realignment and Related Matters." Project 52, 1995.

"Southern Comfort." Katie Davis, director. Docurama/New Video, 2001.

Spade, Dean. *Normal Life: Administrative Violence, Critical Trans Politics, and the Limits of Law*. Brooklyn, NY: South End Press, 2011.

———. "Resisting Medicine, Re/modeling Gender." *Berkeley Women's Law Journal* 18 (2003): 15–37.

Spelman, Elizabeth V. *Inessential Woman: Problems of Exclusion in Feminist Thought*. London: The Women's Press, 1988.

Spry, Jennifer. *Orlando's Sleep: An Autobiography of Gender*. Norwich, VT: New Victoria Publishers, 1997.

Spurlin, William J. *Imperialism within the Margins: Queer Representation and the Politics of Culture in Southern Africa*. New York: Palgrave MacMillan, 2006.

Stacey, Judith. "Can there be a Feminist Ethnography?" In *Women's Words: The Feminist Practice of Oral History*, ed. Sherna Berger Gluck and Daphne Patai, 111–9. New York: Routledge, 1991.

Statistics South Africa. "Total/Gross Employment and Earnings: PO271." www. statssa.gov.za. September 2002.

Stedman, Thomas Lathrop. *Stedman's Medical Dictionary*. Philadelphia: Lippincott, Williams, and Williams, 2000.

Steenkamp, Nicole. Interview by Amanda Swarr and Sam Bullington. Gauteng, South Africa. October 19, 2000.

Stobie, Cheryl. *Somewhere in the Double Rainbow: Representations of Bisexuality in Post-Apartheid Novels*. Scottsville: University of Kwa-Zulu Natal Press, 2007.

Stodel, Jack. *The Jackpot Story*. Cape Town: Howard Timmins, 1965.

Stoler, Ann Laura. "Carnal Knowledge and Imperial Power: Gender, Race, and Morality in Colonial Asia." In *Gender at the Crossroads of Knowledge: Femi-nist Anthropology in the Postmodern Era*, ed. Micaela di Leonardo, 51–101. Berkeley and Los Angeles, CA: University of California Press, 1991.

Stone, Sandy. "The *Empire* Strikes Back: A Posttranssexual Manifesto." In *Body Guards: The Cultural Poetics of Gender Ambiguity*, ed. Julia Epstein and Kristina Straub, 280–304. New York: Routledge, 1991.

Strauss, S. A. "Official Re-Registration of a Female Transsexual Following Medical Treatment." *Forensic Science* 3, no. 1 (February 1974): 19–29.

———. "Transsexualism and the Law." *Comparative and International Law Journal of Southern Africa* 3 (1970): 348–59.

Strother, Z. S. "Display of the Body Hottentot." In *Africans on Stage: Studies in Ethnological Show Business*, ed Bernth Lindford, 1–61. Bloomington and Indianapolis: Indiana University Press; Cape Town: David Phillip, 1999.

Stryker, Susan. *Transgender History*. Berkeley, CA: Seal Press, 2008.

———. "Transgender Studies: Queer Theory's Evil Twin," *GLQ: A Journal of Lesbian and Gay Studies* 10.2 (2004): 212–215.

Stryker, Susan, and Stephen Whittle, eds. *The Transgender Studies Reader*. New York: Routledge, 2006.

Surkan, K. "Passing Rhetories and the Performance of Gender Identity: (Auto)biographical, Visual, and Virtual Representations of Transgender Subjectivity and Embodiment." Dissertation, University of Minnesota, 2003.

Swarr, Amanda Lock. "*The Aversion Project* Interviews: Medical Mistreatment of Gays and Lesbians in the South African Defense Force," report to the South African National Coalition for Gay and Lesbian Equality, October 30, 2000.

———. "*Moffies*, Artists, and Queens: Race and the Production of South African Gay Male Drag," *Journal of Homosexuality* 46, no. 3/4 (spring 2004): 73–89.

———. "Paradoxes of Butchness: Sexual Violence and Lesbian Masculinities in Contemporary South Africa." *Signs: Journal of Women in Culture and Society* 37, no. 4 (summer 2012): 961–986.

———. "*Stabane*, Intersexuality, and Same-sex Relationships in Soweto," *Feminist Studies* 35, no. 3 (fall 2009): 524–548.

Swarr, Amanda Lock, and Richa Nagar. "Dismantling Assumptions: Interrogating 'Lesbian' Struggles for Identity and Survival in India and South Africa." *Signs: Journal of Women in Culture and Society* 29, no. 2 (winter 2004): 491–516.

Swarr, Amanda Lock, and Richa Nagar, eds. *Critical Transnational Feminist Praxis*. Albany: State University of New York Press, 2010.

Swarr, Amanda Lock, Jaye Sablan, and Kai Kohlsdorf. "Transnational Transgender Medical Discourses." *Hypatia's* 25th anniversary conference at the Simpson Center at the University of Washington, Fall 2009.

Swarr, Amanda Lock, with Sally Gross and Liesl Theron. "South African Intersex Activism: Caster Semenya's Impact and Import," *Feminist Studies* 35, no. 3 (fall 2009): 657–662.

Sycamore, Matillda/Matt Bernstein, ed. *Nobody Passes: Rejecting the Rules of Gender and Conformity*. Emeryville, CA: Seal Press, 2006.

———. *That's Revolting: Queer Strategies for Resisting Assimilation*. Brooklyn, NY: Soft Skull Press, 2004.

Taitz, Jerold. "The Legal Determination of the Sexual Identity of a Post-Operative Transsexual Seen as a Human Rights Issue." *Medicine and Law* 7 (1989): 467–74.

———. "The Right to Health: Medical Treatment and Medical Law in South Africa." *South African Human Rights Yearbook* 4 (1993): 124–38.

Taitz, Laurice. "Poor Bill of Health for South Africa." *Sunday Times* (South Africa), June 25, 2000, 1.

Tamtamy, Samia A., Adel H. Loutfy, Foad Hetta, Mostafa Raafat, O.M. Attiya, and Shahira Y. Boulos. "Familial Male Hermaphroditism." *Birth Defects* 10, no. 4 (1974): 243–7.

Tawil-Souri, Helga. "Colored Identity: The Politics and Materiality of ID Cards in Palestine/Israel." *Social Text* 107, 29 no. 2 (Summer 2011): 67–97.

Taylor, Verta A., and Leila J. Rupp. *Drag Queens at the 801 Cabaret.* Chicago: University of Chicago Press, 2003.

"The Third Sex." Directed by Jack Roberts. Films for the Humanities and Sciences, 2000.

Thamm, Marianne. "Not Just Another Murder," *Mail and Guardian* Web site, http://www.mg.co.za/article/2006-02-26-not-just-another-murder, February 26, 2006.

Theron, Liesl. Interview by Amanda Swarr. Cape Town, South Africa. 2007.

Thomas, Lynn. "The Modern Girl and Racial Respectability in 1930s South Africa." *Journal of African History* 47 (2006): 461–490.

Thompson, Leonard. *A History of South Africa.* New Haven, CT: Yale University Press, 1995.

Towle, Evan B., and Lynn M. Morgan. "Romancing the Transgender Native: Rethinking the Use of the 'Third Gender' Concept." *GLQ: A Journal of Gay and Lesbian Studies* 8, no. 4 (2002): 469–497.

Trujillo, Carla, ed. *Chicana Lesbians: The Girls our Mothers Warned us About.* Berkeley: Third Woman Press, 1991

Tucker, Andrew. *Queer Visibilities: Space, Identity, and Interaction in Cape Town.* West Sussex: Wiley-Blackwell, 2009.

Turner, Victor. *The Forest of Symbols: Aspects of Ndembu Ritual.* Ithaca: Cornell University Press, 1967.

———. *The Ritual Process: Structure and Anti-Structure.* Chicago: Aldine Publishing Company, 1969.

Tyler, Carole-Anne. "Boys Will Be Girls: The Politics of Gay Drag." In *Inside/Out: Lesbian Theories, Gay Theories*, ed. Diana Fuss, 32–70. New York, Routledge, 1991.

Valentine, David. *Imagining Transgender: An Ethnography of a Category.* Durham, NC: Duke University Press, 2007.

Valentine, David, and Riki Anne Wilchins. "One Percent on the Burn Chart: Gender, Genitals, and Hermaphrodites with Attitude." *Social Text* 52/53, no. 3/4 (Fall/Winter 1997): 213–22.

Valerio, Max Wolf. *The Testosterone Files: My Hormonal and Social Transformation from Female to Male.* Emeryville, CA: Seal Press, 2006.

Van der Merwe, Andre Carl. *Moffies.* Cape Town: Penstock, 2006.

Van der Westhuizen, Fantie. "Verandering van Geslag is Seuntjie se Enigste Hoop (Sex Change a Boy's Only Hope)." *Beeld* (South Africa), July 21, 1992. Translated by Taghmeda Achmat.

Van Gennep, Arnold. *The Rites of Passage.* London: Routledge, 1909.

Van Onslen, Charles. *The Small Matter of a Horse.* Ravan Press, 1984.

Van Rassel, Jason. "Years of Cases Reviewed after Dr. Levin Charged with Sex Assault." *Calgary Herald* (Canada), March 25, 2010.

Van Zyl, Mikki. "Shaping Sexualities—Per(trans)forming Queer." In *Performing Queer: Shaping Sexualities, 1994–2004—Volume One*, ed. Mikki van Zyl and Melissa Steyn, 19–38. Roggebaai: Kwela Books. 2005.

Van Zyl, Mikki, Jeanelle de Gruchy, Shelia Lapinsky, Simon Lewin, and Graeme Reid. *The Aversion Project: Human Rights Abuses of Gays and Lesbians in the SADF by Health Workers During the Apartheid Era.* Cape Town: Simply Said and Done on Behalf of the Gay and Lesbian Archives, Health and Human Rights Project, Medical Research Council, and the National Coalition for Gay and Lesbian Equality. October 1999.

Van Zyl, Mikki, and Melissa Steyn, eds. *Performing Queer: Shaping Sexualities, 1994–2004—Volume One.* Roggebaai: Kwela Books. 2005.

Vaughan, Megan. *Curing their Ills: Colonial Power and African Illness.* Stanford, CA: Stanford University Press, 1991.

———. "Health and Hegemony: Representation of Disease and the Creation of the Colonial Subject in Nyasaland." In *Contesting Colonial Hegemony: State and Society in Africa and India*, ed. Dagmar Engels and Shula Marks, 173–201. London: The German Historical Institute, British Academic Press, 1994.

Vimbela, Vera. "Climbing on her Shoulders: An Interview with Umtata's 'First Lesbian.'" In *Defiant Desire: Gay and Lesbian Lives in South Africa*, ed. Mark Gevisser and Edwin Cameron, 193–7. Johannesburg, South Africa: Ravan Press, 1994.

Vincent, Louise, and Bianca Camminga. "Putting the 'T' into South African Human Rights: Transsexuality in the Post-Apartheid Order." *Sexualities* 12, no. 6 (2009): 678–700.

Visweswaran, Kamala. *Fictions of Feminist Ethnography.* Minneapolis: University of Minnesota Press, 1990.

Vongai, Cynthia, and Lisa Templeton. "Cross-Dresser Beats the Ladies in Met Fashion Race." *Cape Argus* (South Africa), January 1997.

Vorster, Johann. Interview by Amanda Swarr and Sam Bullington. June 2000.

Wa Ka Ngobeni, Evidence. "Gay Coalition Wants Probe into Levin." *Mail and Guardian* (South Africa), August 18–24, 2000, 5.

Wa Sibuyi, Mpande. "Tinkoncana Etimayinini: The Wives of the Mines." In *Invisible Ghetto: Lesbian and Gay Writing from South Africa*, ed. Matthew Krouse, 52–64. London: Gay Men's Press, 1993.

Wainwright, Joel. *Decolonizing Development: Colonial Power and the Maya*. Malden, MA: Blackwell, 2008.

Waldmier, Patti. *Anatomy of a Miracle: The End of Apartheid and Birth of the New South Africa*. New Brunswick, NJ: Rutgers University Press, 1997.

Walker, Cherryl, ed. *Women and Gender in Southern Africa to 1945*. Cape Town: David Philip, 1990.

Walker, Liz. "Men Behaving Differently: South African Men Since 1994." *Culture, Health & Sexuality* 7, no. 3 (2005): 225–238.

———. *Women and Resistance in South Africa*. London: Onyx Press, 1992.

Weideman, Esmare. *Huisgenoot: 90 Jaar Gedenkuitgawe*. Media24 (2006): 12–15.

Wekker, Gloria. *The Politics of Passion: Women's Sexual Culture in the Afro-Surinamese Diaspora*. New York: Columbia University Press, 2006.

Wells, Julia. "Maternal Politics in Organizing Black South African Women: The Historical Lessons." In *Sisterhood, Feminisms and Power: From Africa to the Diaspora*, ed. Obioma Nnaemeka, 251–62. Trenton, NJ: Africa World Press, 1998.

Weston, Kath. *Families We Choose: Lesbians, Gays, Kinship*. New York: Columbia University Press, 1991.

———. "Lesbian/Gay Studies in the House of Anthropology." *Annual Review of Anthropology* 22 (1993): 339–67.

———. *Render Me, Gender Me: Lesbians Talk Sex, Class, Color, Nation, Studmuffins. . . .* New York: Columbia University Press, 1996.

White, Luise, Stephan Miescher, and David William Cohen. *African Words, African Voices: Critical Practices in Oral History*. Bloomington: Indiana University Press, 2001.

Whitehead, Harriet. "The Bow and Burden Strap: A New Look at Institutionalized Homosexuality in Native North America." In *The Lesbian and Gay Studies Reader*, ed. Henry Abelove, Michele Aina Barale, and David M. Halperin, 498–527. New York: Routledge, 1993 [1981].

Wieringa, Saskia. "Women Marriages and Other Same-Sex Practices: Historical Reflections on African Women's Same-Sex Relations." In *Tommy Boys, Lesbian Men and Ancestral Wives: Female Same-Sex Practices in Africa*, ed. Ruth Morgan and Saskia Wieringa, 281–308. Johannesburg: Jacana Media, 2005.

Wiersma, R. "Management of the African Child with True Hermaphroditism." *Journal of Pediatric Surgery* 36, no. 2 (February 2001): 397–9.

———. "True Hermaphroditism in Southern Africa: the Clinical Picture." *Pediatric Surgery International* 20, no. 5 (2004): 363–368.

Wikan, Unni. "Man Becomes Woman: Transsexualism in Oman as a Key to Gender Roles." *Man* 12 (1977): 304–19.

———. "The Xanith: The Third Gender Role?" In *Behind the Veil in Arabia: Women in Oman*, 168–86. Chicago, IL: University of Chicago Press, 1991.

Wilchins, Riki Anne. *Read My Lips: Sexual Subversion and the End of Gender.* Ithaca, NY: Firebrand Books, 1997.

Williams, Gertie/Johnny, edited by Dhianaraj Chetty. "Lesbian Gangster: The Gertie Williams Story." In *Defiant Desire: Gay and Lesbian Lives in South Africa*, ed. Mark Gevisser and Edwin Cameron, 128–133. Johannesburg, South Africa: Ravan Press, 1994 [1956].

Williams, Peter. Interview by Amanda Swarr and Sam Bullington. July 1997.

Williams, Walter. *Javanese Lives: Women and Men in Modern Indonesia Society.* New York: Routledge, 1998.

———. *The Spirit and the Flesh: Sexual Diversity in American Indian Culture.* Boston: Beacon Press, 1986.

Wilson, Ara. *The Intimate Economies of Bangkok: Tomboys, Tycoons, and Avon Ladies in the Global City.* Berkeley and Los Angeles: University of California Press, 2004.

Wolf, Diane L., ed. *Feminist Dilemmas in Fieldwork.* Boulder, CO: Westview Press, 1996.

Wolpe, Annmarie. "'Where Angels Fear to Tread': Feminism in South Africa." In *Theory and Method in South African Human Sciences Research: Advances and Innovations*, ed. Johann Mouton and Johan Muller, 85–104. Pretoria: Human Sciences Research Council, 1998.

Woods, Donald. *Biko.* New York: Henry Holt and Company, 1978.

Woodward, Wendy, Patricia Hayes, and Gary Minkley, eds. *Deep hiStories: Gender and Colonialism in Southern Africa.* New York and Amsterdam: Rodopi, 2002.

World Currency Yearbook. 171–172. York: Routledge. 1990/1993.

Zwi, Anthony, Shula Marks, and Neil Andersson. "Health, Apartheid, and the Frontline States." *Social Science Medicine* 27, no. 7 (1988): 661–665.

Index

abortion, 80, 270n5
Abrahams, Rashid (pseudonym), 223–24
accountability, 29–30, 36
Achmat, Taghmeda (Midi), 36
Achmat, Zackie, 32, 263n16
addiction, 86, 99, 163
African National Congress (ANC), 15, 18, 51, 64, 65, 240
African Studies, 5–6, 9, 10, 79–80, 118, 184–85
African Women's Life Story Project, 194
AIDS. *See* HIV/AIDS
Alegi, Peter, 222
Alteration of Sex Description and Sex Status Act, 73, 249
Amnesty International, 103, 104
Anglo-Boer War, 14
Anzaldúa, Gloria, 210
apartheid, 239–44; as biopolitics, 262n10; gendered disjunctions of, 4, 11, 43, 51, 57, 239–44; health care under, 81–85, 88–89, 106–107, 189; history of, 14–18
Arondekar, Anjali, 27
Ashforth, Adam, 34, 176–79, 277n47
Association of Bisexuals, Gays, and Lesbians (ABIGALE), 263n23
Aversion Project, 99, 101–103, 242, 272n26
aversion therapy, 16, 50, 80, 98–104, 106, 216, 242

Baard, Sandra (pseudonym), 77, 96–97
Baartman, Saartjie (Sarah), 186–88, 241, 278nn5–8. *See also* Hottentot Venus
Baker, Elizabeth (pseudonym), 52, 63, 89, 93, 126
Baldwin-Ragaven, Laurel, 81, 83–85, 98, 189
Bantustan policies, 51, 83, 270n4
Barnard, Christian, 19
Barnard, Ian, 200, 213
Baxter, David, 207–209
Be Like Others (film), 105
Beaumont Society, 248
Behind the Mask (Web site), 199, 248
Benjamin, Harry, 45–46, 51, 124, 265n8
Besnier, Niko, 261n3
Billings, Dwight B., 47, 105–106, 265n9
biopolitics, 84, 93, 106, 262n10; of colonial medicine, 78–79, 84, 86, 189; Foucault's biopower and, 7, 39, 78–79, 98, 106; necropolitics and, 167–68, 233, 273n2
birth certificates, 59–60, 62–63, 145–46. *See also* identity documents
Births, Marriages, and Deaths Registration Acts, 59–62, 245, 268n28, 268n31. *See also* marriage

319

bisexuality, 45, 166, 194–95, 279n18
Blackwood, Evelyn, 194
Blouws, Kenneth (pseudonym), 223–24
boeremeisie ("farm girl"), 219, 281n18
Bornstein, Kate, 112, 263n25
Botha, P. W., 122, 172–73, 175, 243, 274n12
Brazil, 203, 276n38, 282n22
breast and chest surgery, 116, 127–28, 88, 131, 155, 158, 176, 203. *See also* sex reassignment surgery
Breckenridge, Keith, 51, 71
Bridges, William, 2
Bullington, Sam, 30–37, 208
Butchart, Alexander, 84, 187
butch, 112, 170, 193–97, 200, 224, 279n16. *See also* femme; gender liminality
Butler, Judith, 7–8, 39, 184, 233, 279n22; critics of, 75, 280n4; on death and dying, 110, 273n2; on "heterosexual matrix," 75, 202–203; on performativity, 7–8, 184, 210, 227–29

Cameron, Edwin, 53
Camminga, Bianca, 102
Chatterjee, Partha, 82
Chauncey, George, 200
"cisgender," 28, 170, 264n27
class: colonialism and, 12–15; "deviance" and, 53–54; gender and, 63, 148, 214, 216; health care and, 157, 189; "queens" and, 23, 219–22, 227; race and, 13–18, 44–45, 59, 70, 85, 97, 165, 208–12, 244; social mobility and, 148
Cock, Jacklyn, 103–104
Coetzee, Warren (pseudonym), 218–21

colonialism, 7–9, 61, 82, 187; biopolitics of, 78–79, 84, 86, 189; class and, 12–15; research on, 258; slavery and, 12, 13, 110, 262n9. *See also* racism
Comaroff, Jean, 79
Community Media Health Project, 33
confidentiality, 31–32
consent, informed, 77, 78, 99–105, 161
Constitution, South African, 43, 238; changing sex on ID and, 19, 21, 65, 145, 234, 249; gay/lesbian rights and, 18, 30, 204, 236, 269n42; health care access in, 77–78
Coon Carnival, 213, 214, 281n8
Corbett vs. Corbett, 61, 62
cosmetic surgery, 19–20, 47, 141
Crenshaw, Kimberlé William, 181, 210
Crichton, Derk, 49, 67
cross-dressing, 22–23, 135–37, 158, 207–209; conceptual frameworks of, 209–11; legal issues with, 12, 16, 53–54, 58–59, 143, 207–208, 263n15; in townships, 221–27; violence against, 33–35, 95–96, 137, 197, 204–205. *See also* drag performers; "queens"
Cruel and Unusual (film), 164

Daniels, Chris (pseudonym), 208–209
Davids, Giles (pseudonym), 115, 127–28, 138–40, 152, 160–61, 246
Davis, Madeline, 194
Davison, Patricia, 187
Dean, Tim, 276n37
Delmas Treason Trial, 279n15
democracy, transition to, 1–2, 18, 20, 205, 232, 237–38, 246–56
"deviance," 9, 53–54, 81–82, 191. *See also* sexuality

Dhlomo, Buyani (pseudonym), 192–93, 197, 202
Dillon, Michael, 45
disorders of sex development (DSD), 264n28, 277n1. *See also* intersexuality
Don, Alexander, 49–50, 266n16
Donham, Donald, 185, 201, 202, 204, 213
drag performers, 4, 35; conceptual frameworks for, 209–11; legal issues with, 12, 16, 53; military-sponsored, 215–16; race and, 38, 40, 209–21. *See also* cross-dressing
Drennan, Matthew, 187–88
Drury, James, 187–88
Dube, Daisy, 204, 225, 282n23

Edmunds, Vita (pseudonym), 114, 115, 123–25, 128–30, 137, 143, 168–69, 208–209, 240
Elder, Glen, 4, 9, 13, 44, 75–76, 233
electrolysis, 114, 123, 125, 136, 242
electroshock therapy, 16, 50, 80, 99, 103–104, 216. *See also* Aversion Project
Epprecht, Marc, 10, 27, 44, 233, 263n16, 279n21; on Africanist scholarship, 79; on intersexuality, 278n11; on "mine marriages," 13, 14
Equality Project, 102, 103, 272n25, 283n10
Erasmus, Jean, 104
Erhardt, Anke, 46
Erickson, Reed, 47, 266n11
Erickson Educational Foundation, 47, 266n12
Evans-Pritchard, E. E., 178
"extra-transsexual meanings," 5, 40, 231–32, 256

Fabian, Johannes, 120
femme, 193–97, 200, 224, 279n17. *See also* butch; gender liminality
films, 23, 105, 164; on drag performers, 280n5; on homosexualities, 263n16; on intersexuality, 278n11
fistulas, 88, 131–33, 176, 271n7. *See also* vaginoplasty
Foucault, Michel, 12, 95, 179, 233; on biopower, 7, 39, 78–79, 98, 106; on medical technology, 44; "traveling theory" of, 10, 78
Frederick X (pseudonym), 54–55, 59–60, 268n22
Freeman, Elizabeth, 120–21, 211, 228, 274n10

Garber, Marjorie, 75, 106
Gay and Lesbian Alliance, 207–208, 214
Gay and Lesbian Memory in Action (GALA), 11, 26, 272n23
Gay and Lesbian Pride March, 207–208
Gays and Lesbians of the Witwatersrand (GLOW), 165, 192, 222, 282n21
gender, 3, 54, 70; class and, 63, 148, 214, 216; malleability of, 46; performativity of, 7–8, 184, 210, 227–29; prescribing of, 48–57; "psychological," 52; race and, 4–5, 15–18, 75–76, 80, 104–107, 209–17; sex and, 27, 203, 279n22. *See also* lesbians and gays
Gender DynamiX (organization), 5, 151, 247–48, 252–53, 262n5
gender dysphoria, 48, 51, 55, 124, 125, 138, 159, 164, 266n14

Gender Identity Disorder, 48, 49, 67–68, 112, 138, 163, 255, 266n14, 274n13

gender liminality, 3–4, 135–51; under apartheid, 4, 11–18, 43, 51, 57, 239–44; butch/femme roles and, 112, 170, 193–97, 200, 224, 279nn16–17; community perceptions of, 22–23, 190–92, 195, 197, 236; language for, 28–29, 191, 251–54, 272n29; permanence of, 198; politics of, 231–59; religious views of, 105, 159, 170, 177; research on, 37–38, 45; sexual orientation and, 139, 169–70, 212–17, 236. See also queer; stabane; transgender

Gevisser, Mark, 222

Grace, H. J., 189, 241

Gramsci, Antonio, 78, 102

Greaves, Gloria, 61–62

Green, Jamison, 112

Gross, Sally, 73, 247, 270n47, 278n12

Group Areas Act, 15, 57, 214, 270n4

Halberstam, J., 120–21

Hall, Stuart, 280n3

Hausman, Bernice, 75, 265nn9–10

Hayes, Patricia, 186–87

Hemphill, R. E., 51–52, 54

Hendricks, Donna (pseudonym), 115, 141–42, 148–63, 246, 249

Hendricks, Graeme, 79, 221

Heradien, Simone, 1, 18–25, 34, 69, 73, 221, 233–38, 241, 244–46

hermaphroditism, 186, 192, 195, 198, 200–201; community reactions to, 279n21; definitions of, 277n1; incidence of, 189. See also intersexuality

heteropatriarchy, 4, 9, 44, 75–76, 233

heterosexual matrix, 75–76, 202–204

HIV/AIDS, 164–65, 251–52; activism involved with, 30, 32–34; colonial medicine and, 78–79; health care resources for, 91; intentional infection with, 34, 276n37, 279n18, 279n20

Hoad, Neville, 8, 10, 11, 44, 118, 199, 278n4

homophobic violence, 33–35, 75, 122, 137, 197–98, 204–205, 224–26, 272n21, 275n22, 280n23

hormone treatments, 19, 45–46, 136–37, 162, 232, 251; as aversion therapy, 50, 242; complications from, 87–88, 96–99, 130–31; as medical experimentation, 92, 97–102, 106; secrecy about, 31; self-administered, 163, 203, 276n38

Hottentot Venus, 186–88, 241, 278nn5–8. See also Saatjie (Sarah) Baartman

Hunter, Amy, 86–87

hysterectomy, 114, 128, 140, 145–46. See also sex reassignment surgery

identity (ID) documents: changing name on, 143–44; changing sex on, 18, 21, 43, 54–55, 59–66, 70–74, 100, 145–51; political implications of, 57–58, 72, 138, 234–35, 241, 246–50. See also birth certificates

Internet resources, 153–54, 158–59, 161–62, 175, 247–48, 256

Intersex South Africa, 73, 189, 247, 283n8

intersexuality, 4, 16, 28, 37–38, 74, 264n28; definitions of, 236, 277n1; evaluation of, 49, 269n40; race and, 186–89; transsexualism and, 51, 55; treatment of, 46, 49,

188–89. *See also* disorders of sex development; hermaphroditism; transsexualism; *stabane*
Iran, 105
Isaacs, Nasreen (pseudonym), 223–24
Isitabane, 199, 277n2. See also *stabane*

Jansen, Odessa (pseudonym), 89
jealousy, 176–79, 277n47
Jeeves, Alan, 82
Joost, Michael (pseudonym), 56, 74, 125–26
Jorgensen, Christine, 45
Juridical Matters Amendment Act, 74

Kaplan, Robert M., 99
Kennedy, Elizabeth, 194
Kessler, Suzanne, 46
/Khanako, 186–87, 241
Khosla, Dhillon, 112, 160
Khumalo, Bass John, 36
"kinky politics," 9–10, 40, 210, 211, 233; performativity with, 228–29
Kirk, Paul, 100, 102–103, 272n26, 272nn29–30
Kistner, Ulrike, 78–79, 106
Klein, Thamar, 249
Krouse, Matthew, 215–16
Kulick, Don, 203, 276n38, 279n22, 282n22
Kunene, Thandazo Alice, 192

Lahiri, Madhumita, 280n23
Lalu, Premesh, 81–82, 270n2
Lancaster, Roger, 282n22
Leap, William, 112, 213, 221–22
Leatt, Annie, 79, 221
Legacy, Keiron, 207–208
legal issues, 52; with changing sex on IDs, 18, 21, 43, 54–55, 59–66, 70–74, 100, 144–51, 234–35, 241;

with cross-dressing, 12, 16, 53–54, 58–59, 143, 207–208, 263n15; with gay and lesbian rights, 11, 18, 30, 65, 204, 236, 240; with land-ownership, 14; with pimping, 61–62; with rape, 66; with same-sex relationships, 18, 62; with transsexualism, 18, 57–71, 142–51
lesbians and gays, 183–205, 239–40; aversion therapy for, 16, 80, 98, 99, 103–104, 216, 242; butch/femme roles among, 193–97, 200, 224, 279n19; civil rights of, 11, 18, 30, 62, 65, 204, 236, 240, 246–47; conceptualization of, 55–56; violence against, 33–35, 122, 137, 197, 204–205, 224–25. *See also* queer; sexual orientation
Levin, Aubrey, 99, 103, 104, 272n24
Lewis, Jack, 263n16
Lord, Kristin, 162
Louw, Gene, 63–65

Maart, Herman (pseudonym), 114, 116–17, 140–41, 145–46, 160, 170–71, 244, 246
Mabuza-Suttle, Felicia, 173–75
Makeba, Miriam, 220
Malaysia, 236
Manalansan, Martin, 170, 282n24
Mandela, Nelson, 18, 240
mandrax (street drug), 275n18
Manicom, Linzi, 80
Marais, Charl, 247
marriage: interracial, 15, 17, 110; among miners, 13–14, 215, 262n10; same-sex, 13–14, 61, 62, 215, 262n10; of transsexuals, 61–63, 66–69, 90, 169. *See also* Births, Marriages, and Deaths Registration Acts
Martin, Denis-Constant, 16
Martin, Karen, 11

Masooa, Salome, 282n23
mastectomies, 127–28, 140, 146, 274n17. *See also* breast and chest surgery
Mayibuye Centre, 26
Maynard, G. D., 81
Maynes, Mary Jo, 117
Mbembe, Achille, 64, 95, 168, 171, 202; on "anxious virility," 65; on envisioning freedom, 122, 180–82; on "fantasized objects," 138, 175; on necropolitics, 7–9, 39, 79, 109–11, 162, 167–68, 179, 188–89, 233; on "the postcolony," 151; on "state of injury," 110, 131, 135
McCloskey, Deidre, 112
McLean, Hugh, 185, 196, 201, 202
medical experimentation, 34–35, 38, 47, 50, 57, 68, 77–78, 243–44; on soldiers, 85–104, 216, 237
methodological approaches, 5–11, 26–37, 44–45, 109–21, 208–11
Mfazo, Buyisile (pseudonym), 191
Mince (drag troupe), 217
"mine marriages," 13–14, 215, 262n10
Moffett, Helen, 280n23
moffies, 16, 199, 262n13, 281n6; cross-dressing by, 213–14, 223, 224. *See also* gender liminality
Mohammed, Farid (pseudonym), 224–25
Molobi, William (pseudonym), 115, 163–66
Money, John, 46, 51, 265n7, 266n11
Morgan, Ruth, 101; *Tommy Boys*, 6, 112, 118, 194, 273n5; *Trans: Transgender Life Stories in South Africa*, 2–3, 6, 28, 119, 162, 164, 167, 249–50
Morris, Jan, autobiog *Conundrum*, 76, 112

Mthembu, Zindzi (pseudonym), 190, 193–94
Muñoz, José Esteban, 181–82, 210, 222, 228

Nagar, Richa, 29–30, 36, 151, 273n6
Najmabadi, Afsaneh, 105
Namaste, Viviane, 75, 280n4
National Coalition for Gay and Lesbian Equality, 102, 103, 269n36, 272n25
National Party, 14–17, 64–65, 269n33
National Public Radio (NPR), 32
Native Land Act, 14, 58
Ndana, Phakamile (pseudonym), 195, 201–203
necropolitics, 7–9, 39, 79, 109–11, 162, 179; biopolitics and, 167–68, 233, 273n2; intersexuality and, 188–89; queer, 180
Nestadt, J., 62
Nestle, Joan, 194
Ngcobo, Linda, 185, 195–97, 201–203, 222, 279n20
Nkabinde, Nkunzi Zandile, 257–58
Nkoli, Simon, 165, 197, 279n15, 279n20

Oosthuizen, Jan (pseudonym), 220
Oprah (TV show), 160, 173, 175, 276n34
Ormrod Test, 61–62, 241

Pan Africanist Congress (PAC), 15, 51, 240
Pantazis, Angelo, 5, 71; on extra-transsexual meanings, 5, 40, 231–32, 256
pantsula, 195–98, 279n19
Paris Is Burning (film), 280n5
Park, Yoon Jung, 280n23

passbooks. *See* identity documents

"passing," 59, 146–47, 168–70, 211, 223–24, 277n42; altercations over, 208–209; police harassment and, 123–24; after sex reassignment, 50, 94, 124, 125; stealth versus, 168, 267n17. *See also* "stealth"

passports, 63, 144, 149, 249

performativity, 7–8, 119, 184, 210, 222, 227–29, 233

phalloplasty, 36, 74, 146, 152, 198; complications with, 87, 160–61; prostheses versus, 140–41, 160, 275n23; techniques for, 125–27

"phalloplenthysmography," 188

Phoenix Society, 247, 248, 250

physician-patient relationships, 134–35

Population Registration Act, 15, 57–58, 281n7

Portelli, Alessandro, 119

Posel, Deborah, 15, 17, 75, 218, 268n26, 270n49, 280n23

positionality, 29–30, 36

Prince, Virginia, 273n4

Priscilla, Queen of the Desert (film), 23

Prohibition of Disguises Act, 12, 53–54, 58–59, 216, 263n15

Promotion of Equality and Prevention of Unfair Discrimination Act, 74

Prosser, Jay, 45

prostheses, as part of sex reassignment, 88, 140–41, 275n23

prostitution. *See* sex workers

pseudonyms, 31, 261n1, 272nn23–24, 272n29, 274n7, 281n16

Puar, Jasbir, 93, 180, 273n2

Puerto Ricans, 106

"queens," 38, 85, 207–29; class and, 23; HIV/AIDS and, 165; straight relationships with, 195–96; Thai, 155, 157; violence against, 33–35, 93, 95–96, 137, 197, 204–205. *See also* cross-dressing; *stabane*

queer, 2–3, 28–29, 180, 199–200, 239; visibility of, 211, 225–26, 233. *See also* gender liminality; lesbians and gays

queer temporality, 12, 120–21, 262n10; Muñoz on, 111, 181–82, 210, 222, 228

queer theory, 6, 10, 75, 118, 210, 273n5, 280n4

R vs. Tan and Others, 61–62

race: class and, 13–18, 44–45, 59, 70, 85, 97, 165, 208–12, 244; cross-dressing and, 38, 40, 209–21; gender and, 4–5, 15–18, 75–76, 80, 104–107, 209–17; intersexuality and, 186–89; marriage laws and, 15, 17, 110; sexuality and, 209–21, 227–29; terms used for, 12, 27–28, 75, 281n7

racism, 9–10; in health care services, 81–85, 88–89, 106–107, 189, 244; scientific, 16, 183, 186–88; slavery and, 12, 13, 110, 262n9; "specials" and, 39, 77, 85–88, 92–97, 101, 104–107, 243–44. *See also* colonialism

Raizenberg, Theresa, 36

Rankhotha, Sylvester Charles, 185, 191–92, 196, 279n18

rape, 33–34, 66, 104, 198, 205, 225, 226; of gays and lesbians, 279n16, 279n20, 280n23; incidence of, 231, 282n23

Rassool, Ciraj, 186–87, 278n7

Ratele, Kopano, 9–10, 188, 210, 211, 228–29, 233

Raymond, Janice, 75
Reconstruction and Development
  Programme (RDP), 1, 20, 237,
  238, 246
Reddy, Vasu, 7, 8, 227, 262n7
Rees, Mark, 112
Regulation of Gatherings Act, 207
Reid, Graeme, 6, 11, 118, 205, 213,
  276n39
Reimer, David, 265n7
religion, See spiritual beliefs
representational approach, 29–30, 36,
  113
Riekert, Carmella (pseudonym),
  114–16, 122, 130–35, 144–48,
  153, 157–58, 172–79, 243–44
Roeland, Brandy (pseudonym), 35,
  95–96, 224
Rubin, Gayle, 8
Russell, Diana, 283n5
Ryland, Karen (pseudonym), 3, 63,
  90, 127, 165, 275n27

sadomasochism, 53
Said, Edward, 8, 44, 111, 184, 202,
  210
Salamon, Gayle, 12, 57, 76, 203
Samuelson, Meg, 77
Schilt, Kristen, 267n17
Scott, Joan, 113
Seedat, Aziza, 83
Semenya, Caster, 278n13
sex reassignment surgery, 19–25;
  availability of, 139–41, 152–53,
  237; breast and chest surgery for,
  116, 127–28, 131, 155, 158, 176,
  203; complications from, 86–90,
  92–94, 126–27, 130–34, 156, 176;
  cost of, 90, 91, 131, 140, 155,
  237, 271n8, 275n27, 277n43;
  criteria for, 36, 68–69, 139,

255–56, 266n16; experimentation
  with, 85–98; forced, 16, 38, 39,
  80, 98–107, 237; gender identity
  clinics for, 67–68; history of,
  45–48; legal issues with, 18,
  57–71; motivations for, 68–69;
  phalloplasty and, 36, 74, 87,
  125–27, 140–41, 146, 152, 160–
  61; prostheses and, 88, 140–41,
  275n23; publicly funded, 12,
  19, 51, 72, 85–86, 91, 106–107,
  243; related surgeries for, 274n16;
  research on, 35–36, 46–47;
  reversal of, 198; secrecy about, 19,
  31–32, 93; sexual orientation after,
  55–56, 137; for "specials," 39,
  77, 85–88, 91–97, 101, 104–107,
  243–44; statistics on, 48–49,
  87, 100; stealth about, 49, 50,
  267n17; terminology of, 251–53,
  261n2, 264n1; vaginoplasty for,
  77, 92–94, 123, 129–34, 156–57.
  See also hormone treatments
sex workers, 53–54, 80, 236–37;
  miners and, 14; organizations
  for, 283n10; pimps of, 61–62;
  transsexuals and, 24–25, 39, 67,
  137
sexual orientation: community
  perceptions of, 22–23, 190–92,
  195, 197; gender identity and,
  139, 169–70, 212–17, 236;
  intersexuality and, 200–202; after
  sex reassignment, 55–56, 137. See
  also lesbians and gays
sexuality, 10, 18; bi-, 45, 166, 194–
  95, 279n18; "deviant," 9, 53–54,
  81–82; race and, 209–21, 227–29
Sharpeville massacre (1960), 15, 240
Shelver, Carrie, 269n36
Sigasa, Sizakele, 282n23

Simelane, Eudy, 282n23
Simo, Ana, 100
Singapore, 116, 153, 157–58
Sinnot, Megan J., 194
sitabane. See *stabane*
skesanas, 195–97, 201–202, 213, 223, 224
Skotnes, Pippa, 187
Slapstilli, Lili, 217
slavery, 12, 13, 110, 111, 262n9. *See also* colonialism
Smit, Estian, 73, 90, 91, 118–19, 252, 266n14, 283n6
Somerville, Siobhan, 200–201
South African Law Commission (SALC), 52–55, 60, 66–71, 254–55
Spade, Dean, 73, 240, 275n24
"specials," 39, 77, 80, 85–88, 92–97, 101, 104–107, 131, 133, 243–44
spiritual beliefs: about gender liminality, 257–58; black magic, 176–79, traditional religion, 105, 158–59, 170, 177
Spry, Jennifer, 112
Spurlin, William, 2
stabane, 39, 166–67, 184–85, 190–99; cross-dressing and, 213, 223, 224; definitions of, 184, 190; implications of, 202–205, 254; interpretations of, 198–202, 232; intersexuality and, 201–202, 245; punishment of, 190–91. *See also* gender liminality
"stealth," 113, 117, 152, 168–79, 255–56, 267n17. *See also* "passing"
Steenkamp, Nicole (pseudonym), 114–15, 122–25, 135–37, 143–44, 146–47, 242–44
sterilization, forced, 77, 80, 83–84, 99, 110
Steyn, Melissa, 6, 7–8

Stryker, Susan, 264n27, 264n30
substance abuse, 68, 69, 86, 99, 115, 163, 265n7, 275n18
suicide, 166–68; among soldiers, 99, 104; physician-assisted, 49; among transsexuals, 23–24, 34, 46, 49–50, 67, 89, 111, 137, 181–82, 195, 263n26
Swanepoel, Andre (pseudonym), 165, 233, 251–52

Taitz, Jerold, 60–61, 63–64, 66, 67, 71, 269n38
Tawil-Souri, Helga, 72
Thailand, 194; sex reassignment surgery in, 115, 153–57, 246, 248, 255, 271n8, 271n12, 276n32
Theron, Liesl, 69, 248, 252–53
The Third Sex (film), 278n11
Thompson, Leonard, 240, 283n7
Thompson, Linda, 164
torture, 77, 83, 98, 103, 242
tourism, 200
trans*, 28, 111, 113, 213, 264n29, 282n1
Trans: Transgender Life Stories in South Africa (Morgan et al.), 2–3, 6, 28, 119, 162, 164, 167, 249–50; Alex in, 167, 187, 274n17; Lyndsay in, 104, 164; Marlene in, 248, 250–51, 273n4; Prier in, 254, 257, 258; Tebogo in, 2, 171–72, 276n34; Terrick in, 126–27, 276n34
transgender, 3, 5–6, 28, 37, 40, 45, 203, 261n4; politics of, 231–59; Stryker on, 264n30. *See also* gender liminality
transitions, 1–5, 80–81, 113–21; to democracy, 1–2, 18, 20, 232, 237–38, 246–56; envisioning freedom

transitions (continued)
during, 121–28; "extra-transsexual,"
256–59; histories through, 238–46;
transitioning from, 246–56
transnational connections, 47–48,
151–62, 198–99, 216, 248, 273n4
transsexualism, 5; categorizing of,
44–45, 236, 265n4; class and,
56–57; gender dysphoria versus,
51; history of, 45–48; incidence of,
49; in Iran, 105; legal issues with,
18, 57–71, 142–51; "transexual"
and, 264n28. See also intersexuality
transsexuals: during apartheid,
12–13, 56–59; categorical existence
of, 70–73; children of, 68, 69;
communities of, 22–23, 45, 73,
96, 234, 237, 245, 247; marriage
and, 61–63, 67–69, 90, 169; sex
workers and, 24–25, 39; suicide
among, 23–24, 34, 46, 49–50,
67, 89, 137, 263n26; "true," 36,
48, 56, 68–69, 112, 138, 142,
254–55. See also sex reassignment
surgery
transvestites, 4, 28; legal categories
of, 53; transsexuals and, 22–23,
45–50, 54, 236, 251. See also
cross-dressing; drag performers
Treatment Action Campaign (TAC),
32–33
Triangle Project, 73, 234, 247, 283n8
Trujillo, Carla, 194
Truth and Reconciliation Commission
(TRC), 18, 77, 81, 98–99
tuberculosis, 81, 82, 237
Tucker, Andrew, 6, 23, 169–70, 210,
213, 263n23; on Coon Carnivals,
214; on drag, 216–17, 220; on
queer visibilities, 211, 225–26, 233
Turner, Tina, 217, 281n18

Turner, Victor, 3, 205, 261n3

unions, mine workers', 14
Urban, Thomas, 47, 105–106, 265n9

vaginoplasty, 77, 92–94, 123, 129,
156–57; complications with, 88,
130–34, 156, 176, 271n7. See also
sex reassignment surgery
Valentine, David, 75, 232, 261n4;
on ethnography, 283n14;
on "transexual," 264n28; on
transgender communities, 45
Valerio, Max Wolf, 112
Van der Merwe, Elize, 267n19
Van der Merwe, J. H., 64–65
Van Gennep, Arnold, 3
Van Staden, Martin, 207–208
Van Zyl, Mikki, 6, 7–8, 10, 11, 18,
77, 102
Vaughan, Megan, 78, 86
Verwoerd, Hendrik, 51, 240
Villesky (pseudonym). See Levin,
Aubrey
Vimbela, Vera, 190–91
Vincent, Louise, 102, 267n19
violence, homophobic, 33–35, 75,
122, 137, 197–98, 204–205,
224–26, 272n21, 275n22,
280n23Visweswaran, Kamala, 258
Vorster, Johann (pseudonym), 50, 56,
58, 92, 94

W vs. W, 62–63, 241
Wa Sibuyi, Mpande, 215
Wellbeloved, Joy Rosemary, 167,
250–51, 254–55, 283n13
White, Luise, 175
Wieringa, Saskia, 6, 112, 118, 194,
273n5
Wilchins, Riki Anne, 112

Williams, Peter (pseudonym), 55, 87–88, 91, 93
Wilson, Ara, 194
Winfrey, Oprah, 160, 173, 175, 276n34
witchcraft. *See* spiritual beliefs
Witwatersrand, University of the, 21, 26, 272n23

Women's and Gender Studies, 5–6
World Professional Association for Transgender Health, 274n13

Xhosa, 13, 28, 220, 226

Zulu, 26, 28, 115, 166, 184, 191
Zwi, Anthony, 82